SHADOW EMPIRES

Shadow Empires

AN ALTERNATIVE
IMPERIAL HISTORY

Thomas Barfield

PRINCETON UNIVERSITY PRESS

PRINCETON & OXFORD

Published by Princeton University Press
41 William Street, Princeton, New Jersey 08540
99 Banbury Road, Oxford OX2 6JX

press.princeton.edu

Library of Congress Control Number: 2023931814

ISBN 9780691181639
ISBN (e-book) 9780691253282

British Library Cataloging-in-Publication Data is available

Editorial: Fred Appel, James Collier
Jacket: Chris Ferrante
Production: Erin Suydam
Publicity: William Pagdatoon
Copyeditor: Ashley Moore

Jacket Credit: Enola99d / Shutterstock

This book has been composed in Miller

Printed on acid-free paper. ∞

Printed in the United States of America

10 9 8 7 6 5 4 3 2 1

CONTENTS

MAPS, ILLUSTRATIONS, AND TABLES

Maps

Illustrations

Tables

PREFACE

SHADOW EMPIRES HAD its genesis at a Wenner-Gren Foundation conference, "Imperial Designs: Comparative Dynamics of Early Empires," held in Mijas, Spain, during the fall of 1997. Its seventeen participants were scholars who had written extensively on different empires from an archaeological or historical perspective. Cases included such classic examples as Rome, Achaemenid Persia, and Qin China in the Old World and the Incas and Aztecs in the New World, as well as ancient empires in Egypt, Assyria, and southern India, medieval European empires, and the early modern overseas empires established by Portugal and Spain. I was asked to present the second-century B.C. Xiongnu case, a steppe nomadic empire in Mongolia contemporaneous with the Han dynasty in China. I had written about it and other Inner Asian steppe empires and their relationships with China over the course of two thousand years in my *Perilous Frontier* (1989). While that work was comparative and long term, it was regionally confined to northeastern Eurasia. The opportunity to learn about other empires that emerged in quite different places and cultural contexts from people who knew them in depth was an exciting opportunity. Spending a week in a plush setting in southern Spain close to Granada with all costs covered by the foundation was not too shabby either.

Wenner-Gren conferences have a number of distinctive elements. Participants do not read their papers at the meeting. They are submitted well in advance (the penalty for failure being disinvitation) and printed up in a neat package so that they can be read before the attendees arrive. Everyone stays in the same place, with no guests permitted, for the full five or six days of the conference, and they all eat (and drink) together. The organizers encourage informal conversations among individuals and small groups outside the scheduled meeting times and pay for any late-night bar binges, expresso pit stops, café snacks, and sidebar restaurant jaunts to facilitate that. While the organizers of the imperial designs conference must have had some working definition of empire in mind to choose the cases represented, they did not say what it was. Some participants thought this was a good thing because it avoided drawing arbitrary lines they were uncomfortable setting. Others disagreed and sought to impose imperial order by employing definitions that (not surprisingly) fit their own cases best. Implicit was the question of whether a subset of empires under discussion ought to be excluded as outliers because they were missing something. This was certainly an issue familiar to me because the organization and governance of nomadic steppe empires in Mongolia did not at all resemble those of contemporaneous empires in China, although they consistently made themselves peer polities with China and during the thirteenth century the Mongol Empire conquered most of Eurasia. Could some universal template of empires accommodate them both? And what about maritime empires like those of the Portuguese that occupied very little territory and had tiny administrative footprints? Did Charlemagne's medieval Carolingian Empire pass muster as an imperial successor to Rome in any real sense? And what about the status of Nubian and Libyan dynasties that invaded ancient Egypt and ruled it for a while: interregnums or new empires? If a hypothetical Empires Club employed a blackball system of admission, it was clear that many of the conference participants, including myself, likely represented polities that would be excluded for failing to meet the club's standards.

It was midweek, when people began giving new presentations that responded to what they had heard, that I proposed a model of empires that included two types: primary empires that emerged sui generis in different parts of the world and secondary or shadow empires that came into existence as the products of interactions with primary empires. The former financed themselves by exploiting their internal resources; the latter depended on the extraction of external resources of some type. While primary empires bore striking structural resemblances to one another, shadow empires came in a variety of types. Steppe nomadic empires in Mongolia rose and fell in tandem with powerful dynasties in China to which they were closely connected. Maritime empires used their naval power to create empires that sought economic rather than territorial expansion. Vulture empires emerged when frontier peoples overran collapsing empires and attempted to rule in their ruins. Empires of nostalgia claimed the legacy of a defunct empire to establish a polity that claimed an imperial status more metaphorical than factual. The model provoked a lively debate, and that feedback proved useful when I wrote it up for the conference volume, *Empires: Perspectives from Archaeology and History*, which was published in 2001.

I planned to use that work as the basis for a more detailed research monograph, but world events took me in a different direction just as it was published. My first anthropological research during the mid-1970s in northern Afghanistan had ended abruptly when the Soviet Union invaded the country in 1979. A nation that had known fifty years of peace was now engulfed in wars that continued there long after the Soviets departed in 1989. The possibility of ever working in Afghanistan again appeared remote.

That changed when the Taliban government's long-standing protection of al Qaeda terrorists provoked a U.S. invasion to oust them in response to the 9/11 attacks on New York and Washington in 2001. After a quarter century's absence, I returned to Afghanistan and renewed my academic work in a country whose people had been traumatized by war but in the early days were optimistic about their future. Over the next twenty years I wrote on a wide range of Afghan issues and published a best-selling book (*Afghanistan: A Cultural and Political History*, 2010) that examined how internal and international politics in Afghanistan were interwoven. I soon discovered that even the most prescient analyses of Afghanistan were doomed to be ignored by policy makers in search of simple solutions that could be implemented in short order. Dependent on the military and economic support supplied by the United States and its allies to keep it in power, the Afghan government's venality and incompetence facilitated a resurgence of the Taliban, who retook power in 2021 when the United States withdrew all its forces and abandoned the country to them. It was the fourth time in 180 years that the same scenario had played itself out in Afghanistan.

Before this happened, I had already decided that I needed to take on something different as a new book project. The outline presented in my shadow empires chapter, brief though it was, had been widely cited in the academic literature but needed much more development both to refine the model and to develop the case material in more detail. Taking advantage of a sabbatical in the fall of 2019, I resumed the research and began writing. I was only about a quarter of the way through when the COVID-19 pandemic struck in early 2020 and locked people into enforced isolation for most of the next year. A writer is perhaps better prepared than most people to cope with such an event because writing is a notoriously solitary activity. Indeed, the destruction of normal daily routines that made weekends and holidays the same as any other day increased my productivity since there was nothing else to do. I walked at dawn for exercise, read and wrote during the day, and then binged on Netflix at night—a more healthful habit that binge drinking. Better, though, was the discovery that each of the empires I researched was so fascinating in its own right and full of amazing people and events that it was impossible to be bored. My sadness at leaving one behind was always offset by the excitement of immersing myself in a new one with its own unique story. Although the libraries I needed to consult were closed, thanks to the Hathi Trust I had access to a remarkably large library of scanned books (normally inaccessible for copyright reasons) that was made available to scholars on an emergency basis. University libraries remained closed but scanned book chapters from their collections and provided portals to databases such as JSTOR that gave access to scholarly articles. A working draft was complete before my university required its faculty to end remote Zoom teaching in the fall of 2021. I returned to campus for resocialization with a head of hair and beard that resembled Rasputin's in length and unruliness (now, alas, things of memory). Whether the book would have been any different had conditions been more normal, I cannot say. I can only hope that readers will experience the same sense of discovery that I did writing it but under more pleasant circumstances.

A number of people assisted me in researching and writing the book, but I particularly wish to thank Irina Shingiray for her help in understanding the complex history of the medieval Khazar khaganate, and Michael Khodarkovsky for his informed critique on Russia's relationship with steppe nomadic polities. Charles Lindholm and James Uden served as sounding boards for thinking about how to balance the book's disparate parts, and the endogenous and exogenous typologies emerged during conversations with Nicole Bogott; so I thank them all for that. In a book that draws on comparisons from so many different times and locations, it is impossible to maintain absolute consistency in the spelling of places, people, and terms. There are often competing sets of transliterations that change over time (*Peking* versus *Beijing*), refer to the same places differently (*Kiev* versus *Kyiv*), attempt to follow more exactly the spelling in the original language (*'Abbasid* versus *Abbasid*), use a different English letter for the same phoneme (*Peace of Callias* versus *Peace of Kallias*), or have taken on a life of their own as loanwords in English (*bazaar, assassin, juggernaut, jinseng,* or *kowtow*, among many others). In general, I have chosen the ones most commonly used in the scholarly literature but minimized diacritical marks and accents except when they appear in the sources I quote. Casual readers will not care, and specialists will find fault regardless. The same could be said of the case studies presented in the book: specialists will complain that they are woefully inadequate, while those not already immersed in the scholarly literature may consider the level of detail too high. My goal in writing for both is to present the models in such a way that specialists can better see what I am proposing while those who have no previous background can follow the narrative and appreciate the comparisons without getting lost or confused.

I dedicate this book to the memory of wife, Donna Wilker, who never had a chance to read it and tell me what could be improved.

Thomas J. Barfield
Cambridge, MA

SHADOW EMPIRES

Introduction

EMPIRES WERE THE WORLD'S largest and most durable polities. They dominated Eurasia and North Africa for more than two and a half millennia, only losing the last vestiges of that long hegemony in the early twentieth century. They appeared independently in a variety of cultural contexts worldwide and developed their own distinct imperial traditions. While the success of empires is often attributed to their military might, it is their ability to organize diversity that better explains their long duration and seemingly perpetual reinvention. More than any other type of polity, an empire was of a size and complexity that required tools of governance that set it above and beyond its component parts. Smaller and more parochial city-states and kingdoms, by contrast, maintained narrowly defined boundaries of exclusion between themselves and others that put limits on their size and administrative capacity. Empires too would have insider/ outsider distinctions, but at an entirely different scale and flexibility of measurement. The former was like a local family-run business, the latter like a multinational corporation—your neighborhood coffeeshop versus Starbucks. And while empires might take the name of a founding people or dynastic line, they invariably transcended them.

Empires also left cultural and political templates that survived their demise. Successor states deliberately copied many of them, sometimes claiming to be their heirs. The use of the term *civilization* is often implicitly grounded in sets of high-culture attributes that these empires laid down as distinct and dominant templates in different parts of the world. They were Janus-faced entities simultaneously celebrated for their achievements and condemned for the violence they inflicted on others to sustain themselves.

FIGURE 1.1. *The Distribution of the Eagle Standards* (1810) by Jacques-Louis David.

A Victorian-era Great Britain that put down bloody rebellions against its own colonial rule in India and South Africa could simultaneously celebrate Boudica's equally bloody failed rebellion against imperial Rome in the first century A.D. and eventually erect a statue of her in a fighting chariot outside Parliament in London. In France, Jacques-Louis David's neoclassical painting *The Distribution of the Eagle Standards* celebrated Napoleon's 1804 reintroduction of Roman legionary eagles to inspire his Grande Armée in a style that would have also undoubtedly won praise from Emperor Nero (figure 1.1). Both Russia's Vladimir Putin and China's Xi Jinping appear to long for the glories of empires that the respective revolutions in their countries earlier condemned to the ashcans of history. On the other hand, France's 1960 comic book resister of Rome, Asterix, proved so popular that his exploits were translated into forty different languages and French readers ranked *Asterix the Gaul* itself as number twenty-three in a list of the one hundred best books of the twentieth century in a 1999 *Le Monde* survey.[1]

Definitions: Endogenous and Exogenous (Shadow) Empires

What is an empire, and how does it differ from other types of polities? For the purpose of this study, we will distinguish two basic types of empires: endogenous and exogenous. Endogenous empires emerged through a process of internal development and outward expansion achieved by the forceful incorporation of subcontinental territories inhabited by millions and later tens of millions of people. They were socially cosmopolitan and employed unified administrative systems of governance to rule over their component parts. They extracted the fiscal resources they required internally through systems of direct taxation or tribute payments. Classic examples include ancient Persia, China, and Rome, which we will examine in more detail in chapter 1, but they extended well into the early modern periods with the Ottoman, Spanish, and Mughal Empires. (Endogenous empires were also founded by the Incas and Aztecs in the Americas.) Exogenous empires, by contrast, came into existence as products of their interactions (direct and indirect) with already-established empires, and their persistence depended on such relationships, a form of secondary imperial state formation. Their political and military structures were designed to extract the economic resources on which they depended from external sources rather than internal ones. Their methods for doing so included direct appropriation (raiding and piracy), the establishment of favorable terms of trade, extortion of subsidies in exchange for peace, the receipt of benefits for services rendered, and the scavenging of the ruins of collapsed endogenous empires. Although endogenous empires often dealt with exogenous empires as peer polities, the latter invariably lacked one or more of an endogenous empire's characteristics, such as a large population, high administrative complexity, or a large amount of territory over which it exercised direct sovereignty. Because the emergence and continued existence of exogenous empires were so closely tied to their interactions with endogenous empires, I call them shadow empires.[2]

Shadow empires were not inferior versions or poor, borrowed copies of endogenous empires. They had their own unique structures and can be divided into five different types. The first are maritime empires, which relied on naval power to extract outsize economic benefits from places they did not seek to rule directly. They focused on controlling the means of exchange rather than the means of production, deriving their wealth from the profits of trade rather than the production of the items traded. Maritime empires were significantly smaller in size than endogenous empires or other types of shadow empires. Examples include the Mediterranean-based city-states such as ancient Athens or Carthage and later the Venetian Republic, while Axum may have played a similar role in the Red Sea. Portuguese, English, and Dutch expansion out of the North Atlantic and into the Indian Ocean during the sixteenth and seventeenth centuries created new maritime empires on a much larger scale.

The second type are mirror nomadic steppe empires, whose power was based on horse cavalry militaries and which emerged as an adaptation to the imperial unification of China. In an echo-like fashion, exogenous steppe empires rose and fell in tandem with the endogenous empires established by native Chinese dynasties that supplied them with the resources needed to finance their states. The ancient Xiongnu (second century B.C. to second century A.D.) and medieval Turks (sixth to ninth century) founded the most classic examples of these.

Periphery empires constitute a third exogenous category, which emerged when the power balance between an endogenous empire's margins and its center were reversed and its transfrontier enemies or former clients occupied part or all of its former territories. There were two different types: vulture empires, which sought to maintain the institutional remains of a collapsing empire, and vanquisher empires, whose leaders sought to conquer an intact empire and remake it in their own image. The best examples of vulture empires are those established by dynasties originating in China's northeastern frontier areas after the fall of the Han, Tang, and Ming dynasties in the third, tenth, and seventeenth centuries, respectively. Vanquisher empires, such as those established by Alexander the Great in the fourth century B.C. and the Arab Muslim armies in the seventh century, were much rarer. Unique to the Iranian world, here peoples from the frontier unexpectedly defeated the armies of Achaemenid and Sasanian empires on the battlefield and captured the old empire intact. Unlike the rulers of vulture empires, they sought to impose their own distinct cultural values and ideologies on the newly conquered lands rather than adopting those of the people they conquered.

Empires of nostalgia constitute a fourth exogenous type that was more aspirational than substantive, one reason why they are rarely included in comparative studies. They exploited the remembrance of extinct empires and their cultural legacies to foster an appearance of imperial power that barely existed in any practical terms. While Chinese history during periods of disunion is littered with regional states making outsize imperial claims with hope of growing into them, they either became new endogenous empires themselves or were swallowed up by those that did. In western Europe where no endogenous empire ever emerged after Rome's collapse, Charlemagne's Carolingian Empire in Europe during the ninth century constituted a "next best" option that proved remarkably durable. Although Charlemagne's grandsons divided the empire into kingdoms, its Holy Roman Empire successor based in Germany was more stable and remained intact for 850 years.

Vacuum empires that emerged in the sparsely settled forest zones of northeastern Europe during the medieval period constitute a fifth type of exogenous empire. Here state-level polities of any type were absent before new economic and political interactions with the steppe nomadic empires to their south produced the conditions that could support them. This began with the establishment of the vast nomadic Khazar Empire in the steppe zone north of the Caspian and Black Seas in the mid-seventh century. Khazar demands for tribute and their facilitation of international trade in furs and slaves exported to the caliphate generated a surge of silver into the region that laid the groundwork for the emergence of the Kievan Rus' Empire in the tenth century. It ruled the peoples of the forest zone unchallenged until it was destroyed by the Mongols in the mid-thirteenth century. Interactions in the same region with the Mongol Golden Horde for the next two centuries saw the rise of the Grand Duchy of Lithuania (thirteenth to fifteenth century) in the western forest zone and Muscovy/Russia (fifteenth to eighteenth century) in the east.

If exogenous empires proved overly successful, they could find themselves transformed into endogenous ones. This occurred whenever exogenous empires that expanded beyond their shadow core areas began administering the territories, peoples, or states they had formerly dealt with indirectly. To consolidate their newfound power, they employed the administrative tools of an endogenous empire and, in so doing, became one. The structural DNA of their former shadow empire selves was, however, always reflected in their governing structures even after the transformation was complete. With the exception of empires of nostalgia, each variety of shadow empire produced at least one example of this process: British India (maritime), the Mongol Empire (steppe nomadic), China's Qing dynasty (vulture), the Abbasid Caliphate (vanquisher), and Tsarist Russia (vacuum). Because these five became the largest empires in world history, they are very well known to historians, but their origin as shadow empires has generally been overlooked.

It could be argued that these definitions, discounting size, could apply equally well to large states. This should not be surprising because it appears that empires were the templates for large states and not the reverse. Historically, empires were the crucibles in which the possibility of large states was realized. Indeed, it is difficult to find any examples of large states emerging in areas that were not previously united by some type of empire. It was the experience of empire that created the model, managerial capacity, and mentality needed to rule a large state successfully by employing modified imperial methods of government administration, military organization, and ideology on a smaller scale. Looking at successful large states in the early modern period, we find that their systems of governance drew heavily on the tools first created by empires. It was only in the mid-twentieth century that large states rather than empires became normative, and that may have to do more with their development in the West, where this process was most pronounced, than with any changes in other parts of the world where indigenous and colonial empires ruled supreme, such as South Asia, China, and the Near East, until a century ago. It is also true that with the exponential growth of the world's population in the modern era, many states administered very large populations (forty million people or more) that had been previously found only in the biggest empires of the premodern period. For most of history, there was an order-of-magnitude difference or more between the population size of endogenous empires and that of any other type of state. One difference between large states and empires, however, was their degree of inclusion. Eighteenth-century France or nineteenth-century Germany and Italy attempted to get people within the state to think of themselves as part of a single nation with a common identity; the neighboring multiethnic Austro-Hungarian and Ottoman Empires needed only to convince them they were part of a single polity that maintained order and stability among them.

How many such empires were there? Over a span of 2,500 years, Peter Turchin identified about seventy-five Eurasian and North African mega-empires that he has used in his quantitative research.[3] These include both our endogenous and exogenous types, but because size was his baseline criterion (territories greater than 1 million km^2), this benchmark excludes maritime empires that held relatively little territory and the Holy Roman Empire, which had no clear boundaries. As this is a qualitative study, we will be surveying only a relatively small number of cases in detail, but the appendix provides Turchin's list, with the addition of my characterization of each empire as endogenous or exogenous. If an empire is labeled exogenous, I have also indicated what variety and whether it later transformed itself into an endogenous empire.

Understanding the Significance of Empires from a Comparative Perspective

Although empires have an immensely long history and were the most important polities of their eras, comparative study of them remains relatively underdeveloped. One problem is the absence of agreement on what constitutes an empire and its structural characteristics. Narrow definitions exclude important examples, but adding fundamentally dissimilar polities to the ledger of empires reduces its utility as an analytical category. For example, the contemporaneous steppe nomadic Xiongnu Empire (9 million km^2) and Han China (6 million km^2) were easily peers in size, but the former had a population of less than a million while the latter ruled over fifty million people—not comparable at all. The solution to the problem does not lie in fighting over which empires to exclude from the club but rather in employing Max Weber's sociological concept of "ideal types" as a way to think about them. Weber's ideal type is an artificial construct whose validity is judged by how well it identifies empirical patterned actions. Examining Weber's major synthetic work, *Economy and Society*, Stephen Kalberg wrote that it "never attempts to capture fully any given empirical reality, for this would be an impossible task. Rather, as an analytic treatise it seeks to fulfill a different goal: to formulate ideal types—that is, conceptual tools, or models, for research that chart the patterned meaningful action of persons in diverse groupings."[4] For this reason, no specific case exactly matches an ideal type. Instead the ideal type is to be judged on how well it corresponds to reality or explains the patterns of reproduction in any particular social system. Weber's definition of his ideal types was never a priori (they emerged only after he immersed himself in the case study material) and were employed to build models that elucidated historical social relations and economic developments. This approach can be applied fruitfully to the comparative study of empires.

Endogenous and exogenous empires constitute two ideal types. Both projected hegemony over the people they incorporated into them on an unprecedentedly large scale and maintained that hegemony without constant resort to violence, but they did so in very different ways. Endogenous empires mobilized internal resources to sustain themselves and grew by incorporating new territories. Exogenous empires relied on exploiting external resources of some kind to support themselves, and this could be done without necessarily incorporating new territories into them. While the internal structures of endogenous empires differed from each other in some important respects, they were fundamentally similar. The political structures and economic organization of exogenous empires, by contrast, were not as uniform. They differed sharply not only from endogenous empires but from each other as well. Leo Tolstoy famously wrote that all happy families were alike but that each unhappy family was unhappy in its own way. The same could be said of empires in that all endogenous empires were alike but each exogenous empire was exogenous in its own way. For that reason, I identified five different subtypes of exogenous shadow empires and will explore what made them distinct. In a nice bit of symmetry, by the end of the early modern period all remaining exogenous empires had themselves become endogenous after they adopted territorial expansion models that left no room for shadow exogenous empires of any kind. By the beginning of the nineteenth century, all existing empires were endogenous and could be analyzed as such.

As a comparative study of empires, this book differs from similar works in three respects. First, it focuses on understudied shadow exogenous empires and their relationships with the outside world that sustained them. These are generally deemed worthy of study as empires only after they became endogenous and too large to ignore (the Mongol Empire or Qing dynasty China, for example). Second, it argues that because the templates of both endogenous and exogenous empires originated in ancient and medieval times, cases from those eras should be given analytical priority. In most comparative studies, the opposite is true. Ancient and medieval empires (if presented at all) constitute an introduction to more detailed studies of modern-era colonial empires (mostly European) and their postcolonial legacies. Here these colonial empires will barely be examined except to argue that the majority of them were created by former shadow empires and that their organization reflected that origin. And third, this study decenters Rome as the template for empires. When one lines up all the Eurasian and North African historical cases, it is clear that the most enduring traditions of empire building were not in the West but in China and Persia, where empires emerged earlier, lasted longer, and (most significantly) reemerged after periods of collapse, whereas Rome did not.

The case made in this book is that exogenous empires need to be taken seriously because they were powerful peer polities of endogenous empires and played an enormously significant role in world history. That they are so rarely considered together as a class is likely because they appear so different at first glance. For example, the ancient Athenian maritime empire and the Xiongnu steppe nomadic empire were in many respects polar opposites (navy versus cavalry, urban versus rural, minimal versus maximal territorial size, high versus low levels of literacy, etc.) but had in common the exploitation of other people's resources to finance their states. They also emerged as the direct products of conflicts with neighboring endogenous empires, Persia and China, respectively. The variation in duration of such polities was far wider than of endogenous empires, reflecting the importance of international relations that sustained them. The Athenian maritime empire lasted only a century (508–404 B.C.), but the maritime Venetian Republic survived for more than a thousand years (697–1797). The Xiongnu Empire maintained itself in various forms for five hundred years (210 B.C.–A.D. 304), while the steppe empire created by Huns in Europe (430–469) collapsed soon after the death of Atilla in 453. Charlemagne's Carolingian Empire (800–888) was divided into kingdoms by his grandsons, but the successor Holy Roman Empire (961–1806) survived eight and a half centuries. Successful shadow empires succeeded in the long term either because they transformed their relations with neighboring states into symbiotic ones or because they left the shadows to become endogenous empires themselves. All had coherent political structures and sophisticated strategies that maximized their strengths and minimized their weaknesses. And it is these that deserve more attention from comparative historians and political scientists because their grand strategies, if we may label them that, had very different features from those employed by endogenous empires.

This book also argues that both ancient and medieval empires (endogenous and exogenous) should be given greater analytical prominence because they established the organizational templates employed by later empires. Current historical scholarship on empires focuses instead primarily on European colonial empires, a rather late and unusual type of empire that came into existence in the late eighteenth and early nineteenth centuries and was extinct by the mid-twentieth. Even the best wide-ranging comparative books on empires devote only a quarter of their length to ancient and medieval empires (or none at all) before focusing on the colonial empires of the modern era.[5] The political and economic organization of these modern-era empires is often assumed to be characteristic of empires in general, particularly those that had imperial metropoles separate and distinct from the lands they ruled over. As George Steinmetz notes, while classical land-based empires "combined militarization with restless expansion and various mechanisms aimed at stabilizing and pacifying geopolitical relations," "many (although not all) modern colonies were acquired and discussed in terms of trade, investment, [and] economic exploitation" that entailed "the seizure of sovereignty from locals and the formation of a separate colonial state apparatus."[6] As I hope this book will make clear, these modern-era colonial empires, their modes of administration, and their emphasis on trade and resource extraction employed strategies of rule more similar to those of maritime exogenous empires than endogenous ones. The largest colonial empire of all time was Great Britain's, and it began as an exogenous maritime empire, as did the Dutch and Portuguese colonial empires. The enormous contiguous land-based colonial empires established in Eurasia by Russia and China in the late eighteenth and nineteenth centuries also employed strategies and governing structures they first developed as exogenous empires. For these reasons, historians of colonial empires would be well served by examining these earlier exogenous empires as the templates for those that emerged in the modern era. Ancient Athens in particular developed most of the tools later reinvented by European colonial empires and for that reason alone deserves closer examination.

Finally, this book differs from others by arguing that using the Roman Empire as a template for empires in general is more an obstacle than asset in understanding a type of polity that developed in a wide variety of cultural contexts and took distinctively different forms. Earlier Persian and Chinese models not only provide clearer examples of how empires emerged and were organized, but they also replicated themselves time after time, whereas no endogenous empire emerged to reunite the West after Rome collapsed in the late fifth century. Still, perhaps because it is most familiar to Western scholars and readers, the Roman Empire's evolution is generally presented as if it were universal. For example, in his classic work on empires, Michael Doyle posits an "Augustinian threshold," when a polity became big enough to see itself as an empire, and a "Caracallan threshold," when its parts became thoroughly homogenized.[7] Both of these were real transitions in the Roman Empire that occurred over the course of many centuries and the reigns of many emperors. But Rome's long evolution into an empire was not typical. The Achaemenid Persian Empire of almost 5 million km^2 was conquered by its founder, Cyrus the Great, in the twenty years before his death in 529 B.C. and fully integrated during the reign of Darius the Great (522–486 B.C.). Similarly, the Qin dynasty's founding emperor, Shi Huangdi, united all of China in 221 B.C. and had integrated it uniformly by the time he died in 210 B.C. The templates they created, though modified by their successors, continually reemerged after periods of political and economic collapse. It was the failure of a successor to the Roman Empire to ever emerge in the West that Walter Scheidel argues set its historical development along a different path from Persia, China, or India, where new empires continually replaced old ones.[8] But while Doyle's concept of a distinct Augustinian threshold is not characteristic of other endogenous empires, it *is* characteristic of exogenous empires that transformed themselves into endogenous ones. As will be illustrated in the case studies, this was a process in which rulers of transitioning shadow empires did indeed recognize they were creating something new.[9] Before a truly comparative study of empires worldwide can be said to exist, historians and political scientists alike must endeavor to make themselves as familiar with their histories as they are with that of Rome.

On Structure and Causality

The approach to the comparative study of empires here takes a social science perspective. Its focus on models and patterns of interaction may seem to some to deny the importance of human agency. But as empires were created, maintained, and lost by human beings, obviously their decisions, actions, and responses played a vital role in any historical process. Indeed, the details of each empire hinge on unusual sets of circumstances that differed profoundly from one another. The unification of China under the Qin dynasty was the product of methodical and well-thought-out policies that took a century to realize. The Persian Empire was established by swift conquests and consolidated its diverse territories into a stable empire within only a few decades. Rome's rise, by contrast, was long in coming and had a perpetual ad hoc quality about it. Shadow empires were even more particularistic since they adapted themselves to existing political organizations they had not created. Yet despite their very different origins and characteristics of founding and design, they all fall into the distinct categories of endogenous and exogenous empires I have already outlined. This is not because of some historical determinism, but because these polities had only a few possible pathways to success and many to failure. Since this is a study of empires that were and not empires that might have been, the larger number of failures lies outside our data set— acorns, not oak trees. For example, none of the exogenous empires that became endogenous empires (and only a minority did) anticipated such a transition, as their adaptations to this new status will show. The Mongol Empire's tremendous success, for example, was unexpected by its enemies and initially by the Mongols themselves. Because of these contingencies, the historical models presented here are probabilistic. Given similar structural characteristics, there were regular types of interactions, cycles, or other similarities that reoccurred and that could be expected to reoccur until those conditions changed. However, as a result of the Industrial Revolution, many of the structural features that had been relatively constant for more than two millennia (technology, transport, communications, energy sources, and agrarian economies) changed profoundly and old patterns of interactions ceased or were transformed. Human beings always did have agency in this process but, as Thucydides posited 2,400 years ago when probing the causes of the Peloponnesian War in the ancient Greek world, "human nature being what it is, history will be repeated at some time or other in much the same way."[10] The goal here is to explore empires as polities where interactions with other polities and their own people set the parameters for their decision making over long periods of time. It is a supplement to the study of individual empires and their histories, not a replacement for them.

Looking for broader comparative historical structures is far from a new endeavor. Anthropologists such as Eric Wolf and Marshall Sahlins did pioneering work that has greatly influenced this study, but I have also drawn inspiration from two other particular sources outside my own field.[11] The first is the thinking of the fourteenth-century Arab social historian ibn Khaldun, whose *Muqaddimah* produced models of societies and their interactions in Islamic North Africa and the Near East.[12] He focused on the relationships between tribal societies in economically marginal areas and class-based urban societies in surplus-producing regions that wielded regional political power. His model examined the dynamics of each and explained how it came to pass that so many of the region's ruling dynasties had their origins in marginal places where kinship and descent were the main organizing principles. Once such people conquered cities where power was based on money and institutional authority, they adopted city ways of ruling that they could not sustain for more than four generations before some new group displaced them. Ibn Khaldun himself noted that empires like the Abbasid Caliphate, with their larger financial base, were more stable, but he did not develop a model for them. In some of my earlier work, I also noted that his cogent model of tribal descent groups wielding power assumed they were structurally egalitarian like the Bedouin but that nomadic Turko-Mongolian descent groups were hierarchical, and that type of tribal organization proved far more adaptive to empire building on the Eurasian steppe.[13]

Jumping ahead many centuries, my second major influence is the French Annales school approach, which welcomed a combination of theories and methodologies into history from anthropology, geography, sociology, economics, and psychology. Fernand Braudel's concept of the *longue durée* was particularly valuable in this respect because of its focus on the very long-standing and slowly changing aspects of social life and economic production that framed the relationships between people and the world around them.[14] To an anthropologist such as myself who was interested in societies within their historical contexts, this seemed a productive way to proceed. Anthropologists who only nod in the direction of taking time depth seriously or historians who view comparative social science as marginal for their own work may disagree, but my own ethnographic field-work in northern Afghanistan made me appreciate the value of both. In 1975 the unschooled nomads I lived with along the banks of the Oxus River still recounted the damage Chinggis Khan did to their region in 1221, and they worked up a temper while doing so. When I returned to their community in 2002, the son of the khan who had inherited the family's sheep told me he had doubled their number to 1,500. When I asked how this was possible during a period of brutal wars in which this region was often contested by rival factions, he explained that "people win wars, people lose wars, but the winners always buy sheep." While here I write at the "winners always buy sheep" macro-level, we should not lose sight that it was some particular person who brought sheep to market to sell and another who bought them, each with a tale that deserves telling in its own right. Although they are but sketches, the case studies illustrate the human complexity involved, along with the backstories of at least some of individual men and women who created, ruled, and lost empires.

Book Organization

A comparative study must have categories of comparison, and so I begin chapter 1 by defining in more detail the common structural characteristics of endogenous empires that first emerged sui generis in temperate Eurasia and North Africa during the second half of the first millennium B.C. The largest came to govern territories of 5 million km^2 with populations of more than forty million people. In a world that had previously experienced nothing like them, empires were both acclaimed and condemned but could never be ignored. Even when long gone, the ruins they left behind continued to amaze the living. With newer endogenous empires periodically replacing those that were destroyed, they remained the world's dominant polities until the twentieth century. To understand how they became so dominant, I survey the origin and structural characteristics of the three most significant ancient endogenous empires: the Achaemenid Persian Empire in southwest Asia, the Qin and Han dynasties in China, and the Roman Empire in the Mediterranean Basin. Each created the default model for imperial rule in its respective region using different political structures and styles of administration that were copied by successor endogenous empires. One could easily expand this limited comparison to other endogenous empires, but the primary focus of this book is on the exogenous or shadow empires that emerged in response to them, which are analyzed in subsequent chapters.

Chapter 2 examines exogenous maritime empires using the case of the world's first, ancient Athens, as its primary example. Maritime empires used navies to exert power and preserve their independence, extracting the resources needed to finance them externally from trade profits, transit taxes, tribute payments, and occasionally raiding and piracy. Most, including Athens, emerged in the context of conflict. Its rise to empire began when the Greek city-states in the western Aegean united to fend off two Persian invasions in the fifth century B.C. Athens turned that voluntary alliance into a maritime empire that left its member city-states free to run their own affairs under Athenian supervision as long as they paid their required tribute since they sought economic rather than territorial hegemony. Athens itself ran a democratic political system whose leaders condemned the autocracies found universally in endogenous empires like Persia, a feature it shared with later maritime empires that generally governed themselves through some kind of collective representative body. Although it lasted less than a century, the Athenian maritime empire model was replicated by ancient Carthage and medieval Venice in the Mediterranean and in the sixteenth century by a set of early modern North Atlantic maritime empires: Portugal, Holland, and England. In the late eighteenth century the British would transform their maritime exogenous empire in South Asia into an endogenous one by mounting a series of military campaigns that would eventually bring all of the Indian subcontinent under their rule by the mid-nineteenth century.

Chapter 3 examines the exogenous steppe empires in Mongolia that relied on horse cavalry to exert military power and extract resources from China to finance them. They first emerged at the end of the third century B.C. after the Qin dynasty unified China, drove the nomads out of many of their traditional pasturelands, and built the Great Wall to keep them out. The Xiongnu nomads of the Ordos region responded to this challenge by conquering the other neighboring steppe nomadic groups to create a unified "mirror empire" that then dealt with China as a peer polity. The Xiongnu financed their empire by extracting tribute payments and trading rights from China in times of peace and by raiding China in times of war. Since the nomads avoided occupying Chinese agricultural land that they would have to administer, Chinese policies of appeasement worked rather well to buy peace. Indeed, after periods of initial hostility, the relationship between nomadic empires and China became symbiotic, with the nomads defending weakening Chinese dynasties that paid them from domestic rebels and rival frontier peoples. The two became so closely linked that when the imperial Han and Tang dynasties in China collapsed, so did their mirror images on the steppe. In the thirteenth century Chinggis Khan unified Mongolia but could not strike an appeasement deal with the foreign dynasties then ruling North China and so ended up conquering them—beginning a process that saw his successors transform an exogenous Mongol Empire seeking subsidies into an endogenous empire that would come to rule most of Eurasia.

Chapter 4 explores the exogenous empires that emerged from the periphery of endogenous empires when they lost control over frontier territories where they had previously exerted some kind of hegemony. During periods of imperial state collapse, vulture shadow empires established viable states by expanding into the leftover parts of the old empire. Their rulers combined the old empire's surviving administrative personnel and governing institutions with a military force drawn from their own frontier tribal people. The conquest of North China by the Khitan Liao dynasty from Manchuria in the tenth century after the fall of the Tang dynasty and the expansion of that state by a new Jurchen Jin dynasty in the twelfth provide the clearest examples, but there were many others. As rulers drawn from foreign minority groups, they found it hard to retain power within China after restoring stability there unless they transformed themselves into an endogenous empire by conquering all of China as the Manchu Qing dynasty succeeded in doing in the seventeenth century.

A different type of exogenous vanquisher empire could also emerge from the periphery by conquering a fully intact endogenous empire and reorganizing it with new and innovative political structures. Unlike a vulture empire that developed after an endogenous empire and the order it provided had collapsed, a vanquisher empire took command of a functioning administrative structure and a working economy. They were rare and appeared only in southwest Asia where Alexander the Great toppled the Persian Empire in the fourth century B.C. and the Muslim Arab armies defeated both the Byzantines and Sasanians to establish the Umayyad Caliphate in the mid-seventh century. The caliphate reached the zenith of its power when it became an endogenous empire under new Abbasid rulers in the mid-eighth century and moved its capital to Baghdad. The Abbasid Caliphate adopted many of the governing institutions of the old Sasanian Empire and filled its ranks with a Persian Muslim elite rather than Arabs.

Chapter 5 examines exogenous empires of nostalgia that displayed the outward trappings of an empire without its substance by employing an invented remembrance of an extinct imperial polity. This demanded a suspension of disbelief by rulers and elite subordinate subjects alike for whom a revived fiction of empire created a framework for cooperation that buttressed the state's political legitimacy in a world where they were never entirely sovereign. Rare as vanquisher empires but at the opposite end of a power spectrum, empires of nostalgia emerged only in western Europe where the memory of the Roman Empire was still strong but no polity was powerful enough to re-create it as occurred regularly in China. Charlemagne's ninth-century empire, which was over 1 million km^2 in size with a population of between ten and twenty million, fell into this category before it was dissolved by his heirs a generation later. A successor Holy Roman Empire established in the tenth century proved even more ephemeral as a territorial unit, but its political structure created such a durable framework for cooperation among its component sovereign states that it survived until 1806.

Chapter 6 examines the emergence of exogenous vacuum empires in northern Europe's forest zone, a region that produced no state-level polities until the late eighth century when interactions with the Khazar steppe nomadic empire, the Byzantines, and the caliphate to their south monetized the regional economy. The revenue from trade in furs, slaves, and raw materials enabled warlike outsiders such as the Kievan Rus' to create a large if sparsely populated empire that lasted for 350 years until it was destroyed by the Mongols in 1240. As the power of the Mongols declined, successor states based in Lithuania and Russia vied for dominance in the forest zone, a struggle that eventually led to the emergence of a Russian tsardom in the sixteenth century. Under Peter the Great, Russia transformed itself into an endogenous empire in the eighteenth century, one that became the world's largest by landmass.

Chapter 7 examines the question of why, after a successful run of almost two and a half millennia, all the world's shadow empires either disappeared or transformed themselves into endogenous empires by the mid-eighteenth century. As the previous chapters illustrated, shadow empires were part of a world system in which they wielded independent power that endogenous empires found easier to accommodate than destroy. That balance changed when newly empowered endogenous empires, many former shadow empires themselves, sought to eliminate them. Steppe nomadic empires ceased to exist entirely after their peoples and lands were incorporated by China's Qing dynasty in the east and Russia's Romanov dynasty in the west. Both were former shadow empires that became two of the world's largest endogenous empires by ensuring that none of the territories on their peripheries would ever again wield significant military power. The Atlantic maritime empires (Portugal, Holland, and Britain) all became endogenous empires too after they began ruling colonial territories directly rather than depending on the profits of trade alone. Venice, the only remaining Mediterranean maritime shadow empire that survived from medieval times into the early modern era, was conquered by Napoleon in 1797. Napoleon was also indirectly responsible for the demise of the Holy Roman Empire, an equally long-lived empire of nostalgia, which was dissolved by its last emperor to prevent it from falling into his hands.

The endogenous empires that emerged or expanded in this process, however, all collapsed during the twentieth century. The hypothesis presented here suggests that while endogenous empires were well designed to run large, steady state agrarian economic systems, they proved ill-equipped to cope with the rapid technological changes produced by the Industrial Revolution during the late eighteenth and nineteenth centuries. The capitalist economic system privileged industrial production over agriculture, thrived on constant technological change, and generated serial economic disruptions. While empires might have been able to cope with any one of these elements singly, they proved incapable of coping with all of them simultaneously. Moreover, these new features were incompatible with the values endogenous empires sought to defend: stability over innovation, agriculture over industry, cosmopolitan worldviews over nationalist ones, and sets of conservative social values resistant to change. They all (Ottoman, Hapsburg, Russian, Qing China) fell like dominoes in the first decades of the twentieth century, a process that came to a climax during the First World War. The overseas colonial empires that survived that bloodbath, based on maritime empire templates, proved better adapted to a capitalist economic system but shared the fate of their predecessors after the Second World War when they too dissolved. Nevertheless, the tools that empires used to wield their power did not die with them, and in a final section I discuss their twenty-first-century legacy in world power politics.

CHAPTER ONE

Endogenous Empires

"My name is Ozymandias, king of kings:
Look on my works, ye Mighty, and despair!"
Nothing beside remains. Round the decay
Of that colossal wreck, boundless and bare
The lone and level sands stretch far away.

—PERCY BYSSHE SHELLEY, *OZYMANDIAS*, 1818

ENDOGENOUS EMPIRES WERE STATES established by the forceful incorporation of subcontinental-size territories that exerted sovereignty over millions or tens of millions of people employing a unified and centralized administrative system. From today's perspective, the population threshold may seem easier to achieve than the territorial one, as there are a multitude of modern cities with millions of people. But in 1000 B.C., when the world population was estimated at fifty million, or even five hundred years later, when it had doubled to one hundred million, this threshold was much harder to achieve.[1] While ancient Egypt's Old Kingdom in 2600 B.C. may have been the first to meet the minimum empire size and population measure, its status remained unique for the next two thousand years. Egypt's neighboring Bronze Age competitors, such as the Akkadians (ca. 2300–2200 B.C.) in Mesopotamia and the Hittites (ca. 1400–1200 B.C.) in Anatolia, never reached the territorial threshold and were probably well under the population threshold too. This changed after the middle of the eighth century B.C., when a large number of new empires began appearing in the temperate agricultural zones of Eurasia and North Africa. Their territory sizes and populations rose so explosively that by 100 B.C. just three of them (Roman, Persian, and Chinese) would dominate most of the midlatitude lands between the Atlantic and Pacific Oceans and maintain that dominance, with occasional changes in dynasties, for many centuries.

The explosion of new empires began with the Assyrians (744–612 B.C.), whose center was in the highlands of the upper Euphrates River in today's northern Iraq. At its height in 670 B.C., the Assyrian Empire encompassed 1.4 million km^2 and had incorporated all the core areas formerly held by the Akkadians, Hittites, and Egyptians.[2] It was replaced by one of its subject peoples from highland Iran, the Medes, who allied with the Mesopotamian Babylonians and steppe nomadic Scythians to capture the Assyrian capital of Nineveh in 612 B.C., leading to the collapse of their empire. The Medes (678–549 B.C.) established a new and even larger empire (2.8 million km^2) based on the Iranian plateau, leaving Egypt independent and the Neo-Babylonians (626–539 B.C.) ruling Mesopotamia, the Levant, and northern Arabia. This significant accomplishment is largely forgotten because the Medes were displaced by the even bigger and longer-lasting Achaemenid Persian Empire (559–330 B.C.), which first absorbed the Median base on the Iranian plateau and then conquered both Mesopotamia and Egypt. By 500 B.C. the Achaemenids ruled an empire of 5.5 million km^2 that ran from Egypt and the eastern Mediterranean deep into central Asia and northern India, a hegemony that largely continued under the successor Parthian, Kushan, and Sasanian Empires. The other ends of Eurasia saw similar developments with a bit of lag time. Unlike in the Near East, where a series of ever-larger empires succeeded one another, imperial unification in China was the endpoint of a long process of successive state consolidation. As the Warring States period began around 475 B.C., hundreds of small states in the Yellow River valley had already been absorbed into seven regional kingdoms that would wage war with one another until China was finally unified under the short-lived Qin dynasty in 221 B.C. Its imperial structure was maintained by the succeeding Han dynasty (206 B.C.–A.D. 220), which continued expanding south and west until it encompassed around 6 million km^2. Empire building in the Mediterranean west began with Rome's rather piecemeal expansion during the third century B.C., but by the time the Roman Empire reached its maximum size in A.D. 117, it also ruled an empire of 5 million km^2. These three empires not only dominated most of the Eurasian continent but, with populations of more than fifty million each, ruled over the majority of the world's estimated two hundred million people for many centuries.

Structural Characteristics of Endogenous Empires

Before examining the distinct templates for imperial rule that each of these major endogenous empires created and that were maintained by successor empires in their respective regions, it is useful to examine six internal structural characteristics they all shared.[3]

Endogenous empires were organized both to administer and to exploit diversity, whether economic, political, religious, or ethnic. While empires may have been established through the hegemony of a single region or people, they all grew more cosmopolitan over time with the incorporation of new territories and populations different from themselves. The elite of an empire could be changed or replaced over time without the necessary collapse of the state structure. Egypt's many dynasties were a notable example of this, as was the tendency of Roman emperors to be drawn from non-Italian regions after the end of Augustus's line. Even in China, where preferences were given to a dynasty's home region during the formation of a new empire, once established it soon moved to a countrywide recruitment base to staff it.

It was an empire's ability to incorporate different ethnic, regional, and religious groups into a single governing structure that made it so different from locality-based polities such as city-states that organized themselves on the basis of some common similarity. Empires were not only comfortable with diversity, they thrived on it. The famous Achaemenid frieze at Persepolis, with representatives from all the Persian Empire's many component satrapies lined up in their native dress to present tribute of distinctive local products, was a physical representation of this diversity. Of course, this was not because empires thought well of peoples different from themselves, but rather because their policies were designed to make all groups integral parts of the empire that shared a common political order. It was no missionary enterprise. The first steps were often brutal: to incorporate or destroy any groups that opposed them militarily or politically. This was at times accomplished by wholesale massacres and enslavement, transfers of conquered populations to distant parts of the empire, settlement of imperial troops and immigrants in new territories, and removal of a group's indigenous political leaders or their conversion into the empire's agents. The recognition of such power could lead to preemptive offers of voluntary incorporation in return for special status, a common event in the Roman and Persian world but less so in China. The advantage of getting ahead of the curve was considerable. Local rulers and their descendants not only maintained their power as subordinates within the empire (at least for a time) but could call on imperial forces to put down rebellions against them. Once rival groups were politically neutralized, empires displayed a high tolerance for local variation as long as it did not interfere with good order and the collection of taxes.

Endogenous empires maintained centralized institutions of governance that were separate and distinct from their rulers. While histories of empires focus on their emperors for good reason—decisions were made at the top—these rulers were institutional trustees who administered and commanded resources that were not their private property. Unlike kingdoms, which could be divided among the ruler's heirs as a personal patrimony, empires were normally indivisible, and competition was over who would hold a singular high office to run them, not how the empire could be divided up when its ruler died. In this sense empires were like modern corporations, which are recognized as legal entities distinct both from the people who own their assets and from those who manage their assets. This may be an easy concept to grasp in today's world, where such institutions are common, but it was an innovation that empires pioneered and that set them apart from other polities. Rulers in polities that made no distinction between public and private resources would have endorsed the view reputedly expressed by France's Louis XIV (1638–1715) that "L'état c'est moi" (I am the state). Rulers of empires took more heed of his better-attested deathbed observation, "Je m'en vais, mais l'état demeurera toujours" (I am going away, but the state will always remain).

This structure required an institutional staff to manage the state's business professionally because empires reserved the right to make all important policy decisions from the center and in many cases handled what might seem trivial matters too. This bureaucracy was composed of an elite cadre of literate people who were normally recruited from nonelite parts of the male population whose social statuses made them ineligible to compete for public power, including slaves, freedmen, and eunuchs in societies where such categories of people existed. The authority they exerted was institutional rather than personal, and they worked behind the scenes, often invisible to the general public. These people were particularly important in an empire's intelligence system, such as in the Persian Empire's "Listening-Watch," which was designed so that "the King himself, who had the name of Master and God, might see everything and hear everything," and they were so pervasive that "everyone conducted himself at all times just as if those who were within hearing were so many eyes and ears of the king."[4] Over time, however, these servants of the state were regularly accused of being its de facto rulers. Confucian officials in China argued that, for the good of the state, it was their job to restrain rulers who sought to act too independently. In ancient Rome it might be harder to rein in an emperor once he took power, but getting the job almost always required the support of the palace Praetorian Guard if a contender did not have his own army. Such embedded institutions were invariably at odds with an emperor's relatives and other elite patrimonial members of the court that included powerful women as well as men. While individual officials were vulnerable to dismissal, imprisonment, or even loss of life, they were irreplaceable as an institutional body because an empire could not operate without them. The bureaucracy also provided policy continuity designed to survive incompetent heads of state. As we shall see in their dealings with shadow empires, such officials sometimes parlayed their experience into new jobs with old enemies when the empires they served exiled them or collapsed. But none of this centralized administration could operate unless the systems of transportation and communications, discussed next, were also in place.

Endogenous empires established transportation systems designed to serve the imperial center militarily and economically. Sophisticated and well-maintained transportation systems were characteristic of all great empires. No place in the empire was beyond the center's military reach, and supplies needed for military operations were stored throughout the empire. The Persian, Roman, Chinese, and Incan road systems were particularly impressive in size and all had the capacity to move military forces to the remotest parts of the empire when needed.[5] These roads were supplemented by well-maintained systems of rest stops or caravanserais, as well as bridge or ferry river crossings—services that allowed the empire to oversee who was traveling and on what business. Empires also made large investments in ports to facilitate sea trade and canal systems that linked inland rivers for bulk transport. The level of investment in these infrastructures was well beyond the capacity of all but the richest parts of the empire to finance on their own, particularly in sparsely populated and economically marginal territories. This development was two-edged for the people living in those marginal areas: increased connectivity improved their links to the outside world but left them more vulnerable to the control of the states that built them.

Economically this transportation network allowed imperial centers to support a population and level of sophistication well beyond the capacity of the local hinterland. Where bulk transportation of commodities was possible, the empire's capital (or sometimes dual capitals) became mega-centers that dwarfed all others. Maritime imports of grain from Egypt and North Africa were vital to Rome's survival as a city that reached perhaps a million people.[6] China invested heavily in a series of canals that moved goods to its capitals and provided north–south linkages between its river systems flowing east to west.[7] Aztec success in conquering the lake regions of central Mexico underlay the rapid growth of their capital to a size that astonished the Spanish.[8] Areas that did not have access to such water transport focused on roads and caravan routes using wheeled vehicles or pack animals (except in the New World, where these were both absent). Capitals such as Incan Cuzco or Assyria's Nineveh were impressive imperial centers and covered large areas, but they were subject to much stricter upper limits on their size because they relied primarily on the agricultural surplus derived from their own local hinterlands.[9]

Empires achieved a level of economic integration that facilitated the large-scale expansion of trade and production. Although arising out of bloodshed and conquest, an imperial state was most admired for the peace it gave its component parts. Areas that had suffered endemic warfare could now turn their attention to trade, investment, and production of goods. The market for such products was also greatly increased. The level of domestic production and distribution of goods reached unprecedented scales, to which was added extensive foreign trade in high-value luxury imports. These economic ties bound the empire's component parts together far more strongly than any army. Roads and ports that were first built to ensure the rapid transport of troops and weapons to put down rebellions eventually became the lifelines of civilian commerce that superseded military force as the key to maintaining unity. Whether cause or effect, the world population doubled to two hundred million people (or perhaps even higher) by A.D. 1 after empires had become the dominant polities across Eurasia and North Africa.

Endogenous empires had sophisticated systems of communication that allowed them to administer all subject areas from the center directly. If trade and taxation were the material lifeblood that flowed through the empire's veins, then its communications system could be likened to its central nervous system. All important policy decisions in empires were made at the center, so the expedited flow of information was critical to imperial survival. Roads that transported armies and merchandise also sped information of all types from the very edges of empire to the center for analysis and disposition. Although soldiers on the march were a visible sign of imperial power, the quieter flow of information to the center and instructions from the center was perhaps more impressive. All empires had some sort of fast official postal system that variously included horse riders, runners, or boats. Herodotus famously described the organization and speed of the Persian Empire's messenger service in glowing terms: "Than this system of messengers there is nothing of mortal origin that is quicker. This is how the Persians arranged it: they say that for as many days as the whole journey consists in, that many horses and men are stationed at intervals of a day's journey, one horse and one man assigned to each day. And him neither snow nor rain nor heat nor night holds back from for the accomplishment of the course that has been assigned to him, as quickly as he may."[10] Critical information might travel even faster by beacon towers. With each tower erected in view of the next tower, messages in China during the Han dynasty were recorded as moving as fast as 43 km/hr.[11] Aristotle observed that the Persian Empire was also well staffed "with couriers and scouts and messengers and signals-officers. And such was the orderly arrangement of this, and particularly of the system of signal-beacons which were ready to burn in succession from the uttermost limits of the Empire that the King knew the same day all that was news in Asia."[12]

But a communications system consisted of more than just ways to transmit information over long distances. It required a sophisticated record-keeping system, a permanent bureaucracy that managed the information flow, and a system for dealing with information received in a timely manner. This included rules for deciding which issues could be handled by the staff and which were important enough to pass on to the ruler, who could not attend to every detail. Although some empires were content to let administrators employ regional languages locally, they all adopted shared administrative language or writing systems that were understood by all its officials. This could be accomplished in a number of ways. Some used writing or symbolic systems that worked around spoken language differences, such as Chinese ideographic characters, Egyptian hieroglyphs, or Incan *khipu* knot skeins. More common was the adoption of an official language with standardized grammars and alphabet systems for use throughout the empire. These included Latin and Greek in the Roman world, Aramaic and Persian in various Iranian empires, and Arabic in the Islamic world. Their distinct alphabet systems spread well beyond an empire's borders. (The most common alphabetic scripts in the world today are derived from imperial Latin, Greek, Aramaic, and Arabic models, despite their often uneven correspondence with a language's phonetic structure.) Finally, there were empires that adopted a lingua franca for administration that became a universal second language for members of the political elite, merchants, and scholars who were not born speaking it. These included Greek in the eastern Hellenistic world, Latin in the post-Roman West, Arabic in lands of the Islamic Caliphate, and Persian in the Turkic empires of central Asia and Mughal India. Equally important were empires' impositions of standardized measures (for weight, distance, volume, troop size, and money) and common numerical systems used in official accounting registers. Such systems did not always displace localized usages, but they did serve as common denominators understood throughout the empire and meant that imperial officials at the center did not have to keep track of myriad local variations.

Endogenous empires proclaimed a singular right to rule within their territories and projected their military forces outward. While maintaining a monopoly on the legitimate use of force may be a baseline requirement of all states, empires faced problems of scale because their territories were so vast. Preservation of internal order required an imperial army with a centralized chain of command that could deal with disturbances in any part of the empire. But to the extent that empires regularly relied on military force to preserve internal order, they were short-lived polities. Successful empires better maintained internal order by effective administration, the implementation of common legal systems that could be relied on throughout their territories, and a system of government appointees responsible for carrying out imperial policy. Local officials were often constrained about what they could do without permission from the center. Rebellions by ordinary people were considered signs of administrative failure in well-run empires and continuous rebellions the mark of those on the verge of collapse.

Empires sought to expand well beyond the limits of other types of states. In their growth phases, they generally stopped only when they reached the political frontier of another empire of similar power to their own (Rome and Persia); when they reached deserts, steppes, mountains, or forests that they could not profitably occupy (China and the Mongolian steppe, Rome and the Sahara and Arabian Deserts); where an advance that could be accomplished militarily was forgone as part of a strategic policy designed to create a defensible frontier (China's Great Wall and Hadrian's Wall in Britain); or where the cost of occupation was later deemed to outweigh the benefits (Persia in mainland Greece, China in central Asia, Rome in Germania). Once established, however, imperial borders displayed remarkable persistence and continuity. In part this was because empires eventually stationed the bulk of their troops on the frontiers, not at their centers. Even in decline, empires sought to defend the whole of their territory. Very few (notably the Byzantines) retreated to the core from which they started when pressured on the frontier. Instead empires tended to direct ever-scarcer resources from the center to the frontier to hold the line even at the risk of collapsing the whole system— which it often did.

Endogenous empires sponsored imperial projects that imposed some type of unity throughout the system. One of the reasons empires were so tolerant of diversity was that they expected that some aspects of their own cultural system would eventually overlay and even replace local ones to create an overarching imperial system of values and symbols shared by all within the empire. These were reflected in uniform city plans, architectural styles, symbols, calendars, rituals, art, and fashion that marked an imperial presence even at an empire's margins and sometimes well beyond them. It was a vision that created what we often identify as a civilization. As a project that allowed wide participation, it was implemented in a series of stages that moved from coercion through co-optation to cooperation and finally identification. Today we would call this soft power, and it was fundamentally cultural, often attractive even to an empire's enemies. This cultural legacy and the vision of belonging to something grand and great regularly survived an empire's political collapse and remained alive as a historic ideal to be emulated in the future.

Two Templates for State Authority

It is generally assumed that an endogenous empire exerts direct control over all the territory and people within its borders and administers them with a uniform set of rules and practices that apply from the empire's heart to its farthest margins—one law to rule them all. In this vision of power, the component parts of the empire resemble slices of processed American cheese: each is expected to be uniform in texture and the same as any other. Deviations from this ideal represent a quality-control problem that the state needs to address if it has the power to do so or disguise if it does not. It is a model that was classically employed where an empire's people and economically productive territories were relatively evenly distributed with multiple lines of connectivity among them. The model was ill adapted to parts of the world in which such regions were separated from one another by sparsely populated wastelands in which the population distribution resembled that of islands in an archipelago. Nor did it work well in mountainous areas where exerting direct political control over the people who lived there was both difficult and costly, even when they resided near the centers of imperial power (think the Alps or the Hindu Kush). An empire's best strategy under these conditions was to impose direct control over its productive centers and the lines of communication among them while largely ignoring the rest. This was a Swiss cheese model of governance in which you not only expected to find holes in every slice of cheese but understood that each slice had holes of different shapes and sizes. Moreover, these cheese holes did not constitute defects (as they would in American cheese) but were the natural byproducts of the very process that created Swiss cheese. In other words, in areas where resources and populations were unevenly distributed or not worth the cost of administration, the goal was to rule the cheese and ignore the holes. It made little sense for an empire to fill cheese holes by imposing its direct rule where the return did not justify the investment and more cost-effective alternatives were available. One of these was to apply different administrative rules to people in cheese-hole lands and govern them indirectly. This could be done positively, with friendship alliances and gifts that won people over, or negatively, by punishing hostile behavior with periodic military campaigns and trade embargoes. Rulers who took Swiss cheese as their default judged its value by weight rather than volume and tailored their policies accordingly.

With this distinction in mind, we will turn to a comparison of ancient Persia, China, and Rome as examples of how endogenous empires seeking to impose their rule could produce very different types of imperial governmental structures and policies. It is a fruitful comparison because they not only emerged in close proximity to one another in time and space but also provided the templates that successor empires in their core regions adopted as their own. As noted earlier, one of the biggest comparative differences was the degree of autonomy within the empire that each took as normative. None might be able to completely implement its preferred model of governance or be entirely consistent, but the ideas on which they were based were very different and had great staying power. Persia employed a "king of kings" model in which subsidiary rulers with local autonomy were an integral part of the system and not all the people within its territory were necessarily under direct state control—a classic Swiss cheese template. By contrast, in China there was a firm belief that the emperor should directly command "all under heaven," a concept that excluded the possibility of any even partially sovereign subordinates or local autonomy within the empire. Its governors were expected to ensure that all of its inhabitants recognized the authority of the central state and obeyed its laws. China even went a step further and attempted to assert its ideological primacy in its foreign relations as well. Just as a ruler of all under heaven could have no equals at home, China believed it was only right to demand that other polities accept its theoretical hierarchical superiority before they could engage in diplomatic and trade relationships. While China did not always succeed in these attempts, this concept under-lay its creation of the tributary system that served as the framework for China's diplomacy until the nineteenth century. Rome fell between these two extremes, moving from a Persian-like subsidiary ruler model to one of direct imperial control more like China's as the collective rule based around the Senate that characterized the late Roman Republic gave way to an emperor system beginning with Augustus in 27 B.C. These systems were not the products of arbitrary decisions but derived from strategies each empire developed to govern its vast realms. That successive empires maintained them was evidence of their utility.

A Tale of Three Ancient Empires: Persia, China, and Rome

PERSIA

The Achaemenid Persian Empire (550–330 B.C.) is the least well-documented of the ancient Eurasian endogenous empires because it left few written accounts of its own history. This was in sharp contrast to the Greeks in the fifth to fourth century B.C., when writers such as Thucydides were pioneering detailed comparative histories in which the Greek world was central. China also had a strong tradition of political history dating back many centuries. By the second century B.C., the court itself sponsored an official history that led to the detailed accounts of the Qin and Han dynasties by Sima Qian, a model followed by all successive dynasties in China. For whatever reason, the Persians showed little interest in this type of history or explaining themselves to the world, so we know of them and their empire largely through Greek sources, a few inscriptions, and archaeological evidence.[13] Unfortunately Greek hostility toward the Persians was widespread and reflected negatively on them and their way of life. Even in the twenty-first century the Persian Empire's two invasions of Greece could still inspire such epic comic-book-inspired films as *300* (which grossed an amazing $450 million in 2006) and its 2014 sequel, *300: Rise of an Empire*, which portrayed Persian rulers as monstrous tyrants driving their slavish minions into battle with whips. Fortunately, Xenophon and Herodotus, two of the most important Greek sources, presented some favorable opinions—and indeed were accused by their contemporaries of being too pro-Persian—including the latter's admiration that Persians educated their boys in "three things only, riding and archery and truth-telling."[14] This was hardly a curriculum designed to produce servile whip-driven minions.

The Persians were a tribal subject people of the Medes who rebelled under Cyrus the Great (r. 559–530 B.C.) and replaced them in 550 B.C. Cyrus then expanded east into central Asia, where Bactria and Sogdiana appear to have joined with him rather than fight and held a special status afterward. Persian advances in the west involved greater conflict, with Lydia conquered in 547/6 B.C. and the Neo-Babylonian Empire in 539 B.C. After Cyrus was killed in a battle with the Saka steppe nomads in central Asia in 530 B.C., his son Cambyses II (r. 530–522 B.C.) added Egypt, Nubia, and Libya to the empire in 525 B.C. Darius (r. 522–486 B.C.), from a junior line of descent, won a short civil war to succeed Cambyses and during his thirty-six-year rule both stabilized the empire and saw it reach its maximum extent. In only a single lifetime the Achaemenids had gone from a rebel tribe to the world's largest empire, one that ruled from the Nile in the west to the Indus in the east and from the steppes of central Asia to the shores of the Indian Ocean (map 1.1). A Persian model of imperial rule developed and created institutions that maintained its unity for more than two centuries. It was a model that both survived civil wars over succession and kept distant provinces from breaking away. Persia's failure to add mainland Greece to its collection of provinces was one of its few failures.

According to Herodotus, the Persians had a hierarchical tribal and clan social structure: "Of these the Pasargadae are the noblest, and to them belongs the Achaemenid clan, from which all the Persian kings come. The other Persian tribes are: Panthialaei, Derusiaei, Germanii—they are all agriculturalists; the others are pastoralists: Dai, Mardi, Dropici, Sagartii."[15] Unlike the Scythian and Saka steppe nomads, those in the Zagros Mountain region of Iran were part of an economy and political system in which pastoralists and farmers were interdependent. This dynamic and the complex role nomads played in dealing with states on the Iranian plateau appear to have been similar to those described by modern ethnographers in the same region.[16] The Persians gravitated toward a king-of-kings model of distributed power when building their empire because this was

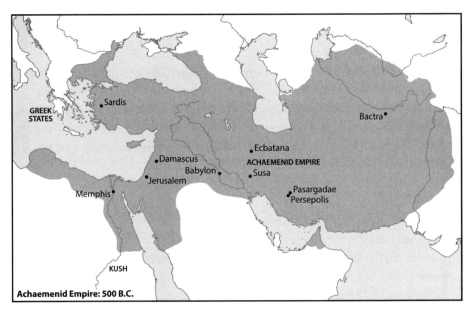

MAP 1.1. The Achaemenid Persian Empire.

how they had previously organized their own tribal political structure. In a political system based on hierarchical descent groups where only members of the royal clans were eligible to compete for power, lower-ranking descent groups and their leaders did not conceive of themselves as possible contenders for supreme rule but could act as allies or enemies of those who were. New royal ruling groups could only be established by outsiders replacing existing ones as the Persians had done to the Medes and Alexander would do to the Persians. Consequently, Persian rulers were comfortable granting autonomy to leaders of subordinate clans and tribes and left them in command of their own people since they did not see them as threats. They took the same attitude toward many of the non-Persian subordinate kings whom they also left in control of their own territories as clients under close Persian supervision. While the Persian Empire experienced many civil wars over succession, the contenders were always members of the royal house. This was in sharp contrast to leaders in egalitarian tribal systems where competition for supreme leadership was open to anyone. Here no ruler could trust subordinates not to use their resources to take power for themselves if the opportunity arose. States established by tribes with hierarchical traditions like the Persians (or later the Mongols and Turks) had very long-lasting dynasties that ruled over large territories; these established egalitarian tribes like those that dominated the Arab world in medieval times, had dynasties that were deposed within three or four generations, and could generally manage to hold only regional territories at best.[17]

The tribal and nomadic origin of the Persian Empire was quite remarkable. Tribally organized people in northeast Asia or the Mediterranean might come to control parts of preexisting but failing endogenous empires (see chapter 4), but they never created any of their own. Or a tribal nomadic group like the fifth-century Huns could have an explosive military expansion but then not survive its leader's death. Moreover, endogenous empires elsewhere all emerged from class-based societies with complex economies, cities, and developed administrative structures. The early Persians had none of these. In the beginning they were organized on the basis of tribal descent groups rather than class; they were a rural mountain people engaged in subsistence pastoralism and agriculture; their highland towns bore no comparison to the cities of Babylonia, Egypt, or central Asia, with their highly developed systems of irrigated agriculture; and they lacked literate professional administrators. Given these deficits, one might have assumed that after a great two-decade run of conquests by Cyrus and Cambyses, the Persian Empire would have experienced an equally rapid dissolution back into its component parts. That it lasted another two centuries is evidence that its rulers' successors, particularly Darius, managed an equally rapid transformation of Persian society, economy, and administrative practices that gave the empire a durable foundation. The Persian tribal elite was transformed into a ruling class in which descent was more institutional than personal. Building projects urbanized the Persian heartland, and the state integrated rural areas into a regional economy that it managed. Most importantly the Achaemenids acquired the needed administrative skills to run an empire. They first adopted bureaucratic practices (and perhaps personnel) from the Elamites, a highland urbanized kingdom they had long interacted with, but later brought their own people into staff positions and shifted to using imperial Aramaic as an administrative language. Although this interaction is not well documented, the later use of literate Persian speakers to administer states in medieval Iran and central Asia by dynasties founded by Turkic and Mongol nomads may provide an analogy. Here rulers who lacked experience in ruling sedentary states found a ready pool of skilled people whose institutions and personnel they adopted as their own.

The tribal structure of the Achaemenids may have actually proved fortuitous because they began their empire building with a different set of principles from those of their urban-based predecessors in neighboring Assyria, Babylonia, and Egypt. Such agrarian states sought direct control over all the people they ruled, and the wealth extracted from them was stored away in walled fortresses for the ruler's use.[18] Those from a nomadic tradition did not concentrate their wealth in one place because the defenses needed to protect it reduced their mobility and deprived them of the option of abandoning territory when attacked. The same was true of concentrating people in one place. In Mesopotamia and Egypt particularly, subject peasant populations working irrigated land produced enough surplus to support large rural populations and cities—easy to access, easy to oversee. Subsistence farmers and pastoralists living in mountainous regions produced little surplus and these regions had comparatively small populations without big cities—hard to access, hard to control. One means of gaining the cooperation of such people was by investing in relationships, which had always been a core principle in tribal societies. Rather than concentrate their wealth in central places and then use the money or other goods stored there to buy needed services and assistance, Persian kings disbursed large parts of their asset base to their clients with the expectation that they could call on their aid when needed in the future. The former was a pure economic transaction, the latter at least partially a social one.

Xenophon recounts a conversation between the legendarily rich King Croesus of Lydia and Cyrus the Great in which this difference was on display. Croesus had advised Cyrus that he could become much richer if he gave less and took more from the people he ruled. Cyrus responded that a "king ought to make his people and his cities happy, if he would derive benefits from them," and that he had access to all the wealth he required by letting his allies and subordinates manage those resources for him.[19] Cyrus then demonstrated this point by having one of his agents obtain sealed letters that acknowledged each promised commitment for a specific amount of money available at his command. When Croesus broke the seals and opened the letters, he discovered that the treasure ready for immediate delivery to Cyrus was far higher than anything he had imagined. In addition, Cyrus was keen to note that there were many advantages to not concentrating his wealth as Croesus had done: "Do you observe, Croesus, that I, too, have my treasures? But you are proposing to me to get them together and hoard them in my palace, to put hired watchmen in charge of everything and to trust to them, and on account of those hoards to be envied and hated. I, on the other hand, believe that if I make my friends rich I shall have treasures in them and at the same time more trusty watchers both of my person and of our common fortunes than any hired guards I could put in charge."[20] Even after the empire's power grew to an unprecedented level, the successors of Cyrus continued the practice of lavish giving because a Persian king of kings never lost his grip on the significance of how such gifts worked to bind people to him.[21] Royal giving was not a form of charity but a political statement of power. While status equality was the hallmark of those engaged in reciprocal gift giving, status inequality was reinforced in hierarchical gift exchanges where a person or group accepted royal gifts with no expectation of ever possibly returning them. This marked the gift takers as inferiors to the gift givers—exactly the message the giving of such gifts was designed to send because it set the king of kings above mere mortals.[22] Of course, Cyrus also had the option of using force on those who were outside the system and had seized Croesus's carefully guarded treasure when he conquered Lydia and had also captured that of even richer Babylonia. But again, thinking more like a tribal leader who valued relationships than an imperial despot, he gave Croesus a pension and new home rather than killing him, just as he had done with his own grandfather Astyages, the former king of the Medes. Rebellion was another story. Achaemenid rulers condemned rebels as liars who had broken their word and deserved only the severest punishment. Darius had to defeat many rivals during his problematic accession to the throne in 522 B.C., all of whom he labeled traitors and had executed publicly in a variety of horrible ways.[23]

The Persians therefore did not attempt to destroy rival tribal groups as they expanded but rather made them junior partners in a larger enterprise if they could. This was a type of segmentary thinking in which enemies in one context might be allies in another. The Persians' level of affinity was highest with groups closest to them geographically and similar to them culturally, as Herodotus explained: "They honor most of all those who dwell nearest them, next those who are next farthest removed, and so going ever onwards they assign honor by this rule; those who dwell farthest off they hold least honorable of all; for they deem themselves to be in all regards by far the best of all men, the rest to have but a proportionate claim to merit, till those who dwell farthest away have least merit of all."[24] At the empire's center geographically and symbolically lay the charmed circle of Persia, Media, and Elam, whose people received the highest positions as common members of the Aryan people. The large eastern part of the empire in Parthia, Drangiana (Seistan), Aria (Herat), Chorasmia (Aral Sea delta), Bactria, and Sogdiana (Transoxiana) might be Achaemenid provinces, but their rich cities and kings were treated more as allies than subjects because they shared so many common customs, Zoroastrian religious beliefs in particular. The rulers of this region also appear

to have had no imperial ambitions of their own. The revolts they participated in were in support of rival Achaemenid contenders for the throne
rather than attempts to break away from the empire. The empire's southwestern flank was another matter. The provinces of Babylonia, Assyria,
Arabia, and Egypt were homes to recent formerly independent states and
empires with their own long-established traditions. They were less happy
with Persian rule, seeing them as newcomers whose culture was both alien
and inferior to their own. The empire's western Anatolian and Mediterranean flank (Greek islands, Phoenicia, Sardis, Ionia, Armenia, Cappa-
docia) consisted of troublesome city-states and regional kingdoms that
were often in revolt but lacked imperial traditions that might challenge the
Achaemenids' right to rule. The empire's southeastern flank of Gandhara
(Kabul-Peshawar), Sattagydia (Sind), Arachosia (Kandahar), and Makran
(Baluchistan) appears to have been its least significant region. (Either that
or exciting places without documentation of that fact.) Beyond the borders
of the empire lay people without the good sense to accept the advantages
of Persian rule, such as the Scythian and Saka steppe nomads, who continually fought the Persians along their northern frontier, and the western
Greek city-states that had fended off their two massive invasions.[25]

It was on the empire's southwestern flank where the Babylonians and
Egyptians had formerly had their own imperial traditions that the Persians abandoned indirect rule in favor of direct administration and military occupation, but in a manner designed to reduce opposition to it. As
Pierre Briant explains,

> The best-known examples show indisputably that the conquerors
> never tried to unify the territories culturally. On the contrary, as we
> have seen, it was by building on the local hierarchy and traditions that
> Cyrus and Cambyses attempted to impose a new authority. The Per-
> sians, for example, did not try to spread either their language or their
> religion. Instead, they exhibited great reverence for the local religions
> and sanctuaries. Each people continued to speak its own language and
> use its own writing system. In Babylonia, the proclamations of Cyrus
> were made in Akkadian and written in cuneiform, and at least begin-
> ning with Darius the royal inscriptions were composed in three lan-
> guages, Persian, Akkadian, and Elamite. When Cyrus promulgated his
> edict on the Jews' return to Jerusalem, it was proclaimed in Hebrew
> and recorded in Aramaic. With only a few exceptions, only the Persians
> spoke Persian, worshiped the Persian gods, and maintained the cul-
> tural traditions of the ruling socio-ethnic class.[26]

Briant continues, "It was by building on the local hierarchy and traditions that Cyrus and Cambyses followed an ideological strategy meant to create conditions for cooperation with the local elites, a most urgent need. This is why, rather than appearing to be outsiders bent on overturning the existing kingdoms and societies, the Great Kings endeavored to appropriate local traditions to their advantage over the long run and to present themselves as protectors of the sanctuaries. At the same time, this strategy required allowing the elites of the conquered countries to participate in the functioning of the new imperial power."[27] Rebellions were always a danger for newly established conquerors, but the Persians believed that these were less likely to occur when the old elites retained a minority stake in a new Persian-administered government. However, whereas Cyrus's policy elsewhere was to leave resources in the hands of local leaders he trusted, in Egypt and Babylonia the Persians reserved the top jobs that set policy for their own people and restricted the role of indigenous officials to implementing them. Some, like Udjahorresnet in Egypt, had served the old regime before siding with the Persians, so it was rarely clear just to whom they were loyal (other than themselves). To oversee such officials and to keep an eye on provinces where the local rulers had more autonomy, the Persian kings appointed personal representatives as satraps who seem to have functioned both as governors and as imperial troubleshooters linking each region to the center.[28]

The origin of the Achaemenid dynasty from a people with a nomadic tradition had another administrative consequence: the imperial court moved seasonally and had multiple capitals. Pastoral nomads viewed seasonal migrations as a normal and natural part of life. They moved their livestock from the hot lowland plains to cool highland mountain pastures in the summer and then returned to the lowlands to avoid the extreme winter cold in the snow-covered mountains. Their dwellings were portable, as were all their other possessions, because they had to be packed on carts or baggage animals. The skills involved in moving whole groups of people and their livestock, including coordinating the migration route with others who were also using it, involved a complex form of logistics. The only thing close to it was moving an army. Part of the Persian success in conquering such a large empire can probably be attributed to the previous experience that at least some of their people had in efficiently organizing such movements. But long after the Persian elite had become fully sedentary and lived in luxurious palaces, they never lost the belief that seasonal movement was more healthy than staying in any one place year-round: "Cyrus himself made his home in the center of his domain, and in the winter season he spent seven months in Babylon, for there the climate is warm; in the spring he spent three months in Susa, and in the height of summer two months in Ecbatana. By so doing, they say, he enjoyed the warmth and coolness of perpetual spring-time."[29] Such seasonal court capitals were characteristic of many dynasties that had nomadic origins long after they had ceased being nomads. (The sixteenth-century Mughal emperor Babur used to spend the winters on the plains of India and his summers in the mountains of Afghanistan.) On the Iranian plateau the Parthians, also of nomadic origin, continued this same tradition by spending their summers in the old highland Median capital of Ecbatana and their winters in Ctesiphon on the Mesopotamian plain, as did their Sasanian successors.

All empires had external frontiers beyond which their writ did not extend, but it is normally assumed that within those boundaries the writ of the state, particularly at its center, should be absolute. One distinguishing aspect of the Achaemenid Empire is that this was not the case in its mountainous core, where some communities remained independent of state control even though they lay in the heart of its territory. Greek military authors believed that this was firm evidence of the Persian Empire's weakness. While many communities in the Zagros Mountains displayed such independence, it was the Uxians in the mountains near Persepolis and the Cosseans in the mountains near Ecbatana who attracted the most attention since they were close to the empire's capitals. As Briant observes,

> The texts indicate that encounters between the Uxians, the Cosseans, and the Great King took place regularly, since the presentation of gifts/tribute was related to the periodic relocations of the court from residence to residence. But it is especially noteworthy that neither the Uxians nor the Cosseans actually controlled the royal roads from Susa to Persepolis or Susa to Ecbatana. Their territories were remote. It must therefore be recognized that every year the Great King (or his personal representative) intentionally detoured to meet the representatives of the Uxians and Cosseans. . . . The bestowal of royal "gifts," here as elsewhere, implied no recognition of royal "weakness"; on the contrary, it created a link between the receiver and the giver. Through this ceremony, the Uxians (in a way) committed their loyalty to the king. The arrangement was advantageous to the King because he received the submission of the Uxians and Cosseans without investment of military resources; furthermore, both groups probably sent soldiers to the king whenever conscription was ordered.[30]

As noted earlier when discussing Cyrus's generosity, the logic of gift exchange allowed each side to get what it wanted in a culturally appropriate fashion that kept the relationship ongoing. By accepting and receiving gifts (although the royal payments were much larger), the empire recognized the autonomy of these tribes as friends rather than subjects. The regularity of their interaction with the Persian court demonstrates it was part of a larger policy, one that was in keeping with the Achaemenids' adoption of what I earlier termed a Swiss cheese model of governance in which the state employed one set of practices for its highly populated regions and a different set for people in marginal areas. To use contemporary computer software jargon, regularly rewarding such people with gifts was not a bug in the program but a feature. The Uxians and Cosseans inhabited the type of cheese holes that did not repay the cost of subduing or administering directly. It was cheaper to pay them off and gain their cooperation peacefully because they were not enemies but rather simple rent seekers whose poor subsistence economy was supplemented by extortion. If they extended their activity to raiding or banditry, the stick was also available. Their proximity to the empire's summer capitals left them vulnerable to punitive raids that could inflict major damage to their camps and villages even if these did not result in an occupation. The Achaemenids also had powerful economic tools at their disposal because mountain villagers required access to lowland markets to meet their basic needs. As ibn Khaldun was to note about similar tribal people in North Africa during the fourteenth century, while they "need the cities for their necessities of life, the urban population needs them for conveniences and luxuries. . . . They must be active on the behalf of their interests and obey them whenever (the cities) ask and demand obedience from them."[31]

Polities that practiced American cheese policies of direct rule had a problem distinguishing the difference between weakness and good sense when confronted with what they saw as extortion and insults to their honor from peoples weaker than themselves militarily. Following the maxim of Greek power politics that "the strong do what they can and the weak suffer what they must," the Macedonians sought to teach the Uxians and Cosseans this lesson after they deposed the Persian Great King.[32] While Alexander the Great succeeded in extracting tribute from them after a surprise winter campaign, these people regained their autonomy after his death because their remote locations and strong defensive positions made wringing regular tribute from them difficult.[33] The American cheese model saw all such ungoverned places as defects to be corrected, whereas the Swiss cheese model took them as naturally occurring, annoying but not particularly dangerous. In mountainous Afghanistan such lands were historically labeled *yagistan*, a term that is equally well translated as "land of rebels" or "land of ungoverned people." Seeing them as rebels demanded some action by the state to change that status, but seeing them as ungoverned did not. Both the problem and the solution were *longue durée* phenomena that would persist on the Iranian plateau for the next two and a half millennia although the people involved changed over time as Iranian tribes were replaced by Turks. The Iranian government only established its full authority over the nomad tribes in the Zagros Mountains in the mid-twentieth century after air power, paved roads, and motor vehicles made it possible to project state power into the region and thus permanently end its autonomy.[34]

While ancient Greek authors chided the Persians for displaying weakness in dealing with their tribal problems, later Great Powers who ventured into areas first ruled by the Achaemenids were forced to conclude that the Persians may have been right. When confronted with similar problems on the northwest frontier of India, even the mighty British Empire decided it was easier to pay off the Pakhtun tribes that threatened the strategic Khyber Pass than continually fight them. Having lost an entire army retreating from Kabul in the winter of 1842, the British became wary of wars with such people. It was an experience replicated in the Hindu Kush by the Soviet Union in the 1980s and the United States in the 2010s. Thus, the British made a strategic decision at the height of their colonial power that all of the Pakhtun tribes living within the hill and mountain zones east of Afghanistan would stay under their own tribal leadership, supervised by British political agents who doled out subsidies and called in military force only when trouble broke out. Like the Persians, they would take direct control of only those Pakhtuns who lived in villages and cities on the flat irrigated plain around Peshawar that was the region's political center.[35] Given their long experience with the complexity of center-periphery relationships, the Achaemenids who dealt with the Uxians and Cosseans would not have felt out of place if suddenly transported to a contemporary international seminar examining twenty-first-century policy options for states in their dealings with nonstate actors.

Achaemenid Persia was spectacularly successful in its ability to organize diversity, the key organizational advantage empires had over other types of polities. Its king-of-kings model worked best on the Iranian plateau and in central Asia because it matched the discontinuous distribution of the region's resources and populations. It had to be modified in conquered areas in the west where resources were more continuously distributed and that had their own imperial traditions its inhabitants wished to restore. The Persians viewed such people as untrustworthy rivals rather than potential junior partners and so either replaced their leaders or put them under close supervision. Nevertheless, by maintaining the cultural identity of each of the areas it conquered, the Persian Empire went with the tide rather than against it. It was a Lego block empire in which each added piece kept its own center, identity, and way of doing things. While attached to one another and the center very securely, they were never melded together into a uniform whole. This made the Persian Empire very resilient. Other empires followed a classic rise-and-fall model—gaining power, reaching maturity, and then collapsing because of internal problems. The Persian Empire rose and stabilized, but it did not fall from its own internal defects. It was murdered midstride by Alexander the Great and his Macedonian successors, who then divided up its Lego brick parts to create their own, smaller set of states, the largest of which was the Seleucid Empire (312–63 B.C.). Although the Seleucids imposed a strong Greek Hellenic stamp on their former Persian provinces, the Achaemenid model remained deeply rooted. The nomadic Parthians (247 B.C.–A.D. 224) reconquered the Persian heartland and Mesopotamia under their ruler Mithridates I (r. 171–138 B.C.) to create a new empire. Proclaiming their ruler king of kings (but allowing more autonomy to their subordinates), they adopted the Achaemenid models of government down to migrating between Ctesiphon, their lowland winter capital near old Babylon, and Ecbatana, their highland summer capital first used by the Medes and Achaemenids. The Parthians were replaced by the more powerful Sasanian Empire (A.D. 224–651), which even more closely followed Achaemenid precedents. In other words, following a Hellenic interregnum initiated by Alexander, successor Iranian empires using the Achaemenid template ruled empires in the highlands of Iran, Mesopotamia, and central Asia for the next eight hundred years. And like the Achaemenid Empire, the Sasanian Empire did not die of old age. It was still expanding at the expense of its old Roman Byzantine rival more than four centuries after it was founded when it too was cut down unexpectedly by outside invaders—the Arab armies of Islam, as described in chapter 4.

Archaeologists often complain that the Achaemenid Empire's policy of accommodation meant that "Persian influence was geographically restricted and socially superficial in all but a very few areas over which they at one time or another had authority."[36] This view may be underestimating its long-term cultural legacy, particularly in its eastern provinces, that was later reinforced by the many centuries of Parthian and Sasanian rule. It survived in a different form through the Abbasid Caliphate (A.D. 750–1258), and its administrative template and language were employed by all the Turko-Mongolian states that established empires there beginning in the eleventh century A.D. Spending his career as one of British India's last political officers managing the Khyber Pass on its Northwest Frontier, Olaf Caroe believed that the legacy of Persia never died out:

> Again and again, when moving in what may be called the Iranian world, I have been struck by the conviction that the influence of Persia over all these lands is a much deeper, older thing than anything which springs from Islam. . . . There is indeed a sense that in which all the uplands of Asia from the Tigris to the Indus is one country. The spirit of Persia has breathed over it, bringing an awareness of one background, one culture, one way of expression, a unity of spirit felt as far away as Peshawar and Quetta. He who has caught that breath has won to the heart of a mystery, and he will not forget.[37]

CHINA

Unlike the Persians, the Chinese had a long tradition of historical writing that became fully developed after their first empires came into being, and it provides a wealth of detail on the process. Here recorded debates on the desirability of having a unified empire to rule China appear centuries before one came into being. In Persia and Rome, the military conquest of an empire came first; how to think about it came later. In China, thinking about what an empire should be came first, and conquering it came later. When China was finally unified under the Qin dynasty (221–206 B.C.), however, the consequences were far more dramatic and rapid than anything that occurred in the Persian or Roman Empire. The Qin dynasty not only unified China, it overturned existing political, social, and economic institutions to create an empire with unprecedented political and military power. It replaced a heterogeneous system of regionally based administration with a centralized government under an all-powerful emperor that employed the same uniform laws and administrative practices everywhere. Its centrally appointed bureaucratic officials supplanted the aristocratic elite that had been China's dominant political class during the Warring States period. The Qin also imposed a uniform set of cultural institutions on the people it ruled even in frontier areas whose inhabitants had not previously shared them. All of these elements would combine to become the aspirational model for Chinese empires thereafter despite the

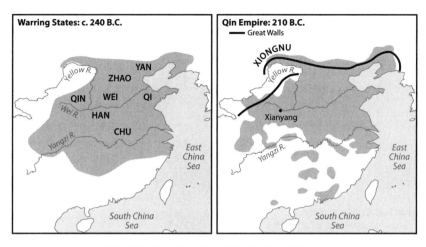

MAP 1.2. The Qin Empire. From Burbank and Cooper, 2010.

many condemnations of Qin policies and practices as immoral. The idea that political power might be shared rather than centralized, a hallmark of the Persian governance and a standard practice in China before the Qin, was now anathematized. No successor dynasty was ever willing to devolve power to autonomous feudatory leaders except under duress. While the Qin dynasty collapsed soon after the death of its founding emperor, the belief that China should be governed by a unitary empire survived and became normative. The succeeding Han dynasty (206 B.C.–A.D. 220) kept much of the Qin structure in place when it established its own, more stable empire, which became China's longest lived (maps 1.2 and 1.3).

The cultural and economic conditions confronting empire builders in China were very different from those the Persians encountered. On the Iranian plateau and in central Asia, people and resources were located in widely scattered pockets, whereas those in North China were concentrated primarily in the Yellow River valley and its tributaries. Agricultural people here lived in densely populated villages, towns, and cities that constituted central places abutting people and economies like themselves. Communities that engaged in subsistence farming in the mountains in the west, pastoralism on the steppe to the north, or rice agriculture in the southern tropical forests were located at their margins and could be excluded from political life in a way not possible in the Persian Empire. Although there were regional differences, all seven of the fourth-to-third-century B.C. Warring States in North China shared a common cultural heritage and tradition. The Persians, by contrast, interacted with Egyptians, Babylonians, Greeks, and Indians who all had their own distinct

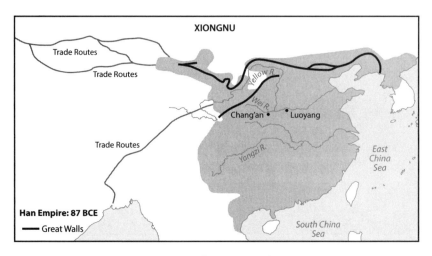

MAP 1.3. The Han Empire.
From Burbank and Cooper, 2010.

civilizational cultures they did not share with others in the empire. The us-them boundary in China was therefore perceived as binary, while in the Persian Empire it was segmentary and shifted depending on the context. For this reason, Chinese empires aspired to do more than just politically unite a set of diverse but similar regional communities. They had an additional goal of seeking to set a common cultural standard for all of China, at least at the elite level, that would fuse this immensely larger whole into a single unit by melting down its disparate parts and recasting them in its own mold—no Lego blocks here![38]

The rulers of the Qin dynasty believed the most effective way to achieve this goal was by replacing the existing system of localized feudal officials with a single ruler whose power extended down directly to every peasant village and household by means of a state bureaucracy. The primary obligation of these appointed local officials was to represent the central government and implement its policies, not further their own interests or those of people they administered as was the case with the feudal aristocrats. In the Qin state, both subjects and officials were expected to serve as interchangeable cogs in a closely supervised machine where the center both set the rules and implemented them. If this description seems more applicable to an army than a society, it is because the Qin dynasty rose to power by organizing itself and its people along military lines. Located in the Wei River valley, a western tributary of the Yellow River, its neighbors viewed the Qin state as not quite fully Chinese and more willing to break traditions that others preserved. But if Qin rulers were more receptive to unconventional ideas than those in other states, it was because their king-dom was initially smaller and weaker than the six regional states to their east that were jockeying for power in the mid-fourth century B.C. Duke Xiao of Qin therefore began his long reign (361–338 B.C.) by welcoming ambitious political advisers to his court from elsewhere in China to hear their plans about how states like his could grow and become more power-ful. While China was awash in political philosophers with bold plans, few rulers were willing to risk making changes that went against their conven-tional ways of doing things. But when newly arrived advisers presented Duke Xiao with radical plans designed to produce a rich state and power-ful army, he acted ruthlessly to implement their programs of reorganiza-tion and transform every aspect of Qin society.

Shang Yang (390–338 B.C.), a philosopher of the Legalist school who wrote extensively on the topic, was the most significant of these Qin state-building advisers. Under his direction, Qin replaced its hereditary officials with centrally appointed governors. It distributed land widely among the peasants and encouraged immigration to bring new land into production. Its taxation system was money based and rewarded productive farmers and brave soldiers, whose occupations were deemed to strengthen state power. It penalized merchants and the feudal nobility as parasitic rent seekers. The Qin legal system was characterized by severe laws and harsh penal-ties. Punishments were inflicted on such a large number of people that the state found itself with a ready pool of convict labor that could be used for its extensive building projects, supplementing the corvée labor it already required of peasants. On the other hand, the Qin law code made a point of insisting that the same rules applied to everyone from peasant to minister, except of course to the ruler, who was above the law. The Qin state's most radical policy, however, was undermining the importance of the extended family as the bedrock of social life by replacing it with groups of five fami-lies who were collectively responsible for each other's behavior. The whole group could be punished for crimes committed by any one of its members, and they had an obligation to inform on one another too.[39]

The Qin military relied on universal conscription to raise troops and employed a complex ranking system based on achievement rather than ascribed social status, a system that made no distinction between military and civil affairs. As Yuri Pines describes it,

> The system of 20 (initially fewer) "ranks of merit" introduced by Shang Yang was one of the most daring acts of social engineering in human history. This system became the cornerstone of social life in Qin. The

lowest ranks were distributed for military achievements, particularly decapitating enemy soldiers, or could be purchased in exchange for extra grain yields; successful rank-holders could be incorporated into the military or civilian administration and thereafter be promoted up the social ladder. Each rank granted its holder economic, social, and legal privileges; and since the ranks were not fully inheritable, the system generated considerable social mobility. . . . The new system attempted to unify the social, economic, and political hierarchy under the government's control, which in turn required the elimination of alternative avenues of enhancing one's socioeconomic and political status.[40]

The structure was designed to manipulate what Shang Yang saw as an intrinsic human desire for economic gain and social advancement by channeling people's efforts into areas that most benefited the state and its ruler. He believed that the efficiencies and productivity generated by this kind of state would create the base for future military expansion and ultimately achieve the as-yet-unmet goal of creating an empire that ruled all of China: "My teaching causes those among the people who seek benefits to gain them nowhere but through tilling; and those who want to evade disasters escape through no other means but war. Within the borders, everyone among the people first devotes himself to tilling and warfare, and only then obtains whatever pleases him. Hence, though the territory is small, grain is plenty, and though the people are few, the army is powerful. He who is able to implement the two of these within the borders will accomplish the way of Hegemon and Monarch."[41] Shang Yang's reorganization of Qin society and its military laid the groundwork for the state's expansion but Duke Xiao's son, King Huiwen (r. 338–311 B.C.), who killed Shang Yang and his whole family after he came to the throne. As a prince, Huiwen had once almost fallen victim to a uniform application of Qin law, and he appears never to have forgiven Shang Yang for that. However, as king he recognized the value of the system that had been created and maintained it. After surviving a number of later succession problems, the Qin state regained its stride as a power player in regional politics with the serial recruitment of a remarkably skilled set of political advisers who again arrived from other parts of China keen to give advice and take revenge on the states that had mistreated them. The first of these was Fan Ju, an exile from the eastern state of Wei who had been flogged almost to death there. He became the counselor-in-chief to King Zhaoxiang (r. 306–251 B.C.) after helping the monarch displace his regent mother from power and rule directly in 266 B.C. He devised the Qin foreign policy of attacking states that were close by and allying with states that were far away—a long-term strategy that worked remarkably well. He also recommended killing as many of the enemy as possible to make it harder for the state that lost them to recover. After his death in 255 B.C., a new set of advisers arrived at the Qin court and set it on the path to becoming China's first empire. The most notable of these were Han Fei and Li Si, both born around 280 B.C. Han Fei was perhaps the most respected of all the Legalist scholars, and his extensive writings refined the theories of Shang Yang with more of a focus on how a ruler should manage his ministers and other subordinates. His rival at court, Li Si, became chancellor to the young King Zheng of Qin beginning in 246 B.C. and served in that post for almost four decades, taking charge of reorganizing the empire in Qin's image after its ruler took control over all of China in 221 B.C. One constant risk all these advisers faced was ending up prematurely dead like Shang Yang if they fell out of favor. As chancellor, Li Si convinced the future Qin emperor that Han Fei was a danger, and Han Fei committed suicide to avoid execution in 233 B.C. Li Si himself later fell victim to a similar plot when one of his rivals got the second Qin emperor to charge him with treason, for which he was executed by being cut in half after torture produced a confession in 208 B.C.[42]

The Qin's organization as a state built for war made it ever more powerful with each succeeding conquest, and all of China was under its control twelve years after it began its attacks in earnest in 233 B.C. While such numbers are always hard to evaluate, the size of the armies on all sides was huge, a mix of infantry and cavalry. The Qin conquest of the southern state of Chu in 224 B.C. and eastern state of Wei in 223 B.C., for example, both reportedly involved invasion forces numbering six hundred thousand men. Casualties could be huge too. It was reported that the victorious Qin had killed four hundred thousand Zhao troops in one battle in 260 B.C. The losing sides' deaths during the series of big battles through which the Qin unified China were regularly listed at one hundred thousand each. Since the Qin system rewarded its troops by paying for the number of heads they took, it was easy enough to kill civilians as well as soldiers to run up such totals.[43] Once unification was achieved, the Qin ruler Ying Zheng, who had ascended to the throne as king in 246 B.C. at age thirteen, proclaimed himself Qin Shi Huangdi (First Emperor of Qin). The Qin empire then replicated its model of state control throughout China. At the top was the emperor, who was served by his court officials, some of whom managed the palace while others handled national administration. The expanding empire eventually encompassed thirty-six commanderies, each with a governor, military commander, and superintendent, that overlay more than one thousand districts. As in most new empires, the Qin's disposition of military forces was designed to deter revolts in its newly conquered territories. Its appointed officials recruited on the basis of merit and loyalty to the new regime took charge of administration. These officials oversaw the demolition of the old elites' family fortresses and the internal walls that had divided each of the Warring States from the others. Because the defeated local nobility had strong historical ties to specific places, the Qin uprooted them from their homes, reportedly sending 120,000 families west to live near the capital city of Xianyang in palaces provided by the state. It was a golden exile that made Louis XIV's transfer of thousands of the French nobility to Versailles in the eighteenth century look puny by comparison. The future prospects for members of this aristocratic class were further diminished by applying the nonhereditary and merit-based Qin ranking system to everyone in the empire.[44]

The Qin expansion led to China's becoming a single economic unit. The dynasty now had a much larger workforce at its disposal, and so the First Emperor oversaw immense new construction projects that produced a 6,800 km network of roads, expanded the empire's system of canals, constructed China's Great Wall, and completed his enormous funerary complex that included a seventy-six-meter-high tomb mound protected by a buried army of life-size terracotta warriors. Standardization was imposed on every aspect of the economy. The roads were all of a uniform width, as were the axles of the vehicles that used them. Qin weights and measures replaced all other units. Qin money replaced all other currencies: round bronze coins with square holes (so they could be strung together) that became the templates for those used by succeeding dynasties in China. Taxes on goods produced and sales in marketplaces were also regularized throughout the empire. Most significant for the future was the standardization of China's ideographic script, a tool that allowed the emergence of a class of literate people who might not understand each other's language or dialect but who could all read the same text. It would serve as the basis of Chinese literature and governance from that time forward. All these changes might be seen as potentially positive for the new people brought into the empire, but not the imposition of Qin's draconian laws. Its organization of people into five-family mutual responsibility units that Shang Yang had first pioneered a century earlier was both new (outside Qin) and undoubtedly highly disruptive to traditional patterns of everyday life.[45] The impact on local communities and families after coming under rule of a regime with such invasive policies can probably be compared only to that of Mao Zedong's period of communes, collectivization, and cultural revolution in the 1950s and 1960s. Both periods were historically short but extraordinarily abusive for ordinary people who had previously been outside politics, and they left indelible wounds.

The military victory of the Qin over its rivals appeared to justify the Legalist philosophers' emphasis on military power but raised the question of what to do with such strength once the conquest of the old Warring States was complete. The Qin used it to move outward against culturally non-Chinese peoples in the south and incorporated many of their territories into the empire as far as Vietnam. In the process they established new Chinese colonial settlements and reorganized local economies to serve the central government. This region was very different from the Yellow River valley of North China in climate, culture, and agriculture. The Qin expansion therefore marked the beginning of a millennium-long process of making the region and its people more Chinese-like, although in the end that would require broadening the definition of what it meant to be Chinese.[46] Armies also moved north to attack the Xiongnu nomads and expelled them from the steppe region south of the Yellow River's Ordos loop. Because the Qin saw the nomads who lived on steppe as a kind of people who could never become Chinese, they sought to seal off this frontier rather than expand into it. They linked the existing walls along the northern frontier to create a single Great Wall that was defended by a string of well-manned military garrisons. The wall also served to separate an idealized agricultural world of civilized China from the steppe pastoral world of the barbarian nomads, a binary opposition that was not reflected on the ground where frontier populations and economies had always combined aspects of both.[47] That binary distinction was not recognized by later foreign dynasties that came to rule over China (or by the current People's Republic of China), but the line of the wall invariably marked China's northern limits under the rule of native Chinese dynasties. Unlike Persia, this was an American cheese model of governance: all places and peoples were treated the same under one set of laws where any holes in the cheese were defects that the state would do its best to eliminate without regard for cost.

The Qin empire collapsed into civil war soon after the death of the First Emperor and was replaced by the Han dynasty (206 B.C.–A.D. 230), whose founding emperor was Liu Bang (Han Gaozu), a leader of peasant origin who defeated a number of more prestigious rivals to reunify China. That the Qin empire could collapse so quickly after moving from strength to strength for more than a century at first seems surprising. But in some ways it is not. As a state geared entirely for war and expansion, it was ill-equipped to cope with its own success. An army rewarded for the number of heads its soldiers took was not easy to repurpose for garrison service after wars within China had ceased. Expeditions to expand the empire's territory in the semitropical south or push the Xiongnu nomads farther north into the steppe could not generate the revenue or prestige that had come with conquering prosperous Chinese kingdoms. Nor was it clear that expanding the harsh Qin laws and taxes to the rest of China was worth the cost of alienating all those they were applied to. Liu Bang, for example, became a rebel only after he unavoidably missed the deadline to appear for military service, a death penalty offense that made the alternative of resistance more attractive. The recent example of the Soviet Union may be instructive here. Like the Qin, its rule under Joseph Stalin maximized economic production for the state, created a powerful military that defeated Nazi Germany, and maintained an oppressive security apparatus that filled its gulags with convict labor used for gigantic building projects. Yet after Stalin's death this system proved incapable of adapting to a long peace and eventually collapsed from internal weaknesses even though its military strength was still fully intact. The very tools that made it so effective in one set of circumstances proved liabilities when those circumstances changed. Watching the dissolution of the Soviet Union, China's Communist Party made economic changes that abandoned Mao Zedong's revolutionary policies to save the state he had created. In some sense the Han dynasty had already set the pattern for such a shift: save the structure of an empire by abandoning the extreme policies that brought it into being and replacing them with more sustainable ones. The Han dynasty was an Empire 2.0 designed for stability and it lasted 426 years—the longest run of all China's many empires. Although the Han dropped many of the most unpopular Qin policies, such as the five-family mutual responsibility system, it retained its basic principles of a centralized government and a bureaucratic administration that recruited on the basis of merit rather than hereditary privilege.

The principles of a centralized government took quite some time for the Han to fully implement. Even though the belief that the best polity for China was a unified empire ruled by one all-powerful emperor survived the Qin collapse, at its founding the Han dynasty discovered it was impossible to maintain that level of centralized rule. Liu Bang had come to power with the aid of a variety of regional allies, and he made many of them semiautonomous kings (*wang*) in parts of the east and south, a system that harked back to China's feudal structure under the Zhou dynasty

(1046–256 B.C.). Over time the Han dynasty replaced them with impe-rial relatives whom they deemed more loyal. Proponents of centralized rule criticized this policy by arguing that such subsidiary kings, whatever their background, had no place in an empire that should be divided only between a single ruler of all under heaven and his undifferentiated sub-jects. Besides, kings with access to independent resources had the capac-ity to revolt. Holders of hereditary kingdoms, on the other hand, believed that it was the central government's unwillingness to treat them as part-ners that was the problem. Both sides were right. Over time successive Han emperors did eliminate many such kingdoms or reduce their power. The tactics they used included subdividing kingdoms among multiple heirs when a holder died, reabsorbing a kingdom if there were no heirs, seizing pieces of territory as penalties for often trumped-up criminal charges, and taking back whole kingdoms as punishment for rebellion. In response, seven of the most important kingdoms organized an upris-ing in 154 B.C. that threatened to bring the dynasty down and return China to its Warring States configuration. It took the central government almost two years to suppress the revolt, which failed in part because the rulers of other kingdoms declined to join the seven already in rebellion. While the losing states were dissolved in the war's aftermath, the dynasty still lacked the power to eliminate all the remaining ones that had not sided with the rebels. That was finally accomplished by aggressive "Martial Emperor" Han Wudi (r. 141–87 B.C.), who succeeded in restoring the Qin status quo ante of a single emperor with no powerful hereditary subordi-nates, although he retained a large number of smaller kingdoms to use as patronage appointments.[48] It is striking that while employing a king-of-kings structure maintained stability in the Persian Empire, it undermined it in China. This was because in Persia the relationship between the center and subordinate kings was symbiotic and an integral component of the empire's scheme of governance. In China the relationship was antago-nistic, an unstable political compromise that was at odds with the basic principle of unitary imperial governance. Subordinate kings in the Persian Empire were regional leaders who had little influence outside their home territories and who sought neither independence nor the throne. Subordi-nate kings in the Han empire, especially when they were members of the imperial clan, periodically sought both.

The Qin bureaucratic administration employed salaried appointed officials with elaborate rules for recruitment, selection, and promotion. Officials received standard rates of pay and were subjected to rigorous performance evaluations. The Han followed its template but recruited officials from a wider range of philosophical schools. These included Confucians who stressed moral relationships, Daoists who took religion as their starting point, and leftover Legalists who still focused on building state power. While Confucianism ultimately became the Han state's authorized philosophical school, there were always a variety of opinions on offer at court for an emperor to choose from. The Daoists' concept of the emperor as the Son of Heaven and their grounding a dynasty's legitimacy in a Mandate of Heaven became deeply embedded in China's political discourse. Even the oft-reviled Legalists could succeed at times with policies that sought to increase the power of the emperor and make the Han state richer. For example, although it was Han Wudi who made Confucianism the official state philosophy, this did not stop him from implementing Legalist policies that imposed state monopolies on salt and iron production to raise revenue for his wars with the Xiongnu. The attraction of the Han dynasty to Confucianism therefore was less its particular set of beliefs (often attacked as vague and impracticable) than its general focus on the maintenance of proper relationships within a fixed hierarchy. It was a conservative ideology that privileged stability over change, an attitude the dynasty shared and that was better suited for an empire in place than one in the making.

The Han bureaucratic system itself was a product of such hierarchical thinking. In this strict system of ranked administrative grades and salaries, each level had its own degree of seniority and responsibility that gave its holder a specific social status. It was a system that required a lot of people. Around 5 B.C. it had a scheduled strength of 130,000 officials and clerks who administered eighty-three commanderies and twenty kingdoms. It was they who implemented a unified set of laws, administrative practices, and tax collection. Making appointments to these positions on the basis of merit rather than hereditary privilege had been a hallmark of the Qin dynasty, and it continued in the Han dynasty. The political significance of hereditary aristocrats declined sharply at the local level during the Han dynasty, and they were replaced by an emerging class of private landowners. This landed class was based on achieved rather than ascribed status and became China's bedrock local elite from that time forward. There was considerable social mobility within this class because an extended family's wealth and landed property (unlike an inherited aristocratic status) could be lost as well as gained over the course of a few generations. What did change from the Qin was the higher percentage of officials recruited from the civilian ranks once wars had ended within China. This coincided with the rise of Confucian scholars at court who urged the emperor to select "men of virtue" with literary training rather than "men of talent" whose practical experience drawn from military service or trade they deemed morally inferior. To this end the Han court established scholarly academies to train such people in large numbers. They became the dominant group in the bureaucracy and, in addition to running the empire, linked the new class of landowners from which they came to the Han court in a symbiotic relationship.[49]

The distinctive template of empire created by the Qin and Han dynasties would become fixed as a Chinese cultural tradition that replicated itself in later dynasties. Its structure of a hereditary emperor who ruled all under heaven could allow for no sovereign subsidiary subordinates. Its expansive view of state control demanded direct rule throughout its territories using centrally appointed officials. While the Qin achieved these objectives by means of a highly militarized state, during the Han civilian administrators became the norm. It was a tradition that expanded in later dynasties with the development of an examination system for recruiting government officials. Native Chinese dynasties following the Han (Sui, Tang, Song, and Ming) explicitly modeled themselves after it. Foreign dynasties, with the exception of the Mongols, also adopted most of its bureaucratic structures and employed a similar class of literate officials to administer the Chinese lands they conquered. Even in periods of disruption when China was divided into regional states, the belief that a unitary empire would eventually reemerge never died. Despite long periods of disunion, it always did, even if it was foreign dynasties like the Mongol Yuan and Manchu Qing that accomplished the task. By Confucian reasoning, any dynasty became legitimate by uniting the Middle Kingdom into a single polity, regardless of its ethnic origin or the status of its founder.

ROME

The Roman Empire (27 B.C.–A.D. 476) is often taken as a model for empires in general by authors from the Western tradition for whom its history and structure are most familiar.[50] Compared with the paucity of historical records on successive Persian empires and the rich but state-vetted histories of Qin and Han China, there is a much wider variety of historical accounts and other written material from many different perspectives for a student of Rome to draw on in addition to a rich tradition of archaeological research. Despite these resources, however, the Roman Empire serves as a poor template for thinking about endogenous empires in general. Whereas all other neighboring empires had identifiable founders, such as Persia's Cyrus the Great or China's Qin Shi Huangdi, who brought them into being during a single lifetime, Roman expansion was more piecemeal and ad hoc. Its empire emerged through a series of conquests made by different Roman generals at different times rather than by a founding king or dynasty. These Roman generals also fought each other in periodic civil wars both before and after the empire came into being. Moreover, although Rome had become a de facto empire during the mid-first century B.C. when it was still notionally a republic (509–27 B.C.), it was not defined as such until Augustus became its first emperor (r. 27 B.C.–A.D. 14). Even after that point, Augustus and his successors maintained the fiction of a republican order by calling themselves *princeps* (first citizen) and retaining the dual consuls appointed annually by the Senate as heads of state. Reflecting this origin, the Roman Empire displayed an evolving mix of structural features that changed substantially over time. It began as a hegemonic empire that employed a distributed sovereignty template similar to that of the Persian Empire before transforming itself into a territorial empire with fixed boundaries and a highly centralized system of direct governance characteristic of Chinese empires. The Roman Empire was thus like an imposing edifice constructed without the aid of an architect that was continually renovated by a series of dissatisfied new owners. It proved remarkably durable despite, or perhaps because of, its ad hoc origins. Its western half dissolved in A.D. 476 but the remainder, the Eastern Roman (or Byzantine) Empire, continued on to become the longest lasting of any endogenous empire (A.D. 330–1453) (map 1.4).

Rome was a late arrival to the business of empire that arose more than five centuries after the establishment of the Achaemenid Persian Empire and two centuries after China was unified. One reason for this was that its western Mediterranean home presented significant obstacles to imperial unification that took the Romans centuries to overcome. Historically it was a region in which independent city-states were the dominant political organization. In the eastern Mediterranean such city-states usually fell under the control of larger kingdoms or empires but maintained their political identity and a degree of self-governance. These included the Greek city-states abutting Thrace and Anatolia as well as Phoenician ones in the Levant that were all incorporated into the Persian Empire in the sixth century B.C. and provided that empire with its naval forces. Mainland Greek city-states such as Athens, Sparta, and Corinth barely avoided a similar incorporation into the Persian Empire by forming alliances that beat back invasions by Darius (492–490 B.C.) and Xerxes (480–479 B.C.). By contrast, the western Mediterranean city-states of

Carthage (founded by Phoenicians in North Africa), Syracuse (founded by Greeks in Sicily), and Rome (founded by its local inhabitants) faced only rivals similar to or weaker than themselves. The mainland frontiers of Rome and Carthage in Gaul, Numidia, and Iberia, for example, were inhabited not by powerful empires or regional states but by tribally organized peoples. Such people might unite to engage in raiding or even attack cities (the Gauls famously sacked Rome in 390 B.C.), but they were not a mortal threat. All such city-states remained relatively small because they were unwilling to assimilate new territories and peoples into a single larger mixed polity. Instead they preferred to dominate others by means of alliances or colonial relationships, a preference that we will see in chapter 2 works better for maritime empires than it does for land-based ones. While city-states in the eastern Mediterranean could mount substantial defenses with such alliances, as their defeat of the Persians demonstrated, Greek and Phoenician city-states were not interested in conquest and direct rule. During the Peloponnesian War (431–404 B.C.), for example, both sea-based Athens and land-based Sparta led leagues of allies that struggled for dominance, but neither ever considered eliminating the other. Rome would break this pattern both by transcending its initial city-state identity and by seeking the destruction of peer rivals rather than just dominating them.

Endogenous empires often emerged in places somewhat at the margins that only later became imperial centers, as we saw with the Qin in China or the Persians on the Iranian plateau. Rome followed this pattern. While the Romans dated the founding of their city to 753 B.C., it was for centuries thereafter a rather small and poor place. Rome became a significant political power only after it completed conquering central and southern Italy in the mid-third century B.C. Previously it had been a marginal player within a larger regional struggle that pitted the numerous Greek colonial city-states in southern Italy and Sicily (what the Romans called Magna Graecia) against Carthage and its allies. They had been at war for centuries, mostly over the control of wheat-rich Sicily. These wars involved a bewildering variety of alliances that finally left Carthage dominant in Sicily and southern Iberia at the beginning of the third century B.C. Between 280 and 275 B.C., failed wars by the Greek king Pyrrhus (he of the unfortunate Pyrrhic victory fame) against both the Romans and Carthaginians had allowed the Romans to expand south. Rome's expansion then set the stage for the three Punic Wars between 264 and 146 B.C. that pitted Carthage's powerful maritime empire against Rome's land-based legions for control of the western Mediterranean.[51]

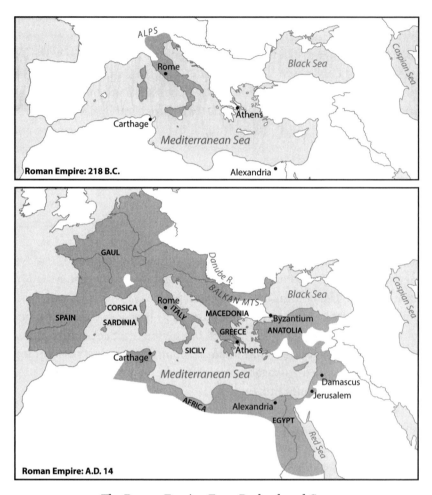

MAP 1.4. The Roman Empire. From Burbank and Cooper, 2010.

In some ways similar to the struggle between Athens and Sparta in the Peloponnesian War, in the Punic Wars each side had to become competent in its rival's way of fighting. In the First Punic War (264–241 B.C.), Rome, a state without a previous maritime tradition, rapidly developed a navy to engage Carthage at sea. The Romans came out on top and gained control of Sicily in 241 B.C., their first overseas possession. Carthage recovered some of its strength by expanding in Iberia, which again put it at odds with Rome and sparked the Second Punic War (218–201 B.C.). As this war began, it was Rome that had naval superiority and Carthage the strongest land army. Famously invading Italy with elephants, the Carthaginian general Hannibal remained there for fifteen years and defeated the Romans in a series of now-classic battles. However, Carthage never provided Hannibal with

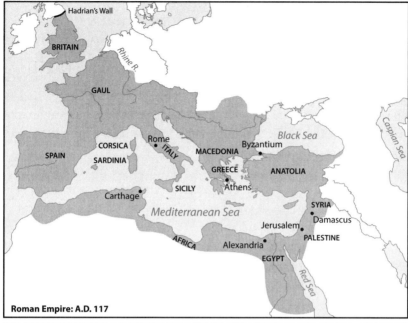

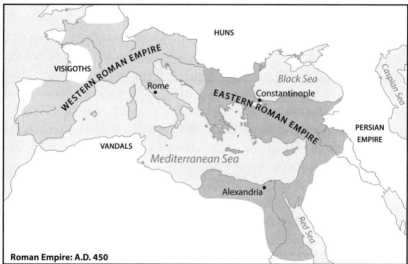

MAP 1.4. (*continued*)

enough troops and supplies to take out Rome itself, a deficiency characteristic of expeditionary forces dispatched by maritime empires that were always wary of overcommitting themselves to distant land engagements. Hannibal had to withdraw his troops when the Romans cut his supply routes and were able to threaten Iberia and then Carthage itself.

In 202 B.C. the Romans landed in North Africa and defeated Carthage's army outside the city. The resulting peace forced Carthage to destroy its still-powerful fleet and pay Rome a large amount of silver, as well as leaving Rome in possession of Carthage's Iberian territories. With Carthage reduced to a disarmed city-state, Rome was now supreme in the western Mediterranean as it moved east against Carthage's former allies in Macedonia. This should have sufficed, given the logic of previous wars in the region, but Rome's move to empire led it to view all potential city-state rivals as polities to be destroyed rather than just defeated, even when they posed little threat. This resulted in a final Third Punic War (149–146 B.C.), in which Roman troops completely leveled Carthage and took the opportunity to do the same to the Greek city-state of Corinth for good measure, enslaving the surviving inhabitants of both cities.[52]

The Roman Empire's size was 1 million km^2 in 133 B.C. after it expanded its holdings in western Anatolia and Iberia. Within a hundred years it would control double that territory with new conquests, and it reached its maximum extent in A.D. 117, when it encompassed 5 million km^2.[53] This growth was a product of gradual territorial acquisition that eventually produced a new definition of who was considered Roman. As noted earlier, Mediterranean city-states were resistant to accepting new people into their polities as equals. For this reason, individual city-states had mobilized themselves into alliances and leagues (sometimes under duress) that retained their local political structures. Rome incorporated many small city-states across Italy that had formerly been parts of such leagues through treaties of perpetual alliance. Under these agreements the Romans imposed obligations on the Italians without granting them the same rights and benefits Roman citizens received even as Roman governance extended down to the local level. Because Italian soldiers made up such a significant part of the army, the Roman tribune Gaius Gracchus proposed extending citizenship in 122 B.C. to all the people in Italy then currently classified as allies (*socii*). Existing holders of Roman citizenship, both rich and poor, rejected this proposal even though the *socii* had fought for the Roman state alongside them for generations. Elite Romans had no wish to dilute their political power by enlarging the ranks of the senatorial and equestrian classes of aristocrats that monopolized the republic's top positions. Poorer Roman plebeians feared the consequences of expanding the pool of people eligible for benefits such as grain subsidies (a set of populist prejudices not unfamiliar to politicians in the European Union or the United States today). The failure of a later attempt to regularize the status of the Italian allies and their long-standing grievances against

Roman rule in general sparked the Social War in 91 B.C., which lasted until 88 B.C. This was a remarkably bloody conflict that contemporary accounts claimed resulted in the deaths of between 150,000 and 300,000 people, an enormous number given the relative size of the population and Rome's historical reliance on these people to man its legions.[54]

Although the Italian *socii* lost the war, they achieved their goal of Roman citizenship when it was extended in stages to all free people in Roman Italy by 84 B.C. This proved to be a fortuitous precedent because it broke the city-state mold of exclusion and allowed the Roman government to subsequently expand grants of citizenship strategically on a much wider basis. While the political rights this entailed lost much of their meaning when emperors came to monopolize power after the end of the republic, the legal status of Roman citizen was still highly sought after and used (not always successfully) to engender loyalty to the Roman state. At the elite level it also allowed for the appointment of prominent wealthy provincials to the Roman Senate who, along with "new men" lacking old Roman ancestral pedigrees, produced a more cosmopolitan body. Thereafter Rome distributed rights of citizenship on an ever-larger scale as the empire expanded to include whole cities, new colonial settlements, and even freed slaves. This piecemeal process reached its conclusion with the Edict of Caracalla (A.D. 211), which extended the right of citizenship to all free people in the Roman Empire.[55]

The success of any long-lived endogenous empire depended on its ability to organize diversity. Persia did this by letting its various peoples maintain their own ways of doing things without ever trying to make them culturally uniform or expecting them to identify with the empire. This was a practical solution since its empire consisted of people who had sophisticated cultures with their own distinct traditions of state-level governance. China took the opposite tack, making its rules uniform everywhere with a focus on the emperor as a necessary symbolic link between heaven and earth. It handled diversity by creating a common elite culture so strong that it expected people to reject earlier regionalisms and see themselves as a naturally unified people. Unlike in Persia, all the rival states within China already saw themselves as part of a larger single cultural tradition, and neighboring regions offered no alternative challenges to it. By calling itself Zhongguo (Middle Kingdom; Central State), China also separated the idea of empire from the dynasties that ruled it. In neither of these polities did the concept of citizenship exist; their rulers had only subjects. For the Romans, however, law and political authority were viewed as coming from the empire's people, and Roman armies marched under banners emblazoned with "SPQR" (*Senatus populusque Romanus*, "The Senate and people of Rome"). Even after de facto power was usurped by Rome's emperors, Roman citizenship retained its importance as a way to bind an ever-larger number of people into the empire by granting them all an equal legal status and rights without making them uniform in culture, language, or religious belief. This was a particularly important element in Rome's Hellenized East, where people saw their own Greek language and culture as superior to that of their conquerors.

In A.D. 155 Aelius Aristides, a champion of Hellenistic values, gave a wide-ranging oration (in Greek) praising the stability of Roman governance compared with that of previous states and empires in the region. He highlighted the wide extension of citizenship as the innovation that underlay Rome's success even before Edict of Caracalla made it universal a half century later:

> But there is that which very decidedly deserves as much attention and admiration now as all the rest together. I mean your magnificent citizenship with its grand conception, because there is nothing like it in the records of all mankind. Dividing into two groups all those in your empire—and with this word I have indicated the entire civilized world— you have everywhere appointed to your citizenship, or even to kinship with you, the better part of the world's talent, courage, and leadership, while the rest you recognized as a league under your hegemony. . . . It was not because you stood off and refused to give a share in it to any of the others that you made your citizenship an object of wonder. On the contrary, you sought its expansion as a worthy aim, and you have caused the word Roman to be the label, not of membership in a city, but of some common nationality, and this not just one among all, but one balancing all the rest. For the categories into which you now divide the world are not Hellenes and Barbarians, and it is not absurd, the distinction which you made, because you show them a citizenry more numerous, so to speak, than the entire Hellenic race. The division which you substituted is one into Romans and non-Romans. To such a degree have you expanded the name of your city. Since these are the lines along which the distinction has been made, many in every city are fellow-citizens of yours no less than of their own kinsmen, though some of them have not yet seen this city. There is no need of garrisons to hold their citadels, but the men of greatest standing and influence in every city guard their own fatherlands for you. And you have a double hold upon the cities, both from here and from your fellow citizens in each.[56]

Such praise of citizenship must be balanced against the Mediterranean world's reliance on large-scale slavery as an important part of its economy. While slavery existed in China and Persia, the number of slaves in the Roman Empire was much larger and constituted a higher percentage of the total population. Walter Scheidel's modeling suggests that the empire's urban slave population amounted to 1.3–1.9 million people, compared with 6.5–7.5 million free people (including freed slaves). The empire's rural population had a larger number of slaves, although they constituted a lower percentage of the population: 3.5–6.5 million slaves versus 49–52 million free people. Given their shorter life expectancies and rates of manumission, to have maintained a continuing presence of 1.2 million slaves would have required the importation of 18,000 new slaves annually, or a total of 3 or 4 million people over the course of two hundred years.[57] Again, unlike in Persia and China, in the Roman Empire the institution of slavery was an integral part of the empire's agricultural, construction, and industrial production as well as what we would today label the service industry from the household to the state level. How order was maintained among those who were slaves and those whose status changed to free person was always an important issue in Roman society, particularly after the suppression of a series of large slave revolts in the late republic, most famously one led by Spartacus (73–71 B.C.), who defeated a number of regular legions. For at least some people the eventual fall of the Roman Empire may not have been unwelcome.

Another reason for promoting the idea of citizenship was that it affirmed people's loyalty to the state that granted it rather than to specific rulers or a single dynastic line. Unlike Persia and China, the Roman Empire did not restrict imperial succession to royal dynasties that were closed to outsiders. In Rome the empire's top job was not hereditary and was filled by a surprisingly diverse array of people. Even what looked like a hereditary succession pattern of the Julio-Claudian line (27 B.C.–A.D. 68) begun by Augustus had not a single case of father-to-natural-son inheritance, and Rome would not see its first until a century later. After the Julio-Claudian line ended with the death of Nero, military leaders rather than civilians were more likely to become emperors because they had troops to back them up. Indeed, of all the ancient empires, only Rome displayed such a preference for military success as a path to supreme power— and these leaders came from many different parts of the empire. To regularize such successions and avoid future conflict, adoption of an heir was regularly employed to create linkages from one emperor to another. Adult adoption had deep roots as a social institution in Roman culture

(Augustus was Caesar's adopted heir), and by using adoption strategically an emperor could pick his successor and turn a potential rival into an ally who knew the job was his next. Whether the transfer of power was peaceful or bloody, people's willingness to accept the legitimacy of whoever won provided an element of stability to the empire. In some respects, the types of imperial power struggles in Rome may seem familiar to the modern reader because they resemble those in a modern multinational corporation—trouble at the top was bad for business, but the institution was not exclusively defined by those who led it. In Persia and China dynastic change of rulership was viewed as a severe political rupture, with all the uncertainty that entailed; in Rome the empire persisted intact even when its top management changed.[58]

The structure of the Roman Empire from the late republic in the mid-first century B.C. until the end of the Julio-Claudian era was a mix of directly governed territories garrisoned by Roman troops and a large number of kingdoms that were subservient to Rome but retained their own rulers. Client kingdoms were old, established states in the eastern Mediterranean that had become independent after the death of Alexander the Great but now saw an alliance with Rome as the best way to preserve themselves. Their rulers had the power to tax their own subjects and maintain their own armies, but they served at Rome's pleasure. The empire's frontier from the Black Sea to Arabia was governed by such client states, serving as a buffer between the Parthians in Iran and Roman provinces in western Anatolia and Syria. This organization was a weaker form of the Persian king-of-kings model since the Persians had both collected revenue from all their territories and had satraps to supervise them.

There was a second type of client leader who led their own tribally organized peoples in the deserts of North Africa and the forests of northern Europe. Unlike the kings of the east, such first-among-equals leaders needed to obtain their people's cooperation to implement their decisions because they lacked the authority to issue commands. Rome recruited such local leaders to organize their own people by providing them with subsidies and recruiting their men as auxiliaries to fight alongside the Roman legions. The total number of these auxiliaries was significant, about equal to the 150,000 men serving in the Roman legions. In addition to manpower, the auxiliaries brought important complementary fighting skills that the Romans needed, particularly cavalry, archers, sling throwers, and light infantry. Tribal client leaders would usually be granted citizenship, and their connection to Rome and the resources it provided allowed them to build up their authority in societies where such leaders had not previously been very powerful. Of course, this process could back-fire. Rome's worst defeats on the northern frontier were inflicted by disaffected German chieftains who had previously served as Roman auxiliaries. The most famous example is Arminius, who ambushed and annihilated three whole legions in Germania in A.D. 9 despite having received Roman citizenship and an education in Rome. Nevertheless, the policy produced enough cooperation from Rome's transborder people that Emperor Claudius (r. A.D. 41–54) granted automatic citizenship to those men who completed their twenty-five years of service as auxiliaries, increasing the number of people on the frontier who had a vested interest in the success of the empire.[59]

As long as the lands along the frontier were protected by clients of various types, this loose form of imperial organization did not require the establishment of fixed borders. An enemy would have to go through them before hitting Roman provincial territory. Rome's own legions were based in mobile camps within Roman provinces, equally able to invade new territories or maintain internal order by suppressing rebellions. The two were not always distinct. While on the map it might appear that these troops were distributed along the frontier looking outward, they could be quickly redeployed within the empire. For example, a massive invasion of Germania was halted and troops redeployed to the Balkans to put down a regional revolt between A.D. 6 and 9. Under the command of the future emperor Tiberius, the Romans soon found themselves engaged in "the most serious of all foreign wars since those with Carthage, which he carried on for three years with fifteen legions and a corresponding force of auxiliaries, amid great difficulties of every kind and the utmost scarcity of supplies."[60] Since the total number of Roman legions was only twenty-eight when the revolt broke out, this meant putting more than half of all the empire's troops in just one sector. More than a half century later, Rome faced another series of rebellions that occurred sequentially in Britain (60–61), Judea (66–70), and the lower Rhine (69). All of these had their roots in the mismanagement of client leaders or auxiliary troops.

Roman troops thereafter moved to fixed bases focused on frontier defense, a change from their previously mobile bases designed for easy redeployment to put down internal revolts. Such revolts had largely ceased when local people began identifying themselves as of the empire rather than as apart from it. In response the empire turned to protecting the lands adjacent to the frontier as its primary responsibility. This shift to identification with Rome was particularly apparent in the western Mediterranean and in the lands south of the Rhine and Danube Rivers where luxuries like wine, baths, and solid buildings were innovations along with literacy, theater, and public games. Such cultural changes had an impact well beyond the territories under Roman control as complex trade networks spread aspects of Roman culture even to people who saw themselves as enemies of the Roman state.[61] These things were not new in the eastern Mediterranean, where high levels of comfort, culture, and complex economies had long predated Rome's rise, but people here benefited from the stability that a Pax Romana brought them. As the power of the empire expanded, Rome abandoned its policy of maintaining client kingdoms and turned them into provinces that now gave the empire fixed linear borders that needed to be demarcated and defended. This change began with the family of Flavian emperors (Vespasian, Titus, and Domitian) who ruled from 69 to 81. Since these emperors had the experience of suppressing rebellions within client kingdoms, a policy of greater centralization would have been more attractive. The empire displayed a final burst of expansion under Trajan (r. 98–117) and reached its maximum size with a victory over the Parthians and a campaign in central Europe. His successor Hadrian (r. 117–138) considered many of these additions too difficult to defend and pulled back to fixed frontier lines manned by Roman troops, a policy followed by his long-lived successor Antonius (r. 138–161) and his adopted son and heir, Marcus Aurelius (r. 161–180).[62]

As in China, in the Roman Empire creating a bounded frontier defended by garrison troops from fixed fortifications was a policy designed to protect the civilian populations behind them rather than fight the people beyond them. If it took many centuries for the Roman Empire to take this form, it was because its population and economic development expanded as the empire did; in China the Qin and Han dynasties consolidated already well-functioning regions and its Great Wall marked their limits. Moreover, as we will see in chapter 3, Chinese expansion was quickly matched by the unification of the Xiongnu nomads, who constituted a severe threat to the Han dynasty even at the height of its power. By contrast Rome faced no such generalized threat from its transborder enemies until much later when it was in decline during the fifth century A.D. When Rome did begin to face problems similar to those of a now-defunct Han China during the reign of Emperor Diocletian (285–306), he reorganized the empire into a more centralized state and changed the structure of the army. His policies and those of his successor Constantine (r. 306–337) hardened the border and relied on stronger fixed defenses. Thus, from the first century B.C. to the fourth century A.D., the organization of the Roman Empire moved from reliance on a Persian-style model of indirect rule with a relatively small but highly skilled military force to a more Chinese-style model of direct rule employing larger numbers of less skilled soldiers backed up by a few elite units. And just as the Chinese came to rely on "surrendered barbarians" to take responsibility for the defense of their northern frontier during the Eastern Han dynasty (25–220), the Romans also became ever more reliant on non-Roman frontier people to meet the higher manpower needs required by this type of defense. In both cases such frontier defenders later became attackers when their respective empires began to disintegrate.[63]

After Endogenous Empires: Aspirational Legacies and Regional Templates

The three endogenous empires described in this chapter all maintained themselves by extracting the resources they needed from inside the polity, organized large and diverse populations, and had complex systems of administration. Whether or not the templates for imperial rule that they created reemerged after they collapsed varied by region. In China the fall of the Han dynasty in A.D. 220 led to centuries of disorder, but empires based on its design always returned, sometimes under native Chinese dynasties such as the Tang (618–907), Song (960–1279), and Ming (1368–1644), or in somewhat different forms under foreign dynasties such as the Mongol Yuan (1271–1368) and Manchu Qing (1636–1912). While the Roman Empire remained an aspirational model, imperial unity never returned to the western Mediterranean and northern Europe, although a few shadow empire variants would claim its legacy. The eastern Mediterranean did maintain a Roman imperial structure in a shrinking territory under the Byzantines (330–1453) for the greatest longevity of any empire. Its ultimate successor, the Ottoman Empire (1299–1923), retained many Roman and Byzantine structures of governance and reunited all of the eastern Mediterranean, Balkans, and Near East into one polity. After displacing Alexander the Great's successors, a pair of endogenous empires using the Persian Achaemenid model of governance ruled Southwest Asia for the next nine centuries under the Parthians (247 B.C.–A.D. 224) and Sasanians (224–651) before becoming incorporated into the Islamic Caliphate (Umayyad, 661–750; Abbasid, 750–1258). As the Caliphate weakened, it was subsumed within empires run by Turkic-speaking peoples founded by Seljuks (1037–1194) and Khwarazmians (1077–1231) before finally being destroyed by the Mongols. The post-Mongol empires in the region included Il-khans (1256–1353) and the Timurids (1370–1507), whose successors also founded the Mughal Empire in India (1526–1857). The adoption of Persian language and administrative practices in all these Arab- and Turkic-led empires was a strong (if often unrecognized) link to a much older regional tradition of imperial rule.

When large endogenous empires collapsed without a peer replacement, the regions under their former control experienced catastrophic falls in the standards of living and the population densities they formerly maintained because smaller successor states could not manage or finance the needed levels of complexity to maintain them. The seeming ease with which such endogenous empires had mobilized available capital, labor, and technology for the construction of transportation infrastructures and monumental building projects distinguished them from other, smaller states (and most shadow empires) that could only achieve such feats on a much-reduced scale, if at all. Later generations could only marvel at their achievements, fostering legends that their people must have been giants, been in possession of secret skills, or had supernatural help. Living in such an age, the medieval Arab historian ibn Khaldun contrasted the Islamic successors with their Persian Sasanian predecessors by noting that the caliphs had been "unable to tear down and destroy many great architectural monuments, even though destruction is much easier than construction," and therefore "we realize that the strength used in starting such a monument must have been immense." As an example, he cited the ill-considered attempt by Caliph Harun al-Rashid (r. 786–809) to demonstrate the superiority of the Arabs over the Persians by ordering the demolition of the massive Sasanian Reception Hall of Khosrow in Ctesiphon. His effort ended in a humiliating failure even after he "had pickaxes applied to it, and he had it heated by setting fire to it, and he had vinegar poured upon it."[64] Successors elsewhere might also implicitly demonstrate their inferiority by repurposing ruins of the monumental structures they could no longer build themselves. The huge Mausoleum of Hadrian in Rome became a medieval fortress that eventually served as a papal refuge and prison from the sixteenth to the twentieth century. Even in a modern era when the world is once again covered with immense buildings and infrastructure projects, the discovery in Xian, China, of an entire army of life-size terracotta warriors commissioned by the First Qin Emperor renewed the wonder of that age.

Powerful as they were, endogenous empires could be challenged by imperial polities established on very different foundations. The structures of these exogenous or shadow empires have received much less attention because they were thought to be just defective versions of endogenous empires unworthy of a historical room of their own. While students of empire will hopefully have found this chapter interesting, they will recognize the terrain of familiar scholarship. In turning to shadow empires, we enter a historical world where this is often not the case. From a comparative perspective, the map from this point on might well read, "Here be dragons!" We will now turn to these seemingly phantasmagoric cases and explore them from within rather than from without.

CHAPTER TWO

Shadows on the Seas

Some went out on the sea in ships;
they were merchants on the mighty waters.
They saw the works of the Lord,
his wonderful deeds in the deep.

—PSALM 107

Maritime Empires

Maritime exogenous empires relied on their navies to exert power and extract the resources they needed to finance their states from peoples and places they avoided ruling directly. If endogenous empires sought to expand their revenue base to amass ever more political power, maritime shadow empires sought to increase their political power in order to amass ever more revenue. To this end they held only the minimum territory needed to wield their naval forces effectively, and thus the size of the territories and populations they ruled fell well below those typical of land-based endogenous empires. Early examples of these include Mediterranean-based city-states such as ancient Athens and Carthage and later the Venetian Republic. In the sixteenth and seventeenth centuries a new set of Atlantic naval powers arose in Portugal, England, and Holland that used improved long-distance sailing ships and gunpowder weapons to exploit the immensely valuable trade in spices and other products from South and Southeast Asia and later from China and Japan. Unlike earlier maritime empires, they advanced the interests of complex private commercial ventures like the British East India Company and the Dutch East India Company that produced enormous profits for both the state and investors. Commercial expansion by the

British East India Company under the protection of India's Mughal Empire turned to conquest when that empire began disintegrating in the mid-eighteenth century and eventually transformed the company, now under British government direction, into the colonial ruler of all South Asia. Despite this, the lure of indirect control was so strong that British government did not divest the private East India Company of its administrative control of India until after the failed Sepoy Rebellion in 1857. In so doing Britain completed its transformation from an exogenous maritime empire into an endogenous one that by the early twentieth century encompassed 35 million km^2, surpassing even the Mongol Empire in size.

Exogenous empires flourished by maximizing exceptional military strengths that enabled them to confront adjacent endogenous empires as independent peer polities. Horse cavalry made the Mongolian steppe nomads powerful enough to take on China despite their small population. It was naval power that enabled the Athenians to keep the Persians at bay and maintain hegemony over the many islands and coastal cities of the Aegean Sea. Both could come to accommodations with their immensely more powerful endogenous empire neighbors because neither the Xiongnu nor the Athenians ever conceived of themselves as possible rulers of China or Persia. Therefore, while both these shadow empires were rising new powers, existing endogenous empires did not view them as existential threats since they showed little inclination to expand beyond the steppes or seacoasts where their power was rooted.

Although shadow empires took advantage of the power vacuums created by endogenous empires, other conditions needed to be present for them to emerge. (The tribes in Germania on the Roman frontier, for example, never created any sort of shadow empire.) In the case of Athens, this occurred when it transformed an alliance of city-states into a centralized maritime empire after Persia withdrew its forces from the Aegean. Athens financed it with tribute payments from member states, commercial taxes on maritime trade, and profits derived from its colonial landholdings. Athens also exploited its dominant position financially by imposing a monopoly on minting silver coinage, politically by requiring that disputes involving allied cities be settled by its courts, and culturally by becoming home to almost every important Greek playwright and philosopher of the era regardless of their origin. In all respects but size of population and territory ruled, the Athenian Empire had the structural characteristics of much bigger endogenous empires (table 2.1) that would also characterize subsequent maritime empires.

Table 2.1. Endogenous empire criteria found in the Athenian Empire

Present	Partial	Absent
Organized to administer and exploit diversity	Centralized institutions of governance that were separate and distinct from the rulers	Size: 200,000–300,000 km²
Imperial project that imposed some type of unity throughout the system with democratic governance and cultural hegemony		Population: 1 million or less
A primate imperial center with transportation systems designed to serve it militarily and economically		
Monopoly of force within its territories, and military force projected outward		
Systems of communication that allowed administration of all subject areas from the center directly		

The Athenian Empire

ANCIENT MARITIME TECHNOLOGICAL INNOVATIONS AND THE EMERGENCE OF SEA POWERS

Although land based, the earliest Bronze Age civilizations, beginning in the fourth millennium B.C., developed in riverine environments with reed and wood boat building traditions. At least some of them had the capacity to engage in long-distance sea voyages by the later part of the third millennium B.C., as documented in cuneiform tablets in Mesopotamia that recorded the arrival of merchant ships from Harappa in the Indus Valley.[1] Farther to the west, Egypt developed large ships for use on the Nile River and the Mediterranean and Red Seas.[2] The opulent Minoan civilization on the island of Crete was the first to base its elite economy primarily on sea trade and sent its ships in all directions from 2400 to 1200 B.C.[3] Although the Greeks in the fifth century B.C., projecting their own time back into the Bronze Age, asserted that the Minoans had founded the first *thalassocracy* (sea-based polity), the Cretans needed no war fleets to police the waters where they sailed unchallenged, and that sea itself was a stronger bar against possible invaders than any walled fortifications.[4] This changed at the end of the second millennium B.C. when invaders and raiders in the Mediterranean littoral began using watercraft specifically designed for war and opened a whole new zone of conflict for Bronze Age land-based polities that would bring about the collapse of many of them between 1200 and 1150 B.C.

This period began with the arrival of the so-called Sea Peoples, who invaded wide swaths of land in the eastern Mediterranean in the early twelfth century B.C. Their lightweight undecked narrow-hulled boats had both sails and oars. They were built for speed and were crewed by 20, 50, or even 120 oarsmen depending on their length. They are best known in literature as the famous "black ships" of Homer's *Iliad* and *Odyssey* that attacked Troy.[5] These boats were not designed to fight other ships at sea but rather to allow the warriors who rowed and sailed them to engage in amphibious operations—raiding villages, markets, and even cities. They would arrive by stealth whenever possible, disembark, and then press quickly inland to fight a hopefully unprepared foe, returning safely to their ships before the enemy could mount a counterattack or retreating more quickly if they encountered unexpected resistance. While many Sea Peoples came only to raid, some of them conquered parts of the eastern Mediterranean and resettled their people there. Even when defeated, they could find themselves reemployed by land powers eager to acquire their maritime skills.[6]

In their style of warfare, tactics, and political organization, these Bronze Age maritime peoples bore a striking resemblance to the medieval Vikings, who also used shallow-draft undecked boats to raid and invade distant lands two thousand years later. They both thrived in worlds on the edge of anarchy where long-established large states were disintegrating and could no longer project enough power to keep raiders from their doorsteps. And like the Vikings, these sea raiders were organized politically as chiefdoms. Boats were owned and built by individuals or local communities and sailed by the followers of the chieftains who led them. A large raid or invasion required the voluntary cooperation of many individual communities, each of which had its own leader who needed to be convinced to participate. What appeared as a single flotilla to an enemy seeing its ships mass on the horizon and then pull its boats ashore (they needed to be beached regularly to avoid waterlogging) was less than met the eye. Composed of independent groups, it did not have so much a chain of command as a chain of consensus, and fleets could disperse as quickly as they assembled. The *Iliad*'s complete accounting of all 1,186 ships participating in the attack on Troy that includes their community of origin, specific commanders, and praise of each illustrates this.[7] Each chieftain's desire for recognition and individual praise demanded no less—no one gets more credit unless everyone gets some credit. War was personal, not institutional, and its heroes had the right to sulk like Achilles in his tent or go home if they did not get the attention or rewards they believed they deserved. It was not yet a world where states took primacy and where the people manning their fleets served anonymously for pay under appointed commanders who themselves could be replaced at any time.

What was also missing from this rich Bronze Age maritime world were warships that could be combined to create true navies and fight at sea. While modified merchant vessels transported troops from Egypt to Syria, for example, there was no naval counterpart to a standing army or any maritime technology that would give its possessors enough of a military advantage to specialize in it. This changed in the eighth century B.C. with the appearance of the first true warships in the Mediterranean. Produced at the behest of city-state polities (or land powers like Egypt and Assyria) rather than individuals or local communities, these multidecked galleys with rams quickly became the mainstay of all navies in the region. Expensive to build, maintain, and crew, they transformed warfare at sea as profoundly as horse cavalry did on land. And just as nomads projected power on horseback from their steppe heartland homes, maritime powers did the same from the sea. Maritime military competition encouraged the rapid spread of improved boat designs regardless of where they originated. This began with the introduction of two-decked ships that could carry more people and equipment and provided a high, stable fighting platform on their upper deck that was absent in more fragile, undecked boats. These biremes had fifty or more rowers divided equally between the two decks and carried about thirty-five marines and sailors who could either defend the ship or board other boats in battle. As significantly, the ship was designed to employ a sheathed metal ram attached to its prow below the waterline that could pierce the hull of another ship and sink it. Lionel Casson stresses that this was something new, a vessel designed to do battle at sea against other ships equipped to do the same:

> Very likely it made its debut during the obscure period after 1000 B.C. that marked the transition from the Bronze to the Iron Age. Its introduction must have had as revolutionary an impact as, say, that of a naval gun twenty-five hundred years later. A warship was no longer merely a particularly fast transport to ferry troops or bring marines

FIGURE 2.1. Bireme relief. Image by Wikimedia user "World Imaging."
Licensed under Creative Commons 3.0.

into fighting proximity with those of enemy ships; it had become an entirely new kind of craft, one that was in effect a man-driven torpedo armed with a pointed cutwater for puncturing an enemy hull. In the wake of the new weapon came, inevitably, far-reaching changes in ship design and construction. From now on, in order to be built more powerfully and of heavier materials, the bow area in particular had to be as massive as possible, for blows were felt here first and hardest.[8]

Decked ships of this design are illustrated in Assyrian war reliefs from the eighth and seventh centuries B.C. and may have been Phoenician in origin, but they were quickly adopted by other maritime powers (figure 2.1). By the fifth century B.C., the dominant warship was a larger trireme that employed 150 rowers on three levels. Although larger boats would be built, the sleek trireme (40 × 6 m) became the centerpiece for Mediterranean war fleets for centuries thereafter because it combined the speed and maneuverability of the slim undecked boats with the lethality of a ram-equipped multidecked ship.[9]

Building and operating multidecked ships required financing that only a state-level polity could provide, and they were owned and manned by states rather than by individuals. In 483 B.C., Themistocles convinced the Athenians to use the windfall from a silver mine bonanza to build two hundred triremes and the port facilities to maintain them, giving them the largest single fleet among the Greeks, which reached three hundred vessels under Pericles in 431 B.C.[10] This was an immense investment for a city-state, even one as rich as Athens. Thucydides gave the cost of building a single trireme as a talent of silver weighing 26 kg (equal to nine man-years of skilled labor); crewing the finished ship when it sailed cost about a talent a month paid in silver. The ships also needed specialized drydocks where they were stored when not in use. Maintaining even just a few triremes proved so unaffordable for smaller city-states that they stopped competing politically as peer polities with those city-states that had them. Employing a navy to engage in war (even assuming not too many boats and crews were lost in battle) was hugely expensive: the nine-month campaign waged by Athens against its rebellious ally Samos in 440–439 B.C. cost it 1,200 talents, which it sought to recoup by seizing Samos's remaining ships and demanding reparations be paid in multiyear installments.[11]

The impact of this trireme transformation was immediate and profound, and as Ian Morris observes, it "completely changed the nature of war and state formation":

> Navies could project state power in ways that had been unimaginable in the sixth century. Thucydides had Pericles remind the Athenians that "With your navy as it is today there is no power on earth—not the King of Persia nor any people under the sun—that can stop you from sailing where you wish. This power of yours is something in an altogether different category from all the advantages of houses and cultivated land." Athens struck with impunity in Egypt, Cyprus, the Black Sea region, and Sicily, as well as all over the Aegean, and naval tactics and training developed even faster than terrestrial ones. As Sparta discovered, the only way to compete with Athenian naval power was to create a similar fleet, but a full summer campaign for such a force would cost at least 600 talents, well beyond the revenue of any normal city-state. The spiraling costs of naval warfare and the need to hire the best rowers were even more important than the rising costs of sieges in speeding up the tempo of state formation.[12]

If changes in military technology created the hardware needed to produce a maritime empire, it was this reorganization and centralization of state power that provided the needed governing software to manage it.

THE PERSIAN ADVANCE INTO THE
AEGEAN FRONTIER AND ITS IMPACT

It was only after 500 B.C. that wielding naval power alone proved sufficient for its users to dominate other city-state polities and keep land rivals at bay, laying the military foundation for the maritime empires established by both ancient Athens and Carthage. This occurred in a coastal Mediterranean environment where most of the many hundreds of small city-states with concentrated populations abutted reservoirs of larger but more dispersed populations of tribally organized peoples on their inland margins— Thracians, Scythians, Numidians, Iberians, and Gauls, to name some of the most important. An exception to this pattern was in the east, where city-states bordered densely populated kingdoms or empires in Anatolia, the Levant, and Egypt. Many Mediterranean city-states had their origins as the colonies of mother states that had sponsored settlements of their own people in places of strategic or economic value whose indigenous inhabitants were too weak to exclude them. These included areas with valuable metal deposits, areas of surplus grain production, and sites of emporiums that captured the trade of inland regions such as Thrace and Scythia. The rise in the number of colonies beginning in the sixth century B.C. also reflected an ongoing maritime rivalry between the Phoenicians in the Levant and Greeks in the Aegean. The Phoenicians became dominant in the southern Mediterranean and as far west as Iberia. The Greeks eventually dominated the Mediterranean north of Cyprus and the Adriatic and Black Seas. Both established beachheads in wheat-rich Sicily. Each of these networks would produce a singularly powerful maritime empire: Athens for the Greeks in the Aegean Sea, Carthage in Tunisia for the Phoenicians. Their rise to this status was a product both of investments in warships that created large navies and of exogenous state formation prompted by the expansion of the Persian Empire, which was extending its reach into the eastern littoral of the Mediterranean Sea.

Without the Persian Empire's advance to the shores of the Mediterranean and into Egypt, it is unlikely that the quarrelsome Greek city-states would have ever created such large naval forces or even agreed to cooperate with one another, much less produced a maritime empire. Although Cyrus the Great conquered Lydia in 547 B.C., the island Greeks in Ionia closest to Anatolia initially had no fear that the Persians would come for them "because the Phoenicians were not yet subject to Persia and Persia herself was not a sea power."[13] This situation changed when Cyrus' successor Cambyses II decided to conquer Egypt and realized that the Persian Empire would need a navy to take it. Cambyses therefore set about subduing Cyprus and Phoenicia to gain control of their naval assets. With these, and a substantial contribution of ships volunteered by Ionian Greek city-states like Samos and Mytilene, the Persians mounted a successful land and sea campaign against Egypt in 525 B.C. According to Herodotus, Cambyses's linked feats of personally establishing the empire's navy and conquering Egypt led the Persians to proclaim that "he was better than his father, because he had kept all Cyrus' possessions and acquired Egypt and the command of the sea into the bargain."[14] And just as the Persian Empire had earlier imposed imperial control over the wide variety of infantry and cavalry troops provided by its satrapies, the Persian navy exploited the existing maritime skills of its new multinational subjects for its own purposes. As Pierre Briant describes it, "The navy was not simply a haphazard conglomeration of regional contingents whose command was left to the local leaders, but rather a royal fleet constructed on the initiative of the central government and commanded by Persian officers. In this process, the subject peoples were required to pay taxes in silver or in kind and to furnish oarsmen." He continues, "The royal administration built the ships (with the help of requisition of manual labor), while the tributary coastal peoples (Greeks, Carians, Lycians, Cilicians, Cypriots, and Phoenicians) provided the oarsmen. This represents a considerable commitment of resources."[15] The resources available to the Persians far outmatched those of any city-state or league of city-states, and so (perhaps paradoxically) the Persian Empire maintained a larger and more powerful navy than did polities with better-established maritime traditions. This was because, while the Persians may have lacked the experience of the Greeks and Phoenicians as sailors and boat builders, they could command the needed capital to build ships on a huge scale and had the ability to conscript or pay the many crews that manned them. Xerxes's invasion of Greece, for example, would pit a Persian fleet of 1,207 triremes against 378 allied Greek triremes at the Battle of Salamis in 480 B.C., a three-to-one material advantage.[16]

Athens's transformation into a leading Greek city-state and then maritime empire began when it took the lead in opposing Persia's expansion into the western Aegean Sea. While Greek historians viewed the conflict as a world-significant "battle of civilizations," the new Achaemenid ruler Darius the Great (r. 522–486 B.C.) did not. His first task had been to gain tighter control of the empire's core satrapies and then hem the empire's ragged frontiers to make them more defensible. These frontier rounding-outs took place in every corner of the empire. They began with better defending Bactria by incorporating the various Saka (Massagetae) steppe nomads living east of the Caspian Sea and along the Syr Darya River in 519 B.C., an attack Darius led in person. The Persians added the rich lowland Indus valley to the empire's holdings south of the Hindu Kush Mountains the next year, and its navy on the Indus then sailed from there to Red Sea. A similar strategic concern about the threat posed by the Scythian steppe nomads on the empire's northwestern frontier moved Darius to mount a punitive campaign against them by way of the Balkans and Ukraine around 513 B.C. While that war ended unsuccessfully, it did keep the Scythians at bay and added new satrapies and client states to the empire that included the strategic Hellespont, the grain-rich western Black Sea littoral, mineral-rich Thrace, and Macedonia. At the same time, Darius's Persian satrap in Egypt solidified the empire's southwestern frontier by conquering Libya, putting it within striking distance of Carthage.[17]

Central to this expansion in the northwest was the cooperation of the Ionian Greek city-states that inhabited the islands and Anatolian coasts of the eastern Aegean. From the time of Cambyses, the Ionians had been ruled by local Persian-backed tyrants who supplied the empire with regular tribute and manned ships in its navy. Such rulers were becoming something of an anachronism in a Greek city-state world where oligarchies and democracies had become the norm. At the beginning of the fifth century B.C., these Ionian autocrats found themselves on the horns of a dilemma, "caught between two irreconcilable ambitions: liberation from Persian protection and retention of their own power" in the face of increasingly hostile populations.[18] In 499 B.C. the islands revolted and sought backing from the Greek mainland that Sparta refused but Athens and Eretria gave. They then assisted the Ionians in an attack on the Persian provincial capital of Sardis that moved the war to the mainland, where the invaders were quickly repulsed. The Persians then deprived the Ionians of access to their landward Anatolian seaports. While the Ionians had an initial advantage at sea and knew maintaining it was the only chance the rebellion had to succeed, the revolt had two critical weaknesses: no unity of command and lack of revenue to finance the fleet. Soon even their advantage at sea was lost when the Persians, according to Herodotus, mobilized 600 Phoenician ships that sailed against an Ionian fleet of 353 triremes. In the ensuing battle at Lade, some Ionian contingents fought while others defected or fled.[19] By 494 B.C. the Persians had regained control of Ionia, destroying cities that resisted them but accepting peaceful surrenders from most. While the Persians restored some of their loyal tyrants in the aftermath, they replaced most of them with democracies that they now deemed more popular with the people. It was always Persian policy to give priority to stable regimes that met with local approval because that better ensured they would pay tribute and not revolt.[20] To this end, in 493 B.C. the Persians recalculated Ionian tribute payments based on new cadastral surveys that measured each island's productive land and added a dose of good governance by requiring that the Ionians bring unresolved disputes to their local satrap for arbitration rather than resorting to fighting among themselves.[21]

The suppression of the Ionian Revolt did not involve any fighting on the Greek mainland, but in its aftermath the Persians focused on the states there that had aided the rebels. In 490 B.C. the Persians expanded their control into the southern Aegean, burning the island of Naxos and sending an amphibious force to attack Eretria and Athens in retaliation for their cooperation with the now-defeated Ionian rebels. The Persians captured Eretria but were repulsed by the Athenians upon landing at Marathon and withdrew. This was less a full-scale invasion of Greece than a probing thrust that, had it been successful, might have induced pro-Persian "Medizers" in Athens to betray the city as their sympathizers in Eretria had done. At the very least, the pro-Persian faction could have pressed for an agreement with the Great King on favorable terms similar to those other city-states had accepted.[22] Because supporting a policy of appeasement with the Persians was more politically mainstream in the wake of the Ionian defeat than it later became after the Persian Wars, Medizers could be likened to pro-Vichy collaborators with Nazi Germany who could reasonably pose as peacemaking patriots in 1940 but were condemned as traitors after France's liberation in 1944.

In 492 B.C. Darius had sent his general and brother-in-law Mardonius into Europe to restore the empire's authority in the Hellespont, Thrace, and Macedonia. But after the Persian failure at Marathon two years later, Darius needed to rethink his strategy. Both Athens and Sparta had turned more violently anti-Persian, and the likelihood of brokering a peaceful accommodation vanished when both cities exiled prominent pro-Persian civic leaders and then murdered the Persian envoys sent to discuss submission terms. Darius determined that the solution to this problem was incorporating the entire Greek mainland into the empire and thus closing the last remaining gap in his western frontier. A successful conquest would eliminate mainland Greece as a base of subversion fomenting unrest in Ionia, give the empire control of the whole eastern Mediterranean from the Nile delta to the Black Sea, and allow the installation of pro-Persian

Greek exiles to maintain order. The imperial logic was impeccable and would require just a limited war to achieve. The main targets (Boeotia, Euboea, Attica, and the Peloponnesus) were territories that encompassed only about 35,000 km², a rounding error of less than 1 percent in an empire that already exerted sovereignty over 5 million km². To this end, Darius "sent messengers to all cities commanding the equipment of an army, charging each to provide much more than they had before provided of ships and horses and provision and vessels of transport. By these messages Asia was shaken for three years, the best men being enrolled for service against Hellas and making preparation therefor."²³ If Darius had been able to mount the attack as planned in 487 B.C., years before Athens added two hundred triremes to its fleet, it is likely that Greece would have been listed as the final satrapy he added to the empire in his long thirty-six-year reign. However, just as these forces were finally assembled, they had to be redeployed to suppress a revolt in Egypt, and the empire was then thrown into further disorder when Darius died in 486 B.C. The usual succession struggles broke out within the Persian court and gave the Greeks a whole decade to prepare for a war that finally began when the new king of kings Xerxes amassed an unprecedented naval and land force to renew the campaign in 480 B.C.

While Herodotus's figures for the Persian army that run into the millions of men may be discounted, it is clear that the empire assumed that its overwhelming numbers would prove decisive. Xerxes led the Greek invasion personally, making a great show of it and Persian power by holding a number of military reviews as the army progressed. Despite being hindered by a series of mishaps, including damage to its bridge over the Hellespont and the loss of one-third of its fleet in storms, the Persian army and navy both advanced in tandem toward the main Greek forces. A Spartan-led defense on land held the strategic pass at Thermopylae, and at sea an Athenian-led defense sought to deny the Persian navy access to the strategic straits of Cape Artemisia in northern Euboea. Thermopylae famously fell after the Persians found a way around it, and the Greek fleet abandoned an inconclusive sea battle when it received news of this defeat. The larger part of the Persian army then marched toward Corinth, ready to invade the Peloponnesus, while Xerxes took the opportunity to burn an evacuated Athens and meet up with his fleet commanders. The Greek coalition was on the verge of disintegration, and had Xerxes simply refused to engage its navy anchored at Salamis, the upcoming pincer movement by land and sea on the Spartan homeland would have concluded the war successfully. Instead, baited by the Athenian commander

Themistocles, Xerxes saw an opportunity to win a flashy sea battle that he could observe personally from a nearby hilltop. He confidently ordered the Persian ships into the narrow waters of a bay where the Greeks had the advantage and his fleet was destroyed. While this was a disaster, his experienced campaign commander Mardonius reminded Xerxes that Persian land forces were still at full strength, unbeaten and ready to conquer the Peloponnesus and add Sparta to Athens in their list of burned cities. But profoundly shaken and in a panic, Xerxes all but fled Greece with most of his army in great disorder, leaving Mardonius behind with a picked force to renew the campaign in the next year. That plan failed after Mardonius was killed at the Battle of Platea ten months later and his expeditionary force disintegrated.[24]

Persia had experience in coping with unexpected military setbacks and anticipated the necessity of periodically mobilizing itself to crush rebellions in places like Babylonia, Ionia, or Egypt. If the Second Persian War was planned by Darius to reverse the failures of the first, one would have expected Xerxes to mount a Third Persian War to at least regain control of the empire's lost satrapies in Macedonia, Thrace, Ionia, and the Black Sea littoral rather than leave these valuable territories under Greek control. Instead the Persians withdrew to mainland Anatolia and abandoned the large chunks of Europe and coastal Ionia that they had formerly ruled. In both cause and effect, this turnabout resembled the consequences of similar military disasters in which an emperor was so personally traumatized by an unanticipated defeat that he erased the peoples who caused it from the empire's mental map. A prime example is Augustus's strategic abandonment of Magna Germania after the loss of three entire legions and their gold-eagle standards to German tribes that ambushed them in the Teutoburg Forest in A.D. 9. Just as Xerxes had carefully planned the conquest of mainland Greece, Augustus was in the process of expanding Rome's holdings in Germania to the Elbe River when the shock of losing those legions induced him to abandon not only the German campaign but all the existing Roman settlements north of the Rhine. That done, none of his successors ever again looked on Germania as potentially Roman even though the empire had digested an equally large and alien Gaul a half century earlier. Similarly, in China, the newly installed Han emperor Gaozu gave up his plan of subduing the steppe nomads that the Qin dynasty had earlier driven from the Ordos and set the Great Wall as China's northern boundary after he was surrounded and almost captured by the Xiongnu horsemen in 200 B.C. In each of these cases, the ruler altered his empire's foreign policy by deploying his forces defensively, setting fixed boundaries beyond which the empire would not expand, and abandoning lands that lay outside them. It was here that the Athenian maritime empire would emerge, as would the Xiongnu steppe empire along China's northern steppe under similar circumstances three centuries later.

FROM ALLIANCE TO EMPIRE

Until 480 B.C. the Athenians existed in a political environment in which the Persian Empire had dominated the eastern Mediterranean for a half century and made life hazardous for the region's remaining independent city-states, forcing them to choose between accepting the empire's hegemony or risking possible destruction. But since no single Greek city-state had the power to resist the Persians, they needed to form alliances. That proved difficult because Mediterranean city-states were notoriously insular and unwilling to cede the authority needed to create a unified force, as the failure of the Ionian Revolt demonstrated. Only fear of Xerxes's massive invasion induced the rival city-states of mainland Greece to establish the Hellenic League in 481 B.C. at Corinth, and then only when news of his impending approach reached them. After the surprising defensive Greek victories at Salamis and Platea, the Hellenic League went on the offensive and destroyed the last organized Persian naval squadron in the Aegean at Mycale in 479 B.C., thereby freeing many of the ports in coastal Anatolia from Persian rule. They then turned north, besieging and then capturing the Persian garrison at Sestos on the Hellespont as well as the strategic city of Byzantium. However, these successes fractured the unity of the Hellenic League because Athens and Sparta had very different ideas on how to proceed in their aftermath. With the Persians having largely withdrawn, Sparta saw an opportunity to declare an end to the war and begin pulling its forces back to the Peloponnesus. The Spartans even suggested that if the Ionians (who had after all fought on the Persian side during the war) now feared for their safety, they should abandon their homes and resettle on the Greek mainland. The sea-based Athenians argued against the Spartans that this was not the time to discuss demobilization since the Persians were bound to strike back and the alliance should therefore be expanded to include the Ionians to make it stronger. Despite the recent string of Greek victories, fear that the ancient world's largest empire would return must have been very real to the Athenians, who were still in the process of rebuilding a home city that the Persians had burned to the ground.

To deal with this threat, the Athenians formed a new alliance in 478 B.C. on the sacred island of Delos with the goal of liberating the remaining

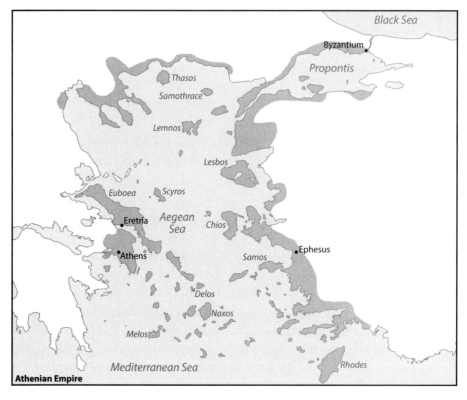

MAP 2.1. The Athenian Empire.

Greek city-states from Persian control, continuing the war to seek revenge and keep Persian naval forces out of the Aegean. This Delian League initially had 20 members from the Aegean islands, 36 from Ionia, 35 from the Hellespont, 24 from the region of Caria, and 33 from the region of Thrace, a number that would eventually grow to 214 (map 2.1). Neither Sparta nor any other of the Peloponnesian city-states that were members of the existing Hellenic League chose to join.[25] The alliance was voluntary but deemed to be permanent, and each state swore to have the same enemies and friends. Athens held its military command and administered the league's finances funded from a common treasury located on Delos, where the alliance met for business. Member cities pledged to contribute either ships with crews or an annual cash tribute payment, the size of which was set by Athens. Although each member had a vote in decision making, the majority of the cash-paying smaller states followed Athens's lead and so effectively gave it the power to set policy even when some of the larger ship-contributing members objected.[26]

The creation of a common treasury supported by annual contributions made this alliance unique, but its naval power could not have been maintained without it. Navies required large capital investments in ships in advance of any conflict, and sending ships to sea demanded ready cash to pay the crews whether they fought or not. By contrast, Thucydides observed that land powers like Sparta saw war preparations as episodic and requiring the mobilization of manpower rather than money. Raising the funds needed for war began only after it was declared and often proved deficient when the cost exceeded normal annual revenues. Land-based Sparta expected its allies to supply troops when asked but did not require any regular tribute money from them.[27] Athens, by contrast, demanded payments of annual tribute even in times of peace and banked them for future use, preparing it to wage a war well before any was declared. Moreover, and unlike Sparta, Athens did not see the military contributions of its allies as assets worth preserving. Instead the Athenians encouraged those cities that initially provided ships and crews to replace them with annual cash payments, reducing their economic and military burden but giving Athens ever greater political and military dominance. Thucydides saw this policy of encouraging annual money payments instead of manned ships as the main tool by which the Athenians transformed the Delian League into the Athenian Empire (*arche*). As the power balance shifted, Athens grew stricter about requiring that tribute payments be made in full and punctually even in times of peace. It also began treating the ever-smaller minority of city-states that still maintained warships less as allies and more as subjects. As Thucydides observed,

Of all the causes of defection, that connected with arrears of tribute and vessels, and with failure of service, was the chief; for the Athenians were very severe and exacting, and made themselves offensive by applying the screw of necessity to men who were not used to and in fact not disposed for any continuous labor. In some other respects the Athenians were not the old popular rulers they had been at first; and if they had more than their fair share of service, it was correspondingly easy for them to reduce any that tried to leave the confederacy. *For this the allies had themselves to blame; the wish to get off service making most of them arrange to pay their share of the expense in money instead of in ships, and so to avoid having to leave their homes. Thus, while Athens was increasing her navy with the funds which they contributed, a revolt always found them without resources or experience for war.*[28]

Athens was the natural leader of the Delian League not only because it had the most ships and best naval commanders but because it was by far the largest Greek city-state. Its population had reached a high of about 337,000 in 431 B.C., at the time the Peloponnesian War began, when the populations of most other Greek city-states numbered only in the thousands. The total Athenian citizen population was about 200,000 (including 60,000 adult males who were politically active), 40,000 resident aliens (metics), and perhaps 97,000 slaves.[29] From the beginning Athens took advantage of its access to the league's resources to increase its economic, political, and military dominance. Its first campaigns were not against Persians on the Asian mainland in the east but in Thrace and the Aegean in the west. Targets seem to have been chosen as much for their value to Athens as for the military threat they posed to the alliance, since some of the Persian garrisoned cities in Thrace were never attacked. The first league action was taken in 477 B.C. against the city of Eion in Thrace, a valuable trade emporium that exploited resources from farther inland. Its Persian defenders were defeated after a siege, its population was enslaved, and it became an Athenian colony. At the same time, the Athenians captured the central Aegean island of Scyros, which had never been under Persian control but was a center for piracy any new master of the seas would wish to end. The population was enslaved and the island occupied by the Athenians, who then established a colony and strategic naval base to police the neighboring sea lanes. The small city of Carystus on the island of Euboea was attacked next. Although it had no Persian garrison, it had sided with the Persians during the war and declined to join the Delian League when the war ended. It was captured and forcibly enrolled in the league, in part to prevent free riders from taking advantage of the alliance's security without paying for it. The benefit to the league of acquiring this new member (particularly by force) may have been marginal, but it increased Athenian dominance within Euboea, which was to become one of Athens's most important sources of imported grain. Member states that objected to Athens's priorities could not simply quit the alliance if they were dissatisfied but had to rebel. The first to try, around 470 B.C., was the island of Naxos, a founding member of the league and a city-state that still had an active navy. The Athenians put down the rebellion, took Naxos's ships, and made it pay cash tribute from that point on.[30] While the league may have begun as a voluntary alliance, this attack set a precedent that Athens increasingly employed against any member state that attempted to withdraw or did not make timely tribute payments.

Any complaints that Athens was not paying enough attention to the Persian threat were silenced soon after the Naxos revolt ended. The Persians had massed a large land and naval force at the mouth of the Eurymedon River in southern Anatolia with the intention of retaking Ionia. The Athenian commander Cimon took a fleet of two hundred triremes and attacked it in 469 B.C. As at Mycale, the Persian fleet retreated and beached its boats, expecting to be protected by the army. Cimon sent his marine forces ashore, destroyed two hundred beached triremes, and routed the Persian army as well. It was a spectacular victory that produced an immense amount of booty. It also eliminated the immediate threat to the coastal Ionian cities that were unwalled and vulnerable to a land attack. On the other hand, many of the league's members could now again question the need for its continuation as the Persian threat receded. That debate became academic as Athens moved relentlessly to consolidate its power. By 462 B.C. the Athenians had entered into wars with Sparta and its allies as well as making attacks on Persian provinces in the eastern Mediterranean and Egypt. The campaigns in mainland Greece were inconclusive, but the Egypt expedition ended in disaster when the Persians returned in force in 455 B.C. and Athens may have lost as many as two hundred triremes. A successful attack on Cyprus prevented a Persian surge back into the Aegean and laid the groundwork for a peace deal in the spring of 449 B.C. It was a realpolitik compromise: the Persians recognized the autonomy of the coastal Greek city-states and agreed not to sail their ships into the Aegean north of Cyprus, while the Athenians agreed not to attack any places ruled by the Great King. Under Pericles's famous leadership, the league's treasury at Delos was transferred to Athens. The existing funds from that and the annual tribute payments still funded the navy, but large sums were now diverted to non–war related projects such as the expensive construction of the Parthenon and its upkeep.[31]

Athens had created a maritime empire financed by the contributions of the city-states it came to rule. Enemies could call it tyranny, but Athens had met both major goals of the Delian alliance: keeping the Greek states safe from Persian attack and allowing the vast bulk of them to run their own affairs locally. It was only after the 449 B.C. agreement, known as the Peace of Callias, that league members could truly object that the alliance was no longer necessary. However, since Athens continued to provide internal security in the region and on the seas where conflict among city-states had formerly been rife, many argued it was a fair exchange, or at least the Athenians did. As we will see, the Athenians also created an integrated economic zone that produced larger markets with better terms of trade than had existed at the time of the Persian Wars. Despite a number of revolts against Athens by subject city-states during the Peloponnesian War with Sparta (431–404 B.C.), its grip remained remarkably strong throughout that war until it was brought to a sudden end after a Spartan victory in 405 B.C. at the Battle of Aegospotami near the Athenian naval base at Sestos on the Hellespont. Even after the formal dissolution of its empire in 404 B.C., Athens would continue to play a leading regional political and economic role, going so far as to create a second, similar alliance system against Sparta and its allies from 378 to 355 B.C. when its coercive power was far weaker.[32]

THE LOGIC OF MARITIME EMPIRES

Just when Athens became an empire is subject to a debate similar to that about when an acorn becomes a sapling and then an oak tree. What is clear is that the Athenians saw the opportunity to create an empire at the time the Delian League was established and worked relentlessly toward that goal. This was something they recognized themselves when they justified keeping their empire to the Spartans on the eve of the Peloponnesian War:

> Surely, Lacedaemonians, neither by the patriotism that we displayed at that crisis [the Second Persian War], nor by the wisdom of our counsels, do we merit our extreme unpopularity with the Hellenes, not at least unpopularity for our empire. That empire we acquired by no violent means, but because you were unwilling to prosecute to its conclusion the war against the barbarian, and because the allies attached themselves to us and spontaneously asked us to assume the command. And the nature of the case first compelled us to advance our empire to its present height; fear being our principal motive, though honor and interest afterwards came in. And at last, when almost all hated us, when some had already revolted and had been subdued, when you had ceased to be the friends that you once were, and had become objects of suspicion and dislike, it appeared no longer safe to give up our empire; especially as all who left us would fall to you. And no one can quarrel with a people for making, in matters of tremendous risk, the best provision that it can for its interest.[33]

Part of the animosity directed against Athens, and maritime empires in general, was due to the primacy they gave to economic rather than military or political domination. Endogenous empires violently conquered and ruled in ways that were at least clear and direct, seeking new land, people, and revenue to augment their military might and defray the cost of administration. Maritime empires achieved their goals indirectly by using political and military power to preserve and increase their economic opportunities. They came into being with a minimal use of force and occupied only the small amount of land needed to control the economic assets they targeted, not seeking to expand into ever-larger new territories that would then have to be unprofitably defended and administered. While the world viewed a great conqueror sucking the wealth out of a land taken by force as a legitimate use of power, building and maintaining an economic system (by force when necessary) that did the same for its creators was at best seen as devoid of honor and at worst as a type of cheating. Two millennia later, endogenous empires like Habsburg Spain, Mughal India, Qing China, and Napoleonic France would have the same opinion of the Dutch and, even more emphatically, the British maritime empires. Adam Smith, the eighteenth-century Scottish political economist, highlighted the unusual nature of such polities and their leaders: "To found a great empire for the sole purpose of raising up a people of customers may at first sight appear a project fit only for a nation of shopkeepers. It is, however, a project altogether unfit for a nation of shopkeepers; but extremely fit for a nation whose government is influenced by shopkeepers. Such statesmen, and such statesmen only, are capable of fancying that they will find some advantage in employing the blood and treasure of their fellow-citizens to found and maintain such an empire."[34] Athenian leaders were of course not responding to pressure from shopkeepers in the agora, but they did have to respond to the demands of their democratic system of governance, in which both wealthy and poorer citizens alike expected to benefit. They were willing, as Smith suggests, to use state power to create and preserve a political economy that rewarded the people who kept them in office. In this sense the power and stability of a maritime empire's government depended on servicing the needs of a larger elite that benefited from the use of state power for the acquisition of private wealth—wealth that would not later be seized by autocrats to make their states more powerful. Maritime empires were therefore almost always governed by representative bodies with strong mercantile interests, not autocrats.[35] Such states did little if any trading or commodity production themselves, which is not surprising because they were controlled by people who wanted those businesses for themselves. This was not the case for the endogenous empires we examined earlier that were all founded by autocrats or (as in Rome) became autocracies where state power was not shared. In endogenous empires the state often took a large and direct role in the economy, particularly in China, where governments were historically hostile to the merchant class.

Thucydides famously concluded it was Sparta's fear of Athens as a rising power that was the root cause of the war between them.[36] But one might say that it was the fear generated by the different type of power Athens was wielding, particularly the economic transformations that it was making within the places it controlled, that was a greater concern. Neither Athenian military power based on its warships nor its use of political power to dominate other city-states was new, and such power historically ebbed and flowed. What was new and thus potentially revolutionary was Athens's drive to integrate its empire into a single economic whole with Athens at its hub. City-states within the empire might retain their political identity but only within a transformed political economy of Athens's making. Those that fell within its grasp could never again act independently, particularly after Athens stripped them of their ships, nor could they fence off their economic assets from exploitation by Athens without risking destruction. Even when the empire fell (as it was to do), the economic structure the Athenians created would not fall with it, making it impossible to revive the old status quo. If some time-traveling fifth-century B.C. Greek readers were to stumble upon Karl Marx and Fredrik Engles's *Communist Manifesto*, which portrays the capitalist bourgeoisie as having an unrelenting drive and engaging in "naked, shameless, direct, brutal exploitation" undisguised by conventional religious and political illusions, they would immediately think of Athens.[37] Indeed when the Corinthians were attempting to convince the Spartans to join them in declaring war on Athens in a speech recounted by Thucydides, they described Athenian character and goals in terms not unlike those used by today's business rivals of Google, Amazon, or Facebook who complain they seek disruptive change in order to undermine and then replace them.

> They are swift to follow up a success, and slow to recoil from a reverse. Their bodies they spend ungrudgingly in their country's cause; their intellect they jealously husband to be employed in her service. A scheme unexecuted is with them a positive loss, a successful enterprise a comparative failure. The deficiency created by the miscarriage of an undertaking is soon filled up by fresh hopes; for they alone are enabled to call a thing hoped for a thing got, by the speed with which they act upon their resolutions. Thus they toil on in trouble and danger all the days of their life, with little opportunity for enjoying, being ever

engaged in getting: their only idea of a holiday is to do what the occasion demands, and to them laborious occupation is less of a misfortune than the peace of a quiet life. To describe their character in a word, one might truly say that they were born into the world to take no rest themselves and to give none to others.[38]

This is not to say that the Athenians were proto-capitalists or seeking to change the world, only that running maritime empires like Athens required a mental flexibility and constant energy that other Greeks found disturbing. If they wanted a classical literary analogy, it would be to Homer's Odysseus *polytropos*, a man of twists and turns who was often deemed too clever for his own good. The Athenians' propensity to act when others sat still, their exploitation of every new opportunity, and their spurning of lazy leisure as they got richer ran against the cultural ethos of the time. But the Athenians made no excuses for their actions and proudly proclaimed their superiority over other Greek states such as Sparta that held different values. In his Funeral Oration, Pericles would call Athens a "school of the Hellas" that needed no Homer to sing its praises because its accomplishments were so self-evident: "For we have opened unto us by our courage all seas and lands and set up eternal monuments on all sides both of the evil we have done to our enemies and the good we have done to our friends."[39]

The evil done to their enemies included a hard realpolitik applied to any who stood in their way. In 416 B.C. the Athenians determined that the neutrality of the island of Melos in the ongoing Peloponnesian War set a bad example for the city-states within their own empire seeking to opt out of this Great Power conflict. They therefore commanded the Melians to abandon their neutrality and join the Athenian Empire or expect a war if they did not. It was a nonnegotiable demand backed by an unapologetic pure power threat, as the Athenian envoys made clear to the Melians:

> For ourselves, we shall not trouble you with specious pretenses—either of how we have a right to our empire because we overthrew the Mede, or are now attacking you because of wrong that you have done us—and make a long speech which would not be believed; and in return we hope that you, instead of thinking to influence us by saying that you did not join the Lacedaemonians, although their colonists, or that you have done us no wrong, will aim at what is feasible, holding in view the real sentiments of us both; since you know as well as we do that right, as the world goes, is only in question between equals in power, while the strong do what they can and the weak suffer what they must.[40]

The Melians refused, and the Athenians destroyed their city, enslaving the population and sending their own citizens to take control of the island's land.

HOW ATHENS IMPOSED ITS WILL

Athens managed its growth primarily by expanding its economic boundaries without enlarging its territorial base. Lisa Kallet explains that "the way in which the Athenians extended Athens/Attica outwards . . . is not to be understood as political annexation, but rather in terms of an economic zone controlled by various instruments and authorities."[41] This allowed Pericles to describe Athens as "sufficient for herself both in peace and war," a statement that would otherwise make no sense for a city well known for importing the majority of its grain and for boasting that "because of the greatness of our city the fruits of the whole earth flow in upon us; so that we enjoy the goods of other countries as freely as of our own."[42] This economic prosperity allowed Athens to become the unrivaled cultural center for the entire Greek world, a city that attracted poets, philosophers, and playwrights who would produce the finest works of the classical era. Just how this came to be was the product of a half dozen interlocking policies that individually seemed unrelated but collectively created a viable and stable maritime imperial structure. It took full advantage of Athens's control of the seas and required only a relatively small application of force to maintain. These policies included (1) eliminating economic rivals, (2) creating an ever-larger number of cleruchies (colonies placed in foreign lands whose residents retained full Athenian citizenship), (3) sending officials to oversee local city-state administrations without actually running them, (4) imposing a common coinage and system of measurement to create an integrated regional market with Athens at its center, (5) making Athens the legal center for regional dispute resolution, and (6) reducing an initial dependency on income derived from direct tribute payments with taxes on trade.[43] These policies all centered on increasing Athens's control of commodities, money, and trade rather than expanding its territory.

Removing Economic Rivals

Athens's first campaign as leader of the Delian League ousted the Persian garrison and resident population from the Thracian city of Eion in 476 B.C. and annexed it as a colony. Thrace was renowned for its "abundant forests for ship-building, much wood for oars, [and] mines of silver" and was populated by a mix of both Greeks and native Thracian tribes.[44] Eion was strategically located at the mouth of the Strymon River and served as both an access point to inland Thrace and an important emporium in its own right for goods coming from there to the coast. Athens's goal here was apparently to take control of an existing regional trade network and expand it, but that proved difficult. This was because the Athenian new-comers did not have well-established connections with the fractious Thra-cian tribes in the hinterland and because they were in competition with the rich island of Thasos off the coast, which did. Thasos "drew a yearly revenue from the mainland and the mines of two hundred talents on aver-age, and three hundred when the revenue was greatest," receipts so large that it levied no taxes on farming.[45] It had used these funds to maintain a navy and build substantial city walls. Endogenous empires like Persia taxed such rich indigenous economies but left their owners free to man-age them because, as Kallet concludes, "it was in the Great King's interest (and thus, in turn, his satraps') to encourage local and regional prosperity in order to maintain royal revenues throughout the empire; in the case of Thasos, this meant not impeding commercial activity . . . and allowing the Thasians control of their mines." By contrast, a maritime empire like Ath-ens was not content to leave a rival in control of such valuable resources, so it "sought, in varying degrees and ways, to exert direct control over local and regional economic activity."[46]

Thasos revolted against the Athenians in 465 B.C., seeking never-delivered Spartan aid a year later. Most of the rebellions that occurred against Athens's hegemony beginning with Naxos in 470 B.C. were rooted in discontent over the annual tribute payments owed to the Delian League or weariness among states still contributing ships and crews for Athens's many wars. The Thasian revolt was different because it was based on an economic dispute, Thucydides attributing its outbreak to the Athenians' belief that Thasos was "over profiting from the emporia on the mainland and the mine under Thasos' control."[47] Kallet argues that while these par-ticular issues may have provoked the revolt, the war should be seen in the context of a long-running competition between the two states over which would control Thrace's natural resources and trade networks: "The revolt is an endgame, the culmination of the Athenians' ruthless agenda, beginning in 476 and over the next several years taking over the entire Thasian commercial sphere, threatening production, revenue from taxa-tion, imports and exports, profit, and thereby Thasos' prosperity and strength."[48] Defeating Thasos proved no easy task. An Athenian attempt during the war to found a large new colony upriver from Eion located in the area where the important city of Amphipolis was later established failed when local Thracians killed most of the settlers. And while Athens quickly eliminated the Thasian fleet defending the island, the city itself withstood a siege of almost three years before it surrendered on terms that included pulling down its walls and giving up its remaining ships, together with paying an indemnity and making future annual tribute payments. Thasos also agreed to give up its claims to territories on the mainland and to the silver mines it had been working there. It should be noted what Athens did not do: it did not expel its people or establish an Athenian cleruchy as it did elsewhere. It was as if because the causes of the revolt were economic rather than political, so was its resolution—just another Athenian hostile takeover that did not demand the physical destruction of a now-toothless former business rival.

Cleruchies

One of the most important if generally overlooked institutions that Athens employed to expand its economic control within the empire was cleruchies. They were an old and distinctively Athenian form of colonization in which Athens seized some or all of the land of another state and divided it into defined plots of public land (*kleros*) that were then distributed to its own citizens in exchange for rent payments based on the value of the land. Unlike in ordinary colonies, which Athens also established, cleruchs and their land were considered extensions of territorial Athens itself and governed by Athenian laws and officials. Cleruchs retained their Athenian citizenship, paid their taxes directly to Athens, and owed military service to the cleruchy. Disputes between cleruchs and local residents were adjudicated in Athenian courts using Athenian law. Poor Athenians who got such plots soon found themselves with the income required to serve as hoplites in the army. While some cleruchs might remain permanently settled on their plots overseeing a subject workforce, others were absentee landlords who derived income from their cleruchy holdings while still living in Athens, and still others moved back and forth between their residences in Athens and their holdings abroad. The state received substantial revenue from cleruchies because it owned the land and could efficiently tax each allotment by means of an assigned annual assessment.[49] While there is considerable debate about how many Athenian possessions during the fifth century B.C. were cleruchies rather than colonies, the total number of beneficiaries was large, with between fifteen thousand and twenty thousand Athenian citizens possessing cleruchy landholdings of some type.[50]

The process of establishing cleruchies took two forms, both of which relied on harsh exploitation of the local population. In the first, Athens seized the entire territory and enslaved or deported its population; in the second, the Athenians annexed part of the land within a self-governing city-state to create a cleruchy and reduced that city's annual tribute obligation to compensate for the lost tax revenue. In both cases slaves or hired farmers worked the seized plots of land for the new Athenian cleruchs.[51] In looking for historical analogies, the cleruchies employing slave labor might best be compared to eighteenth-century French and English sugar plantations in Haiti and Jamaica, while cleruchies where owners leased land to tenants or used hired workers resembled eighteenth-century Ireland, where the estates of English landlords occupied nine-tenths of the island's arable land and relied on the labor of the poor resident Irish to farm it. There is another commonality with these eighteenth-century examples as well: like them, Athenian cleruchies were commercial enterprises designed to produce export crops, specifically the wheat and barley that fed the people of Athens. To make this happen, the Athenians needed to clear the land of excess people and introduce monocropping regimes that could produce larger surpluses with fewer workers. As Alfonso Moreno describes the process,

> After the local populations had been expelled or enslaved, these territories were calculatingly divided up into very few and very large landholdings, with a population large enough to cultivate them but small enough to generate large food surpluses. We have seen in the case of Scyros that this would translate into a population density less than one tenth of that of contemporary Attica. Contributing to the depopulation of the islands was the additional fact (as we have seen) that after receiving a *kleros* any Athenian cleruch who wished to do so could return to Attica, and that this is in fact what many did.[52]

Athens imported around forty-three thousand metric tons of wheat annually, worth 1,300 talents in the fifth century B.C., much of which was derived from "an empire of cleruchies with Euboea as its crown jewel," a large (3,700 km^2) and fertile island just north of Attica and separated from it by only a narrow strait of water.[53] After Athens suppressed an Euboean revolt in 446/5 B.C., it divided most of the island into cleruchies. This created an opportunity to add more resident cleruch settlers (the law banning Athenian citizenship for the children of foreign spouses was lifted for them) and an even greater opportunity for the rich who were absentee landlords. The expansion was also popular with the poorer citizens of Athens, the demos, because politicians promised them an unending flow of free grain from these state-owned landholdings. However, in what might appear an all-too-familiar pattern to citizens of democracies today, the rich ended up with most of the profits and the poor with very little free grain. Such bait-and-switch benefits of empire were satirized by Aristophanes in his play *The Wasps* when his character Bdelycleon asks why, with such riches in the hands of the politicians running the Athenian state, the demos remained mired in poverty:

> If they wished to assure the well-being of the people, nothing would be easier for them. We have now a thousand towns that pay us tribute; let them command each of these to feed twenty Athenians; then twenty thousand of our citizens would be eating nothing but hare, would drink nothing but the purest of milk, and always crowned with garlands, would be enjoying the delights to which the great name of their country and the trophies of Marathon give them the right; whereas today you are like the hired laborers who gather the olives; you follow him who pays you.

And as for the free grain, "When [the politicians] are afraid, they promise to divide Euboea among you and to give each fifty bushels of wheat, but what have they given you? Nothing excepting, quite recently, five bushels of barley, and even these you have only obtained with great difficulty, on proving you were not aliens, and then *choenix* by *choenix*."[54] For maritime empires that sought hegemony primarily in the economic rather than the political sphere, cleruchies enabled the efficient exploitation of foreign resources previously shielded from ownership by outsiders, and for this reason they were widely hated by other Greek city-states that feared falling victim to them. In maritime empires the state created and maintained an economic system that was profit oriented rather than power oriented, although the two were closely intertwined. For Athens, as Moreno concludes, "although the dependence on imported grain by the dêmos demanded an articulated ideology of public control, the cleruchic project always remained a public/private quid pro quo. There always remained, in particular, the guiding presence of the Athenian elite in the extension and exploitation of cleruchies and their resources."[55] While they may not have employed cleruchies, it was a quid pro quo that would be found in all maritime empires.

Athenian Officials Abroad

The Delian League was founded as an alliance of equal states. This changed as Athens took on an increasingly imperial role after the Peace of Callias and developed a system to oversee the states now under its control. It assigned seven hundred Athenian officials to manage overseas relations using four different offices: magistrates, garrison commanders, heralds, and overseers. Magistrates (archons) were resident in subject city-states that still maintained their own governments and supervised local tribute collections as well as keeping close watch over its people. Garrison commanders (*phrourarchoi*) resided in subject cities where the Athenians had occupation forces or naval bases. Heralds (*kerykes*) were imperial officials sent out from Athens to announce new decrees to subject states that were then required to implement them. Overseers (*episkopos*) were nonresident civilian officials initially assigned to supervise the foundation of new cities or the reorganization of existing ones but whose roles expanded to include the continual supervision of member city-states. Jack Martin Balcer sees this position, in which civilians served as roving imperial officers, as a borrowing from the Persian Empire's "eyes of the king," high-ranking officials whose job it was to report back personally to the center on conditions in the provinces and sniff out possible rebellion by the locals or a satrap.[56]

These officials were not distributed equally. Magistrates were appointed in the more populous places, and military officials took charge in places where they were absent. Garrison commanders of course were found only in places where Athens had stationed occupation forces after putting down rebellions or maintained naval bases because of their strategic value. Overseers worked a circuit of places that they undoubtedly came to know well, and heralds appeared only periodically, moving from city to city with their decrees. For this system to work, it needed links to the local population. The most prominent of these were the *proxenoi*, resident friends of Athens in other cities who had demonstrated their ties of affection over a prolonged period (often generations by inheritance) and performed services for Athenians who were visiting or living there. This type of city friend position had an old history from a time when outsiders needed protection and hospitality provided by locally prominent families that could vouch for them and help with any problems.[57] It was a very widespread phenomenon, and most city-states had their own *proxenoi* in places where they did business. *Proxenoi* also served as political intermediaries between their own city and those of their foreign friends. It worked well in a political world of equals but much less so in a world where Athens began to set the rules to its own advantage. In such a situation, it was easy for Athenian *proxenoi* to be viewed as disloyal collaborators in their home cities. Perhaps for this reason, Athens issued a decree that Russell Meiggs explains provided for "a collective penalty of five talents to be paid by a state for the killing of an Athenian in its territory, and special protection for an Athenian proxenos." Meiggs continues, "Such measures presuppose strong anti-Athenian feeling and attacks on individual Athenians and friends of Athens. It may be mere coincidence that no evidence which must be dated earlier than the forties survives, but the reaction of the Aegean world to the Peace of Kallias would be a very appropriate context."[58] The Athenian imperial structure described earlier required relatively few people to operate and exerted control by using existing institutions where possible. It was a type of organization preferred by maritime empires precisely because it was indirect. Athenians intervened directly only when putting down rebellions and usually reconstituted local governments staffed with allies to avoid the cost of permanent occupation unless they wanted to create a cleruchy. Compared with endogenous empires, the lines of political authority in maritime empires were deliberately opaque. The pattern was to leave subject polities autonomous in theory but under the control of its political agents in practice. Maritime empires used military force only when other avenues of coercion failed.

Creating an Economic Commons:
Money, Measurements, and Markets

If maritime empires were content to maintain the facade of existing political institutions within their subject states and colonies, they moved in the opposite direction when it came to economic affairs. Here they gave priority to enforcing uniform policies that applied to all territories under their control. This included abolishing barriers that impeded the development of integrated markets with themselves at the center.

In the Athenian Empire this was most clear in its "decree enforcing use of Athenian coinage, weights and measures."[59] Although just when the decree was issued is still subject to intense debate, it proclaimed an Athenian monopoly on the minting of silver coins and required their use in all transactions (with an exception given for electrum coins minted in the Black Sea area). The decree also required the use of a common system of weights and measures. Explanations for issuing the decree have been economic (Athens's mint profited) and political (Athens was throwing its weight around), but practicality was a strong reason too.[60] As I noted in chapter 1, empires specialized in organizing diversity, but that diversity had to be managed. The imposition of standardized measures for weights, grain, land, and money helped make that possible. Policies of standardization were found in all endogenous empires, if not at their origin then during periods of their consolidation. The taxes and tribute collected by Athens needed to be accounted for in a common unit of currency, and it was easier to collect the money in that currency than juggle the value of different ones. Distributing and collecting grain, allocating units of land, and taxing commodities by weight also required common standards of measure because they varied from city to city. However, even if administrative practicality was the basis for such a project, the standardization of money and measures had a positive impact on trade, and for maritime empires that was a goal as well. Athenian measures and coins became a mercantile lingua franca whether or not Athens could actually enforce their use.

Athens was already ancient Greece's largest city, but control of a maritime empire made it one of the biggest trading centers in the Mediterranean as well. Writing at the height of the empire's power, the Athenian comic poet Hermippos praised in mock grandiose style the wide range of luxury goods flowing into the city from every corner of the Mediterranean world:

> From Cyrene silphium-stalks and ox-hides, from the Hellespont mackerel and all kinds of salt-dried fish, from Thessaly salt and sides of beef. . . . Syracuse provides hogs and cheese. . . . These things then come from those places; but from Egypt we get rigged sails and papyrus, from Syria frankincense, while fair Crete sends cypress for the gods, and Libya provides plenty of ivory to buy. Rhodes provides raisins and dried figs, while pears and fat apples come from Euboea, slaves from Phrygia, mercenaries from Arcadia. Pagasai furnishes slaves, and branded rascals at that. The acorns of Zeus and glossy almonds come from the Paphlagonians, and are the ornaments of a feast. Phoenicia provides the fruit of the palm and the finest wheat flour, Carthage supplies carpets and cushions of many colors.[61]

What is noticeable from this list is how many of the places mentioned lay beyond the Athenian Empire proper. Trade within the empire was less flashy but more significant because it provided the city with grain to eat, wood for boats, metal for tools, and cloth to wear. It constituted part of an immense seaborne trade that Morris estimates had a value of eighteen thousand talents per annum.[62] Athens imposed a 1 percent tax on all goods passing through its port of Piraeus that included not only commodities destined to be consumed in Athens but those that were reexported from there as well. As a clearinghouse that linked the entire region, Athens was a place where cities that specialized in the export of single products could sell them and then pick up what they lacked before returning home. In creating this trade network by using its naval power, Athens imposed sets of rules that even its rivals needed to respect in order to do business there. For this reason, the Athenian Pseudo-Xenophon, usually called the

Old Oligarch, wrote that while Athens's maritime superiority did allow it
to extract tribute revenue from subject states, its real power lay in determining who could move goods, to where, and under what conditions on
the seas it now controlled, because "there is no city which does not have to
import or export, and these activities will be impossible for a city unless it
is subject to the rulers of the sea."[63] This was the foundation of Athens's
trade-based prosperity. The Old Oligarch noted,

> Wealth [the Athenians] alone of the Greeks and non-Greeks are capa-
> ble of possessing. If some city is rich in ship-timber, where will it dis-
> tribute it without the consent of the rulers of the sea? Again if some city
> is rich in iron, copper, or flax, where will it distribute without the con-
> sent of the rulers of the sea? However, it is from these very things that
> I have my ships: timber from one place, iron from another, copper from
> another, flax from another, wax from another. In addition, they will for-
> bid export to wherever any of our enemies are, on pain of being unable
> to use the sea. And I, without doing anything, have all this from the land
> because of the sea; yet no other city has even two of these things: the
> same city does not have timber and flax, but wherever there is flax in
> abundance, the land is smooth and timberless. There is not even copper
> and iron from the same city, not any two or three other things in a sin-
> gle city, but there is one product here and another there. Furthermore,
> every mainland has either a projecting headland or an offshore island
> or some strait, so that it is possible for a naval power to put in there and
> to injure those who dwell on the land.[64]

Such active maritime economies facilitated a social leveling that allowed
people to engage in business without much concern about rank or legal
status. "For this reason," the Old Oligarch opined, "we have set up equality
between slaves and free men, and between metics and citizens. The city
needs metics in view of the many different trades and the fleet. Accordingly, then, we have reasonably set up a similar equality also for the metics." However, for a conservative such as himself, such economic and legal
equality had its downside: "Now among the slaves and metics at Athens
there is the greatest uncontrolled wantonness; you can't hit them there,
and a slave will not stand aside for you."[65]

Athens as a Legal Center

Athens's chosen path to domination came not by empowering its officials
abroad to resolve disputes but rather by requiring they be resolved in

Athens by Athenian courts. While it appears not all cases involving Athens and Athenians demanded resolution in Athenian courts, many did, and it was the Athenian demos that adjudicated the cases brought by the allies.[66] That made it clear the demos outranked the Athenian officials posted abroad because the litigants had to come personally to Athens and make their cases before them. The Old Oligarch argued that this was one of the strongest assertions of Athens's democratic-based authority and that it served to maintain political balance in the empire:

> [The Athenians] force the allies to sail to Athens for judicial proceedings. But they reason in reply that the Athenian people benefit from this. First, from the deposits at law they receive their dicastic [jury] pay through the year. Then, sitting at home without going out in ships, they manage the affairs of the allied cities; in the courts they protect the democrats and ruin their opponents. If the allies were each to hold trials locally, they would, in view of their annoyance with the Athenians, ruin those of their citizens who were the leading friends of the Athenian people. . . . In addition, were the allies not to go away for judicial proceedings, they would honor only those of the Athenians who sail out from the city, namely generals, trierarchs, and ambassadors. As it is now, each one of the allies is compelled to flatter the Athenian populace from the realization that judicial action for anyone who comes to Athens is in the hands of none other than the populace (this indeed is the law at Athens); in the courts he is obliged to entreat whoever comes in and to grasp him by the hand. In this way the allies have become instead the slaves of the Athenian people.[67]

Litigants also spent considerable amounts of money in Athens on lodging and services as they waited to get their cases resolved, and that benefited the resident Athenians who provided them.

Taxes

Tribute payments provided Athens with most of its regular external income at the beginning of the empire, and those tribute assessments increased when it went to war. With time, however, the empire's revenue base grew larger and more diverse. Cleruchies brought in substantial tax income from foreign holdings, as did state-owned mines, rents from land dedicated to temples, and indemnities paid to Athens by defeated city-states. So did more irregular revenue-raising ventures such as "money-collecting ships" that appear to have engaged in a type of state-sponsored

piracy and extortion in which small fleets of ships raided targets of opportunity in places like the Black Sea and Caria.[68] Such revenue collections by
force may have had more in common with the rough methods used by the
Afghan state early in the nineteenth century than the peaceful collection
of a European Union value-added tax in the twenty-first:

> In central Afghanistan during the 1830s, the revenue of Beysoot under
> the kings of Cabul was seventeen thousand rupees. Dost Mahomed
> increased it to the enormous sum, comparatively, of eighty thousand
> rupees, which was an assessment of two rupees for each family! This
> tax is levied upon the villagers by their own chiefs. A body of one
> thousand cavalry is annually sent to collect the revenue. This corps
> is dispersed over the district in small divisions, each one with orders
> to collect, and is quartered upon the husbandman, who is obliged to
> subsist the soldiers so long as the revenue remains unpaid! This custom
> of purveyance adds greatly to the expense of the subject, who is liable
> to many vexatious processes and exactions and to injury and abuse of
> person and property, to enforce a speedy settlement. The revenue is
> collected in kind, the amount being paid in sheep, horned cattle, goats,
> horses, slaves, grain and berricks [wool cloth], etc. The accumulated
> mass is dispatched to Cabul, which is the nearest mart of general com-
> merce; a portion is sold for necessary cash expenses, another portion
> is traded off by means of reciprocal necessities and much of the grain
> is retained for family use. The slaves are sold by private contract, but
> the government levies, at the chebotter or customs office, a percentage
> upon the amount of sale![69]

But from the perspective of the development of a maritime empire,
Athens's most innovative revenue-raising scheme was its decision to
replace tribute payments with an empire-wide tax on trade in 413 B.C.
at a rate "of a twentieth upon all imports and exports by sea, which they
thought would bring them in more money."[70] Athens previously imposed
such taxes in specific places, like the 1 percent tax on trade through Piraeus
and a 10 percent tax on goods transiting the Bosporus, but these did not
demand too much effort to collect. Piraeus was Athens's own home port
and had an administration that could observe what was brought in and
out of it. The Bosporus is a very narrow strait linking the Black Sea with
the Mediterranean, a choke point that made it easy to observe, control,
and tax any shipping through it at Byzantium—a lucrative revenue source
that was often imposed by regimes there. An empire-wide tax on trade,

however, was orders of magnitude more difficult. It required that Athens have detailed knowledge of all the transit trade occurring in hundreds of ports as well as the ability both to access its value and to collect payment. That it imposed this type of tax in the wake of a military disaster in Sicily displayed just how confident Athens was in its mastery of the empire's economic sphere. It is also evidence that Athenian citizens and its city-friend allies were to be found everywhere and had the detailed local knowledge to implement such a tax. Although tribute payments were revived a number of years later, and it is unclear whether the trade tax remained, Athens's ability to propose and implement it is evidence of just how integrated the empire's economic production and trade had become by the end of the fifth century B.C. Even though the empire itself would fall in 404 B.C., this network with Athens at its center would have a long afterlife. What Athens could no longer command by force in the fourth century B.C., it obtained by favorable trade connections that particularly expanded in the Black Sea region north toward Crimea, which became its major source of grain.[71]

THE END OF THE ATHENIAN EMPIRE

Why did Athens not use its power to establish what we would call an endogenous empire as Rome was later to do? I have argued here that this was never the goal of any maritime empire because they had a particular aversion to engaging in the manpower-heavy land wars that would be required to create such an endogenous empire and, more importantly, they saw little profit in it. They were, however, vulnerable to the temptation of using their sea power to engage in distant and risky expeditions against rich territories with the collusion of local factions in such places. For Athens these adventures nearly always ended in costly failures because those seeking their aid exaggerated either how easy such places would be to conquer (Sicily) or how easy it would be to hold them against a counterattack (Egypt). Both Egypt and Sicily were renowned for their grain production and hence attractive targets, but invasions targeting them proved too difficult to sustain and ended with the destruction of the Athenian expeditionary force and its ships. Nevertheless, even after these immense losses, Athens was able to maintain its empire because it continued to rule the sea. In the aftermath of the Egyptian debacle it was still able to strike a peace with Persia and rebuild its strength under the leadership of Pericles. The calamity in Sicily, combined with the renewal of the Peloponnesian War by Sparta, made this more difficult but not impossible, as Thucydides explained:

> And yet, after they had met with disaster in Sicily, where they lost not only their army but also the greater part of their fleet, and by this time had come to be in a state of sedition at home, they nevertheless held out ten years not only against the enemies they had before, but also against the Sicilians, who were now combined with them, and, besides, against most of their allies, who were now in revolt, and later on, against Cyrus son of the King [of Persia], who joined the Peloponnesians and furnished them with money for their fleet; and they did not finally succumb until they had in their private quarrels fallen upon one another and been brought to ruin.[72]

The Persian alliance helped pay for the needed additional ships to take on Athens's weakened fleet, and this time Spartan commanders took aim at economic targets in Euboea, Thrace, and the Hellespont that had far more impact on Athens than earlier Spartan invasions of Attica did. The Battle of Aegospotami in 405 B.C. unexpectedly destroyed most of Athens's remaining ships, allowing the Spartans to cut off the city's food supply by blockading Piraeus and forcing Athens's surrender in 404 B.C. Still, if Athens had maintained the one-hundred-ship reserve restricted exclusively to city's defense as Pericles had advised, it could have likely warded off this naval attack and the war would likely have continued. The Spartans stripped a surrendered Athens of all but a few ships, dissolved its remaining empire, and put the city under the rule of a client regime for a time, but they left the city itself intact and commercial activities continued as before. Unlike Rome, which determined to destroy Carthage utterly, Sparta just wanted Athens off its back. Over the next century Athens once again became a major political player but was never again hegemonic after power shifted north to Macedonia under Phillip II (r. 359–336 B.C.) and his son, Alexander the Great (r. 336–323 B.C.).

The British in India: Transformation from Exogenous to Endogenous Empire

A second wave of maritime empires emerged along Europe's North Atlantic coast in Portugal, Holland, and England during the sixteenth and seventeenth centuries with the development of large sailing ships, improved navigation tools, and ship-mounted cannons, as well as the discovery of new maritime routes to Asia and the Americas. They pioneered the expansion of European maritime trade into Asia by sailing around the southern end of Africa, thus getting direct access to the producers of high-value goods in India, China, and islands of Southeast Asia. This ended the Islamic world's former monopoly over the transit trade of Asian luxury goods like spices and silk coming into Europe from the east and undermined the prosperity of their Italian trading partners. It also reduced the profitability of existing overland trade networks because bulk carriage of goods by ship was cheaper, involved fewer middlemen, and avoided the taxes levied by states along the way. This new trade generated extraordinarily high profits, and many former luxury goods like spices and tea eventually became items of mass consumption in the West as well. These maritime polities had some transatlantic interests in the areas not already dominated by Spain's earlier conquests in the Americas: Brazil (Portugal and Holland), the Caribbean (Holland and England), and eastern North America (England). However, unlike Asia, these territories required settlement and economic development to generate profitable exports like sugar and tobacco and were far less valuable as markets, at least initially. What all these emerging maritime empires had in common with their Mediterranean predecessors was the goal of seeking economic rather than political domination, light administrative footprints that employed indirect rule using local intermediaries where possible, and the occupation of only the minimum amount of land needed to secure their power. In the case of the British in India, these policies changed in the late eighteenth century and were abandoned in the nineteenth as they conquered ever larger swaths of territory and became rulers of a de facto endogenous empire. The resistance to accepting this reality was so strong, however, that the British government in London only reluctantly took responsibility for ruling India directly in 1859 as the crown jewel in a then-world-spanning colonial empire on which "the sun never set."

THE INDIAN OCEAN WORLD IN THE
EARLY MODERN GLOBAL ECONOMY

The discovery of the Americas and new sea routes from the North Atlantic into the Indian Ocean both occurred at the close of the fifteenth century during voyages sponsored by the rulers of Spain and Portugal. These Iberian powers then moved aggressively to exploit that new knowledge, but in very different ways. After establishing bases in the Caribbean, Spain sponsored freebooting conquistadors who attacked Mexico in 1519 and then Peru in 1532, where they quickly conquered the Aztec and Incan empires and made themselves fabulously wealthy. The lethality of Old World diseases for New World populations that had no immunity to them may better explain the completeness of Spain's success than its conquistadors' guns and horses, since they caused population declines as high as 90 percent.[73] The Spanish Crown took direct control of these and other overseas territories like the Philippines (in 1564) to create its own endogenous empire that in the Americas stretched from today's southwestern United States to southern Chile. Spanish colonial administration there relied on appointed viceroys who were the personal representatives of the Spanish king and implemented policies set by the Crown.[74] It was the Americas' rich silver mines that financed the empire and allowed Spain to fight a series of expensive (if less than successful) wars against the English and Dutch in the North Atlantic and maintain a galley fleet that kept the Ottoman Empire out of the western Mediterranean. The flow of American silver extracted by Spain was so vast and poured out of Spain so rapidly that it sparked an international trade boom with a worldwide impact.[75] Despite having created an empire whose largest and most valuable territories were overseas, Spain was not a maritime empire. Like other land-based empires such as Persia or Ming China that also built navies, Spain constructed its large fleets principally for defensive purposes: to protect its land assets from attacks by sea, suppress piracy, police trade monopoly zones, transport troops to war zones, and enable the safe transfer of overseas wealth back to Spain.[76]

The Portuguese expansion into the Indian Ocean was quite different. It was entirely maritime and focused on trade that required domination of the sea routes rather than conquests on land.[77] This the Portuguese achieved at the Battle of Diu off the west coast of India in 1509 against an alliance of local Muslim states aided by the Ottomans. But while the Portuguese won such sea battles by employing cannons on their sailing ships, that military superiority was far from absolute because these weapons were not new to Asia and on land their rivals could field much larger armies.[78] Moreover, the Muslim states in the region were not in decline, as 1500 marked a renewed period of empire building in Iran by the Safavids, in India by the Mughals, and in the Mediterranean, the Balkans, and Egypt by the Ottomans. Establishing a maritime empire was therefore a counterstrategy of expansion that avoided wars with powerful continental states. The Portuguese extracted wealth from the region by dominating its local trade networks that linked its spice-producing islands and by regulating the region's shipping. The first was achieved by the Portuguese conquest of Malacca in 1511, made possible because of the power vacuum created when the Chinese withdrew from this region seventy years earlier. The second they accomplished by controlling maritime access to the Indian Ocean from Egypt and Mesopotamia. This they did by building a fort abutting the Persian Gulf's narrow Strait of Hormuz in 1514 and by actively patrolling the entry to the Red Sea at Bab-el-Mandeb. Traders wishing to move goods needed either to employ Portuguese vessels or to obtain their permission to use local ships. From their colonial capital at Goa on the southwest coast of India, the Portuguese ran a network of widely separated fortified settlements from Africa to the South China Sea manned by around fifteen thousand people in total, a seemingly tiny footprint to claim the status of empire.[79] But as with other maritime empires, Portuguese success was measured in economic terms rather than in the amount of land or numbers of people they controlled. This had the advantage of allowing them to strike deals with neighboring territorial states that were bigger and stronger but whose "land-centrism" led them to underestimate the potency of maritime empires that they often viewed more as nuisances than peer polities.

Until the beginning of the seventeenth century, the Portuguese were able to sustain their trade monopoly in the Indian Ocean, but that was breached after they entered into a dynastic union with the Spanish Crown that lasted from 1580 to 1640. Before that time Catholic Portugal had been on good terms with both Protestant England and Holland, whose merchants could do business in Lisbon even when their countries were in conflict with neighboring Spain. The union upended that relationship and drew Portugal into Spain's wars against these two Protestant states, particularly after the Spanish sailed a huge armada into the North Sea in 1588 to support troops already fighting the Dutch with the intention of invading England. This aggressive move famously failed after the fleet lost a sea battle with the English and was subsequently sunk by violent storms. In the aftermath both Dutch and English ships entered the Indian Ocean, first to attack Portuguese shipping and then more aggressively to take over the spice trade themselves.[80]

While the Portuguese employed government officials to organize and regulate their international trade in the East, the English and Dutch governments ceded that responsibility to two private chartered companies: the English East India Company (EIC), established in 1600, and the Dutch United East India Company (Vereenigde Oost-Indische Compagnie, VOC), established in 1602. Both these companies were granted the authority to build navies, make war, seize territory, and in general act as surrogate governments in the Indian Ocean realm. While the English and Dutch would soon become fierce rivals, they both saw the need to break Portugal's trade and shipping monopoly in the Indian Ocean.[81] When the VOC was condemned for acting illegally after it plundered a rich Portuguese merchant ship full of Chinese goods in 1603, it countered with an argument that was to have enormous implications for the future. The Portuguese claimed the VOC had no right even to be in the Indian Ocean, let alone attack their shipping, because the Portuguese king had exclusive sovereignty over all the seas there (*mare clausum*). The Dutch political philosopher Grotius rebutted this argument by asserting that no single nation could claim sovereignty over the world's oceans, which by right should be open to the ships of any nation that chose to sail upon them (*mare liberum*).[82] This eventually became an accepted world standard, a boon for maritime states, and meant the competition between Europeans in the Indian and Pacific Oceans thereafter would be multipolar. The only upside for the Portuguese was that freedom of the seas allowed them to service their remaining regional trading ports even after the Dutch and English became the overwhelmingly dominant players in the Indian Ocean and South China Sea. Indeed, the Portuguese would have the distinction of being the last of the Europeans to lose their Asian enclaves: it was only in 1961 that India forcibly incorporated Goa, Daman, and Diu; and China did not reclaim Macau until 1999 after 442 years of Portuguese rule there.

Maritime empires exploited trade to finance themselves, and that required a sophisticated economy in which investment at the center was key. Like ancient Athens, Holland and England would build economic systems in which Amsterdam and London would become trade centers, cultural hubs, and sources of capital for both governments and private investors. Unlike Mediterranean maritime empires whose economic catchment basins were regional, these new maritime empires were global in scale and produced vastly larger commercial profits and government revenues. The Portuguese had merely sought to regulate the flow of trade to their advantage; the VOC would move to own it. Much like ancient Athenians described earlier, the Dutch were uniquely positioned to combine both state and private interests into a singularly powerful economic machine. Their "VOC was a unique politico-commercial institution, and one that could be imitated nowhere else in the world, because the United Provinces were the world's only federal republic in which a collectivity of town governments, committed to the advancement of trade, industry, and navigation, also wielded great military and naval power."[83]

Many of the VOC's strategies might have been drawn from an Athenian playbook as it created an Indian Ocean *arche* by subordinating the indigenous rulers of islands and coastal city states, enforcing its own rules for regional trade and shipping, and establishing cash-cropping plantations run by its own citizens. After moving to a permanent headquarters at Batavia (today's Jakarta) on the island of Java in 1619, the VOC made alliances with existing rulers who were sometimes more powerful than the Dutch but who needed help to fend off the Portuguese and English. The VOC then drove the Portuguese out of Malacca in 1641 and from Ceylon by 1658, and limited English access to the spice trade. In the process, the VOC turned its former native allies into clients, controlling their lands and politics without having to administer them directly.[84] Employing a commercial settlement policy that an Athenian cleruch would have recognized and perhaps admired, the VOC massacred indigenous island populations and replaced them with slave labor under Dutch supervision to create cash-cropping plantations that produced nutmeg, mace, cloves, and cinnamon.[85] It also moved relentlessly to cut off alternative supplies of these spices by destroying all the trees that produced them on the islands the VOC did not control, so that by 1656 the company had an effective monopoly. This allowed the VOC to set prices that were both stable and hugely profitable (as high as 1,000 percent).[86] In addition to exporting spices back to Europe, the Dutch became major participants within the intra-Asian regional maritime economy. They monopolized transport between the east coast of India and the Indonesian archipelago, maintaining trading bases on both sides, and carried Chinese silks to other Asian markets like Japan in exchange for silver, gold, and copper.[87] This internal regional trade was a vital revenue source for the VOC and helped offset its many expenses.

BRITISH EXPANSION AND
TRANSFORMATION IN SOUTH ASIA

Roughly speaking, the prime of Portuguese power in the Indian Ocean ran from the middle of the sixteenth century to the middle of the seventeenth, and the Dutch from the middle of the seventeenth century to the middle of the eighteenth, at which point the British became ever more dominant until, by the middle of the nineteenth century, they ruled all of South Asia. In that process the British in India found themselves responsible for administering a land-based endogenous empire (map 2.2) that was even larger than that of the Mughals. However, because maritime empires put

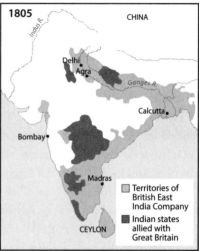

MAP 2.2. British expansion in India, 1767 and 1805.
From Burbank and Cooper, 2010.

profit before power, this achievement was not the endpoint of some master plan of conquest but rather a by-product of the EIC's relentless drive
to exploit the region's trade that drew the British ever more directly into
Indian affairs. Since expanding that economic reach demanded ousting
rivals who stood in its way, the EIC (like the Mongols) eventually found
itself a master of vast territories it had initially only intended to profit
from economically. As Edmund Burke complained in 1788, "The constitution of the Company began in commerce and ended in empire."[88] By the
end of the eighteenth century the British Parliament was so appalled by
the EIC's actions that it enacted laws that empowered British government
in London to set its policies in India and to appoint viceroys to implement
them. However, it declined to take direct responsibility for governing what
was now Britain's most valuable colonial possession and continued to pre-
tend that it was an EIC responsibility. Even after the defeat of the Sikhs
brought Punjab under British control in 1849 and completed the conquest
of the entire subcontinent, it was divided into a patchwork of hundreds
of princely states bound to the British by treaty, some entered into voluntarily and others imposed after military defeats. And London also continued to maintain the legal fiction that the EIC was just an intermediary
administering India as a recognized vassal of the Mughal emperor. The
British government only abandoned that wilted fig leaf in the wake of a
massive failed revolt by the EIC's own sepoy troops in 1857, at which time

it both abolished the Mughal dynasty and revoked the EIC's authority to rule in India.

After the Dutch took control of the spice-producing regions in the Indian Ocean during the mid-seventeenth century, England refocused its own maritime efforts on schemes of settler colonization along North America's Atlantic seaboard and expanding its access to the Indian cotton and silk cloth trade. Although Indian textile production and commerce were in the hands of private merchants, entry to Indian ports and markets required the permission of political authorities on the coasts or farther inland. The most important of these inland sovereigns was the Mughal emperor, whose dynasty (1526–1857) had been founded by horse-riding Turks under the leadership of Babur, a descendant of Tamerlane. Originally from central Asia, the Mughals had conquered North India and created a powerful endogenous empire that was still expanding south and east when the British arrived. The Mughals employed Persian as the language of government administration and, in the fashion of Iranian empires, were comfortable devolving authority to local leaders who swore allegiance to them. Although themselves Sunni Muslims, the Mughals were very cosmopolitan and their elites included large numbers of Hindus and Shia Muslims. At the height of their power in the late seventeenth century, they governed 90 percent of India's 125 million people and occupied a territory of 4 million km^2 from Afghanistan to Bengal and from the Himalayas to southern India.[89]

The Mughal ruler parceled out power and revenue to subordinates by issuing firmans (Persian *fermān*), imperial edicts or orders that granted their recipients specific rights. These could range from relatively routine business (permission to travel or trade, accept an inheritance, a change in status) to highly political (governorship appointments, authority to collect taxes, grants of state land). Local governors, nawabs, could issue their own firmans, but these had a more limited remit. In 1615 British monarch James I sent Sir Thomas Roe as an envoy to the Mughal court of Emperor Jahangir to negotiate a wide-ranging treaty. This failed to materialize in part because the Mughals did not see distant non-Muslim European states as peer polities worthy of binding agreements. Still, Roe did finally get a specific firman in 1618 that granted the English permission to reside and trade in the city of Surat in Gujarat, to travel freely into India's interior, and to seek the redress of the injuries inflicted on them by the local officials in exchange for protecting Mughal shipping from pirate attacks and their sea raids on Indian ports.[90] The EIC soon realized that a strategy of working within the Mughal system of governance gave it an advantage not shared by the Dutch or Portuguese. The relationship protected EIC profits and property more securely, gave it access to a much larger market, provided Mughal-guaranteed security against the seizure of their factories (trading centers) by the Portuguese and Dutch, and allowed the EIC to act independently of London at a time when England was consumed by a civil war and its aftermath. As William Wilson Hunter observes,

> However low the fortunes of the Company sank under King or Commonwealth in England, the Surat factory grew with a strength of its own. In 1657 the Company decided that there should be but one Presidency in India—and that Surat. . . . It also illustrates the position which the English quickly secured in the economy of the Mughal Empire: as a sure source of revenue, a sea-police for the coast, and the patrol of the Ocean path to Mecca, gradually developing into negotiators on behalf of the native Government. Surat forms the type of an early English settlement under the strong hand of the Mughal Emperors.[91]

In choosing to operate under Mughal protection, the EIC avoided loss-producing military obligations that Roe himself declared were undermining the competitiveness of its Portuguese and Dutch rivals:

> By my consent you shall no way engage yourselves but at sea, where you are like to gain as often as to lose. It is the beggaring of the Portugal, notwithstanding his many rich residences and territories that he keeps soldiers that spend it, yet his garrisons are mean. He never profited by the Indies, since he defended them. Observe this well. It hath been also the error of the Dutch, who seek Plantation here by the sword. They turn a wonderful stock, they prowl in all places, they possess some of the best; yet their dead payes consume all the gain. Let this be received as a rule that if you will profit, seek it at Sea, and in quiet trade; for without controversy, it is an error to affect garrisons and land wars in India.[92]

After establishing itself in Surat, the EIC expanded its presence in India by opening three additional regional administrative centers (presidencies) as it grew: Madras, Bombay, and Bengal. Madras, founded in 1639, was the EIC trading center for Southeast India on the Coromandel Coast, which became a permanent presidency in 1694. Bombay, founded in 1639, replaced Surat as the EIC's western regional presidency in 1694 after conditions in Gujarat deteriorated because of civil unrest there.

Bengal was first opened to the EIC with a Mughal firman in 1650, but the company lacked a significant urban center there until Calcutta was founded in 1690, a city that soon grew so important that it became the EIC's paramount presidency in 1772 and would remain the capital of all British India until that was moved to Delhi in 1911.

This expansion was conducted with the consent of the Mughals or, in the case of Madras, the inland state of Golconda, which was not then part of the Mughal Empire. Each of these new centers began investing considerable sums to erect fortifications, much to the displeasure of the London head office, because they could see what London could not: the powerful Mughals were beginning to lose their iron grip on India. Trouble began with an insurgency led by the charismatic Hindu Maratha Confederacy warrior commander Shivaji (r. 1674–80), who expanded out of central India. The long-lived Mughal emperor Aurangzeb (r. 1658–1707) responded by mobilizing a huge army and fighting a prolonged war with the Marathas that began in 1681. In the process Aurangzeb conquered Golconda in 1687 and temporarily ended the Maratha threat in 1689 after Mughal forces ambushed and killed Shivaji's successor Sambhaji and his most important followers.[93] During this war the English were threatened by the Marathas in both Surat and Bombay and by a rapacious Mughal governor in Bengal. In response they decided to make themselves a more independent power within India by recruiting soldiers and building forts. Breaking its long-standing policy of avoiding military adventures, the EIC began attacking Mughal positions on land and at sea in 1686, sending its largest force by ship to Bengal. This proved an ill-considered (or at least premature) endeavor because the English were no match for the Mughals on the ground in Bengal, where they were expelled, and Aurangzeb deployed hired ships to attack Bombay. He also canceled the EIC's right to trade, seized its goods, and arrested its agents in Mughal-controlled territories. The EIC sought terms for surrender in 1689 by petitioning Aurangzeb for a pardon that he granted in 1690 after the EIC agreed to pay a large fine and restore all property taken from the Mughals.[94] The Mughals and the English reconciled because the Mughals still depended on the English to secure the sea routes to the Red Sea and the English now concluded they could not do business in India without Mughal cooperation.

Aurangzeb's defeat of the Marathas and his conquests in the south were the high-water mark of Mughal power in India. However, the widespread destruction caused by that long-running conflict damaged the economy, and the conquered territories proved hard to integrate into a Mughal political structure that was already under stress. Aurangzeb could still hold it together and demonstrate to the English that he was not to be trifled with, but following his death in 1707 the empire experienced a series of succession struggles that gave its enemies time to recover and weakened the central government's grip over outlying provinces. By the mid-eighteenth century the Mughal Empire was close to collapse after it was attacked from multiple directions. Its capital of Delhi was regularly captured and looted: by the Marathas (1737, 1757, 1771), by Persia's Nadir Shah Afshar (1739), and by the Afghan Ahmad Shah Durrani (1757, 1761). Delhi never fully recovered from the destruction caused by these attacks, but each of these invaders decided it was more advantageous to keep a recognized Mughal emperor on the throne there than to abolish the dynasty.

The Mughal dynasty survived in this weakened form because its shared sovereignty structure acted as a barrier against complete collapse and because its emperor still retained an unmatched cultural and political prestige. In highly centralized systems like China where the emperor was the ruler of all under heaven, the entire political structure dissolved when the dynasty that ruled it fell. And since there could be only one ruler of all under heaven, each new dynasty sought to eliminate any surviving heirs of the old one lest its own legitimacy be called into question. The Mongols hunted down the last Song royal heirs as they conquered southern China in the thirteenth century, and in the seventeenth century the Manchu Qing dynasty made recovering the Ming princes who had fled to Taiwan a priority. By contrast, the Persianate king-of-kings imperial system in India had granted subsidiary sovereignty to many of its numerous governors. Such governors legitimized their authority by being part of an imperial system in which they combined their appointments from the center with strong local connections to the regions they ruled (inherited or established while governing). It was, as André Wink observes, "a system of concurrent rights" within a "shifting structure of sovereignty" that passed commands down and tax revenue up when the empire's center was strong.[95] But during succession struggles for the Mughal throne, or when the general authority of the center declined or ceased to exist, having a local power base allowed these governors to maintain themselves as autonomous rulers. Even after the Mughals in Delhi lost their coercive power to demand obedience, it was in the interests of those in technically subordinate positions to maintain the facade of an imperial government to which they continued to swear fealty while keeping local tax revenue for themselves and commanding their own armies. Invaders from the margins like the Marathas, the Persians, the Afghans, and later the British also saw advantages in working through a captive Mughal emperor who was deemed more legitimate than themselves. The historic success of the Mughals in creating an inclusive elite culture that transcended sectarian, linguistic, and regional divides (at least in the north) continued to give their emperor an exalted status that the parvenus attacking Delhi could never hope to equal. While a Mughal emperor could be forced into exile without funds or an army, or be abused by those with more actual power, he could never be deprived of his inherent imperial aura, which commanded respect from Hindus and Muslims alike. His firman recognizing a petitioner's right to rule a territory or collect its taxes, even when obtained by coercion or bribery, could legitimize actions that would otherwise be judged illegal usurpations of power and property.

The EIC was just one, and far from the strongest, of the regional players expanding their reach throughout India during what was called "the great anarchy" of the mid- and late eighteenth century. The Marathas had come to dominate western and central India, the governor of Bengal was ruling independently in the northeast, the Afghans were in and out of the Punjab, and the French king created a rival state-backed trading company that was providing military aid to its allies in southern India. As the richest and most populous part of India, Bengal became the prime target for EIC expansion that reflected a change in its investment strategies. The EIC had historically focused on trade in cloth and other Indian products that were purchased with gold or silver and sent back to London. By the mid-eighteenth century, tea transshipped from China had eclipsed the value of that trade and opium grown in Bengal had become the main product sold back to the Chinese to pay for it. When the Mughal governor of Bengal attacked and seized Calcutta, the EIC's commander Robert Clive counterattacked and defeated him at the Battle of Plassey in 1757. Fortuitously, because EIC forces were ill equipped to counter the governor's aggression alone, it had the aid of a British navy flotilla that had been dispatched east during the worldwide Seven Years' War (1756–1763) then being fought between France and Britain. The EIC oversaw the appointment of a new Mughal governor for Bengal who agreed to reimburse the company for its war costs and property damage. He also agreed to ally his government with the company against the EIC's Indian and European rivals, facilitating the expropriation of French property the British had already seized. In 1764 EIC forces, again under Clive's command, won the Battle of Buxar against a successor nawab of Bengal, the nawab of Awadh, and the Mughal emperor Shah Alam II. In the soon-signed Treaty of Allahabad (1765), the EIC agreed to pay a subsidy to Shah Alam in return for his grant of a *diwani* (right to collect taxes on behalf of the emperor) for the eastern provinces of Bengal, Bihar, and Orissa. The nawab of Awadh was given his territory back after agreeing to pay a war indemnity and accepting the supervision of his government by the EIC.

The Treaty of Allahabad, in the words of a contemporary Mughal historian, Ghulam Husain Khan Tabatabai, "was done and finished in less time than would have been taken up for the sale of a jackass, or a beast of burden, or a head of cattle," but it was a foundational document in the EIC's creation of the British raj in India.[96] As William Dalrymple notes,

> With one stroke of the pen, in return for a relatively modest payment of Rs2.6 million, and Clive's cynical promise on behalf of the Company to govern "agreeably to the rules of Mahomed and the law of the Empire," the Emperor agreed to recognize all the Company's conquests and hand over to it financial control of all north-eastern India. Henceforth, 250 East India Company clerks backed by the military force of 20,000 Indian sepoys would now run the finances of India's three richest provinces, effectively ending independent government in Bengal for 200 years. For a stock market-listed company with profit as its main raison d'être, this was a transformative, revolutionary moment.[97]

However, giving a profit-making company such a valuable prize soon led to economic disaster for both Bengal and the EIC when the latter engaged in coercive and unsustainable levels of tax collection. The EIC's fixed tax assessments on which its profits now depended were high and left no margin for error in a land where periodic floods and droughts could reduce annual harvest yields by half. That next occurred when monsoon rains failed in 1769 and produced a severe famine the next year during which the population declined by one-third, leaving the EIC with far less tax revenue than expected and an economy that would take years to recover fully.[98] This led to a financial panic in London that, as Dalrymple explains, threatened to bankrupt the EIC and ruin its many investors: "Only seven years after the granting of the *Diwani*, when the Company's share price had doubled overnight after it acquired the wealth of the treasury of Bengal, the East India bubble burst after plunder and famine in Bengal led to massive shortfalls in expected land revenues. The EIC was left with debts of £1.5 million and a bill of £1 million in unpaid tax owed to the Crown. When knowledge of this became public, thirty banks collapsed like dominoes across Europe, bringing trade to a standstill."[99] The British government stepped in with a massive bailout of £1 million in 1773 and in exchange took command of EIC decision making in India, although subsequent government-appointed viceroys proved just as imperialistic as their private EIC predecessors. Despite continual opposition from London, they employed the same template that Clive had pioneered in Bengal and Awadh to take over ever-larger chunks of India in what Robert Travers labels conquest by treaty: "Treaties with states that were conquered or defeated in battle by the East India Company were often used to impose burdens on subordinate allies considered 'dependent' sovereigns. Typically, these dependent Indian states were compelled to have their territories garrisoned by the Company's forces and to pay a corresponding tribute. In these cases, treaties established a form of indirect rule or empire by proxy, in which the Company outsourced its military costs without taking on new administrative burdens and tried to establish a 'ring fence' of buffer states around its territories."[100] The British also used alliances to win wars against the most powerful remaining independent states in the south and west, conquering Tipu Sultan's well-armed and French-backed southern state of Mysore in 1799 and then defeating the Marathas in a second war, after which the EIC occupied Delhi in 1802. More conquests would come, but the British in India had completed their transformation from a maritime exogenous empire exploiting India's economy at a distance into an endogenous Indian empire supported by its own tax revenue and civil administration. From a base of only a few forts with small garrisons in the 1740s, by 1805 the EIC controlled much of India's land mass (map 2.2) with a land army of two hundred thousand that was twice the size of the regular British army at home. The vast majority of these troops (88 percent) were locally recruited Indian sepoys trained and equipped in European fashion.[101] By the middle of the nineteenth century, with its conquests in the Sind and Punjab, Britain's maritime empire in South Asia had transformed itself into an endogenous empire that was responsible for the governance of the entire region.

COSMOPOLITAN SOCIETIES, PAROCHIAL RULERS: THE PARADOX OF LEADERSHIP IN MARITIME EMPIRES

In examining Rome's rise earlier, we saw that there was a tension between an aspiring endogenous empire's need to assimilate new territories and peoples into a single larger mixed polity and a Mediterranean city-state's ingrained resistance to expanding its citizen base. This was true even in cases where the restrictions that determined who could be a citizen were so limiting that they led to a demographic crisis. An extreme example is the severe decline of male Spartan full citizens from around eight thousand in the mid-fifth century B.C. to less than one thousand a century later.

That decline resulted in the collapse of Sparta's military power since they constituted the core of its army.¹⁰² We saw that Rome solved this problem by expanding its definition of Roman citizenship ever more broadly, breaking its link to the actual city of Rome after the Social War ended in 88 B.C. Athens took the opposite course. While it was a much more populous and cosmopolitan city-state than Sparta, the expansion of its empire led not to an increase in the number of Athenian citizens but rather to stricter regulations on who would be accepted as one. For example, in 451 B.C. Pericles introduced a new law tightening Athens's citizenship requirements that would in the future exclude children of foreign spouses.¹⁰³ Such a law was distinctly anticosmopolitan because it effectively blocked upper-class Athenians from broadening their connections with elites in other city-states through marriage. This had helped the Athenians on many occasions when such direct ties to different regions, particularly in Thrace, facilitated cooperation with the people who lived there. Indeed, had this law been imposed earlier, two of Athens's most capable military leaders, Themistocles and Cimon, would have been denied citizenship because their mothers were foreign. There was also an increased scrutiny of the city's existing citizenship rolls for possible past fraud. Given that benefits accruing to citizens in Athens's democratic system included the right to receive state payments for service and grain allotments, own land and houses in Athenian territory, be protected by Athenian law, and (if men) the right to participate in politics, those who held citizenship opposed extending these rights to others.¹⁰⁴ Fortunately for Athens, the successful expansion of maritime empires was compatible with this type of restrictive citizenship and insular elite management in ways that it was not in endogenous empires.

The ruling elite in Athens and other maritime empires minimized the number of territories under their direct administration. While goods and money increasingly poured into the center, managing the flow of that wealth did not require the manpower-heavy administrative infrastructures found in endogenous empires. Nor did it require the expansion of elite status to include people from other parts of the empire or outside it. Recruitment of such "new people" was common in endogenous empires even when existing powerholders opposed their inclusion, but maritime empires successfully restricted membership in their elites to people like themselves. Struggles for power at the center were invariably insular and sometimes just family feuds. Maritime empires therefore presented a seeming paradox: cosmopolitan in their economy and culture, but surprisingly parochial in their politics. This was possible because maritime empires had alternative means of political and economic integration that did without territorial provinces with centrally appointed governors found in endogenous empires.

The leadership of the British raj in India displayed similar characteristics even after it became an endogenous empire. Its ruling class in London retained the soul and self-image of its maritime shadow empire past, as if imagining its skinny younger self was more real than the portly gentleman it now saw reflected in the mirror. In part this was because maritime empires were able to change their economic and administrative structures abroad without making equivalent changes at home. The British Empire's insular governing elite remained just as closed to outsiders before and after it became an endogenous empire, although it did open its ranks to those who amassed great fortunes abroad.[105] That elite could never conceive of its vast colonial holdings as anything other than alien appendages inhabited by ungrateful subjects. This paradox of British political insularity within an economy and cultural life that was cosmopolitan bears strong similarities with the ancient Athenian maritime empire, and perhaps suggests the trajectory that Athens would have taken had it been longer lived and more militarily successful in Egypt and Sicily.

On the cosmopolitan side of the ledger, both Athens and London were unrivaled primate centers that grew ever more diverse as their empires grew, becoming the largest cities of their age with a high percentage of foreign-born residents.[106] They were both renowned for a vibrant cultural life that attracted all manner of thinkers and artists from other parts of the world. As Samuel Johnson said of the city in 1777, "Why, Sir, you find no man, at all intellectual, who is willing to leave London. No, Sir, when a man is tired of London, he is tired of life; for there is in London all that life can afford."[107] Both empires set the rules for international trade that became normative beyond the areas they controlled politically so that even foreign merchants would value their goods in British pounds or the Athenian silver drachmas and use the idiosyncratic measurement systems that each mandated. Yet even as their empires grew larger, the size and composition of the political elites who ran them remained narrow. Both empires resolutely refused to extend political rights to the people they ruled over, in spite of congratulating themselves on running democracies (popular and parliamentary) at home that they boasted were superior to neighboring polities ruled by tyrants, oligarchs, or oriental despots. Athens restricted political participation to male citizens, and these had to meet increasingly strict standards of descent. The British had an elected parliament, but that represented only legally enfranchised male citizens of England, Scotland (added by the 1706 Treaty of Union), and Ireland (added by the 1800 Treaty of Union), and voting was long hedged by exclusionary property criteria and religious qualifications. There was no representation provided for those outside the British Isles.

This city-state mentality at the center of a large empire might be understandable for Athens because it was a city-state in a world of city-states. But Britain was already a globe-spanning empire when it faced a similar choice to that confronted by Rome after its early first-century B.C. Social War when Roman citizenship was finally extended throughout Italy. Although that extension was opposed by Rome's existing elite and the poor alike, granting it more broadly eventually opened the door to participation in politics and administration by people throughout the empire and gave them a common imperial identity. Britain was confronted with the same choice in the late eighteenth century, first in North America and then India. Having been edged out of the spice trade by the Dutch in the seventeenth century, Britain shifted its primary colonial investment to the Atlantic coast of North America, where it established a large number of settler colonies (the British gave a spice island to the Dutch in 1667 in exchange for Manhattan). By the 1770s its American colonists were demanding participation in a government that was making policies and collecting taxes without their consent. Unlike the Roman Republic after the Social Wars, however, the British Parliament refused to expand the empire's representative political base to include its colonists in North America even though they still thought of themselves as British. In 1776 the Americans severed their ties with Britain and declared independence, creating a new state that would be more inclusive if only because it was keen to attract additional immigrants to a place where land was plentiful but labor in short supply.

The British army that the Americans defeated in their War of Independence was led by General Charles Cornwallis, who surrendered to them at Yorktown, Virginia, in 1781. With the loss of its most valuable North American colonies, the EIC expansion into India took on greater economic importance for Great Britain. And it was the same Earl Cornwallis who was sent to India in 1786 as governor-general to reform the EIC's administration in Bengal. Perhaps mindful that the American colonists sought independence when they were refused participation in running the empire, he was determined to make sure no such people emerged in India, particularly through intermarriage. In 1791 he enacted a law similar to that passed by the Athenians in 451 B.C. that denied the children of foreign spouses inheritance rights, citizenship, and employment by the EIC: "No person, the son of a Native Indian, shall henceforward be appointed by this Court to Employment in the Civil, Military, or Marine Service of the Company," and like the Athenians he required that job candidates present proof of ancestry.[108] India thus became an Athenian-style cleruchy in which the British there were trained to think of themselves as having no true connection to its people or its culture. Although these servants of the raj were often born in India and spent their lives working there, it was driven into their heads that "home" would always be Britain, a place they rarely saw and whose cold, damp weather might cut their lives short should they retire there.

CHAPTER THREE

Shadows on the Steppe

There is not a person in the whole nation who cannot remain on his horse day and night. On horseback they buy and sell, they take their meat and drink, and there they recline on the narrow neck of their steed, and yield to sleep so deep as to indulge in every variety of dream. . . . Sometimes when provoked, they fight; and when they go into battle, they form in a solid body, and utter all kinds of terrific yells. They are very quick in their operations, of exceeding speed, and fond of surprising their enemies. With a view to this, they suddenly disperse, then reunite, and again, after having inflicted vast loss upon the enemy, scatter themselves over the whole plain in irregular formations: always avoiding a fort or an entrenchment.

—AMMIANUS MARCELLINUS, *ROMAN HISTORY*, 31.6, 8 (ca. 390)

Steppe Nomadic Empires

The polities established by horse-riding nomads in Mongolia were distinctive shadow empires that arose as secondary phenomena when native Chinese dynasties unified China and took control of the entire southern steppe frontier. Although the details of their founding might differ, the stability of such nomadic empires depended on extracting wealth from China on a continuing basis (through pillage, tribute payments, border trade, or reexport of extorted luxury goods) and not by taxing the limited resources of their own steppe nomad populations. When China was politically centralized and prosperous under the Han (206 B.C.–A.D. 220) and Tang (618–907) dynasties, so were Xiongnu and Turkic nomadic empires on the steppe. When China experienced prolonged political anarchy and economic depression after these dynasties collapsed, so did the unified steppe polities that had prospered by their extortion of them.

Steppe nomadic societies had economies based on mobile forms of animal husbandry that supported only small and scattered populations organized largely on the basis of kinship and descent. That way of life stood in stark contrast to neighboring sedentary polities whose economies were based on peasant agriculture that supported dense populations and large cities. Their dispersed populations and lack of urban centers would appear to have made steppe nomads poor candidates for achieving even state-level political organization, let alone imperial hegemony. Yet beginning in the third century B.C., the nomads along China's northern frontier managed to create a series of empires that controlled immense territories under the rule of powerful, long-lived dynasties. For two thousand years they and other steppe nomads like them to the west terrorized rival states in northern China, central Asia, Iran, South Asia, and eastern Europe. The thirteenth-century Mongol Empire founded by Chinggis Khan would grow to become one of the largest empires in Eurasian history.

The Xiongnu Empire

ORIGINS OF STEPPE PASTORALISM
AND ITS MILITARY POWER

Pastoral nomadism in central Eurasia depended on the exploitation of extensive but seasonal steppe grasslands and mountain pastures. Since humans cannot digest grass, grazing livestock is an efficient way of exploiting the energy of such a grassland ecosystem. This required moving the animals from one seasonal pasture to another over the course of an annual cycle, so the regular movement of the whole population was considered a normal and natural part of life. Sheep and cows raised primarily for milking were the most important subsistence livestock, although they were slaughtered for their skins and meat as well. Sheep and goats also provided wool and hair that was used for cloth, ropes, and varieties of woolen felts, a product whose insulating qualities made life possible in severely cold places. Bactrian camels that could carry loads up to 240 kg transported the steppe nomads' heavy baggage. Alternatively, camels and oxen could be harnessed to pull carts and wagons where those were in use. The horse, however, took pride of place because steppe nomads defined themselves culturally as horse riders and horse raisers, and so did outsiders who observed their way of life.[1]

This form of steppe pastoralism first emerged on the grasslands of western and central Eurasia at the end of the Bronze Age around 1200 B.C. and spread east to Mongolia in later centuries. Adding to the numbers of already-existing pastoralists were forest hunters in southern Siberia and sedentary subsistence farmers in eastern Europe who also moved into the steppe and adopted this new way of life. Despite the disparate origins of the people engaged in it, by the middle of the first millennium B.C. the material culture of the steppe pastoralists was strikingly similar across the entire Eurasian steppe zone.[2] Men, women, and children all now rode the horses that were raised in large numbers. This habitual and universal use of horse riding proved to have great military potential once a way was devised to fight effectively from horseback. That occurred with the adoption of a new form of archery that employed a recursive compound bow. Using such a bow, a rapidly moving horse archer could shoot more arrows from the saddle with greater accuracy over longer distances and with greater penetration power than ever before (figure 3.1).[3] Already skilled riders, steppe nomads began deploying well-disciplined groups of mounted archers working as coordinated units, attacking at a distance and only closing with the enemy if the odds were in their favor. This produced a revolution in warfare that had its echo in the neighboring sedentary world, where horse-drawn chariots had previously been the preeminent weapons of war:

> The defining feature of [the steppe nomadic] Iron Age cavalry was that it attacked and retreated as a body, in which individual riders became anonymous. An ideological model of fighting that was appropriate for a state, under the leadership of a general, was grafted onto tribal horseback riders armed with a new bow-and-arrow technology. That shift in the identity of the warrior, combined with the new recurve bows and standardized arrows, changed the effectiveness of mounted fighters somewhere in the steppes between about 900 and 700 B.C. After this happened cavalry swept chariots from the battlefield and a new era in warfare began.[4]

The emergence of complex sedentary states and then endogenous empires at the time of this military revolution created new opportunities for steppe nomads living at their margins. Inside sedentary states lay concentrated resources ready to be exploited either by raiding or more peacefully by trading. These opportunities had existed previously, but the scale of the resources and the scope of new trading networks were now much larger. As the spread of more mobile forms of pastoralism and mounted

FIGURE 3.1. Illustration of a Mongol archer on horseback.

archery expanded rapidly from the Black Sea and Kazakh steppes in the west to the Mongolian Plateau in the east, it laid the foundation for subsequent shadow empires. Beginning with the first written records of this type of warfare in the seventh century B.C. with the Scythians fighting the Assyrians, the Saka and Scythians fighting the Persians in the sixth and fifth centuries B.C., and the Xiongnu fighting the Chinese in the third century B.C., all historical written accounts paint identical pictures of steppe societies with similar pastoral nomadic economies, common material cultures, and uniform styles of warfare regardless of their disparate origins or languages spoken. James Scott describes the emergence of this new system of interaction as qualitatively different from what had existed previously. He also notes its emergence in parallel with the rise of Eurasia's first great endogenous empires, whose frontier relationships with steppe peoples were as much economic as military: "What was unique was the unprecedented magnification of scale: of the confederations of mounted warriors, of the wealth of the lowland states, and of the volume and reach of trade. The emphasis on raiding in most histories is understandable in view of the terror it evoked among elites of the threatened states who, after all, provide us with the written sources. This perspective overlooks the centrality of trade and the degree to which raiding was often a means rather than an end in itself."[5] But the defensive military power of sedentary states was growing rapidly as well, and that put less well-organized groups of nomads at a disadvantage. If the Scythians had been able to raid the Near East with impunity in the middle of the seventh century B.C., their expulsion was just the start of a process that soon saw the establishment of the enormously more powerful Achaemenid Persian Empire (550–330 B.C.) in the west and the imperial unification of China under the Qin and Han dynasties (221 B.C.–A.D. 220) in the east. These endogenous empires had the capacity to campaign against the steppe nomads directly and control the flow of trade. Steppe nomads responded by creating peer polities of their own to achieve and maintain power parity with the much more populous sedentary states on their frontiers.[6] Although livestock-based economies could thrive without such complex political organizations, the only way the nomads could successfully confront neighboring sedentary states was by matching their level of military and political organization. In explaining the wide variation in political structures found among nomadic societies, the anthropologist William Irons concludes that the key variable was the level of complexity of the sedentary state they interacted with: "Among pastoral nomadic societies hierarchical political institutions are generated only by external relations with state societies and never develop purely as a result of the internal dynamics of such societies."[7] Chinese empires were among the world's largest and most populous states whenever they emerged—the nomads in Mongolia facing off against them would create their peer steppe empires to match beginning with the Xiongnu.

THE POLITICAL ORGANIZATION
OF THE XIONGNU EMPIRE

The Xiongnu Empire was founded in 210 B.C. under the leadership of Maodun, its first *shanyu* (emperor), contemporaneously with the civil war that reestablished a unified China under the Western Han dynasty (206 B.C.–A.D. 9). Maodun's unification of the steppe tribes set the pattern for future nomad empires in which a military conquest by a charismatic tribal leader raised his own people to power. He created an imperial confederacy that was autocratic and statelike in foreign affairs but consultative and federally structured internally, a model that would be adopted by all succeeding nomadic empires with the exception of the Mongols under Chinggis Khan. Its political structure had three levels. At the top was the supreme shanyu, who was always chosen from the ruling lineage of the group that founded the state. That lineage maintained a special royal status, and only

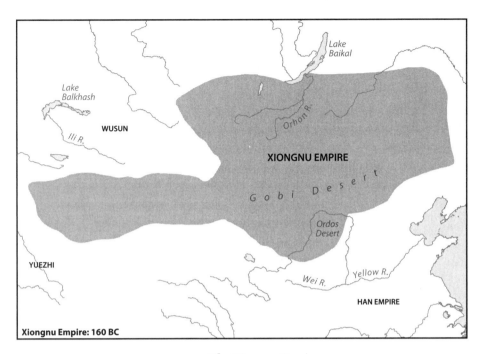

MAP 3.1. The Xiongnu Empire.

members of this "golden clan" could compete for the office of shanyu. The shanyu served as the imperial confederacy's supreme military commander and maintained a monopoly over Xiongnu foreign relations, particularly its dealings with China. At the second level were imperial governors who supervised the indigenous tribal leadership. The most important commanded the large eastern and western wings of the empire and were usually patrilineal relatives of the shanyu (brothers, uncles, and sons). These imperial appointees served as the key links between the central administration at the center of the empire and the local tribal leaders of its component parts. Such local tribal leaders constituted the third level of organization and were drawn from the indigenous elites of each tribe, some of whom were also linked to the ruling dynasty by marriage alliances. Although structurally inferior to imperial appointees, they retained considerable autonomy. If the imperial commanders overstepped their authority or threatened local interests, such leaders could raise their own people in revolt against them, organize an emigration to territories beyond the empire's control, or defect to China and take their people with them.[8]

This Xiongnu steppe shadow empire arose with amazing rapidity immediately after China first unified under the Qin and Han dynasties

Table 3.1. Endogenous empire criteria found in the Xiongnu Empire

Present	Partial	Absent
Size: 9 million km²	Systems of communication that allowed administration of all subject areas from the center directly	Population: 1 million or less
Organized to administer and exploit diversity		Imperial project that imposed some type of unity throughout the system
Monopoly of force within their territories, and military force projected outward		Centralized institutions of governance that were separate and distinct from the rulers
		A primate imperial center with transportation systems designed to serve it militarily and economically

at the end of the third century B.C. and proved extremely long-lived. It ruled the entire eastern Eurasian steppe from the end of the third century B.C. through the middle of the first century A.D. and maintained itself as a regional power into the fourth century A.D. As table 3.1 illustrates, it did without the administrative institutions and large populations that were central to the stability of endogenous empires like China. Nevertheless, the territory it ruled was immense (almost twice as large as Han China (map 3.1), and its fearsome military capacity made the Xiongnu China's only significant external threat for more than two centuries.

The Xiongnu imperial confederacy model may remind readers of the Achaemenid Persian Empire. Its ruling elite had also evolved out of a hierarchical tribal political tradition, employed a king-of-kings administrative model, and used gift giving to reinforce political bonds. There was one very large structural difference, however. The subordinate leaders in the Persian Empire collected taxes from their own people that funded the central state, whereas in steppe imperial confederacies the central state funded the subordinate leaders. As an endogenous empire, the Persian Empire's tax and tribute revenue was generated internally even if some of it was later redistributed to favored groups. The steppe nomadic imperial confederacy in Mongolia was designed to extract external resources for redistribution to its subject nomad groups. It did not depend on regular tax revenue from its nomadic components but instead demanded their military services when needed. The flow of gifts and trade opportunities were payments in advance for such services. The stability of imperial political organizations in Mongolia therefore depended on the successful exploitation of neighboring sedentary societies, the only way they could continually finance such a structural domestic revenue deficit.

Success in incorporating the many formerly autonomous steppe nomad tribes into a single polity was only the first step in building an effective empire because maintaining that unity could not depend solely on military force; it also had to offer economic and political benefits to the tribes now within it. The bargain was this: in exchange for accepting imperial leadership and subordinate political positions, the confederacy's component tribal leaders received access to new flows of Chinese luxury goods for themselves and trade opportunities for their people that they could not get when the nomads were divided. The foreign policies of all imperial confederacies in Mongolia therefore focused on extracting resources from China and, to a lesser extent, the non-Chinese sedentary oasis states to the southwest in today's Xinjiang. This could be done directly by raiding, indirectly through the receipt of subsidy payments, or cooperatively through the establishment of institutionalized border trade agreements that allowed ordinary nomads to acquire goods through peaceful exchange. The nomad rulers of Mongolia devised specific strategies to achieve each of these goals. The first was a hostile "outer frontier strategy" that relied on violence and coercion to extract revenue from even the most powerful dynasties in China. The second was an "inner frontier strategy" that obtained revenue by either allying with stronger Chinese dynasties or protecting weaker Chinese dynasties against internal and external enemies. The first was characteristic of relationships between rising new states in both China and Mongolia; the second evolved as the relationship between the two became more symbiotic.

The Xiongnu Outer Frontier Strategy: A Predatory
Approach to Foreign Relations

The number of steppe nomads in the Xiongnu Empire was relatively small, never exceeding a million people distributed over a huge area. They were seeking to extort a Chinese endogenous empire with a population of perhaps fifty million people during the Han dynasty. To succeed they had to influence decision making at the very highest levels of government because Chinese foreign policy was made at court and not by frontier governors or border officials. To this end the nomads implemented their terroristic outer frontier strategy to magnify their power. Taking full advantage of an ability to strike suddenly deep into China and then retreat before the Chinese had time to retaliate, the steppe nomads could attack the frontier from many different points. The consequences of such violence and the disruption it produced encouraged the Han dynasty to negotiate agreements favorable to the Xiongnu in return for peace.

The outer frontier strategy had three major elements: violent raiding to terrify the Chinese court, the alternation of war and peace to increase the size of subsidies the nomads received or gain access to trade, and the deliberate refusal to occupy Chinese land that the nomads would then have to defend. The threat of future violence always lurked beneath the surface of even the most peaceful interactions. Zhonghang Yue, a Chinese eunuch defector working for the Xiongnu in the second century B.C., once warned a Han dynasty diplomatic mission of the danger China faced in stark terms: "Just make sure that the silks and grain stuffs you bring the Xiongnu are the right measure and quality, that's all. What's the need for talking? If the goods you deliver are up to measure and good quality, all right. But if there is any deficiency or the quality is no good, then when the autumn harvest comes we will take our horses and trample all over your crops!"9 Chinese dynasties had three policy options to deal with such threats: (1) ignore the demands and respond defensively by fortifying the frontier; (2) appease the nomads with expensive peace treaties that provided them with subsidies and border trade; or (3) respond aggressively by raising an expeditionary cavalry force to attack the nomads on the steppe. Each approach produced its own set of problems. The nomads could continually raid the frontier if demands were ignored, looting to get what they wanted and wreaking havoc on China's border population, sometimes even threatening lands near the capital itself. But the alternatives of appeasement or aggressive military action were only slightly less problematic. Seeming to pay tribute to horse-riding barbarians violated the very essence of a Sinocentric world order in which the Chinese emperor was deemed uniquely paramount. Attacking them was expensive and never conclusive.

The Han dynasty (and later Chinese dynasties too) found that it could drive nomads away from the frontier temporarily but with little effect because they were mobile and avoided battles they might lose. Nor was it feasible to resettle their lands with Chinese farmers (a common policy on China's southern frontier) because the vast bulk of the steppe was unfit for agriculture—too dry, too cold, too salty, or covered with a grass sod too tough to break with existing plows. As a result, the Xiongnu needed only to move themselves and their animals out of harm's way until invading Chinese armies eventually withdrew, a tactic by which the Scythians had stymied the Persians centuries earlier. Although nomad attacks could be repulsed by large armies posted on the border or preempted by campaigns on the steppe, frontier warfare was costly and disruptive to China's economy. It drained the treasury and strained the peasantry with ever-increasing demands for taxes and conscript soldiers. By contrast, steppe nomadic households were always prepared for war and had the needed horses, weapons, and supplies readily available. Because all its men (and some women) were trained as warriors, the nomads could mobilize a far higher percentage of their adult population for war than China could. For them wars cost little and did not disrupt their domestic pastoral economy. Indeed, the loot individuals collected from raids on China made them popular and profitable. Attacking Chinese expeditionary forces invading the steppe itself was less lucrative but offered young men an opportunity to raise their personal prestige.

How this relationship played itself out can be seen in the evolutions of Han-Xiongnu relations. Maodun founded the Xiongnu Empire in 210 B.C. while China was being torn apart by a civil war that occurred with the fall of the Qin dynasty and the establishment of the Western Han dynasty. Although the Xiongnu took no part in that conflict, they did attack the border regions and plotted with the new dynasty's less loyal frontier commanders against the central government. Such raids and border intrigues provoked Liu Bang, the founding Han emperor Gaozu, into personally leading a large army north to attack Maodun in 200 B.C. Gaozu may have been inspired by the success of the Qin dynasty campaigns against the Xiongnu led by the famous general Meng Tian in 215 B.C. He had swiftly driven the Xiongnu out of their Ordos homeland south of the bend of Yellow River and then began the construction of the Great Wall to keep them out of China permanently. Gaozu's hastily organized campaign turned out very differently. The Xiongnu had returned to the Ordos during China's civil war and were now much stronger after their recent conquest of rival nomad tribes living in the east. The Han expeditionary force not only failed to restore the old border, it suffered a stunning reversal when the Xiongnu lured the Han emperor into an ambush and then encircled him and his army for seven days. The besieged emperor cut a deal that allowed him to escape and the humiliating defeat made the dynasty wary of taking on the Xiongnu in battle thereafter.

To avoid future conflicts, Gaozu sent envoys to the shanyu to negotiate a peace that established the *heqin* (marriage alliance) policy as a framework for relations between the two states that lasted from 198 to 135 B.C. The heqin policy had four major provisions:

(1) The Xiongnu and Han recognized each other as coequal states.
(2) The Great Wall was the official boundary between the two states.
(3) The Han court gave a princess in marriage to the shanyu.
(4) The Chinese agreed to make fixed annual payments in goods to the Xiongnu, which at their maximum in later decades amounted to around one hundred thousand liters of grain, two hundred thousand liters of wine, and ninety-two thousand meters of silk.[10]

In exchange for these benefits, the Xiongnu agreed to keep the peace and not attack China. With this victory in hand, Maodun turned his attention to the Yuezhi, a powerful confederation of steppe nomads on the western border of the Xiongnu. After Maodun killed the Yuezhi ruler in 176 B.C. and made his skull into a drinking cup, he was master of the whole Mongolian Plateau.[11] The Xiongnu then resumed raiding China despite the existence of the heqin peace treaty. While the Chinese believed that the treaty provisions were more than generous, the Xiongnu were always keen to increase them, and employing violence after periods of peace was one means to that end. When the Chinese complained to Maodun, he put the blame for the trouble on China's aggressive border officials and chastised the Han court for failing to respond to embassies he had sent earlier to resolve the matter. "As a result the Han has broken off peaceful relations and our two neighboring countries are no longer bound by the alliance."[12] Nevertheless, Maodun expressed his willingness to restore peace, noting that he had now extended his empire far to the west, had incorporated many nomadic tribes in addition to the Yuezhi into the empire, and had taken control of the twenty-six oasis kingdoms in the Western Region of today's Xinjiang: "All the people who live by drawing the bow are now united into one family and the entire region of the north is at peace. Thus I wish to lay down my weapons, rest my soldiers, and turn my horses to pasture; to forget the recent affair [of raiding China] and restore our old pact, that the peoples of the border may have the peace such as they enjoyed in former times, that the young may grow to manhood, the old live out their lives in security, and generation after generation enjoy peace and comfort."[13] The shanyu's peace offer displayed the dual prongs of the outer frontier strategy in full flower. The Xiongnu welcomed a peace in exchange for subsidies, but their series of raids had demonstrated the damage they could cause if their demands were not met. Ministers at the Han court all agreed that the Xiongnu were far too powerful to attack and so advised Emperor Wen (r. 180–157 B.C.) to strike a deal. "Since the *Shanyu* has just conquered the Yuezhi and is riding on a wave of victory, he cannot be attacked. Moreover, even if we were to seize the Xiongnu lands, they are all swamps and saline wastes not fit for habitation. It would be far better to make peace."[14]

An important part of the renewed peace treaty was the establishment of regular border markets. After Maodun's peaceful death in 174 B.C., the Xiongnu made expanding access to these official markets their most significant negotiating demand. While the redistribution of heqin subsidy payments benefited the Xiongnu political elite, these goods could never adequately compensate the much larger number of ordinary nomads who were forced to forgo raiding in times of peace. Without the guarantee of regular access to border markets where the Xiongnu could trade live animals and other pastoral products for grain, cloth, and metals, the shanyu could not expect his people to observe the peace. The Han court was opposed to increasing the size and number of border markets since it was believed that closer economic links between their own frontier people and the nomads would likely lead to political subversion. The Xiongnu were therefore forced to extort increased trade privileges the same way they extorted increased subsidies: by raiding or threatening to raid China. Loot from such raids kept the Xiongnu tribespeople appeased until China finally agreed to liberalize its trade policy under Emperor Jing (r. 157–141 B.C.). Once the Chinese agreed to expand such markets, the Han court did its best to control them by regulating the location and timing of trade fairs and restricting just what items could be sold. Not that edicts issued in the capital had much of an impact on the behavior of corrupt frontier merchants: contraband iron and other prohibited goods flowed onto the steppe in bulk despite the death penalty inflicted on those caught engaging in such trade.[15] Still, the stronger economic ties brought stability to both sides of the frontier and old hostilities were gradually forgotten: "From the *Shanyu* on down, all the Xiongnu grew friendly with the Han, coming and going along the Great Wall."[16]

Although the heqin policy successfully maintained stability along the frontier for three generations, critics at the Han court had always attacked it as a humiliation that China needed to reverse. They complained that Gaozu's agreement to recognize the Xiongnu Empire as an equal state violated the very essence of a Sinocentric world order, a view well expressed by Jia Yi, who was a prominent official at the court of Emperor Wen:

> The situation of the empire may be described just like a person hanging upside down. The Son of Heaven is at the head of the empire. Why? Because he should be placed at the top. The barbarians are at the feet of the empire. Why? Because they should be placed at the bottom. Now, the Xiongnu are arrogant and insolent on the one hand, and invade and plunder us on the other hand, which must be considered an act of extreme disrespect toward us. And the harm they have been doing the empire is extremely boundless. Yet each year Han provides them with money, silk floss, and fabrics. To command the barbarian is a power vested in the Emperor at the top, and to present tribute to the Son of Heaven is a ritual to be performed by vassals at the bottom. Now the feet are put on the top and the head at the bottom. Hanging upside down like this is something beyond comprehension.[17]

Jia Yi went on to explain that such a reversal should be easy to correct. He estimated that the whole Xiongnu population was no larger than a Chinese district and so should be forced into submission rather than placated. Despite the obvious violation of a Sinocentric world order, however, successive Han emperors ignored these attacks on the heqin policy because buying off the Xiongnu was less disruptive than fighting them, since the goal of Xiongnu was to be appeased, not to take Chinese territory. While the Xiongnu welcomed Chinese defectors, who crossed the frontier into their territories and did stir up trouble in border provinces, they had a policy of staying out of internal Chinese politics because established dynasties that paid subsidies were preferable to rebels who did not. When the seven autonomous kingdoms within China rebelled against the dynasty in 154 B.C. and sought a Xiongnu alliance, the nomads stood by as the central government crushed them. Had the Xiongnu intervened, the outcome might have been different.

This relatively peaceful situation lasted until 133 B.C. when, under the aggressive leadership of Emperor Wu (r. 141–87), the Han court abruptly abandoned the heqin policy for a policy of military confrontation. This began with an attempted surprise ambush of the shanyu. He was lured into China by a frontier merchant who had long traded contraband goods with the Xiongnu but was now in the pay of the Han court. The merchant promised the shanyu an easy pillage of the major border market of Mayi, where Han forces secretly lay in wait to attack him. The plot went awry when the suspicious shanyu smelled a trap and captured a Han official who spilled the beans. That event opened a period of more than a half century of constant frontier warfare between China and the Xiongnu, although both sides found it advantageous to continue trading at the border markets.[18]

The Han dynasty's turn to war came at a time when it was at the height of its power and attempting to undo the political compromises it had made under duress earlier in its history. It was the view of many in the Han court that China was now powerful enough to make a Sinocentric world order a reality by invading the steppe and destroying the power of the nomads forever. Despite a huge military investment, however, these attacks failed to subdue the Xiongnu. While the Chinese periodically defeated the Xiongnu in battle and engineered the defection of some of their component tribes, Han armies found nothing to conquer in Mongolia but empty land and no expedition there could stay longer than three months before running out of supplies. Moreover, the expense of these wars in men, horses, and money was so high that the dynasty practically bankrupted itself financing them. China's conquest of the Western Region oases in today's Xinjiang deprived the Xiongnu of tribute from that region but, because it required the Han dynasty to post troops there and provide gifts in silk to local leaders, it also proved to be a costly money pit that drained the treasury. Nor did the Han attacks destroy the stability of the Xiongnu Empire, since the invasions reinforced the shanyu's position as protector of the nomads against Chinese aggression. After decades of war, the Han court reluctantly concluded China had no more chance of removing the Xiongnu from the steppe than they had of driving the fish from the sea. By 90 B.C. the Chinese had abandoned their attacks on the steppe and adopted a completely defensive position that involved cutting off trade while repulsing raids.[19]

The Xiongnu Inner Frontier Strategy: Inventing the Tributary System

The Xiongnu had long understood that the absence of peaceful relations ultimately worked to their disadvantage, and so throughout the war they sent envoys to China requesting a resumption of the heqin treaties as a way to restore the status quo ante. But China rejected such peace offers, insisting that any future agreement take place within its new "tributary system" framework in which the shanyu would be required to pay homage to the Han emperor, send his heir as a hostage, and make tribute payments to China. It was a relationship the Xiongnu considered unacceptable and

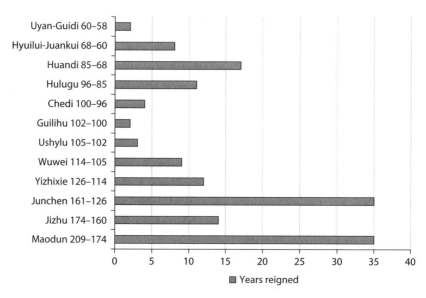

FIGURE 3.2. Xiongnu Shanyus, 209–58 B.C.

explicitly rejected in 107 B.C.: "'That is not the way things were done under the old alliance!' the *Shanyu* objected, 'Under the old alliance the Han always sent us an imperial princess, as well as allotments of silks, foodstuffs, and other goods, in order to secure peace, while we for our part refrained from making trouble at the border. Now you want to go against the old ways and make me send my son as hostage. I have no use for such proposals!'"[20] However, the ensuing decades of continual war with no subsidy payments made it ever more difficult for succeeding Xiongnu rulers to maintain both the empire's equilibrium and its dominance over the non-Xiongnu steppe tribes that Maodun had first conquered. For example, while there were only five shanyus in the century between 209 B.C. and 105 B.C., during the next forty-five years six shanyus would succeed to the throne, and only half of these survived more than four years (figure 3.2).

Worse for the Xiongnu, many of the conquered tribes, such as the Wusun in the west and Wuhuan in the east, were emboldened by support they received from the Han court to attack the Xiongnu, a policy better aligned with China's more defensive policies after 90 B.C. As a result, the Xiongnu were compelled to mount a punitive campaign against the Wusun in 80 B.C. and then pivot to the other side of the empire to attack the Wuhuan after they pillaged the Xiongnu royal tombs in 78 B.C. The situation became much worse in 71 B.C. when the Xiongnu engaged in a winter campaign and lost a significant number of troops in a severe blizzard. In the aftermath of this disaster, the Xiongnu experienced simultaneous attacks mounted by China in the south, the Wusun in the west, the Wuhuan in the east, and the Dingling in the north. The empire survived but in a much weaker condition that was exacerbated by a famine in 68 B.C.

Losing control over some component tribes and suffering ongoing economic difficulties were significant setbacks to the once all-powerful imperial confederacy, but a more existential threat came from divisions within the Xiongnu elite that manifested themselves under such conditions, particularly whenever a shanyu died. In 60 B.C. a violent succession dispute resulted in five rival factions warring upon one another for the throne until only two brothers remained. The weaker, Huhanye, decided that his only chance of political survival was to come to terms with China, but many of his people questioned this choice.

> The general expression of opinion was:—"By no means! It is the character of the Xiongnu to value independence and disparage submission. By mounting our horses and fighting for the national cause, we have gained a renown for courage among all the nations, whose sturdy warriors fight to the death. Now we have brothers striving together for the supremacy; and if the elder is unsuccessful, it falls to the lot of the younger. Although they die in the contest, yet they leave an unsullied reputation for courage to their children and descendants, excelling all other nations. Although China is strong, that is no reason why the Xiongnu should be annexed to it. How should we thus subvert the institutes of our ancients, becoming subject to the Chinese, disgracing the former *Shanyu*s, and being made the laughingstock of all nations. Although we should obtain peace at this price, how can we any more be looked upon as the head of the nations?"[21]

This point of view was grounded in a long history in which any nomad leader who surrendered to China and fell under the control of Han frontier administrators then disappeared from the steppe political scene. But others argued that the current situation was so dire that it required accepting new risks: "Ever since the time of Yizhixie *Shanyu* [r. 126–114 B.C.], the Xiongnu have been gradually whittled down and can never regain their former status. Although we could exhaust ourselves striving after that, we shall never enjoy a day's repose. Now if we submit to China, our nation will be preserved in peace; but if we refuse to submit, we are running into perdition. We cannot avert this by our plans."[22] So Huhanye broke with Xiongnu tradition and accepted the Chinese demands to make peace in 53 B.C. Surprisingly, this proved a stroke of genius because the feared tributary system was more symbolic than real. Huhanye maintained his autonomy as a sovereign shanyu and, in terms of protocol, was ranked above all Chinese nobles and only below the Han emperor himself. In return for his formal compliance, Huhanye and his allies received a flood of gifts and better border markets. During his first visit to the Han court in 51 B.C., Huhanye received 5 kg of gold and an equal value in Han coins (200,000 cash), seventy-seven suits of clothes, eight thousand pieces of silk, and 1,500 kg of silk floss. More significantly, the Han government supplied his followers with five thousand metric tons of rice. His brother Zhizhi, the northern shanyu ruling in Mongolia, was so impressed by the benefits Huhanye received for doing so little that he immediately asked that the Han court make him a tributary as well, something the crafty Huhanye lobbied against.[23]

Realizing that the Han tributary system effectively traded valuable gifts for symbolic actions, Huhanye implemented a new inner frontier strategy in steppe politics. In essence he used Han wealth and military protection to reestablish unity within the Xiongnu Empire. The Chinese did not expect this outcome. They had congratulated themselves on their astute statecraft in aiding one faction over another in a Xiongnu civil war and "using barbarians to fight barbarians" to keep the steppe divided. They also believed Huhanye's entry into the tributary system would allow China to maintain control over the southern Xiongnu permanently through him. While in the short term such a goal could be realized, Chinese aid enabled Huhanye to restore a unitary Xiongnu Empire. After receiving Chinese patronage for a decade, in 43 B.C. Huhanye decamped north to his Mongolian homeland, where "his people all gradually came together from various quarters, so that the old country again became settled and tranquil." His brother Zhizhi retreated far to the west, where Chinese troops eventually killed him near Lake Balkhash in 36 B.C. The Xiongnu Empire was again politically stable and the continued flow of Chinese resources would keep it intact for another century.[24]

Even after the Xiongnu regained their unity and power, they never again demanded a return to the more equal heqin agreements because the tributary system paid them so much more. (Nor, it should be noted, would later nomadic empires have objections to the tributary system framework.) The shanyu was more than willing to accept the ritual symbolic superiority of the Han emperor as long as the Chinese were willing to pay him to do so. And many aspects of the old heqin agreements appear to have continued under the tributary system, including the annual subsidies

Table 3.2. Silk payments to the Xiongnu shanyu on visits to the Han Chinese court

Year of visit	Silk floss (kg)	Silk pieces (number)
51 B.C.	1,500	8,000
49 B.C.	2,000	9,000
33 B.C.	4,000	16,000
25 B.C.	4,800	20,000
1 B.C.	7,300	30,000

Source: Yu, *Trade and Expansion*, 47.

and the provision of a Han princess in marriage to the shanyu. Xiongnu sovereignty was recognized by allowing the shanyu to continue to take hostages and tribute from tribes and small states still subject to the Xiongnu Empire. Nor was the old sticking point of sending the shanyu's heir as a hostage to the Han court any longer deemed a problem. The Chinese paid for his lavish upkeep and knew war would break out if they dared harm him.

One reason the nomads played the role of shameless tributaries so effectively was that they never accepted the Chinese cultural values that the scheme was designed to inculcate. The nomads declined to adopt China's ideographic writing system or its philosophies, calendars, and court rituals that were the core of its soft power even in lands hostile to its political control, such as Korea and Vietnam. The Xiongnu never judged themselves by Chinese cultural standards nor saw themselves as in any way inferior. Their participation in the tributary system was practical—the imperial gifts they received were far more valuable than the nominal tribute they paid, and as tributaries they had access to Chinese markets that had previously been closed to them. The Xiongnu regularly visited the Chinese court on tributary visits for the remainder of the Western Han dynasty once Huhanye began the tradition. Those in which the shanyu came in person generated the largest gifts and were quite expensive to his Chinese hosts because the shanyu insisted on bringing a large entourage that also needed costly accommodations and gifts of their own. Each shanyu made at least one visit during his reign if he could, and with each visit the size of the gifts increased (table 3.2).

Far from acting like submissive vassals in awe of the Han emperor, the Xiongnu now actively set about exploiting the tributary system for their own ends. (The steppe nomads' perceived lack of sincerity would be a persistent complaint made by Chinese officials running the tributary system during the Han and subsequent Chinese dynasties.) China had created its own sorcerer's apprentice problem: having demanded the Xiongnu make these tributary visits to prove Chinese superiority, it could find no easy way to end them as their costs rose ever higher. The Chinese also began to view the arrival of the shanyu at the Han court as an ill-omened event after two reigning Han emperors died unexpectedly in 49 and 33 B.C. immediately after the Xiongnu departed. But if the shanyu were denied permission to present tribute, then China feared the Xiongnu might respond by raiding the frontier again. This point was made clear in 3 B.C. when a prominent official and political philosopher, Yang Xiong, outlined the likely consequences of such a refusal when the Han court was on the verge of telling the shanyu to stay home:

> Now the *Shanyu*, reverting to right feeling and cherishing an unfeignedly sincere heart, wishes to leave his palace and take his place at the audience before the august presence. This is a custom that has been handed down from early ages and is favorably regarded by the spiritual intelligences. Although it may be costly to the State, it is a thing that must not be dispensed with. Why should he be repulsed as one bringing an evil influence, thus, on account of an uncertain impending event, nullifying the favors of the past and opening up the way to a quarrel in the future? To quarrel with those who have good intentions is to engender heartfelt hatred; repudiating their former expressions, they will look to our declarations in the past, and imbibing a bitter hatred against China, will sever every connecting bond, and never more to the end will they respect the imperial presence. It will be impossible to overawe them; it will be useless to address them. . . . Now, in governing the Xiongnu, if the laborious efforts of a hundred years are to be lost in one day—if one is to be secured at the expense of ten—it is your servant's humble opinion that this will not tend to the peace of the country. May your Majesty reflect a little on this subject, so that calamities may be averted from the people on the borders, ere the turbulence has broken out, or war has been declared![25]

The 1 B.C. visit by the Xiongnu shanyu proceeded as planned, but the death of Emperor Ai the same year surely reinforced the fear that such visits were indeed ill omened.

The policy of lavish tributary payments continued and became even more regular after turmoil in China led to the establishment of the Eastern Han dynasty (A.D. 25–220). When it first came to power, the Xiongnu were united and had moved south into frontier regions that Chinese troops had abandoned. However, beginning in 47, the Xiongnu became divided in their first violent succession struggle in a century. As during the previous civil war, a southern shanyu allied himself with China and employed the inner frontier strategy of using China's wealth to check his northern rival. Because this civil war would last for more than forty years, the lineage of southern shanyus maintained their close connection with China throughout and were content to leave the northern steppe fragmented, maintaining control only around the immediate Great Wall frontier in order to dominate the flow of goods to the steppe and thus stop the northern Xiongnu from gaining access to the system. The northern Xiongnu were later defeated by a rising new steppe power, the Xianbei nomads, who invaded from the east in 83 and then brought all the tribes in northern Mongolia under their rule. As a result, China expanded the tributary system beyond the southern Xiongnu to include the Wuhuan and Xianbei in the east, as well as the Qiang tribes on edges of the Tibetan plateau and the oasis kingdoms in the Western Region. This involved substantial transfers of wealth from China to the frontier peoples that were intended either to buy peace or to keep them divided. From A.D. 50 to 100 the southern Xiongnu received the equivalent of US$100 million annually, the rapidly expanding Xianbei almost triple that amount, and the oasis states of the Western Region got about US$75 million. Working from revenue records cited in the histories of the Eastern Han dynasty, Ying-shih Yu estimates that the annual cost of these direct tributary payments (mostly in goods) amounted to US$750 million (18,300 kg in gold), which was equal to one-third of the Eastern Han government payroll, or 7 percent of the empire's total revenue. And this did not include the military and administrative costs of operating the system or gifts made outside the subsidy system.[26]

By the end of the first century A.D., the relationship between the Eastern Han dynasty and the southern Xiongnu had become so close that the latter now played the role of "frontier guarding barbarians" who protected China from attacks by other tribes on the steppe in return for more subsidies. Although the southern Xiongnu eventually fell under the control of Han frontier officials who could determine succession to leadership by supporting favored candidates, the southern Xiongnu never lost their identity as an independent state. The system began to unravel as China experienced domestic political troubles during the mid-second century. The Yellow Turban Rebellion in 184 opened a period of particularly violent turmoil within China that lasted even after the Eastern Han dynasty collapsed in 220. In this situation frontier nomadic groups adopted different policies toward China depending on their location. The southern

Xiongnu continued to employ the inner frontier strategy and its leaders remained allies of the dynasty to the end, but the powerful Xianbei nomads in northern Mongolia employed the outer frontier strategy and attacked China's ever-weakening provincial defenses.

Neither strategy was viable without a prosperous and stable China to extort. By the time the Eastern Han dynasty was formally abolished, these surplus resources no longer existed. China's population and cities were in steep decline and its economy was in ruins. Aggressive Chinese warlords battled one another for the control of territory and were keener to fight the nomads than pay them off. In the absence of Chinese subsidy payments, with no rich provinces to loot, and with old trade networks collapsing, nomadic rulers lost their ability to maintain centralized polities and the tribes in Mongolia reverted to anarchy. A nomadic empire as powerful and centralized as that of the Xiongnu would not reemerge for another three hundred years, when the Turks (Tujue or Göktürks) were again able to exploit a reunifying China under the Sui and Tang dynasties in the sixth century to establish a relationship structurally analogous to that of the Han and Xiongnu. Like that relationship, unity on the steppe again disappeared with the collapse of the Tang dynasty in 907.

A XIONGNU LEGACY: DUAL UNITY, DUAL DISSOLUTION

The centralized Xiongnu exogenous empire that emerged on the Mongolian steppe was economically dependent on exploiting a prosperous and united China, and so were successor nomad empires in Mongolia. They came into existence in parallel with the unification of China and disappeared when China's political and economic infrastructure dissolved in periods of anarchy. As table 3.3 shows, there was a close correlation between the unification of China under native Chinese dynasties and the rise of nomadic empires in Mongolia. This was particularly true of the relationship between the Han dynasty and the Xiongnu just described, and it would be true again in the relationship between the Tang dynasty and the Turks/Uighurs during the sixth through ninth centuries. They were dyads in which the shadow empires of the steppe nomads extracted resources from China's endogenous empires without having to rule China itself. With the exception of the Mongol Empire, a case that I will take up later in this chapter, all the foreign dynasties that successfully ruled China were a different type of shadow empire, vultures from Manchuria that did best when both the empires on the steppe and those in China

Table 3.3. Major dynasties in China and steppe empires in Mongolia

Native Chinese dynasties	Foreign dynasties	Steppe empires
1. Qin and Han (221 B.C.–A.D. 220)		*Xiongnu* (209 B.C.–A.D. 155)
2. Chinese dynasties during the Period of Disruption (220–581)		Xianbei (130–180)
	3. Toba (Tabgatch) Wei (386–556) and the other foreign dynasties directly before and after	*Rouran* (402–555)
4. Sui and Tang (581–907)		*First Turkish* (552–630) *Second Turkish* (683–734) *Uighur* (745–840)
5. Song (960–1279)		
	6. Khitan Liao (907–1125)	
	7. Jurchen Jin (1115–1234)	
	8. Mongol Yuan (1279–1368)	*Mongol* (1206–1279)
9. Ming (1368–1644)		Oirats (1399–1454) Eastern Mongols (1478–1635)
	10. Qing (1616–1912)	Zunghar (1632–1757)

Notes: Italics indicate nomadic empires that controlled the whole steppe. With the exception of Mongol Yuan, all foreign dynasties are from Manchuria.

simultaneously fell into political anarchy and economic depression, which I will analyze in chapter 4.[27]

Shadow empires of whatever type relied on exploiting economic resources that they did not control directly. In the case of the nomadic empires and China described earlier, the goal of both sides was normally securing relative peace at an acceptable price. A bipolar world was the typical political outcome because both sides believed their cultures and economies were too different from one another to meld into a single stable political unit. To make the point on a grand scale, the Chinese had first built the Great Wall to delimit their respective spheres of influence. But in periods following simultaneous imperial state collapse in both China and Mongolia after the Han and Tang dynasties ended, emerging frontier states from Manchuria that straddled these boundaries came to power and ruled both North China and southern Mongolia (see chapter 4). These so-called foreign dynasties, the Toba Wei, Khitan Liao, and Jurchen Jin (table 3.3, middle column), did not see China's northern frontier as impermeable. They created armies that combined Chinese infantry troops and steppe nomad horse cavalry. They employed a dual administrative structure that used Chinese officials and law within China proper but governed its northern steppe and forest zones (as well as its own people within China) with non-Chinese elites using their own traditions. Most significantly, foreign dynasties originating in Manchuria did not look on the steppe nomads in Mongolia as alien others but rather saw them as rival cousins who could be dominated with a judicious use of force, a sophisticated system of alliances, and keen appreciation of tribal politics that they manipulated. For them, unlike the Chinese, it was a southern frontier along the line of the Yangtze and Huai River systems that constituted a seemingly impermeable political frontier. Their fast-moving cavalry troops that so effectively dominated the dry plains of North China and the steppelands of Mongolia and Manchuria could make far less headway in the wet semitropical marshlands and lake systems of southern China, which required the deployment of both naval forces and infantry troops.

When North China was ruled by these foreign dynasties, the steppe nomads in Mongolia found it very difficult to unify. Such dynasties had active divide-and-rule policies that supported weaker groups against stronger ones, regularly switching their support to the rivals of old allies if they got within striking distance of unifying the steppe. And unlike native Chinese dynasties, foreign dynasties refused to pay the nomads off in return for peace, preferring to go to war instead. For these reasons, Mongolia remained politically divided after the fall of the Tang dynasty in 907. In the ensuing three hundred years, the foreign policies implemented by both the Khitan Liao dynasty (907–1115) and the Jurchen Jin dynasty (1115–1234) successfully prevented the rise of any nomad empire in Mongolia until Chinggis Khan suddenly created one in 1206.

The Mongol Empire: Transformation from Exogenous to Endogenous Empire

A Mongol steppe nomadic leader, Temüjin (1162–1227), founded what became the world's largest empire under the title of Chinggis Khan in 1206. He was an unlikely unifier, let alone world empire builder. At the time of his birth, the Mongols had fallen victim to the Jurchen Jin dynasty's policy of side-switching that shifted away from them and to their Tatar enemies. In the aftermath, the Tatars murdered Temüjin's father and the Mongols he formerly led deserted his family. The hard lesson Temüjin learned from this and similar experiences was that shared bonds of kinship and descent fragmented easily under pressure and could never be relied on. He therefore sought out personal patrons from more powerful tribes such as the Kerait's Toghrul Khan, a steppe ruler who fortuitously owed a political debt to the young Temüjin's dead father. Toghrul eventually helped Temüjin recover leadership of the Mongols around 1190 and brought them within the Kerait confederation. Temüjin returned the favor in 1196 by defeating Toghrul's brother, who had seized power in a coup two years earlier, putting his patron back in control of the Kerait confederation. Their relationship soured after this highpoint because Toghrul's sons believed that Temüjin was positioning himself to become the elderly leader's successor at their expense. When Temüjin proposed a marriage between his eldest son and a Kerait princess in 1203, Toghrul not only insultingly refused the request but (at the urging of his sons) exiled him too. In response Temüjin used his small remaining force to mount a surprise attack on the Kerait leaders when they were feasting. He routed them and a fleeing Toghrul was beheaded by a rival tribe, leaving Temüjin in charge of the Kerait confederation, whose princesses he then married to his sons.[28] The Jurchens attempted to rally the remaining tribes in Mongolia against him, but Temüjin defeated them all in a series of battles. He was formally recognized as the imperial ruler of the steppe in 1206 with the title of Chinggis Khan, the first nomad leader to achieve that level of sovereignty over Mongolia since the fall of the Uighur Empire in 840.

Unlike the nomadic empires established by the Xiongnu and Turks, the Mongol Empire was not an imperial confederacy. The founders of these earlier empires had been elite members of existing ruling dynasties within their own powerful tribes. They gave the most important imperial positions to their own relatives and were content to let the subordinate tribes in the confederation maintain their own identity and local political leadership. Although he came from a descent group that had previously led the Mongols, Chinggis had been deserted by them and even his close relatives on many occasions. As a result, he refused to share power and reorganized the existing steppe tribal system to reduce the influence of the old elite that previously led it. Chinggis avoided giving military commands to his relatives (including his own sons) and instead chose men with demonstrable talent who had previously proved their loyalty to him. These men, whose humble social status and disparate origins would have relegated them to herding livestock or other menial tasks in the old system, became some of the most successful military commanders in world history under Chinggis's direction. He broke the cohesion of the enemy tribes he conquered by dispersing them among nested sets of decimally based military units (ten, one hundred, one thousand, ten thousand) without regard to kinship or genealogical descent. Chinggis appointed the commanders of these units, and soldiers were prohibited from leaving their assigned units without permission on pain of death. This must have been a fairly widespread division: the most common request made to Chinggis by successful commanders of one thousand he wished to reward was to be allowed to reunite their own people. At the same time, Chinggis cleverly divided the steppe aristocracy by recruiting the sons and younger brothers of existing tribal leaders into an imperial bodyguard (*keshig*) numbering ten thousand men. It was an elite group whose members outranked all others, including their fathers and elder brothers. Their future lay with the empire, not the old tribal system, and they later became its generals and administrators.[29]

If Chinggis's internal organization of his steppe polity was different from his predecessors', his foreign policy was not. Like rulers of earlier steppe shadow empires, he needed to extract resources from surplus-producing agrarian economies to finance his state and reward his followers. Like them, he intended to employ a classic outer frontier strategy of violent raiding to terrify his enemies and produce loot for his followers, threaten further war to obtain treaties that would provide his state with regular subsidies, and eschew the occupation of heavily populated agricultural land that would then have to be defended and administered. As we saw earlier, this strategy succeeded in creating a stable bipolar world when implemented by the Xiongnu against the Han dynasty and by the Turks against the Tang dynasty. Had the Mongols been facing the native Song dynasty that then ruled South China, we might have seen a similar set of developments and the emergence of a new stable bipolar frontier. But between the Song and the Mongols lay a North China ruled by the Jin dynasty of Manchurian origin, which responded to nomad threats of war with bigger wars rather than appeasement. The result would be twenty-five years of intense conflict that led to the destruction of the Tangut Xi Xia kingdom and Jurchen Jin dynasty in China, as well as the Khorasmian khanate in central Asia. In the aftermath of this unanticipated success, the Mongol Empire transformed itself into an endogenous empire that drew its resources directly from the sedentary lands it conquered and administered. Following Chinggis Khan's death in 1227, the Mongols added ever more sedentary territory to their empire, which at its maximum extent included all of China, central and southwestern Asia, and eastern Europe (map 3.2). These later conquests would themselves become independent endogenous empires after the unity of the Mongol Empire fractured in the 1260s.

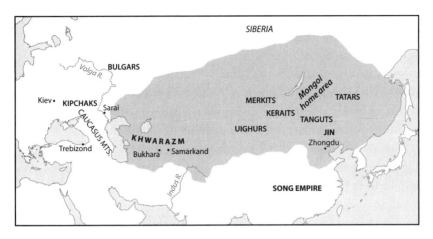

MAP 3.2: The Mongol Empire at the death of Chinggis Khan.
From Burbank and Cooper, 2010.

There were two rival states ruling North China when Chinggis united the steppe in 1206, the Tangut state of Xi Xia in the west and the Jurchen Jin dynasty in the east, both of which had strong historical ties to the nomads in Mongolia. Chinggis attacked the weaker Tanguts in 1209. As would be typical in all the Mongol campaigns, the Tangut defenders greatly outnumbered the invading nomads. Moreover, they maintained fortresses at strategic passes and protected their cities with high walls. Nomad cavalry forces in previous eras had easily looted undefended villages and sent their populations fleeing, but they were never able to reduce well-garrisoned fortresses or engage in siege warfare against walled cities, both of which they simply moved around. The nomads retreated back onto the steppe when large Chinese armies eventually arrived to counterattack. The Mongols proved different. First, Mongol troops operated under a stricter central command than earlier steppe nomadic armies, with all units silently advancing or retreating in unison following flag signals. Any individual soldier who broke ranks, retreated or advanced without orders, or engaged in personal looting could be executed. While the Mongols often used tactical feigned retreats to lure an enemy into planned ambushes, they did not attempt to avoid pitched battles even when outnumbered as had the Scythians, Xiongnu, and Turks. Second, and the biggest departure from previous nomadic empires, was Chinggis's addition of a corps of professional military engineers to his ranks so that he could either lay siege to walled cities or breach their fortifications. There was of course a learning curve involved in this new approach, as could be seen during the Mongol siege of the Tangut capital of Yinchuan in 1210 when their engineers attempted to divert a river to wash out the city's thick earthen defensive walls but ended up flooding the Mongol camp as well. Still, the attempt was impressive enough to induce the Tanguts to choose submission to avoid further fighting. The Tangut ruler agreed to become a client of the Mongols and provided them with valuable gifts, a princess in marriage, and a promise of future military aid. The Mongols then evacuated their forces and returned to the steppe with their plunder.[30]

Things at first seemed to follow the same pattern with the Jurchen Jin. Long having been the dominant power manipulating the tribes of Mongolia, a new Jin emperor sent an envoy demanding that Chinggis submit to his authority after he had returned from his Tangut campaign. Chinggis refused and mobilized his troops for an attack on the Jin frontier in 1211. His invasion was aided by the border tribes there who were familiar with the region's mountain passes and fortifications, by Jurchen defectors who provided both tactical and strategic advice, and by disgruntled Khitan tribes who allied themselves with the Mongols to remove Manchuria from Jin control in 1212. The initial Mongol attacks ebbed and flowed (Chinggis was wounded and returned to Mongolia in 1212), but their tempo increased in 1213–1214 when they looted across North China and surrounded the Jin capital of Zhongdu (today's Beijing). The Jin emperor was deposed and his replacement agreed to become a Mongol client, gave Chinggis a princess in marriage, and provided the Mongols with so many luxury goods that "as for the satin and goods, our troops loaded as much as their horses could carry and moved away, tying up their loads with bands of heavy silk fabric."[31] The Jin emperor was left in place as the Mongols withdrew to the steppe.

For the Mongols, this new relationship, in which the Jin dynasty would pay not to be invaded, was the successful endpoint of an outer frontier strategy, not an intermediary step in the conquest of North China. For the Jin dynasty, however, paying off the Mongols was a stopgap measure designed to get them to withdraw while it prepared itself for a new war. Within months the Jin emperor abandoned his vulnerable northern capital and moved the court to Kaifeng, a city on the south bank of the Yellow River as far away as he could get from the Mongolian steppe. From there the Jin reasserted its right to act as an independent state by blocking Mongol envoys from making diplomatic contact with the Southern Song dynasty. Chinggis responded by reinvading North China, declaring the Jin actions a violation of a peace agreement that was less than a year old: "After they had already submitted themselves, how could they hinder the envoys sent to [Song emperor Ningzong]?"[32] The old Jin capital of Zhongdu surrendered to the Mongols in 1215 after a brutal siege and experienced such a great loss of life that a Khwarazmian envoy arriving in the aftermath recoiled in horror at what he observed. He recounted that on the road to the city, he "saw a white hill and in answer to his query was told by the guide that it consisted of bones of the massacred inhabitants. At another place the earth was, for a long stretch of the road, greasy from human fat and the air was so polluted that several members of the mission became ill and some died."[33] And this was only the first of a series of bitter campaigns between the Mongols and the Jurchens over the next two decades that ended with the destruction of the Jin dynasty in 1234.[34] This constant warfare had a devastating impact on North China's agricultural population. The last Jin census, taken in 1195, estimated that the dynasty ruled a population of 50 million people; the first Mongol census, in 1235, found only 8.5 million people remaining in the same territory.[35]

Had Chinggis Khan truly been interested in conquering China, he would have exploited the capture of Zhongdu in 1215 by immediately striking south to eliminate the Jin dynasty. Instead he left China for Mongolia before the city fell and never returned, leaving the fighting in North China to his subordinates and allied troops. His attention had turned west, where battles with remnant nomad groups in central Asia put Mongol troops on the borders of Khwarazmia whose envoys had then traveled to North China to gain intelligence about the situation there. Chinggis was initially keener to create trade links with Khwarazmia than to invade it, but that changed in 1218 after the Khwarazmian governor of Otrar massacred several hundred merchants coming from Mongolia and seized their goods. When Chinggis sent a delegation seeking the governor's punishment and compensation, the Khwarazm shah Ala ad-Din Muhammad executed the envoys, leaving one to return to Mongolia to inform Chinggis of his displeasure. The Mongol response was swift and massive: a full-scale invasion to take revenge that began in 1219 and ended in 1225. Mongol armies took every city in the region and destroyed most of them with great loss of life in 1220–1221. Units then chased the fleeing Ala ad-Din Muhammad across northern Iran, where he died on an island in the Caspian Sea. They then moved west and made their first contacts with the Christian state of Georgia, the Kipchak nomads on the Black Sea steppe, and Kievan Rus' before rejoining the main Mongol force in central Asia in 1223. Another force under Chinggis's personal command had pursued the Khwarazm shah's son Jalal ad-Din across today's Afghanistan to the banks of the Indus River, where he escaped into India after they defeated him in battle in 1221. Chinggis then returned to central Asia and began his slow march home in 1225, withdrawing all Mongol troops and abandoning the territory he had overrun, leaving only a local governor in Khwarazmia.[36]

That the Mongols would inflict such destruction and then depart made
no sense to people in a region where the goal of military action was to add
functioning territories to the state, not annihilate them. The strategic violence of the outer frontier strategy was being employed with no appreciation that the region's population base and economic infrastructure were
more fragile than in North China and would take far longer to recover. A
goal of destruction rather than control also characterized Chinggis's last
war against the Tanguts in Xi Xia. They had broken their agreement to
send troops for his campaign in the west, telling Chinggis that he should
not undertake such a venture if he did not have enough of his own. Rather
than simply ousting its insolent ruler and taking charge of the territory
himself, Chinggis sought personal revenge. As he came back to Mongolia,
he ordered his army to destroy every city in the region and return the place
to desert. That destructive process was almost complete when Chinggis
fell from his horse and died in 1227, having created an immense empire
without ever quite appreciating the full significance of his accomplishment. It would take the Mongols more than a generation to give form to
what its founder had only outlined.

Shadow empires did not seek to become endogenous empires; rather
they sought to create a stable equilibrium with the states they extorted
that maximized their strengths and minimized their weaknesses. When
an exogenous empire did become an endogenous empire, it was because
its strategy of exploitation proved overly successful—the would-be parasite became its own host and needed to adapt to that role reversal. The
question of whether the Mongols could continue to avoid the responsibilities of direct imperial rule split the elite: conservatives wanted to preserve
the steppe institutions of the past, while innovators were keen to graft
steppe military power to a sedentary economic base. It took civil wars and
a generational change to complete this transformation, but it began with
acceptance of at least minimal responsibility for the administration of conquered territories and then the expansion of them. It was Chinggis Khan's
third son and successor, Ögedei, who began the process, albeit at a fairly
basic level. He relied primarily on foreign advisers who had the required
administrative skills but were aliens to the populations they ruled. In
North China the Mongols employed Muslim officials from central Asia
who ran an abusive system of tax farming to raise revenue in the lands
that had been allocated as fiefs to prominent Mongols. It more closely
resembled raiding the economy than administering it. But even this was

initially opposed by those who believed that taxing conquered farmers was not worth the effort. In 1229 they broached the idea of exterminating the peasants and letting the land in North China revert to horse pasture. It was Ögedei's Khitan prime minster Yelü Chucai (1189–1243) who put an end to this talk by asserting he could deliver double the tax revenue on an annual basis if the agricultural population was protected and administered as previous dynasties had done. Talk of killing off peasants ceased as the promised flow of goods and silver poured into the Mongol capital of Karakorum and Yelü Chucai's administrative reforms reduced the worst abuses.[37] In the west Ögedei dispatched Mongol armies that advanced deep into Europe from 1236 to 1241, although after his death they withdrew to Russia and the Kipchaq steppe.

It was only in the 1260s under the grandsons of Chinggis Khan that the process of becoming an endogenous empire was finally completed. Up until that point, the empire's political center was its capital city of Karakorum in central Mongolia, which was quite near the long-deserted city built by Uighur nomads during the Tang dynasty. It was here that policies were set, Great Khans chosen, and armies dispatched from one end of Eurasia to another. Subject rulers and diplomatic envoys journeyed to this distant and inconvenient place (to everyone but the Mongols) to treat with its rulers, whose favor or disfavor had life-or-death consequences.

Karakorum received a constant flow of luxury goods and captives from conquered lands that attracted merchant caravans eager to do business there. This high-profit trade got more attention than the more prosaic arrival of daily wagon trains loaded with the imported food from China that fed its people. Karakorum reached its height under the last universal Mongol ruler, Möngke (r. 1251–1259), who came to power after displacing the heirs of Ögedei. It was he who focused on expanding the empire into more distant and heavily populated agricultural areas. Möngke first assigned his brother Khubilai with the task of ruling North China from where the Mongols began their conquests of the southwestern states abutting Song China and then Song China itself. The fighting in the south forced the Mongols to adapt to a terrain and climate ill-suited for their horse cavalry by recruiting large numbers of Chinese infantry troops into their ranks. They had to build a navy as well because so much of the fighting and troop transport in this lake and riverine environment required the use of boats. While China was Möngke's first priority, he also allocated troops to his brother Hülegü for the conquest of Iran, Iraq, and Syria, which the Mongols had only partially overrun in the 1220s. Hülegü accomplished this task between 1256

and 1260, destroying Bagdad and the last remains of the Islamic Caliphate in the process. Only stiff Mamluk resistance prevented the Mongol
Empire from expanding onward into Egypt.[38]

Whether Möngke had intended this or not, his deployment of imperial forces to conquer and rule ever-larger sedentary regions shifted the
empire's center of gravity from the steppe to the conquered sedentary
regions of China and Southwest Asia. Mongol rulers based there had
better access to locally produced goods, weapons, and more secure revenue streams than their relatives remaining on the steppe. This became
immediately apparent during the succession struggle between Möngke's
brothers, Ariq Boke and Khubilai, following his unexpected death in 1259.
In previous succession struggles, the faction that occupied Karakorum
had the strategic advantage, so when they both declared themselves rival
Great Khans in 1260, Mongol odds makers would have placed their money
on Ariq Boke, whom Möngke had left in charge of Karakorum, and not
Khubilai, who was based in North China.

However, because the nomads in Mongolia had become so dependent on access to resources from sedentary lands to feed themselves and
equip their soldiers, Ariq Boke found himself in dire straits when Khubilai
stopped the Chinese supply trains to Karakorum. He desperately sought
an alternative source of food and troops from the neighboring Chagatai
Khanate in central Asia. But Khubilai cut off that avenue as well by getting
its new ruler, Alghu, to switch sides in return for de facto autonomy. Khubilai made a similar deal in distant Iran with his brother Hülegü, who recognized him as the empire's ruler in return for his own region's autonomy.
Ariq Boke was forced to surrender to Khubilai in 1264 and died a few years
later.[39] It was now clear that Mongol forces ruling sedentary areas were
more powerful than those remaining in its old steppe homeland, although
the latter continued to mount insurgencies against their cousins in China
for many years afterward. As a result, the rationale that formerly justified
maintaining a unitary empire with its political center in Mongolia disappeared. The Mongol Empire then devolved into four independent successor khanates, each with a different sedentary core region: the Golden
Horde (1259–1480) spanning the Black Sea and Kazakh steppes (including
Russia and Khwarazm), the Il-Khanate in Southwest Asia (1256–1335),
the Chagatai Khanate in central Asia (1260–1370), and the Yuan dynasty
in China (1271–1368) (map 3.3).

Each Mongol successor state was now an endogenous empire in its own
right, and although they all adapted to the distinct cultures of the people
they ruled, they never abandoned their steppe traditions of governance.

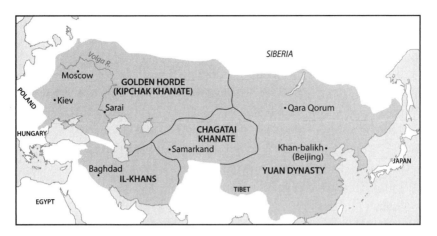

MAP 3.3. The Mongol Empire in 1294. From Burbank and Cooper, 2010.

The Golden Horde in Russia remained the most nomadic and retained its mobile pastoral economy while extracting tribute from the surrounding agricultural population. Its rulers continued to live in mobile yurt camps that moved with the seasons, but they also established a fixed capital at Sarai on the lower Volga River.[40] Both they and their Il-Khan rivals in Iran eventually became Muslims. At the opposite end of the spectrum, the Mongols in China became the most sedentary and aligned themselves more closely to Chinese cultural values, with one major exception. Unlike any previous or successor foreign dynasty, the Mongols marginalized China's literati class and the written Chinese language in favor of outsiders: Mongols, western Asians, and those in North China with links to the previous foreign dynasties there. Still, under Khubilai's direction, the Mongols began the process of adapting their regime to a Chinese value system that previous Mongol Great Khans disdained. Khubilai gave the Mongol state a Chinese dynastic name, the Great Yuan, and its collaborators could argue it achieved a standard of Confucian legitimacy after the Mongols finally defeated the Song dynasty and united all of China in 1279, an ideal that had not been attained since the fall of the Tang dynasty in 907.[41]

But it was Khubilai's earlier reaction to the Song dynasty's attempt to buy peace with the Mongols that marked the watershed moment of change from exogenous to endogenous empire. Chinggis would have undoubtedly been willing to trade peace for the vast flow of wealth the Song was willing to offer, as he had originally done with the Jurchen Jin dynasty in North China. This was an arrangement favored by previous Xiongnu shanyus and Turkish khagans and one that would have relieved them of the responsibility governing additional sedentary people. Chinggis's grandson Khubilai rejected the Song offer because he was no longer content with mere extortion. His vision for the Mongol state in East Asia was to rule all of China and its neighbors too. The Mongol Empire that began its life as a disruptive startup extortion business had by now become an aggressive monopolist that did not play well with others. Think Google, Facebook, or Amazon on a slower time scale.

The Demise of Steppe Empires

Steppe empires were the products of interaction with neighboring sedentary states. They reached the height of their power when the Mongol Empire became an endogenous empire that spanned most of Eurasia. Upon the fall of the Mongol Yuan dynasty to the Ming dynasty in 1368, the frontier reverted to its previous bipolar status as China poured resources into static walled defenses along its northern frontier and devoted most of its military effort to keeping the nomads out of China. Unlike the Han and Tang dynasties, the Ming refused to pay off the nomads until the late sixteenth century, fearful they might be seeking to reconquer China. This produced the longest period of frontier unrest in China's history, during which the nomads relied primarily on raiding China to get what they wanted. At the other end of the steppe, the Golden Horde successor of the Mongol Empire remained a powerful endogenous empire for a century longer, until it broke up into rival khanates during the mid-fifteenth century.

In the seventeenth century steppe pastoralists throughout the Eurasian steppe began to feel pressure from two new expanding empires, the Manchu Qing dynasty in the east and Tsarist Russia in the west. The Qing dynasty began as a vulture empire from Manchuria that quickly conquered all of China to become an endogenous empire. But unlike native Chinese dynasties (Han, Tang, Song, or Ming) that viewed the steppe nomads as aliens who must be excluded rather the governed, the Manchus viewed the Mongol tribes as frontier relatives whose horsemen could be incorporated into their own armies. The Qing governed their Mongol territories with native Chinggisid princes whom they treated as junior partners in the dynasty's scheme of rule. The non-Chinggisid Zunghar Mongols in the west attempted to conquer Mongolia in 1688 to create a new steppe empire but were met with force rather than appeasement. The Manchu Qing emperors were comfortable campaigning on the steppe, often in person, and mounted a series of wars against them that lasted close to a century.

In 1757 they finally destroyed the last Zunghar strongholds in the Altai Mountains region and occupied their territories, including the subject oasis cities of Xinjiang's Turfan Basin. Qing China now directly controlled the entire steppe region from Manchuria in the east to the Altai in the west, leaving no place for any remaining steppe nomads to regroup. At the same time, a Russian vacuum empire was expanding into the Black Sea steppe zone and settling it with an ever-larger number of farmers. Russia's incorporation of the vast Kazakh steppe on its Siberian frontier continued until it reached the border of the Qing empire. As the nineteenth century began, the entire Eurasian steppe was now divided between Russia and China, and the remaining steppe nomads were their subjects rather than politically autonomous communities. The two-millennia pattern of mirror steppe empires wielding power as peer polities with their sedentary neighbors was extinguished, never to return.

CHAPTER FOUR

Shadows on the Horizon

And some of our men just in from the border say
there are no barbarians any longer.
Now what's going to happen to us without barbarians?
Those people were a kind of solution.

—C. P. CAVAFY, "WAITING FOR THE BARBARIANS," 1904

Empires from the Periphery:
Vultures and Vanquishers

Periphery shadow empires emerged in frontier areas over which endogenous empires had previously exerted some kind of hegemony before they weakened or collapsed. Unlike the steppe and maritime exogenous empires that sought a favorable modus vivendi with neighboring endogenous empires, those arising from the periphery saw themselves as possible replacements for them. They had no vested interest in preserving the status quo and reaped dividends in periods of chaos. They filled a niche that lay somewhere between state-destroying anarchy and imperial restoration. There were two distinctive types, each of which had its own dynamic.

Vulture shadow empires were founded by invading groups from the periphery when an endogenous empire collapsed and were particularly common in North China. Taking on imperial trappings after the demise of a formerly dominant endogenous empire, its rulers left their homelands and assumed control over parts of an old empire. They were vultures feasting off a corpse, not lions bringing down prey. As a consequence, their primary objective was to restore basic political order and economic productivity by combining the remains of a preexisting imperial order with their own traditions of governance. In that process they made themselves the governing elites of states in which many of their majority subjects were more culturally sophisticated than themselves and whose cooperation was needed to administer their more complex economies and larger populations. It was a shaky synergy that came with high risks. Failure led to further political disintegration and territorial devolution. However, success in reestablishing order made those regimes vulnerable to replacement by the indigenous elites who administered them. The only way to avoid this fate was by leaving the shadows and transforming themselves into endogenous empires.

The idea that endogenous empires were naturally subject to such collapses is one of history's oldest paradigms, deeply embedded in both Western and Chinese tradition, as well as in contemporary social science.[1] Commonly attributed to barbarian invasions destroying the empires they overran, in reality these collapses were by-products of disruptions generated by domestic civil wars, plagues, severe economic depressions, and population declines that brought endogenous empires to the point of breakdown long before any barbarians arrived. The different outcomes afterward depended on the nature of the center's collapse and the resources available to any successor state. But this decline-and-fall scenario was not universal. In the ancient Persian world, powerful empires did not decay and slowly die; instead they were murdered in midstride by vanquisher empires from the periphery while still securely governing all of their territories, the surprise victims of blitzkrieg wars that gave them no time to recover. These vanquisher empires inherited a still-functioning structure of governance and a solid economic base that they reorganized to suit their own purposes. They were lions taking down prey and not vultures stripping corpses.

Successful takedowns of fully functioning empires by outsiders from the periphery were as rare as they were impressive. In the 1,200 years from the foundation of the Achaemenid Empire in 550 B.C., they occurred only twice: when Alexander the Great conquered the Persian Empire in 330 B.C. and ended 220 years of Achaemenid rule, and in 651 when Arab Islamic armies took control of the Sasanian Empire that had been in power for 425 years. Had Alexander not died in 323 B.C., so soon after conquering all the Persian Empire's old provinces, perhaps his grand vision of a new mixed Greco-Persian imperial state might have taken root. Instead his Macedonian generals divided the empire into smaller successor states, the largest of which was the Seleucid Empire in the Persian heartland, which was reduced to marginality by the rise of the native Parthian Empire in less than a century. The Arab Caliphate avoided this fate by transforming itself into an endogenous empire when it adopted a Sasanian imperial structure in Muslim dress after the Abbasid Caliphate replaced the Umayyad Caliphate in 750. At its height the caliphate controlled a territory of over 11 million km^2, although that included large tracts of desert. It would remain a powerful but smaller imperial state until 946, and the prestige embodied by the caliphate remained so high that it continued on in a diminished form until it was finally destroyed by the Mongols in 1258.

Vulture Empires

Vulture empires were created by leaders of frontier provinces, client states, or tribal groups who sat on the geographic and cultural periphery of an empire. They were formed after the internal collapse of their imperial neighbors when leaders on the periphery were able to seize the remains and form their own new empire. Frontier regions were always considered to be places apart culturally and administratively, even when they had strong economic and political ties to the empire. Depending on administrative preferences, frontier lands might be formally incorporated into the empire and occupied by imperial garrisons or ruled indirectly by client leaders. The latter was common even in highly centralized endogenous empires that compromised their usual policies of direct rule and cultural assimilation in frontier areas by recruiting local elites as partners. Although such frontier rulers became familiar with the dominant imperial culture, they retained strong links with their unassimilated coethnics in the hinterland, who could be used either for or against the empire.

Long experience with the dominant empire transformed the local culture and political organization in frontier areas. During times of centralization, participation in the imperial system allowed cooperating leaders to overcome rivals with the economic and military aid they received from the empire. However, when the empire weakened or withdrew from a frontier, a struggle invariably ensued between those who wished to return to a more autonomous and less hierarchical political structure and those who wished to employ the tools of the withdrawn imperium to create their own centralized state. This contest often took generations to resolve. If it resulted in the emergence of a new centralized state, it was one that combined elements of an indigenous political culture with an administrative system modeled on the old empire (and sometimes employing its leftover personnel). If the center was weak enough, particularly if civil wars had generated regional anarchy, leaders from such marginal territories could seize control of the center themselves and found new imperial dynasties. In the process these new rulers recruited ever-larger numbers of people of disparate origins into their polity who then took on a common ethnic identity that superseded older parochial identities based on actual kinship and descent. Imperial withdrawals created opportunities for them to expand into new territories and to rule over a subject peasantry. Although such a new polity might be named after its elite's frontier homeland, its success depended on maintaining domination over the existing administration of the fallen empire. In this new environment, rulers developed their own hybrid states that adapted aspects of their own cultural traditions with existing models of imperial administration.

FRONTIER DYNASTIES IN NORTH CHINA: THE KHITAN LIAO AND JURCHEN JIN DYNASTIES

The largest number of vulture empires (and the most successful) were found straddling China's northeastern frontier. After the fall of the Han, Tang, and Ming dynasties, it was groups from Manchuria that created stable transfrontier states. Some eventually succeeded in establishing control over enough people and territory to cross the imperial threshold and rule all of North China. With the exception of the Mongol Yuan dynasty, all of China's non-Han "conquest dynasties" came from the northeast (see table 3.3).

The process began when loosely organized tribal confederations with collective leadership were transformed into centralized states by autocrats who then proclaimed themselves Chinese-style emperors. They employed a dual organizational structure that used, on the one hand, Han Chinese officials and administrative structures to govern their Chinese subjects and, on the other, indigenous leaders who followed customary traditions to govern their tribal people. The military was run by commanders with tribal roots and Chinese officials controlled the civil administration, with the emperor using each to check the power of the other. It took generations for these emerging states to develop fully and successfully compete for power within North China as the stronger ones swallowed others like themselves until only a single state remained. For example, dozens of weak polities battled one another in the third century after the fall of the Han dynasty before the northern Toba Wei (386–535) succeeded in unifying North China and pushing the steppe tribes back into northern Mongolia. When the Tang dynasty fell at the beginning of the tenth century, the process moved faster and with fewer players: the Khitan Liao dynasty (916–1125)

Table 4.1. Endogenous empire components in the Jurchen Jin vulture empire

Present	Partial	Absent
Population: 50 million	Size: 2.6 million km² (only North China—did not meet the historic Chinese unification standard)	Imperial project that imposed some type of unity throughout the system
Organized to administer and exploit diversity	Centralized institutions of governance that were separate and distinct from the rulers (dual organization that kept both Chinese and tribal institutions)	A primate imperial center with transportation systems designed to serve it militarily and economically (had sets of capitals rather than a primate center)
Monopoly of force within their territories, and military force projected outward		
Systems of communication that allowed administration of all subject areas from the center directly		

first unified the frontier regions, and the succeeding Jurchen Jin dynasty (1115–1234) incorporated it and expelled the Chinese Song dynasty from most of North China, occupying its capital of Kaifeng in 1125. The Manchus, who rose in the early seventeenth century, were the last and most successful vulture dynasty in Chinese history. They seized Beijing with the help of Ming defectors in 1644 and went on to occupy all of China within two years, setting into motion its transformation into China's largest endogenous empire, which I will examine in more detail later.[2]

The structural characteristics of the vulture dynasties (table 4.1) that combined both Chinese and tribal elements were effective in governing multiethnic states in which the ruling ethnic groups constituted only a small minority of the population. This mixture of different structural elements worked well to establish order when they first came to power but proved harder to maintain over time unless, like the Manchu Qing dynasty, they transformed themselves into endogenous empires.

The Khitans were originally pastoral nomads and the major tribal power in the northeast during the early sixth century at the end of the Toba Wei dynasty and the rise of the Tang (map 4.1). However, every one

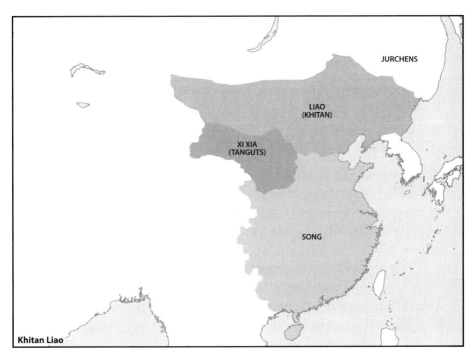

MAP 4.1. The Khitan Liao dynasty.

of their numerous attempts to create an autonomous state during succeeding centuries was put down by either Tang China or its Turkish steppe
empire counterpart because neither was willing to permit a third frontier
power to come into existence. As long as the steppe and China remained
united polities, they maintained a bipolar world in which the northeastern frontier peoples fell under the sway of one of the two powers. Maintaining a bipolar frontier was so important that when rebellions against
Chinese control in Manchuria began to succeed, they were put down by
the nomads from the central steppe, so at some times the Khitans were
ruled by the Turks in Mongolia and at others by Tang China. At the end
of the ninth century the Khitans were organized as a confederation with
a supreme khagan and eight autonomous tribes whose elected leaders
served three-year terms. If, as Chinese records state, the Khitans were
descendants of the Han dynasty–era Xianbei, it would seem that their old
tradition of elective political leadership and local autonomy still remained
deeply rooted in the northeast.[3]

Khitan political structure changed after the Tang dynasty fell and the
ambitious Liao dynasty founder Abaoji (r. 907–926) created a centralized
state that reduced the autonomy of the confederation's component tribes

and also eliminated power sharing with his close relatives. He began this process as a local tribal chief in 901 when he attacked the Chinese frontier, capturing ninety-five thousand people and one hundred thousand animals. He then settled these people in a city run by Chinese officials who had defected to his cause and employed Tang Chinese models of administration. Abaoji's success raised his prestige among the Khitans but also led to a fear that he was growing too powerful, a threat that was realized in 907. According to a hostile Song dynastic account,

> The Chinese told Abaoji that there was no case of a Chinese ruler being replaced on the throne. Thereupon Abaoji made increasing use of his power to control the tribes and refused to be replaced. After nine years the tribes reproached him for not being replaced after such a long time. Abaoji had no choice but to pass on his banner and drum [symbols of authority]. But he said to the tribes, "The Chinese whom I have obtained during the nine years of my rule are numerous. I should like to organize an independent tribe to govern the Chinese City. Is this permissible?"
>
> The tribe consented to it.
>
> The Chinese city which was situated southeast of Mount Tan and on the Luan River, enjoyed the advantages of salt and iron. . . . Its land was suitable for the cultivation of the five grains. Abaoji led the Chinese in cultivating the land and constructed a city, houses, and markets after the system of Yu prefecture. The Chinese were satisfied with this and had no thought of returning.
>
> Abaoji, realizing that people could be used, followed the plan of his wife Shulü and sent emissaries to inform the tribal chieftains: "I own the salt-lake from which you eat [salt]. But though the tribes know the advantages of eating salt, you do not realize it has an owner. Is that fair? You should compensate me."
>
> The tribes considering this to be right, all assembled at the salt-lake with oxen and wine. Abaoji placed soldiers in ambush nearby. When the wine had begun to take effect, the hidden soldiers came forth and killed the tribal chieftains. Then he set himself up and was not replaced.[4]

This massacre of tribal leaders placed Abaoji in an unchallenged position as he declared himself khagan of the Khitans, a title he upgraded to emperor in 916. The addition of literate Chinese officials to his government played a decisive role in creating an imperial structure in which the emperor could have no peer and succession was limited to sons rather than brothers. These changes were most strongly resisted by Abaoji's brothers and uncles, who mounted a series of failed rebellions against his autocratic rule. As one later-executed rebel uncle explained, "At first I did not realize how exalted a Son of Heaven is. Then Your Majesty ascended the throne. With your guards of attendants, you were extremely dignified and in a different class from the common run of people."[5] Still, the Khitan elite never fully accepted the Chinese model of imperial succession and the dynasty was plagued by fights over the throne throughout its history.

The power of the Khitan Liao dynasty lay in Abaoji's combination of a Khitan cavalry military with a Chinese agricultural and manufacturing economic base. As the state grew under Abaoji's successor, Yaogu (Emperor Taizong, r. 927–947), this informal division of labor was made explicit in a legal dual administrative structure, as described in its official dynastic history:

> In the old Khitan way of life their affairs were simple, their official duties specific, and their governmental system plain and unsophisticated and not confused by terminology. Their rise was rapid indeed. In 921 an edict was issued concerning the regularization of grades and ranks. When Taizong came to rule over China, he divided the government into North and South. The Khitans were governed according to their own national system, while the Chinese were governed according to their own system. The national system was plain and simple. In the Chinese system the usage of traditional terminology was preserved.
>
> The government of the Liao state was divided into a Northern and a Southern division. The Northern Region administered the affairs of the camps, tents, tribes, lineages, and tributary states, while the Southern Region administered the taxes and the military affairs of the Chinese prefectures and counties. To govern according to custom is indeed to achieve what is proper.[6]

For its first forty years the Liao state confined itself largely to campaigns in Manchuria and Mongolia. Its strategy for dealing with China's many successor states that had arisen after the fall of the Tang dynasty was one of alliance or neutrality. It was not until they collapsed that the Khitans attempted to conquer North China and overran Chinese territory as far south as Kaifeng by 947. However, Emperor Taizong died within months of this success, and the Khitans withdrew back north when faced with both local rebellions and a struggle for succession. North China remained in the hands of local warlords until the establishment of the Song dynasty in 960. From its capital in Kaifeng, the Song was able to seize a number of important kingdoms allied with the Khitans without substantial

opposition. In 979 and then in 986, the Song attacked the Khitans themselves. They were repulsed on both occasions, the second time disastrously.
In addition to a tenacious military defense, the Khitans responded politically in 990 by recognizing the new Tangut kingdom of Xi Xia, located in
northwestern China, whose existence threatened the Song frontier there.
The balance of power then began to shift in favor of the Liao. By 1004,
the Khitans were strong enough to counterattack, forcing the Song to sue
for peace on the Liao's terms. A treaty signed in 1005 required the Song
to deliver two hundred thousand bolts of silk and one hundred thousand
ounces of silver annually to the Khitans in exchange for its recognition of
the existing frontier. This effectively ended fighting between the Song and
the Khitans for a century.[7]

The Liao court abandoned policies of expansion and worked to preserve the status quo after making peace with the Song. This invited trouble
because while payments extracted from a Chinese dynasty might be sufficient to support a nomadic imperial confederacy, these could not cover all
the costs of the Liao state's more expensive dual organization. Nor could
they cover the costs of increasingly frequent wars along its northern flank
with frontier people, which drained the Liao treasury and alienated the
local population. In spite of a new treaty signed with the Song in 1042
that greatly increased the amount of payments from the south, the Khitans experienced a fiscal crisis in the latter half of the eleventh century.
Vulture dynasties had always treated their Chinese territories as places to
be exploited rather than nurtured and maintained strong military forces
to ensure their dominance. But during the long peace with the Song, the
Khitan elite that had previously devoted itself to military affairs progressively abandoned the hard work of war to become a class of rent-seeking
landlords exploiting a subject Chinese peasantry. Because the amount of
Chinese agricultural land that the Liao state controlled was limited, the
diversion of tax revenue into private hands undermined its finances and
incited rebellions among peasants who were victims of land grabs. By 1087
banditry and widespread migrations by displaced people were so endemic
that the Liao government declared the situation in many rural areas to be
out of control.[8]

The situation was no better on the northern frontier, where harsh Khitan rule provoked revolts by its Jurchen subjects living in the Manchurian
forest zone, whose mixed economy was based on hunting, fishing, horse
raising, agriculture, and the export of wild ginseng root. The Jurchen
people there had long complained of abusive officials and the dispropor-
tionate work they expended to provide the Liao court with exotic furs and

animals as tribute payments. They revolted in 1114 under the leadership of a tribal chief, Aguda, who then declared his establishment of a new Jin dynasty. The Khitan responded by sending an imperial army (exaggeratedly reported as seven hundred thousand strong) to counterattack in 1115, but it disintegrated after losing a battle to a much smaller number of Jurchens and the dynasty then lost control of Manchuria. Jurchen expansion afterward was swift and relentless. The Liao central capital fell to the Jurchens in 1120, and they extinguished the Liao dynasty entirely after capturing and deposing its emperor in 1125. One reason for the Liao's quick demise was the defection of its Khitan tribal leaders and Chinese officials who saw better prospects for themselves with a rising Jurchen Jin dynasty than with a failing Khitan Liao. They were not disappointed because the Jurchens needed their skills and gave them high ranks. Even more opportunities opened up after Aguda died and his younger brother Wuqimai (Emperor Taizong, r. 1123–1135) invaded Song dynasty territories in 1125. In retrospect, an early Song alliance with the Jurchens against the Khitans proved ill-conceived because it led to the replacement of a conservative status quo power with an aggressive new revisionist regime. In 1226 the Jurchens swept through all of North China and captured not only the Song capital of Kaifeng but the reigning emperor too. The Song government paid for a peace treaty and withdrew south to the Yangzi River basin. This left the Jurchen in command of almost all China north of the Huai River, far more Chinese territory than the Liao had ever ruled (map 4.2).[9]

Governing North China demanded a level of expertise the new Jin dynasty lacked, so it readily adopted the existing Khitan model of dual administration, which was particularly attractive since it allowed tribal groups to be ruled differently from the Chinese population. To staff the administration, the Jin recruited officials who had previously worked for the Song and Liao dynasties in China and the Bohai Kingdom in Manchuria. Jurchen traditional values, customs, and even language were lost at a rapid rate in the new environment in spite of periodic government programs and edicts designed to protect Jurchen culture. This was not because the Jurchens had a greater affinity for Chinese culture than had the Khitans but because, over the course of a single generation, they transferred their three million people out of the frontier and into China proper, where they constituted only about 10 percent of the population. The issue of adopting Chinese culture became part of the political struggle over who should control the state: the emperor or the tribes. From 1123 to 1150, cliques whose power depended on the emperor struggled against Jurchen warlords who had effectively established their own fiefdoms in North

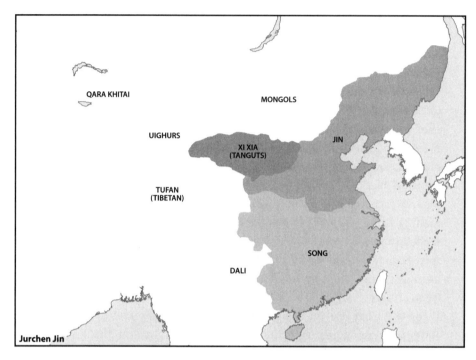

MAP 4.2. The Jurchen Jin dynasty.

China. Jurchen custom viewed political power as a shared patrimony, and important decisions were brought before a council of tribal leaders. Chinese statecraft rejected such devolutions of power and, as imperial authority grew stronger, the Khitan dual system of administration was replaced by a more classically Chinese system of centralized rule.

It was one of Aguda's grandsons, Digunai (Wanyan Liang, r. 1150–1161), who took the strongest steps in this centralizing and Sinicizing direction by moving the capital from Manchuria to today's Beijing, establishing an examination system for official appointments, and ending the privileged status of the Jurchen tribal elite (many of whom he also murdered). These were only the first steps in a grander plan to conquer the Song in the south and refurbish Kaifeng as the capital of an empire that ruled all of China, a feat last accomplished by the Tang dynasty. Had Digunai succeeded, he would have transformed a vulture exogenous empire into a foreign-ruled endogenous one. However, he was assassinated by his own officers when his costly invasions of Song territory failed. He was posthumously stripped of his imperial title, and regime historians painted his actions in the worst possible light. Although Digunai's administrative changes remained in place, his successors abandoned his Sinicizing policies in favor of a

Jurchen nativism that set them further apart from the Chinese majority they ruled. But the traditions the dynasty was attempting to revive were already dead or dying, and it fought a losing battle against the disappearance of the Jurchen language in China.[10]

This situation left the Jin on the cusp of a transformation into a cosmopolitan endogenous empire that it never quite completed, rejecting a butterfly future to maintain its existing caterpillar identity. As we saw in chapter 3, the same type of dispute would arise a century later within the Mongol third-generation elite who replaced the Jurchens as the rulers of North China in 1234, but with the opposite outcome. Declaring the establishment of a China-based Yuan dynasty in 1279, Khubilai Khan's armies would first defeat a bid for the throne by his nativist brother in Mongolia and then proceed to conquer the Song dynasty and unify China under a single ruler. Despite its failure in execution, Digunai's ambitious plan to unify China was not without potential for an ambitious vulture shadow empire, and in 1644 the Manchu Qing dynasty would accomplish it. In the process it created China's largest endogenous empire by adding Manchuria, Mongolia, Tibet, and the oases of eastern central Asia to China's core provinces. Moreover, the Manchus accomplished this feat with remarkable speed: the establishment of vulture empires within North China had taken a century to complete after the fall of the Han dynasty in the third century and decades after the fall of the Tang dynasty in the tenth century, but would prove instantaneous after the fall of the Ming dynasty in the mid-seventeenth century.

THE MANCHU QING DYNASTY: TRANSFORMATION FROM EXOGENOUS TO ENDOGENOUS EMPIRE

Creation of the Manchu State

The political history of what later became the Qing dynasty began with murders and revenge plots worthy of Shakespeare's contemporaneous play *Macbeth*, had it been set in Manchuria rather than Scotland. Nurhaci (1559–1626), the dynasty's founder, came to power as a young man when he succeeded in killing and replacing a powerful Ming dynasty–supported Jurchen tribal khan in 1586 whom he blamed for his father's death. Nurhaci's career from that point may be divided into a tribal phase lasting until 1618 and a border conquest phase that occupied him until his death in 1626. The first and longer period was characterized by his unceasing efforts to control the Jurchen tribes. He employed the traditional tactics of wars, marriage alliances, trade deals, and exploitation of the Ming Chinese tributary system as means to this end. For much of this time he shared power with his brother and then his eldest son but eventually came to view both with suspicion. Nurhaci executed his brother in 1611 for challenging his primacy, and his eldest son was sacked and imprisoned for plotting a coup in 1612, dying three years later. (His other fifteen adult sons fared little better: seven were executed, forced to commit suicide, or posthumously disgraced, and five were cut off for political crimes or relegated to minor posts.) Nurhaci declared himself khan of the new Jurchen Later Jin dynasty in 1615. It was a move that distanced him from the existing tradition of Jurchen collective rule and staked out an imperial claim, albeit an aspirational one.[11]

Nurhaci's most enduring innovation during this tribal period, and one that laid the foundation for a future state, was his reorganization of the military. In 1601 he created standard companies of three hundred households each called arrows that were combined into battalions consisting of five companies. They in turn were assigned to four color-coded groups called banners (red, white, yellow, and blue) of ten battalions each. In 1615 four additional banners (bordered red, white, yellow, and blue) were added, to bring their total to eight. The banners were initially commanded by Nurhaci's brother, sons, and nephews, who held the rank of senior or junior *beile* (chief). Banner membership became hereditary, and its leaders wielded considerable political power that would later display itself most prominently at times of dynastic succession.[12]

Nurhaci's frontier expansion began with the 1618 surrender of the Chinese trading city of Fushun (Mukden), whose Ming commander and garrison defected to the Jurchens. Beginning a policy that would later pay dividends during the conquest of China, its military officers received high ranks and their troops joined Nurhaci's army. The Ming responded by sending a large expeditionary force against him but it was defeated. From his new base Nurhaci conquered the neighboring Chinese province of Liaodong in 1621. This victory was not universally welcomed back home because it meant an end to popular looting raids there. Tribal leaders also resented Nurhaci's refusal to share the spoils of war with them. The distribution of captured people was a major source of wealth for tribal leaders, who then owned them as slaves. Insisting that conquered Chinese territory and people (and the revenue they produced) belonged to the state, Nurhaci recruited Chinese administrators to help him govern its large Chinese population (about a million people), which included both farming villages and cities. Nurhaci initially believed he could integrate Liaodong's Chinese population directly into the Jurchen state as he had earlier done with various Mongol and transfrontier Chinese communities. Indeed, the Chinese may have appeared to Nurhaci as a useful counterweight to his relatives who commanded the Jurchen banners and whose influence he was keen to curb. To this end he ordered Jurchen and Chinese families in Liaodong to live together within the same villages, where they were to work the land together as equals. However, the Jurchens treated the Chinese farmers as servants, and the latter revolted in 1623 after a major crop failure. Although quickly suppressed, this rebellion generated mass paranoia within the minority Jurchen population when it was learned that some Chinese villagers had secretly poisoned their Jurchen neighbors, resulting in the establishment of separate Jurchen villages and exclusive Jurchen quarters within the region's cities.[13] A confidential letter outlining how this new separation policy should be applied in criminal cases provides both an unvarnished picture of Nurhaci's style of rule and the problems of building a frontier apartheid state:

> Let the *beiles* and officials live happily. If I am angry now and spit in your faces, it is because your way of judging crimes is wrong. Why do you let Chinese in leading positions be equal to you? If a Jurchen has committed some crime, look to his merits. Ask what he has accomplished. If there is any little reason, use it as a pretext to pardon him. If a Chinese has committed a crime deserving of capital punishment, if he did not make an all-out effort as he should, or if he stole things, why not kill him and all his descendants and relatives instead of letting him go with a beating? The Chinese who have been with us since Fe Ala [i.e., before 1619], judge on the same basis as a Jurchen. Once a sentence has been decided upon, you cannot change it back again, it is like a mule that does not know how to go backwards. You Eight *Beiles* read this letter in secret to the banner *beiles* and officials. Do not let the people hear of it. Do you not know that they [the Chinese] poisoned our women and children at Yaozhao after our troops left?[14]

Under the new rules, the Chinese were forbidden to carry arms, whereas Jurchens were obligated to. Many former Ming officials retained in office to govern the local population were demoted although they had remained loyal during the 1623 revolt, which had been the work of the local Chinese peasants. Believing that the Jurchens had broken their promise that defecting Chinese officials would retain their old ranks and titles, they started a new revolt in 1625 that, like the first, was quickly suppressed, and a large number of Chinese officials were removed from office in the aftermath. That purge was tempered by the Jurchens' need for Chinese experience in administration and for Chinese labor for agriculture and war. When large numbers of Chinese fled the province following the 1625 rebellion, Nurhaci warned his commanders against wholesale killing: "If the Liaodong people rebel and escape they are committing a crime. But why kill them? Take them as soldiers and let Chinese fight Chinese. It will be to the benefit of the Jurchen."[15] Although this dual administrative system strongly resembled that established by the Khitan centuries earlier, it was not because Nurhaci was copying it but because he faced similar problems and devised similar solutions.

At the time of Nurhaci's death in 1626, the Jurchens found themselves facing walled Ming defenses protected by heavy cannons that blocked their further advance into China. While he had created a viable frontier state, it remained a poor one that was often short of food. Moreover, Nurhaci's worldview remained tribal rather than imperial. In his will he called for his successors to govern the state as a cooperative confederation administered by a council with rotating leadership. His successor Hung Taiji (r. 1626–1643) rejected his father's posthumous command and instead moved to consolidate his own power. He foiled a cousin's attempt to make himself and his bordered blue banner independent, lest it set a precedent for the other banner leaders to do the same: "If I let him go outside, then also the two red, the two white, and the Plain Blue Banner could all go across the border and live outside. Then I am without a country and whose emperor would I be? If I follow this suggestion the empire will fall apart."[16] He then stripped the most powerful *beiles* of their banners and cowed the rest into submission. Moving away from Jurchen tradition already undermined by his father, Hung Taiji introduced Chinese-staffed bureaucratic institutions that both favored his centralization of power and promoted the supremacy of the emperor over his relatives.[17] The process reached its culmination in 1636 when Hung Taiji declared himself emperor of the new Manchu Qing dynasty, abandoning his father's title of khan, the dynastic name of Jin, and the name of his people as Jurchens. All three were legacies of a small-minded frontier mentality Hung Taiji deemed unsuitable for the upcoming great enterprise of conquering China. Rebranding the Jurchens as Manchus and his dynasty as the Great Qing, he cut the historical links with the twelfth-century Jurchen Jin dynasty that Nurhaci may have seen as reflecting needed glory on his nascent state but that were no longer grand enough for Hung Taiji.

Hung Taiji expanded his power base by creating new Chinese and Mongolian banners to dilute the power of the original eight Manchu banners and give the Qing state a more robust fighting force. The first Chinese banner was established in 1630, a second in 1637, four by 1639, and eight by 1642. Following the Manchu conquest of Inner Mongolia, eight Mongol banners were created there in 1635. The Manchus treated the Mongols they incorporated as junior partners in the emerging Qing empire and not conquered subjects, a status that would only grow in importance after the conquest of China.[18] Because Chinese and Mongol banners were attached directly to the imperial government, their leaders never had the historic autonomy of Manchu banner officials. For Hung Taiji and his successors, they were tools the emperor could employ to keep Manchu *beiles* in line. This had a profound impact on the importance of the original Manchu banners, the majority of which were still tied to individual *beiles* who often had their own political agendas. It also highlighted the Qing dynasty's cultivation of a multiethnic enterprise that would aid in its transformation into a fully endogenous empire, albeit one in which the Manchu imperial line carefully guarded its superiority over all other groups.

The Manchu Conquest of China

Vulture empires filled the voids produced by the collapse of endogenous empires, and in the case of Ming China that collapse and void filling were simultaneous. The Ming dynasty was destroyed from within by peasant rebellions that had begun in the 1630s and culminated in the fall of Beijing and the suicide of the Ming emperor in April 1644. On taking control of the capital, the rebel leader Li Zicheng proclaimed himself emperor of the new Shun dynasty. This created a dilemma for Ming general Wu Sangui, who was keeping the Manchus at bay at the strategic Shanhaiguan Pass three hundred kilometers northeast of Beijing: accept the authority of a usurping Chinese peasant rebel or defect to the alien Manchus. Wu chose the latter after learning Li had arrested and tortured his father. The combined Ming and Manchu forces quickly routed the rebels, who fled Beijing in June. The Manchu forces were led by Dorgon, who had taken power as regent upon Hung Taiji's death in September 1643 and the succession of his five-year-old son Fuyi to the throne as the Shunzhi Emperor (r. 1643–1661). It was Dorgon who restored order to Beijing and installed the Shunzhi Emperor as the ruler of China, declaring the Qing now held the Mandate of Heaven.[19]

The Qing conquest of the rest of China was mostly complete by 1650, although pockets of Ming loyalists fought on for another decade and a remnant based in Taiwan survived until 1683. Had Ming loyalists been better organized and acted more aggressively, things might have turned out quite differently. Faced with similar invasions out of the northeast, the Song dynasty had driven the Khitans back to the edge of the frontier and later prevented the Jurchens from expanding into South China. This was a real concern for the Manchu leaders, whose military was relatively small, lacked the amphibious riverine warfare capabilities required for fighting in the south, and did not have enough administrative capacity to properly govern the territories they had conquered. Unlike the Khitans and Jurchens, however, the Manchus had quickly recruited large numbers of ex-Ming Chinese officers, soldiers, and officials into their ranks. They did have such skills and also provided the needed extra manpower to engage in large infantry battles. These Chinese additions facilitated the Qing reunification of China in record time, a task that had taken the Mongols more than fifty years of destructive warfare to achieve. As Pamela Crossley observes, "The conquest was effected by a diverse group of people, the overwhelming majority of whom would by any definition simply be called Chinese men—most of whom had lately been serving in the Ming armies or militia. Their leaders were largely, but not exclusively, Qing bannermen, and of the bannermen a (declining) portion were registered as 'Manchu.' The conquest, then, was primarily a phenomenon of Chinese fighting Chinese."[20] However, it should be noted that invading minorities successfully exploiting subject majorities was the rule rather than the exception when victorious exogenous empires transitioned themselves into endogenous ones. For example, most of the soldiers in the British Indian Army were native sepoys, and that army was bigger than the one Britain maintained at home. Although the structures they employed were very different, both the British in India and the Manchus in China succeeded in governing peoples unlike themselves in ways deemed legitimate enough to hold power for a couple of centuries. The British did this by portraying themselves as vassals of the Mughal emperors long after that dynasty was defunct, and the Manchus employed Chinese rituals and political institutions to align themselves with majority Han values. After both were challenged by rebellions that threatened their rule, they adopted government policies to make such revolts less likely in the future.

Once in China, the Qing dynasty experienced disputes over the level of Sinification it should allow to develop, an issue that had divided earlier foreign dynasties. Emperors had a bias in favor of Chinese institutions and ideologies because they reinforced the power of the state and its unitary ruler. Those seeking to preserve tribal ways opposed them for that reason and were keen to preserve traditions that distributed power and economic benefits widely within the ruling Manchu elite. These factions alternated in power during the Qing's first twenty-five years in China. As regent,

Dorgon set policy favoring the traditional faction and limited the use of Chinese institutions until his unexpected death in 1650. At that point the young Shunzhi Emperor began ruling in his own name and reversed Dorgon's priorities by adopting a wide range of Chinese institutions until his own death from smallpox a decade later. His demise permitted the tribal faction to reemerge under the Oboi regency when they declared Xuanye (Shunzhi's seven-year-old son, who had survived smallpox) the Kangxi Emperor (r. 1661–1772). Oboi and his faction took the regime in a nativist direction and rolled back Shunzhi's policies, vesting more power in the Manchu banners. That period ended when a now fifteen-year-old Kangxi arrested Oboi in 1669 and took personal control of the state.[21] He would become the longest-reigning emperor in Chinese history, and it was he who completed the Qing dynasty's transformation into an endogenous empire. In doing this Kangxi struck a balance that emphasized preserving Manchu cultural values as distinct from the Han Chinese while using classic Chinese institutions of governance to reduce the influence of Manchu bannermen in setting policy. Lawrence Kessler notes that, with an impact that might be compared to that of his contemporary Louis XIV of France, Kangxi's "major achievements and the essence of his rule are easily perceived in a fifteen-year seminal period from 1669 to 1684 when he succeeded in consolidating Manchu rule over China." Kessler continues, "By the end of this period, Kangxi had reversed the general direction of government policy, exercised mature judgment in political crises, crushed a major enemy on land and another at sea, secured China's northern frontiers against foreign encroachment, harnessed both Manchu and Chinese talents for government service, opened China to Western scientific knowledge, patronized literary compilations, and dissipated the anti-Manchu hostility of a large group of Chinese scholars."[22] The crucible for this transformation was the Rebellion of the Three Feudatories from 1673 to 1681, where Kangxi's deft handling of the crisis secured Manchu power in China and made him all-powerful. The revolt had its roots in a political deal the Manchus struck with their Chinese collaborators when they first came to power. At that time the Manchus rewarded their most important ex-Ming generals, such as Wu Sangui, with fiefdoms in southern and eastern China that they had helped conquer. While they were theoretically under the authority of the Qing emperor, these men commanded their own troops, collected taxes for themselves, and handled local administrative affairs. They received large subsidies from the Qing treasury even when they acted at cross-purposes with imperial appointees in their regions. Their titles as subordinate kings (*wang*) also violated an exclusive sovereignty principle long embedded in classical Chinese political thought. And going back to the Han dynasty in the second century B.C., the tension between the imperial court and such subordinate sovereigns always produced rebellions when the central government attempted to eliminate them. For the Qing this occurred after Wu Sangui petitioned the court to retire from his governorship of Yunnan with the proviso that the position be transferred to his son, effectively creating a hereditary kingdom. He revolted in 1673 when that demand was rejected, and he was quickly joined by the Chinese rulers of Guangdong and Fujian Provinces, who held similar positions. The rebellion soon engulfed all of South China from along the coast, west to Sichuan, and then north into Shaanxi. After Manchu banner forces sent to suppress the rebellion were defeated, Wu sent Kangxi an insulting message suggesting he and his dynasty return to their Manchurian homeland. While many at court favored compromise, Kangxi reorganized his military command and made good use of Chinese Green Standard troops who completed retaking the rebel parts of southern China by 1677. Wu died in 1678 just after he had declared himself emperor of the new Zhou dynasty, and his successors fought a losing battle to hold Yunnan in the west that they lost to Qing forces in 1681.[23]

The termination of this eight-year struggle finally put the Qing dynasty in direct control of all China with no internal rivals. The failure of the Manchu military leadership and the effective use of Chinese Green Standard troops increased the emperor's power within the Qing government. Neither Manchu banner leaders nor old ex-Ming allies could any longer act as if they were exempt from Kangxi's authority. The Manchu bannermen in particular had demonstrated they were no longer the military backbone of the empire after failing the dynasty in this crisis. From now on they could only maintain their positions by supporting Kangxi in hope of receiving imperial favor, and he was free to employ Chinese in military or civilian positions as he pleased. This allowed Kangxi to reconcile the traditionalist Chinese bureaucracy to life under Manchu rule. The Qing was no longer a vulture dynasty feasting off the corpse of China but a powerful tiger hungry for new prey. The war had left Kangxi with battle-hardened troops and a well-oiled military machine that he used to expand into Inner Asia. When threatened by the Zunghars with the rise of a new nomadic empire in western Mongolia, the Qing did not restore the old Ming walls but combatted them on the steppe itself by allying with their Khalka Mongol enemies in the east. When the Zunghars were finally defeated in 1757 under the great Qianlong Emperor (r. 1735–1796), the Qing empire had almost doubled in size to include all of China's old frontier lands plus Manchuria, Mongolia, Tibet and Turkestan (map 4.3).[24]

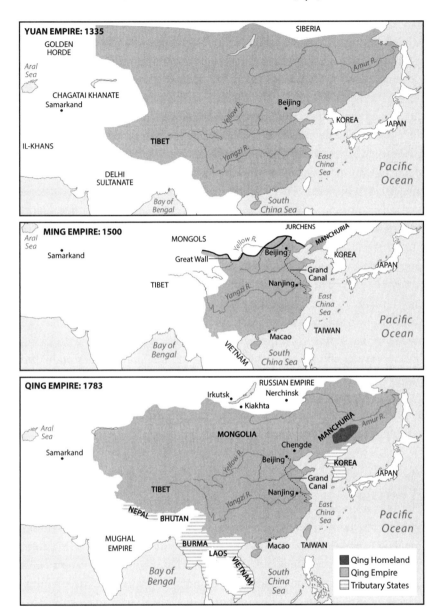

MAP 4.3. The Manchu Qing Empire. From Burbank and Cooper, 2010.

The ruling elites of exogenous empires that transformed themselves into endogenous ones all maintained the distinct values of their former shadow selves. The British retained a classic maritime strategy of indirect rule that gave primacy to trade and avoided assuming formal sovereign authority even as they came to control all of South Asia. Moreover, India was just one piece in a colonial empire that in some ways resembled the Athenian *arche* on a globe-spanning scale. Similarly, the Mongol conquest of China produced a regime prone to policies of predatory extortion it found hard to shake. Unlike any other dynasty (native or foreign) ruling China, it refused to employ the Chinese language and the literati class as the core of the civil service, giving preference to foreign Mongolian, Persian, and Turkic peoples and their languages. Perhaps as a consequence, the Mongol Yuan dynasty lasted less than a century, the shortest lifespan of any of China's major dynasties. When Ming rebels in the south threatened the dynasty's existence, the Mongols responded with a classic steppe nomadic strategy: in 1368 they just decamped for their old homeland rather than attempt a costly last-ditch defense of North China they were sure to lose. The Qing dynasty, by contrast, proved to be one of China's longest lived, 276 years, but it too retained its frontier roots. While China remained the core of the empire, the dual organizational structure allowed the Manchus to administer the Chinese in Chinese ways while applying different laws and political structures in non-Chinese areas. Unlike the preceding Yuan dynasty, which was never at home in China, or the Ming dynasty, which saw non-Chinese as too alien to be part of their state, the Qing created a successful endogenous empire that included both comfortably. It is a balance that the current People's Republic of China, the inheritor of the Qing's territorial base but not its cosmopolitan outlook, has found more difficult to maintain.

Vanquisher Empires

Vanquisher empires arose when relatively weak frontier polities on the periphery attacked and conquered much more powerful and fully functional endogenous empires, reorganizing them under an alien ruling elite. Unlike a vulture empire that developed after an endogenous empire and the order it provided had collapsed, a vanquisher empire took over a functioning administrative structure, transplanting itself into an existing host body primed to reject it. Given the negative power imbalances involved, successful vanquisher empires were quite rare. Their founders needed to win almost every risky bet they took, since a major defeat or the death of a leader could bring about their collapse. Vanquisher empires also needed to complete their conquests within a short time period because the advantage shifted to endogenous empires during prolonged wars. If able to recover their balance, endogenous empires could strike back effectively under new leadership even after losing a series of battles or territories. As black swan events that took everyone at the time by surprise, the successes of vanquisher empires have had idiosyncratic explanations.[25] The success of Alexander the Great's vanquisher empire was classically attributed to his unique military genius. The Arab armies that established the caliphate attributed their own victories to miracles wrought by Allah, who rendered the impossible inevitable. Modern historians have found it easier just to denigrate the empires they defeated as weak polities on the verge of collapse anyway. But that assumption is questionable: both the Achaemenid and Sasanian Empires were intact and wielded immense military power when they were conquered respectively by Alexander and the Arabs.

While vulture empires appeared in many parts of the Afro-Eurasian world where frontier people advanced into the chaos generated by an endogenous empire's collapse, vanquisher empires emerged only on the edges of the ancient Iranian world because endogenous empires there appeared immune to the cycle of rise, decline, and fall that characterized Rome in the west and China in the east. Despite civil wars over succession and rebellions within their empires, they displayed a remarkable stability and staying power. For 1,200 years, three long-lived indigenous Iranian empires (Achaemenid, Parthian, and Sasanian) would continuously rule the whole region, with only one 150-year break filled by Alexander the Great and his Seleucid successors. And just before the Sasanian Empire fell to the Arabs in 651, it had been expanding rather than contracting. Thus, if vanquisher empires were remarkably rare, so was the strength and stability of the empires they overthrew—ones that in antiquity never suffered the types of internal collapse that were the incubators of vulture empires elsewhere. A possible explanation may lie in what they all had in common: a king-of-kings model of governance and systems of succession to rulership that were competitive but not chaotic.

Employing a king-of-kings model of distributed authority served to protect Iranian empires from the periodic crises on their frontiers that produced systemic collapses in North China and the Roman west. Losing outer parts of their empires temporarily was a common occurrence in the Iranian world and did not immediately endanger their overall integrity or stability. Iranian empires also had a more robust political structure that managed a better balance than either China or Rome in how their emperors came to the throne. China's strict hereditary succession system avoided civil strife but at the cost of promoting many weak boy emperors to the throne. Rome's imperial succession system had the opposite problem. It largely ignored the principle of hereditary succession after the end of the Julio-Claudian line and instead permitted an open competition where anyone proclaimed emperor was ultimately deemed legitimate if he succeeded in fending off rivals. There were no child emperors here, but such an open succession system encouraged Roman generals and their armies to pit themselves against one another whenever an opportunity arose, to the detriment of the empire as a whole. The ancient Iranian systems fell between these two extremes. Like China, they strictly limited succession to a royal house but, more like Rome, allowed any adult member within that house to compete for the throne, better ensuring that talent (even if of a sanguinary sort) would rise to the top. Thus, while there were repeated wars of succession in Iranian empires, the number of competitors involved was small and the competition ended after the winners proved their superiority by killing or exiling their rivals in a bloody tanistry selection process.[26] It was a balance that kept a ruling house from becoming so insular and unworldly that it could no longer govern effectively, as often occurred in China, but avoided the free-for-all civil wars that periodically debilitated the Roman Empire.

ALEXANDER THE GREAT

Even after more than two millennia, Alexander the Great (356–323 B.C.) remains a world figure who inspires ever-new popular and scholarly interpretations of his life. Having already traversed and conquered the entire Persian Empire (map 4.4), Alexander was still in the midst of reorganizing his new state and adding to it when he died in Babylon at age thirty-two. While the empire was then divided up among his generals, the fusion of Hellenistic and Persian culture he set in motion had a more lasting impact, albeit of a colonial type in which a Greek speaking elite imposed itself on a diverse substrate in a manner similar to the nineteenth-century British in India. Nevertheless, unlike most conquerors who are praised in the histories of their own people and excoriated in the histories of those they conquered (think Chinggis Khan), Alexander's reputation as a heroic figure inspired both Greeks and Persians to claim him as their own after his death, although as a Macedonian he was neither. A popular fiction of his life, *The Alexander Romance*, was translated into many languages during Hellenistic times, survived the collapse of the ancient world that produced it, and continued on in medieval Latin texts as well as in classical Persian poetry still loved and recited today.

Alexander became the ruler of Macedonia in 336 B.C. after the assassination of his father, Philip II. During his twenty-three-year reign, Philip transformed Macedonia into a regional power with conquests in Thrace

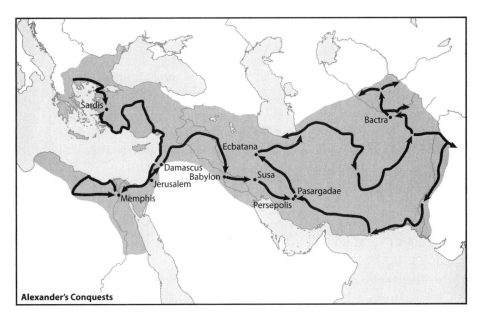

Alexander's Conquests

MAP 4.4. Alexander the Great's empire.

and mainland Greece that included all its major city-states but Sparta. In 338 B.C. he organized a new Hellenic League at Corinth with himself as head for the avowed purpose of mounting a war of revenge against the Persian Empire. However, much had changed in Greece since the original Hellenic League repulsed the invasions of Darius and Xerxes a century and a half earlier. By imposing his hegemony over the mainland Greek city-states, Philip had proved himself a more immediate threat to their independence than the Persian Empire. It was now a status quo power content within its existing borders and, far from seeking its overthrow, the Greeks were supplying the Persians with a steady flow of mercenary troops who served the Great King and his satraps loyally, often in elite positions. Any war with Persia would inevitably pit Greeks against other Greeks, many of them Athenian. Moreover, cold calculation suggested that invading the world's largest empire would be a high-risk enterprise. The Great King Artaxerxes III (r. 356–338 B.C.) had just restored the empire's lapsed authority in the eastern Mediterranean by suppressing a rebellion of Phoenician city-states (345 B.C.) and regaining control of Egypt (343 B.C.). As a result, Persia once again had a large fleet at its command that could threaten the Ionian coastal and island city-states Philip was attempting to woo to his side. That strategy was upended by Philip's assassination and a subsequent Persian victory over his Macedonian advance guard that had invaded parts of Asia Minor in 336 B.C. Athens and Thebes also revolted upon Philip's death, forcing his son and successor, Alexander, to invade Greece in 335 B.C. to bring them and their allies back in line. In a swift campaign he leveled the city of Thebes after fierce fighting and enslaved its people—a shocking act of violence that immediately induced the surrender of Athens. With that and a preemptive strike in Thrace to protect his rear, Alexander crossed the Hellespont into Asia Minor in 334 B.C. He landed with thirty-two thousand infantry and five thousand cavalry to join the thirteen thousand Macedonian troops dispatched there earlier. With an elite phalanx core numbering twelve thousand at its center, his fifty thousand troops were the largest invasion force ever to come out of the West. With this army, which was unlike any the Persians had faced before, Alexander's goal was not to liberate a part of the empire but to conquer all of it.[27]

The empire Alexander was attacking had formidable resources at its disposal and was politically stable, Darius III having just won the violent succession struggle that ensued following the death of Artaxerxes III. Yet because ancient Greek authors always portrayed the Persians as corrupted by luxury and united only in their servile embrace of tyranny, it has long been assumed that the empire must have been on the verge of economic and military collapse when Alexander invaded—requiring only a strong, manly push to bring it crashing down. This was far from the case, as scholars like Pierre Briant, who come to the war from the perspective of Achaemenid history, make clear:

> Contrary to a commonly held idea, the Achaemenid empire had not fallen into a state of accelerated decline in the fourth century [B.C.]. Nor is there any sign of an economic crisis or of widespread discontent. The Great King was always able to rely on the loyalty of the great Persian families and on the cooperation of local elites. This does not mean, however, that the empire was in a state of total tranquility. There had been revolts, including a recent one in Egypt (the so-called revolt of Khababash), but overall imperial authority was accepted inasmuch as the unity of the empire rested on the recognition of its regional and local diversity. . . . The Great King's financial resources were also virtually limitless, since he had the accumulated treasures of Susa, Ecbatana, Persepolis, and Babylon at his disposal, as well as the provincial treasuries (for example in Sardis and Tarsus), and the many mints in the western satrapies.[28]

Paradoxically it was the very stability and wealth of the Persian Empire that made Alexander's conquest of it possible. While it relied on conventional warfare to defeat a unitary state, a vanquisher empire could not conclude such a military campaign successfully without exploiting the stored wealth and the administrative structure of the empire it was attacking. The first financed and supplied the army as it made its rapid conquests; the second provided the new regime with an efficient way to govern its conquered territories without disruption. In such a zero-sum game, the more of an old empire's resources an invader acquired through conquest, the harder it was for that empire to regain its stability. When the leaders of the now-wounded empire could no longer command enough resources or authority to continue the war, its own elites abandoned them for positions in the new regime that needed their administrative skills and deep connections with the local population. This recruitment heralded the transition from conquest in war to administration in peace, which required a different set of political priorities. Attention paid to the installation of an alien set of rulers at the top obscures the degree of continuity remaining among the people who staffed the government's lower levels and the persistence of existing institutions of governance. During such periods, the conquerors' rank-and-file troops habitually complained their leaders were being "corrupted" by adopting too much of the culture of the defeated empire and its hierarchical values. Choices of clothing, court ceremonial practices, and marriages with indigenous elite families provoked particular ire, but the clearest example of the new world emerging was realization by the rank and file that their leaders had no intention of ever returning themselves or the new empire's capital back to their old frontier homeland.

Alexander was well aware of this dynamic, and it was reflected in his military campaign. While he had an excellent source of manpower in Macedonia, he did not have the economic reserves to keep them in the field for very long. These he first obtained after his victory at the Battle of the Granicus River in May 334 B.C., which resulted in the defection of the Lydian satrap and the treasure he controlled in its capital of Sardis. Alexander then moved his army south to Cilicia, although he was less successful in gaining the defections of other Persian garrisons along the way. In the meantime, Darius III responded to the defeat of his satraps' locally recruited forces by taking personal charge of the war, leading an imperial army west from Babylon to link up with the remaining Persian and mercenary troops who had retreated south. Alexander and Darius then confronted each other directly at the Battle of Issus in November 333 B.C., where the Persians were defeated, in part because they fought on ground favorable to Alexander that limited the deployment of their larger numbers. Darius fled east back to Babylon to mobilize a new army while Alexander moved south to take control of Syria, the Levant, and Egypt. While critics have faulted Alexander for not immediately pursuing Darius after his victory at Issus, such a course would have been reckless because the Persians still had active forces in play behind him, their navy commanded the eastern Mediterranean coast, and Sparta was plotting with Persia to play a fifth-column role in Greece. By seizing the Phoenician city-states and Egypt, Alexander deprived the Persians access to their ports and ships, undermining the empire's capacity to support the Persian garrisons still in Ionia or to conduct amphibious attacks on his rear.

The Persians had policies in place for putting down revolts and recovering lost territories. The king of kings would order his satraps to raise troops for him, and when everything was in order he would march against his foes with overwhelming numbers. This could take some time. Herodotus wrote that Darius the Great had taken three years to assemble his army and navy for a second invasion of Greece, which was delayed another seven years by his death and a war in Egypt before Xerxes took it up again.[29] But because the empire's center was never in danger, Persia had the luxury of choosing when to go to war. If its armies were defeated, the setback could be remedied in new wars mounted months or years later. Egypt, Ionia, or Babylon might throw off the Persian yoke for a time, but the empire always struck back. The war with Alexander was different because he was taking the initiative and his aim was to conquer the empire itself. Although Alexander had fewer troops, they were more experienced in battle and moved faster than the Persians, whose imperial armies were assembled only periodically as the need arose. The Persians partially compensated for this by dipping into their immense wealth to employ large numbers of Greek (and other) mercenaries who augmented their satrapal forces, a rare practice in the fifth century that had become commonplace by the late fourth century B.C. Alexander executed or enslaved many thousands of these mercenaries after they surrendered at the Battle of the Granicus River with the excuse that Greeks fighting on the Persian side were traitors deserving no mercy. This alienated their natal Greek cities (particularly Athens) that were supposed to be his allies and gave those Greeks still fighting for the Great King a good reason not to abandon him. Although Alexander's victories over the Persians at Granicus and Issus were impressive, they had only given him control of the non-Persian satrapies in the west that were least loyal to the empire. The next phase of the war would require the invasion of Mesopotamia and the adjacent Iranian plateau, which constituted the Persian Empire's core and contained its most important cities, Babylon, Susa, Persepolis, and Ecbatana, that were also the gateways to the empire's eastern provinces, about which the Greeks then knew very little.

With time to prepare in Babylon and well in advance of Alexander's arrival, Darius amassed troops and carefully chose their next battlefield at Gaugamela on the upper Euphrates River. It was a wide, flat plain suitable for deploying a large number of troops where the Persians would have a tactical advantage. Darius even ensured that it was raked clear of stones so that he could deploy scythed chariots. In October 331 B.C. the armies of Alexander and Darius met for their second set-piece battle in which both commanders personally led their troops. On horseback, Alexander charged the Persian center held by Darius and forced him to flee the field, leading to a rout of the remaining Persian forces. This defeat induced the satraps of Babylon and Media, two of the empire's richest provinces, to surrender to Alexander. Alexander then made a quick winter march east into the mountains and captured Persepolis in January 330 B.C., putting the bulk of the empire's stored treasure in his hands. Having reappointed the satraps of Babylon and Media to their existing posts, Alexander won more defectors from the Persian elite by letting them continue to rule their satrapies as well. Allowing no time for Darius to regroup at Ecbatana, Alexander pursued the Great King relentlessly until he was murdered by his own satraps in July 330 B.C. This marked the formal end of the Achaemenian Empire, and Alexander now styled himself king of Asia. While his Macedonian army would have been happy to declare victory and return home at this point, Alexander saw his work as unfinished because more than half of the Persian Empire's territory still lay untraversed to his east.[30]

Alexander had needed to win only three major battles over the course of four years to defeat the Great King and gain control of his empire, the world's largest. This was a conventional war and it resulted in a conventional victory. After Darius's death, however, it became clear just how much of Alexander's success was due to having a single fixed target to attack. Local leaders in Bactria and Sogdiana, who had always acted more as the Great King's allies than his subjects, refused to accept Alexander's rule and mounted a bloody insurgency against him from 329 to 327 B.C. Alexander responded with a scorched-earth policy directed not just at the combatants but at the general population. He divided his army into smaller groups "and gave orders that the fields should be set on fire and that all who were of military age should be killed."[31] Alexander's troops, accustomed to fighting conventional battles with identifiable enemies and clear outcomes, grew dispirited fighting a dirty war that had neither. In the end, both sides saw this war as unwinnable and struck a deal for peace. It included positive acts of reconciliation such as Alexander's marrying Roxanna, the daughter of one of the rebel leaders, and bringing large numbers of Bactrian cavalry into his own army. It also had a punitive side. Alexander left a large garrison force in central Asia to preserve order that was augmented by European colonists he settled in new cities at various strategic sites in the region.[32] Alexander then set out for India, where he captured new territories east of the Indus River but had to end his campaign after his troops mutinied in August 326 B.C., fearful that he would otherwise never stop. After sailing down the Indus River and conquering cities there en route, Alexander completed a grueling march west across today's Baluchistan and arrived back in Susa in early 324 B.C.

Not since Darius the Great had a ruler personally led troops to every corner of the Persian Empire as Alexander had done. But, again like Darius the Great, Alexander realized that bringing political order and stability to his immense empire was a bigger task. This new structure would require the Macedonians to accept a high but subordinate status within a hierarchical system in which they would all be subjects of Alexander, imperial king of Asia, not the boon companions of a Macedonian monarch. It would require the Persians to accept that his empire had permanently replaced their old one, much as the Medes had been forced to do by Cyrus when he established the Achaemenid dynasty two centuries earlier. Alexander also had to merge Macedonian and Persian traditions in ways that increased his authority rather than undermining it. Thus, he refused to wear the high tiara crown of a Persian king of kings but did adopt other royal regalia, symbolically distinguishing himself from the Great Kings he had replaced while sending a message to the Macedonians that he was free to wear other varieties of imperial Persian dress they associated with oriental despots.[33] Sometimes the clash of cultural expectations could not be immediately bridged. Nowhere was this clearer than in the controversy over the court ritual of *proskynesis*, the Persian custom of kneeling or inclining the upper part of the body accompanied by a hand gesture when approaching the king. While this was a regular way of acknowledging a superior that had no particular religious overtones for the Persians, the Greeks had long objected to performing the ritual when visiting the Persian court, arguing it was a form of abject submission appropriate only when paying homage to the gods. Briant notes that Alexander's demand that the ritual be performed by both groups while in Bactria in 327 B.C.

provoked an angry response from the Macedonians: "The Macedonians' refusal, whether expressed openly or concealed, was not merely a theoretical issue. It showed that they continued to regard the Iranians as beneath them, the vanquished foe, and they were intent on treating them as such. Alexander was sensible enough not to insist on the ceremony, and proskynesis was evidently not demanded again from the Macedonians."[34] Alexander must have realized then that creating a truly cosmopolitan empire under his personal management would require a generational time frame to accomplish, and this may help explain the flurry of activity he engaged in at Susa to lay its foundation. Before this began, however, he conducted a political purge as he was returning from India by dismissing or executing a number of powerful satraps who had taken advantage of his absence. The charges against the Macedonian satraps centered on their abusing power, stealing personal and state property, and acting as if they were autonomous; the charges against the Persian satraps centered on suspicions that they were seeking to restore Achaemenid power. The only men still holding satrapies after the purge ended were Persians who had personal ties with Alexander and Macedonians who lacked the political stature of their predecessors. Alexander also commanded that the mercenaries hired by his satraps as garrison troops in Asia Minor be dismissed in 325 B.C. and sent east to seek employment in his own army. With the empire secure militarily, Alexander saw little need to bear the added expense of such garrisons, and taking troops away from provincial governors reduced their capacity to oppose him.

Once in Susa, Alexander made his boldest moves to begin the transformation of his shadow vanquisher empire from the periphery into an endogenous empire with its center in the old Persian heartland. In February 324 B.C. Alexander married two Achaemenid princesses, Stateira (daughter of Darius III) and Parysatis (daughter of Artaxerxes III), women of much higher rank than Roxanna. Because he had no Macedonian wife, Alexander's future heirs would all be of mixed nationality and some descended from the most prestigious Achaemenid royal lineages. Alexander's best friend and alter ego, Hephaestion, married Stateira's sister Drypetis at the same time so that their children would be related. In addition to these marriages, Alexander organized a lavish mass wedding where eighty of his Hetairoi (Companions) also took elite Persian wives. (Unlike Alexander, they were not enthusiastic about the arrangement, and all but one, Seleucus, divorced them after he died.) While the Macedonians may have seen these marriages as demonstrating his favoritism to the Persians, Alexander was sending a different message: his empire's center and its rulers would remain in the lands of Persia. Over the course of the coming decades, Alexander could expect that membership in his empire's political elite would come to be defined by social class rather than ethnic origin. In this process Macedonian and Greek prejudices against the Persians (and Persian hostility toward them) would gradually recede with the emergence of a new bilingual and multiethnic generation that would have eventually viewed such prejudices as parochial and old fashioned.[35]

For Alexander, the primary means to this end was not the creation of happy mixed families but the reorganization of the empire's military. He had stopped campaigning in India only when his Macedonian troops refused to follow him any farther, making the point that a Macedonian king was in some ways still a first among equals who needed to maintain his army's political support. Unlike a Persian king of kings, he could not demand blind obedience. Access to Iranian wealth and manpower allowed Alexander to change that equation. He raised new Iranian units, trained and equipped to fight as the Macedonians did, and added these to existing units that had already become more mixed as local replacements had filled their manpower gaps during the India campaign. At the time of the Persian marriages, Alexander raised their status by promoting auxiliary Iranian units into his elite Companion cavalry and recruiting a new Iranian cavalry unit armed with Macedonian lances rather than the Iranian javelins. Alexander also welcomed the arrival in Susa of the thirty-thousand-man Iranian phalanx he had ordered trained in Bactria in 327 B.C. Giving that unit the name of Epigonoi (Successors) was an ominous sign to the Macedonians who had previously viewed themselves as irreplaceable. Their anger came to a head in a mutiny at Opis on the upper Euphrates in the summer of 324 B.C. "when Alexander announced to the army that the men no longer fit for service (due to wounds or age) would be sent back to Macedon with substantial severance pay. The infantry took this as proof that Alexander no longer wanted their service and would, henceforth, rely exclusively on the Iranian phalanx."[36] Alexander's response was to raise the status of even more Iranian units, and within a few days the Macedonian troops capitulated and begged to be reconciled. Alexander then sent the veterans home after paying off their substantial debts and promising to care for the mixed-marriage children they left behind, another future source of military manpower that would be loyal to him alone. As Briant concludes, "In the space of two years (324–323), Alexander succeeded in mobilizing a completely new army in which Macedonians and Iranians served cheek by jowl. In the short term, this made it possible for him to contemplate his immediate plans for further conquests with renewed optimism, as he was well aware that Macedon was exhausted by his continuous manpower levies. As for his chances for long-term success, the best guarantees would be seeing the territories gathered into a unified empire and Macedonians and Iranians collaborating in a combined army."[37] Had Alexander lived another twenty or thirty years, he might have had an empire that also included Arabia and North Africa (his next targets) and surpassed the Achaemenid Empire in its capacity to organize diversity to its own advantage. That would have created a multinational Hellenistic world that ran from North India to Spain, a unified cultural zone only comparable to the Muslim Caliphate established in the same region a thousand years later. But the process of becoming an endogenous empire ceased abruptly when Alexander died of fever in Babylon in June 323 B.C. and power fell into the hands of his Macedonian generals (known collectively as the Diadochi), who had never shared his vision. Most of them were interested only in the western regions of Egypt, Asia Minor, and Macedonia/Greece, where they established successor kingdoms and fought one another. The eastern parts of the Persian Empire eventually fell under the control of the long-lived Seleucus (358–281 B.C.). He was the only one of Alexander's Companions who retained his Persian wife, Apama, from the 324 B.C. mass marriage at Susa, and she would eventually become a queen whose son succeeded Seleucus upon his death. The Seleucid Empire (312–63 B.C.) maintained the Iranian model of government and was the largest polity ruled by any of the Diadochi.[38] The Seleucid Empire soon lost control of its eastern territories to the Iranian Parthians in today's Turkmenistan, to the Greco-Bactrian Kingdoms in today's Afghanistan, and to the Indian Mauryan Empire. It would be the Parthians under Mithridates I (r. 171–132 B.C.) and Mithridates II (r. 124–91 B.C.) who ended their empire and forced its retreat into Anatolia and Syria, where it was eventually swallowed up by the Romans.

THE ISLAMIC CALIPHATES: TRANSFORMATION FROM EXOGENOUS TO ENDOGENOUS EMPIRE

A newly established vanquisher empire always had factions within its elite that pulled in opposing directions. One sought to transform it into an endogenous empire by recruiting new people into its ruling class who could provide stronger local connections and missing administrative skills. The other sought to preserve the privileges of the conquest elite even if this resulted in the fragmentation and ultimate dissolution of the empire. Those intent on making the empire endogenous saw their initial victories as first steps in a longer building process that forwent short-term profit taking in favor of long-term investments in the places they now ruled. They had no intention of returning to the poor backwaters from which they had emerged. Their opponents, by contrast, were much keener on reaping those short-term profits immediately and sharing them with as few people as possible. They saw returning home as no bad outcome, and if they did have to live in foreign lands, it would be as resident expatriates lording it over the locals. This faction suspected that their "jam tomorrow" rivals would produce the promised jam at their expense for an empire that could then do without them. As we saw earlier, it was Alexander who sought the endogenous path, which his generals abandoned upon his death. The next vanquisher empire, that of the Muslim Arabs a millennium later, would face the same problem but would succeed in transforming itself from an exogenous empire of exclusively Arab composition focused on warfare under the Umayyads (661–750) into a multinational endogenous empire focused on governance under the Abbasids (750–1258) in which Islam itself would become a universal rather than exclusively Arab religion.

The Rise of the Arabs and Creation of an Islamic State

The empire established by the Umayyad dynasty had its origin in the deserts of central Arabia where Muhammad, a native of Mecca, proclaimed the receipt of a new monotheistic revelation from God. Associating himself with earlier monotheistic prophets such as Abraham for the Jews and Jesus for the Christians, Muhammad declared that Allah had sent this new message to the Arabs, commanding them to follow the one true God. This message was not well received in pagan Mecca, reconfirming Jesus's observation (Luke 4:25) that "no prophet is accepted in his own country." Muhammad and his followers had to flee the city to seek refuge in Medina in 622, a flight (*hijra*) that now marks the beginning of the Muslim calendar era. There Muhammad became its ruler and gained religious followers among a number of Arab tribes. He conquered Mecca in 630, at which time the city's Qureshi tribal elite adopted Islam. Much to the displeasure of the prophet's earliest supporters, they would later take the lead in the formation of an Arab empire that came into being after Muhammad's immediate successors unified the tribes in the Arabian Peninsula following his death in 633. Under Islam's first two caliphs, Abu Bakr (r. 632–634) and Umar (r. 634–644), these tribes attacked the Byzantines in Syria and the Sasanians in Iraq. Byzantine forces suffered a major defeat at the

Battle of Yarmouk in 636 that led to the loss of Syria to the Arabs and their permanent occupation of Damascus. Sasanian forces were routed at the Battle of al-Qadisiyyah at the same time and the Arabs captured their capital of Ctesiphon the next year, giving them control of Mesopotamia. Such rapid expansion exacerbated internal political tensions within the Muslim community, which was already divided both over the choice of Muhammad's successors and by preexisting rivalries among the Arab tribes that served as its military. This unrest led to Umar's assassination in 644, opening an era of sectarian conflict in which his two immediate successors, Uthman (r. 644–656) and Ali (r. 656–661), also died violently. That period of turmoil (*fitna*) ended after Ali's death with the establishment of a more stable successor government, the Umayyad dynasty led by Caliph Mu'awiya I (r. 661–680). Under Mu'awiya, who had been the governor of Syria since 639 and was a scion of the old Qureshi Meccan elite, the empire's center of gravity shifted away from Arabia to Syria with Damascus as its center.

The tribal peoples in Arabia had never previously endangered the long-established (more than six-hundred-year-old) Roman/Byzantine and Parthian/Sasanian empires to their north. Historically these empires were more focused on dangers from each other and those posed by a succession of horse-riding nomads coming out of the Inner Asian steppe zone. However, despite their military capacity, none of these steppe nomadic groups ever threatened Iranian or Byzantine core territories. The Parthians and Sasanians lost a number of eastern provinces in Sogdiana, Balkh, and the Hindu Kush to invading Kushans (30–270), Kidarites (350–450), and Hephthalites (450–550) who established states there, but none ever conquered territories on the mountainous Iranian plateau or in Mesopotamia, and eventually most of these eastern provinces reverted back to Iranian control. The Huns, who experienced an explosive growth of power under Attila (r. 434–453), were more interested in extracting gold from the Byzantines than replacing them, and their polity disintegrated soon after Atilla's death. The western Turk khaganate (552–657) and Khazars (650–850) had close relationships with both empires (and their Islamic successors) reinforced by strong trading ties.

The tribes in Arabia (whether nomadic or sedentary) were organized quite differently from those on the Eurasian steppe, where a tradition of hierarchical social organization facilitated the formation of centralized political structures with autocratic hereditary leaders. By contrast, the tribes in Arabia were organized into egalitarian lineages that united only to fend off outside attacks and fractured once the threat receded.

Anthropologists refer to this process as segmentary opposition: "Me against my brothers; my brothers and me against our cousins; my brothers, my cousins, and me against the world." Such segmentary lineage organizations developed most commonly in regions where people engaged in subsistence agriculture or pastoralism that produced little in the way of a surplus that might allow for the development of class divisions. Both leaders and their followers lived lives of relative poverty, reinforcing cultural values that emphasized equality of status. As a result, such tribal leaders lacked what ibn Khaldun called royal authority, the ability to command. They could neither resolve a dispute nor go to war without first mustering a group consensus on the rightness of the action—and the larger the group involved, the harder this was to achieve. While divisions into autonomous tribes preserved local independence, its major shortcoming was an inability to ensure people's safety. Without any centralized leadership to preempt violent acts committed by rival groups, blood feuds were endemic, raids on livestock were common, and access to collective resources such as land or wells was never secure. From the perspective of the Byzantine and Sasanian Empires they bordered, however, the persistence of political anarchy and tribal infighting in Arabia was not a bad state of affairs. As long as people there were busy clashing with one another, the only threat they posed to imperial order was as raiders of caravans and frontier settlements who could be deterred by engaging in punitive counterraids, creating networks of local allies, and denying disfavored tribes the right to trade.[39]

Muhammad was far from the first religiously inspired leader to emerge in this region with a message of unity through common faith. Indeed, what we now call the Middle East was the home to more revolutionary religious movements than any other place in the world, some of which grew well beyond the people and cultures in which they originated. In the centuries before the coming of Islam, both monotheistic Christianity and dualistic Manichaeism had emerged as major religions in the Roman/Byzantine and Sasanian Empires, respectively. However, because these empires took a dim view of social movements that threatened their absolute supremacy, the founding prophets of both religions fell victim to state violence: the Romans crucified Jesus in 33 and the Sasanians executed Mani in 277. Despite this unpromising start, both religions eventually came to an accommodation with the states that killed their founders and later wielded considerable influence within them. Christianity would become the state religion of the Roman/Byzantine Empire in the fourth century, and its followers were also found in growing numbers in the Sasanian Empire. While

Zoroastrianism remained the Sasanian state religion, Manichaeism successfully competed for adherents in both empires and spread east into central Asia and China as well. Empires also violently suppressed adherents of long-established religions whenever champions of unrest arose among them. Rome fought a series of Jewish Wars, the last of which led to the destruction of Jerusalem in 70. And when a heterodox interpretation of Zoroastrianism known as Mazdakism sparked a radical social movement in Iran during the late fifth century, the Sasanian Empire ended it by killing Mazdak and a large number of his followers in 528.[40]

Islam took a different path from previous religious movements in the region because of where it arose and how it was organized. Christianity and Manichaeism were faiths that emerged in the densely settled towns and villages of Greater Syria and Iraq that were ruled by powerful states, but Islam recruited its first adherents from among the stateless tribally organized people of central Arabia, many of whom were nomads. Once their religions were established, Christians and Manichaeans (and the more ancient Zoroastrians and Jews of the Second Temple period in Jerusalem) constructed hierarchical institutionalized ecclesiastic organizations whose ordained clerics set themselves apart from the mass of ordinary believers. It was a structure that resembled the hierarchical administrative systems of the empires in which they practiced. Islam had no such institutional ecclesiastic structure or even an ordained clergy set apart from other believers, all of whom were held to be of equal status. It was a structure that reflected the traditional local autonomy and egalitarian beliefs that were normative among the tribes in Arabia where the faith began.[41] These egalitarian values and the equality of all believers proved harder to maintain when Islam expanded into societies with deeply rooted class hierarchies whose cultural values differed markedly from those of the religion's desert Arab founders.[42]

But perhaps Islam's sharpest divergence from patterns displayed by Christianity and Manichaeism was in the role played by its founder. While the founding prophets of Christianity and Manichaeism restricted themselves to seeking religious adherents, they were still eventually arrested and killed by state authorities running the empires in which they resided. Although Muhammad's life was threatened by his enemies in Mecca after he began his preaching there, he had nothing to fear from Byzantine and Sasanian authorities, who would have undoubtedly ended his career prematurely had he begun it in their territories. Mecca and Medina, however, lay in the central Arabian desert region of the Hejaz, well beyond the control of Egypt and Greater Syria to the north and the Sasanian-administered territories along the Persian Gulf and in Yemen. The absence of any strong state presence in the Hejaz, indigenous or foreign, provided Muhammad a unique opportunity that he exploited after arriving in Medina as a refugee prophet from Mecca in need of sanctuary. The city's residents, in need of a leader acceptable to its many factions, eventually appointed Muhammad as their ruler. As a charismatic prophet, Muhammad stood outside and above the tribal system he was asked to govern in Medina, free to break with customary practices and existing norms. In serving as both a religious prophet and political leader, Muhammad ensured that these two roles would become thoroughly entangled and inseparable. Unlike Christianity or Manichaeism, whose founders never wielded secular authority, Islam was as much a political movement as it was a religious one. This melding of secular and religious authority was evident in the changing content of earlier and later Quranic chapters (suras). As Theodor Nöldeke writes, the suras produced in Medina deal much more with law, political divisions, and changing alliances than do the more spiritual verses attributed to Muhammad's earlier time in Mecca when he (like Jesus or Mani) held no political position: "Since Muhammad was unable to distinguish precisely between religious and mundane matters, he frequently used the authority of the Koran to issue ordinances that are not at all related to religion. When reviewing these facts, it must not be overlooked that at that time religion and the social order were closely connected, and that by involving God in the most human affairs daily life thus became elevated to a higher, divine sphere."[43] Islam's future leaders would, like the faith's founder, continue filling the dual roles of a supreme leader of the faithful and a chief executive officer of what became an imperial state. The tension between these two roles was a perennial source of conflict. Political disputes cloaked themselves in religious garb and no religious debate was ever free of politics. Unlike Christians dealing in the Roman Empire who heeded Jesus's admonition (Mark 12:17) that believers should "render to Caesar the things that are Caesar's, and to God the things that are God's," for Muslims government and religion were inseparable. Many states sponsored an established religion, but only Islam sponsored its own state.

The transformation from a group of fractious tribes into the nucleus of a powerful empire under the banner of Islam occurred when Muslims began to view themselves as members of a single *umma* (community) with a shared religious identity that transcended tribal divisions. This, ibn Khaldun concluded, permitted Arab tribes that would never willingly take commands from leaders of a rival tribe to unite in the name of God and willingly follow his prophet's orders:

Bedouins can acquire royal authority only by making use of religious coloring, such as prophethood or sainthood, or some great religious event in general. The reason is because of their savagery, the Bedouins are the least willing of all nations to subordinate themselves to each other, as they are rude, proud, ambitious, and eager to be leaders. Their individual aspirations rarely coincide. But when there is religion (among them) through prophethood or sainthood, then they have some restraining influence upon themselves. The qualities of haughtiness and jealousy leave them. It is easy then to unite (as a social organization). This is illustrated by the Arab dynasty of Islam. Religion cemented their leadership with religious law and its ordinances, which, explicitly and implicitly, are concerned with what is good for civilization.[44]

In the early days of Islam, however, religious laws and ordinances that were good for civilization proved less significant than the opportunities unification gave for conquering others. Segmentary lineages were organizations well designed for predatory expansion because it was always easier to achieve unity by attacking outsiders than insiders.[45] Patricia Crone puts this issue at the forefront of her polemical answer to the question, "Why did the Arabs in Muhammad's time find the vision of state structures and unification so attractive?" and asserts it was the promise of wealth and power in this world, not salvation in the next, that was the prime motivator: "God could scarcely have been more explicit. He told the Arabs that they had a right to despoil others of their women, children, and land, or indeed that they had a duty to do so: holy war consisted in obeying. Muhammad's God thus elevated tribal militance and rapaciousness into supreme religious virtues: the material interests were those inherent in tribal society, and we need not compound the problem by conjecturing that others were at work. It is precisely because the material interests of Allah and the tribesmen coincided that the latter obeyed him with such enthusiasm."[46] If this appears a bit harsh, remember that all empires in their conquest phase were rapacious and keen to take what belonged to others. But all other empires defined conquered territories and peoples as the exclusive property of the state, not that of the armies that fought its battles or the community at large. The early Muslim armies divided captured property and people among themselves in a rigorously equal manner, infamously cutting up an enormous Sasanian palace carpet into small pieces so each soldier could have an equal part of it.[47] Only when that phase was complete did a state structure emerge that was then able to subordinate the people who produced it. This was the reverse of the pattern seen among the nomads in Mongolia, where the unification of the steppe and the incorporation of its component tribes within a centralized political structure was completed well before their shadow empires took on China.

The Early Islamic Conquests

Muhammad died in 632 with no surviving sons. His four immediate successors were all men with affinal ties to the prophet, two as fathers-in-law (Abu Bakr and Umar) and two as sons-in-law (Uthman and Ali).[48] The first, Abu Bakr, was faced with a series of revolts known as the Ridda Wars (Wars of Apostasy), some of which stemmed from a simple refusal to pay taxes while others (seemingly taking a page from Muhammad's own handbook) recognized their own prophets and rejected Islam's political-religious hegemony. Both posed challenges to a regime that had just lost its charismatic leader. The first threatened its political stability and the second challenged its religious authority, and because Muhammad had combined the two, they could not be treated separately. Abu Bakr responded with force and quickly succeeded in bringing the rebel tribes back into line. This done, his successor Umar turned his attention to the rich lands of the north ruled by the Byzantine and Sasanian Empires.[49] The dates and details of the Arab invasions of Syria and Iraq are surprisingly elusive. Debates about the locations of battles or army movements that occurred during Alexander's campaigns all fall within a narrow range, but similar debates about the early Arab invasions involve different years and different places, and sometimes question whether they occurred at all. Here I set this aside and simply note that these successful wars in Syria and Iraq created a new empire and solidified the caliphate's hold over the Arabian heartland (map 4.5). It was also when the new Muslim polity became a vanquisher empire by defeating two of the superpowers of the age.

There has always been a question of how the Arabs managed to defeat both the Byzantine and Sasanian Empires, a feat never managed before by invaders from Arabia. Neither was on the verge of collapse when the Arabs attacked them. (Had that been the case, the Arabs would have resembled vulture empires picking up the pieces in North China or the Germanic tribes moving into the Western Roman Empire.) A century before, both the Sasanian and Byzantine Empires had contemporaneously produced two of their most outstanding emperors, Khosrau I (r. 531–579) and Justinian I (r. 527–565), who reformed their respective administrations and militaries. Both ousted

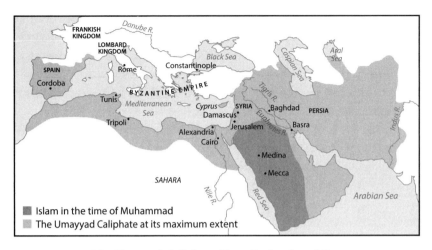

MAP 4.5. The Umayyad Caliphate. From Burbank and Cooper, 2010.

invading tribes that had long occupied territories on their periphery: Justinian regained North Africa, southern Spain, and Italy for the Byzantines, while Khosrau had restored Sasanian hegemony in central Asia by defeating the Hephthalites in alliance with the western Turk khaganate.

Between 602 and 628 the two empires engaged in a war that ended up weakening both of them, although each scored some great victories during it. The conflict began when a low-ranking military officer, Phocas, seized the Byzantine throne after murdering Emperor Maurice, who was the brother-in-law of the Sasanian emperor Khosrau II (r. 591–628). Khosrau declared war on the Byzantines, and Phocas's poor military leadership in that war led to his downfall in 610 when Heraclius (r. 610–641), the son of the governor of Carthage, ousted him and began the slow process of restoring the empire's military capacity. This was not easy, as the Sasanians continued to overrun one province after another, giving them control over territories in the west that had not been under Persian rule for nine hundred years. In 614 they conquered Syria and Palestine (hauling off the Christian True Cross from Jerusalem) and in 619 occupied Egypt. They also had armies in Armenia and Anatolia that reached the gates of Constantinople in 626. This string of victories ended when the siege of Constantinople failed to produce the expected surrender of the city and Heraclius went on the offensive. He invaded the Sasanians' core territories from the north and his troops were at the gates of their capital city of Ctesiphon in 628. A coup then toppled Khosrau II, and his successor agreed to a peace deal that restored the old boundaries between the two empires in 629 (and returned the True Cross to the Byzantines).[50] During the next four years there were as many shahs, with the political situation only stabilizing when the rival military factions combined to put the young Yazdegerd III (r. 632–651) on the throne. Aware of brewing trouble from the tribes in central Arabia, the Sasanians and Byzantines formed an unconsummated military alliance against them in 635.

For many centuries the frontier borderlands between Arabia and the empires in the north had been occupied by client Arab tribes whose leaders had established confederations there, the most important of which were the Byzantine-allied Ghassanids located on Syria's southwestern frontier and the Sasanian-supported Lakhmids in southern Iraq. They played two strategic roles. The first was as a barrier against incursions by other desert tribes to their south; the second was as fighters of proxy wars on behalf of their state sponsors. As was typical in such relationships, client confederations and their leaders were periodically at odds with their patrons. The Lakhmid confederation was dissolved and its territory absorbed by the Sasanians in 602 as they began their long war with the Byzantines. The Ghassanid confederation was also in conflict with the Byzantines before that war began and appears to have dissolved when the Sasanians captured Syria in 614. Whatever the political status of these confederations, their component tribes were the first targets of the Muslim armies when they began attacking north. Because the expansion of the caliphate was so rapid, these campaigns are generally viewed as clearing operations that allowed the Islamic armies to engage the Byzantines and Sasanians directly. However, unlike Alexander, who had a clear strategic vision of how he would conquer Achaemenid Persia, Abu Bakr and Umar do not appear to have had any such plans. It is more likely that they only intended to occupy the territories of the Ghassanids and Lakhmids as bases for future frontier raids and wars with the Byzantines and Sasanians. Just as the Byzantines and Sasanians had used these territories and their people to project power into the desert, the Muslims could use them to project desert power in the opposite direction. It was also an area bordering the desert that would allow for a safe retreat south if Muslim troops were defeated. Evidence for this can be seen in the fact that the initial battles in Syria were all east of the Jordan River, which was the old Ghassanid heartland, and that the early campaign in Iraq lay in the Lakhmids' home territory in the deserts west of the Euphrates River. As in Syria, where the Ghassanids allied with the Byzantines, many of the tribes in Iraq fought against the Muslim forces either as Sasanian allies or simply to preserve their autonomy. These earlier conflicts were

eclipsed by Arab victories at the Battle of Yarmouk against the Byzantines and the Battle of al-Qadisiyyah against the Sasanians around 636,
which gained them direct control of towns and cities in Syria and Iraq.
However, both these battles were fought in the heartlands of these old
Arab kingdoms, the Golan Heights south of Damascus in Syria and near
the old Lakhmid capital of al-Hira in Iraq. After their victories, the
invaders made these regions their own centers of gravity. They made the
new desert margin city of Kufa (adjacent to al-Hira) their ruling city in
Iraq rather than stay in Ctesiphon. In Syria they made Damascus, the
closest city to Ghassanid territory, their capital in preference to the old
Roman/Byzantine capital of Antioch.[51]

The Arab conquests in Byzantine-administered areas relied less on
winning battles than on accumulating the surrenders (on good terms)
of ungarrisoned cities and towns that had only recently returned to Byzantine control after fourteen years of Persian administration. As Walter
Kaegi describes the situation,

> Islamic tribesmen did not simply overrun a static and gravely weak-
> ened Byzantine Empire. Instead, their invasions occurred while Byz-
> antium was still in the process of restoring her authority over the
> full extent of the former eastern borders of the empire. Heraclius
> [the Byzantine emperor] was in that region because he was person-
> ally involved in overseeing that restoration and reunification. If he
> had had more time, he might have succeeded. The Muslim invasion
> caught him and the empire off-balance at a very awkward time, and
> kept them off-balance. The exertion of minimal pressure at the critical
> moment and place was able to bring the Muslims maximal rewards in
> terms of military victories and territorial conquests, with a minimum
> of casualties. The Byzantines were just restoring their authority in the
> Syrian cities and countryside, but that process of restoration and cre-
> ation of lines of authority and a viable power structure with conscious
> identification with Byzantium was even more tenuous in the area east
> of the Jordan and the Dead Sea when the Muslims began their own
> probes and raiding, which they very soon greatly intensified.[52]

While the Arab conquest of Syria, the Levant, and then Egypt was a
major setback for the Byzantine Empire, it had weathered their earlier
loss to the Sasanians and the region was not as vital as the Balkans or
Anatolia for its continued survival. Arab attempts to expand north into
Anatolia failed because its Bedouin armies were not equipped to remain
in mountainous regions during seasons that were too cold and wet for

their dromedary camels. They could and did raid the region during the summer, but raids did not expand the size of the empire. Later attempts to capture the Byzantine capital by sea also failed, in part because of the distance involved but mostly because Constantinople's walled defenses were impregnable as long as the empire had troops to man them and ships to harass the besiegers.

The war in Iraq was initially deemed less significant than that in Syria, although its outcome would have a bigger impact. The Arabs of Mecca and Medina knew the Greater Syrian region well and some even owned land there. They were intimately familiar with its cities and had long-standing trade connections with them. Muhammad himself had traveled there on business earlier in his life and had later declared Jerusalem a city holy to Islam, a status it had long held for Jews and Christians. Iraq was a more alien and less familiar place to the Arabs from the Hejaz. It was part of a different trading network and within an empire where dualistic religions (Zoroastrianism and Manichaeism) were more common than monotheistic religions (Judaism and Christianity) or the pagan faiths prevalent in Arabia. Perhaps for these reasons, tribes from Arabia's east and south that had formerly been under Sasanian colonial rule took the lead in volunteering to campaign there. The first Muslim incursions on the frontiers of Iraq (similar to their advance into Syria) were designed to control the Arab desert tribes that had formerly been part of the older Lakhmid frontier confederation, not attack Sasanian strongpoints. Although the Sasanian Empire had just been through a period of political turmoil, it had fended off many frontier incursions like these over its previous four centuries of existence. At the Battle of the Bridge in 634, the Sasanians routed the Muslim army and inflicted a large number of casualties, forcing the Arabs to retreat back into the desert. The situation changed dramatically only after the Muslim victory at the Battle of al-Qadisiyyah in 636 led to the capture of Iraq's irrigated Mesopotamian plain (*sawad*) and the fall of the Sasanian winter capital of Ctesiphon in March 637. M. Morony explains that the occupation of these territories gave the Muslims a strong base for further expansion:

> The capital at al-Madā'en [Ctesiphon] had been the apex of [the Sasanian] administrative system, and Iraq had provided about one-third of their annual tax revenues. In addition, they lost the royal treasure, substantial military forces that perished defending Iraq, and the leadership of many high-ranking nobles. The Muslims now held these resources and were assisted by former members of the Sasanian army

and administration who had defected. By . . . the 640s, Muslim armies based in Iraq were as well organized, provisioned, and equipped as the Sasanians themselves.[53]

Although both the Byzantines and Sasanians lost territories and battles to the invading Muslim Arabs, only the Sasanian Empire collapsed, and for the same reason that the Achaemenid Empire fell to Alexander: it could not survive the loss of its center. After such a loss, Yazdegerd III, like Darius III, had no stable rearguard area from which to make a stand as the Arabs pursued his forces. By the time he was killed in 651, his empire no longer existed and his heir had fled to Tang China. Ibn Khaldun was perhaps the first to note that empires were designed to survive territorial losses on their frontiers but not the loss of their core territories:

> A dynasty is stronger at its center than it is at its border regions. . . .
> When the dynasty becomes senile and weak, it begins to crumble at its
> extremities. The center remains intact until God permits the destruc-
> tion of the whole (dynasty). Then, the center is destroyed. But when a
> dynasty is overrun from the center, it is of no avail to it that the outlying
> areas remain intact. It dissolves all at once. The center is like the heart
> from which the (vital) spirit spreads. Were the heart to be overrun and
> captured, all the extremities would be routed. This may be observed
> in the Persian dynasty. Its center was al-Mada'in (Ctesiphon). When
> the Muslims took over al-Mada'in, the whole Persian empire dissolved.
> Possession of the outlying provinces of the realm was of no avail to
> Yazdjard. Conversely, the center of the Byzantine dynasty in Syria was
> in Constantinople. When the Muslims took Syria away from the Byz-
> antines, the latter repaired to their center in Constantinople. The loss
> of Syria did not harm them.[54]

If the Muslim Arab armies moved from success to success on the battlefield and quickly took control of new territories in the wake of their
victories, they suffered from increasing disunion internally. As the new
Islamic state was becoming an empire, the question of who should rule
it generated succession struggles made worse because each occurred
in the wake of an incumbent's assassination: Umar in 644, Uthman
in 656, and Ali in 661. Because Muhammad had fused the state with
the religion, these disputes were both sectarian and political. The three
main religious factions were the Sunnis, Shias, and Kharijites. The
Sunnis asserted that succession was nonhereditary but limited to men
from the prophet's Quraysh tribe chosen by the leaders of the Muslim

community. The Shias argued for a hereditary succession limited to Ali and his heirs. The Kharijites took the radical position that the Muslim community could choose any person as caliph regardless of their social status or origin, even a slave, if they were pious and moral. Civil war, the First Fitna (656–661), broke out when Ali's ascension to the caliphate was challenged by Mu'awiya, the longtime governor of Syria. This was in part a struggle between factions with competing regional interests that included the old guard in Medina, Mu'awiya in Syria, and troops based in Iraq, where Ali had moved the capital to Kufa. The conflict seemingly presaged the division of the empire into independent kingdoms similar to those established by Alexander's generals after his death and in much the same places. This did not occur, however, because after Ali's forces won a set of initial victories, Mu'awiya was able to get him to arbitrate the dispute and then outplayed him politically. This alienated Ali's Kharijite allies, who then fought as an independent faction and assassinated him in 661. Mu'awiya became caliph, picked up the pieces, and moved to shore up the institutions of government. His twenty-year reign laid the foundation for a more stable empire and the emergence of the hereditary Umayyad dynasty.

The Umayyad Caliphate

It is with the Umayyad Caliphate that the empire vastly expanded to eventually encompass 11 million km², one of the world's largest by area. Despite its enormous size, the Umayyad Caliphate would retain its exogenous orientation until it was replaced by the endogenous Abbasid Caliphate, for which it had laid the foundation. The rulers of exogenous empires saw themselves as separate from the territories they dominated and attempted to use indirect forms of administration whenever possible. For the Umayyads this meant separating the Arab Muslim population socially and politically from the people they ruled in a type of ethno-religious apartheid regime. This could be seen in where they chose to settle, how they expanded and administered their territories, and their policies of social and religious exclusivity. While the Arab Muslim population in Syria settled on properties abandoned when the Byzantines withdrew, the Arabs avoided long-established population centers everywhere else. Instead they built new fortress cities (*rabat*) for themselves and their clients on the edges of the desert from which they could project their military power at a safe distance from the alien people whose taxes financed their empire.

Kufa and Basra replaced Ctesiphon in Iraq, Fustat (Cairo) replaced Alexandria in Egypt, Kairouan replaced Carthage in Tunisia, and in central Asia the Arabs concentrated themselves in Marv and avoided Samarkand, Bukhara, Balkh, and Herat. Even in Syria, the Umayyad capital of Damascus was a replacement for the region's Byzantine provincial center at Antioch since Damascus had well-established links with Arabia that Antioch did not.

The Umayyad Caliphate resolved many of its internal tensions by expanding into new territories from North Africa and Spain in the west to central Asia and the borders of India in the east. Discontented factions could find wealth and power in new lands rather that fight over existing ones. Unlike the Mongols, who planned their military campaigns centrally and provided imperial troops for them that were then withdrawn to fight elsewhere, the Umayyads ran a franchise empire. Leaders sought authorization from the caliph to engage in new conquests and then recruited their own troops who were promised a large share of the loot and landed estates in the territories they helped conquer. Thus, while the Umayyad equivalent of McDonald's golden arches appeared to be everywhere, the new territories (franchises) were operated by their governors (franchisees) and not by the Umayyad caliph (McDonald's head office), who collected a percentage of their revenue. And like McDonald's, these new governorships could adapt to local customs as long as they maintained basic commonalities.[55] In describing the role of Umayyad governors, Hugh Kennedy explains,

> It was not an absolute government in which governors were appointed and dismissed by a central authority but almost a confederation of different leaderships acknowledging one overall authority. From his provincial governors the caliph demanded that they accept his authority, that they keep order and that, in some cases, they forward revenues to the central government: it is recorded, for example, that of 60 million dirhams collected in the province of Basra, only 4 million were sent to Damascus, all the rest being spent in the province, mostly on paying the local military. Beyond that governors were allowed to establish their own power bases and assure the fortunes of their families and friends.[56]

Lacking their own civil officials and taxation system, the Umayyads were fortunate that both the Byzantine and Sasanian governmental structures remained functional in the areas they had conquered. As a result, the Umayyads saw no need to create a common empire-wide system of administration—the hallmark of an endogenous empire. They simply followed the procedures employed by the previous regimes implemented by an existing network of non-Muslim officials whose work they oversaw. This was a patchwork system where tax rates and administrative procedures developed in an ad hoc fashion during the conquest period without any attempt to standardize them. Even the old coinage was retained. The gold solidus (dinar) remained the standard unit of currency in Byzantine areas, while the silver Sasanian dirham was used in its former territories, and the Arabs only slightly modified existing coin designs when they later started to mint their own. Conquered settled areas provided the empire with a surplus of tax revenue, the extraction of which the Byzantines and Sasanians had raised to a high art. They had both imposed heavy poll taxes (a tax levied on every adult without reference to income or resources) and high fixed land taxes on all agricultural production. The Arabs, who required far less annual tax revenue to run their government than the old empires did, won popularity by reducing the existing levels of annual taxation from these high levels. Revenue flows were high enough to allow the Umayyads to levy lower land taxes on Muslim-owned estates than non-Muslim ones. Muslims were also exempted from the poll tax (*jazia*) applied to the *dhimmi*—Christians, Jews, and Zoroastrians, who were deemed "People of the Book," a protected but inferior status.[57]

A common misperception of the early Islamic conquests is that the Arabs were keen to spread their new monotheistic religion as widely as possible, by force if necessary. In reality, although they declared their God unique and universal, the first Muslims believed this revelation had been given to the Arabs alone and that Islam was distinct from both monotheistic Judaism and Christianity, whose prophets they recognized, not to mention the various dualistic religions that competed with them throughout the region. By fusing Arab tribal identity with the Muslim faith, early Islam more closely resembled the Judaism of the Torah (a religion limited to the Twelve Tribes of Israel) than it did the Christianity of the New Testament (a universalistic religion that actively recruited new believers). The wars within Arabia that sought conversions were thus aimed at pagan tribes that had no excuse for rejecting Islam, literally "submission to the will of God." Once they were united, God had promised the Muslim Arabs victories against their enemies that would bring them wealth and power. After those victories were achieved, they had no desire to share either their religion or their new riches with non-Arabs. So tight was the Arab-Muslim link initially that the only way for non-Arabs to become Muslims was to be simultaneously adopted into the Arab tribal system as clients (*mawālī*), thereby also becoming a kind of Arab themselves. Because God had rewarded believers alone, allowing non-Arabs to join the faith made the conquered and the conqueror equal, entitling Muslim converts (at least in theory) to the same benefits and elite status as the Arabs themselves—making conversion a source of political and economic advantage. Such conversions first took place among the large number of captured people who served the Muslim community and lived with them and later among a large number of non-Arabs who flocked to the new Arab centers, particularly Iraqi Kufa and Basra, to seek work or join the army.

In some ways, as Edward Luttwak concludes, this religious exclusivity facilitated the acceptance of Islamic political rule by its non-Muslim subject populations:

> With the Muslim Arabs few and mostly ensconced in their garrisons, everyone could live much as they pleased. Muslim discrimination, moreover, had the immense advantage of being nondiscriminatory— all categories of Christians and Jews were treated equally, whether well or badly. That was highly desirable for most of the population in the Byzantine territories that came under Muslim rule, starting with a majority of the Christians themselves: the Monophysites of Syria and Egypt. They had been harshly persecuted by the Byzantine authorities to persuade them to accept the christology of the Council of Chalcedon of 351 . . . whereby both divine and human natures coexist within the single essence of Christ. But most native Christians of Syria and Egypt were and remain Monophysites, adhering to the one-nature doctrine of their Coptic and Syriac Orthodox churches, while only a Greek-speaking and elite minority was Chalcedonian and therefore unpersecuted by the Byzantine authorities.[58]

When the Roman Empire was governed by pagans, it never attempted to impose a religious ideology of any type on the empire's subjects. While it suppressed religious sects deemed a danger to the state or fomenters of social disorder, Edward Gibbon famously observed that its basic rule was to stay out of religious affairs: "The policy of the emperors and the senate, as far as it concerned religion, was happily seconded by the reflections of the enlightened, and by the habits of the superstitious, part of their subjects. The various modes of worship, which prevailed in the Roman world, were all considered by the people, as equally true; by the philosopher, as equally false; and by the magistrate, as equally useful. And thus, toleration produced not only mutual indulgence, but even religious concord."[59] Such toleration disappeared when Christianity became the Roman Empire's state religion, for Christianity saw itself as not only a universal faith but an exclusive one. It tolerated no polytheists or dualists and barely tolerated the Jews, who worshiped the same God but had failed to transfer their allegiance to Jesus Christ. After suppressing pagans and dualists, Christian clerics then harnessed the power of the Roman state to enforce their own standards of religious orthodoxy, which defined many of the empire's otherwise loyal Christian citizens as heretics. This created political problems for the empire where none previously existed. Centuries before Muhammad created a state based on Islam, his Christian clerical predecessors had already wielded the power of state to fuse politics and religion. It would be a model soon adopted by the Muslims as Islam was transformed from a parochial faith of the Arabs into an aggressive universal religion that, like Christianity, would seek to convert nonbelievers to the true faith and punish existing believers deemed to have fallen into heresy. Of all types of religious believers, monotheists would prove the hardest to reconcile with the demands of cosmopolitan diversity that were the foundations of endogenous empires. It is perhaps no accident that the major Turko-Mongolian empires that appeared in their wake were not religiously based and, when they adopted a monotheistic faith, they did not impose it on others. China avoided the problem by never taking on a sectarian religious identity and maintaining a wary watch on all religious institutions within its empires.

Despite the huge size of the Umayyad Caliphate, it remained an exogenous empire because its rulers saw themselves as outsiders long after their rule had been accepted by the local populations (table 4.2).

Under the Abbasid Caliphate, all the missing endogenous elements listed in table 4.2 would be added by adopting an Iranian model of governance that would make Baghdad a primate imperial center and institutionalize government functions in a bureaucracy run by appointed viziers. Far more significantly, the Abbasids would make the spread of Islam as a universal religion their imperial project and create an Islamicate world in which Muslim identity superseded tribal Arab identity.

Table 4.2. Endogenous empire components in the Umayyad Caliphate

Present	Partial	Absent
Size: 11 million km²	Systems of communication that allowed administration of all subject areas from the center directly	Imperial project that imposed some type of unity throughout the system (kept Islam confined to Arabs)
Population: 62 million		Centralized institutions of governance that were separate and distinct from the rulers
Organized to administer and exploit diversity		A primate imperial center with transportation systems designed to serve it militarily and economically
Monopoly of force within their territories, and military force projected outward		

The Abbasid Revolution

Empires needed to organize diversity and did so by becoming equal opportunity oppressors. Any group that opposed imperial authority or incited rebellion became a target, regardless what motivated that opposition (religion, politics, ethnicity, social status, or economic condition). Endogenous empires, however, leavened that repression by eventually creating ways for conquered groups to enter their elite in some fashion so that they became more cosmopolitan over time. In chapter 1 we saw that Rome did this by expanding its definition of citizenship ever more widely and having emperors who came from different parts of the empire. The Persian king-of-kings system could always provide more slots for new subordinate kings, and China's creation of an empire-wide elite culture eventually erased the parochial regional identities that characterized the Warring States period. Exogenous empires, by contrast, resisted expanding their elites, a prejudice that could be maintained only if they ruled over relatively small populations and remained within their core area (Athens's maritime empire, the Xiongnu steppe empire). However, if they expanded into areas outside their core and had to rule over very large populations, their unwillingness to open their ruling elite more widely eventually led to their demise (vulture empires in North China, the Seleucid Empire in Iran) or to their transformations into endogenous empires that could incorporate a broader variety of people at the elite level even if their rulers were still drawn from the empire's creators (Mongol and Manchu China). After a half century in power, the Umayyads were confronted by this challenge, one that had profound implications not only for the structure of the empire and who ruled it but also for whether Islam would remain an exclusive Arab faith or become a universal one.

The position of caliph was again contested following the death of Muʿawiya in April 680 because he had insisted that his son Yazid succeed him, an innovation that was seen as illegitimate in many quarters. Husayn, a prime contender to become caliph as the last surviving son of Ali and Fatima, attempted to move himself and his family to Kufa in Iraq, where his allies were keen to support his claim. However, he and his small group of followers were intercepted by Yazid's forces and massacred at the Battle of Karbala in October. Yazid then turned his attention to the Hejaz, where ʿAbd Allāh ibn al-Zubayr had declared himself a caliph in Mecca. Umayyad troops went after him and his supporters first by capturing Medina in the summer of 683 and looting the city before attacking Mecca itself in the fall. During the siege the city's sacred Kaaba burned down, but the war ended when Yazid died in November. In the aftermath a collateral line of Umayyads under the leadership of the elderly Marwan I took control of the caliphate in 684. The dynasty regained its balance under his long-ruling son, ʿAbd al-Malik (r. 685–705), who both expanded the empire and increased its centralization. The Umayyads first tightened their military control over Iraq by sending troops from Syria to garrison its cities, but the dynasty's greatest innovations were organizational. The Umayyads now standardized their coinage and made Arabic the language of administration—an aspect of endogenous imperial thinking that eliminated local differences and forced existing Persian and Greek officials to work in the language of the conqueror rather than their own. More surplus tax revenue was sent directly to Damascus, a blow to the Iraqi cities that had grown rich by retaining the taxes collected in Mesopotamia.[60]

The Umayyad policy of expansion continued apace and reached its maximum extent with additions in the west from North Africa into Spain and in the east from central Asia to the Indus Valley. However, the new conquests failed to end the growing political divisions within the caliphate. The Arabs in Iraq no longer wanted to leave home to fight on distant frontiers regardless of the rewards on offer, and those who were conscripted anyway proved open to subversion once they got there. There were also unresolved conflicts between the Arabian tribes that came from the north (Qays) and those originally from the south (Yaman) that often verged on civil war. And Arab forces in central Asia and Spain were now so distant from Damascus that they saw themselves as autonomous actors and made deals with local non-Muslim allies to govern. But perhaps the dynasty's biggest structural problem was the growing number of non-Arab converts to Islam. In order not to lose tax revenue, the government refused to recognize them as equal to Arab Muslims and they continued to pay the same poll and land taxes as non-Muslims. This naturally produced discontent. In a process similar to Christianity's break with Judaism so that it could include gentiles in its ranks, non-Arab converts (and increasingly the descendants of such converts who were born Muslim) asserted that Islam was a universal religion in which a believer's membership in the Muslim community (*umma*) transcended any tribal, regional, or racial differences. While the Arabs might well take pride of place as Islam's first followers and the custodians of the holy sites of Mecca and Medina, they could not continue to act as if Islam were an exclusively Arab religion or assert a God-given superiority over other believers. If this had been purely a religious problem, it could have been handled relatively easily. Indeed, Umar II (r. 717–720) reformed the tax code to end the collection of poll taxes from converts and applied the land tax uniformly no matter who owned the property. These moves encouraged more people to become Muslims, and in some places officials began demanding they do so, but it is notable that these reforms took place a half century after the dynasty was founded and were reversed in many places after Umar II died.[61] What changing the tax system could not resolve was the issue of Arab political hegemony within the caliphate and the growing inability of the Umayyad's Syria-based political center in Damascus to manage the rising discontent emerging from the old Persian-speaking centers in Iraq, the Iranian plateau, and most importantly Khorasan (today's Afghanistan and central Asia).

Throughout the Umayyad Caliphate it had been the Arabs who took the lead militarily and politically. Thus, its history was one where the main action revolved around conflicts among its various factions: regional (Syrian and Iraqi), tribal (Qays and Yaman), and sectarian (Sunni, Shia, and Kharijite). Non-Arabs on the frontiers of the caliphate like the Berbers in North Africa or the Persian landowning nobility of eastern Iran appeared either as allies of these factions or as rebels opposed to them but always as responders to Arab actions. This began to change when the Persians challenged a century of Arab hegemony in general and the political dominance of Syria over Iraq and the Iranian east in particular. Just as the Parthians

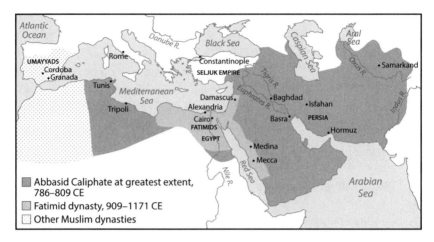

MAP 4.6. The Abbasid Caliphate. From Burbank and Cooper, 2010.

displaced the Seleucids to restore Persian rule over Iraq and the Iranian plateau, a similar transformation was taking place in Khorasan, where non-Arabs took the lead in toppling the Umayyad Caliphate in 750 and installing the first Abbasid caliph. Although the position of caliph would remain in Arab hands, the Arab tribes and the urbanized heirs of the Arab conquest elite who formerly ran the empire would be pushed to the margins. The result was a restoration of Persianate power and a transfer of the caliphate's political center from Damascus in Syria to Baghdad in Iraq, a new city located in the vicinity of the previous Achaemenid, Parthian, and Sasanian winter capitals of Babylon and Ctesiphon (map 4.6). While the Abbasid revolution is often described in sectarian terms because it began as a populist religious movement and justified its cause in Islamic terms, following its overthrow of the Umayyads it might be better seen as an Islamic state under new Iranian management or an Iranian empire with a new state religion. If the latter, it was following the cultural and religious trajectory of the Roman/Byzantine Empire, which had by the fifth century become a defender of a single monotheistic faith whose cultural values and religious symbolism came to define it.

The Abbasid revolt in Khorasan was led by a shadowy figure of probable Iranian origin whose identity and background are still subject to debate. Abu Muslim was the name he received from an Abbasid imam when he joined their cause as a young man and was made responsible for recruiting supporters to their cause in Khorasan. The Abbasids were one of many dissident groups based in Kufa, an Iraqi hotbed of anti-Umayyad politics. For a generation they had dispatched secret missionaries to distant Khorasan and other frontier areas in an attempt to start an insurgency against the Umayyads, asserting that they were tyrants who had usurped the caliphate from its rightful heirs.[62] Despite his youth Abu Muslim proved himself a charismatic leader, skilled military commander, and effective alliance builder. In 747 he raised the movement's black banner in Khorasan and began attacks on the Umayyad government there. In less than a year Abu Muslim had taken their center at Marv as well as the cities of Herat and Balkh. While the revolt is sometimes glossed as an ethnic Persian-Arab conflict, the situation in Khorasan was complicated since both the Umayyads and Abbasids had members of each group supporting them. In the view of Elton Daniel, Abbasid success there was based on mobilizing the power of two discontented multiethnic and anti-Umayyad populations: "(1) the bloc of 'middling class' Arab colonists, their *mawali* [clients], and the Iranian *dahaqin* [local landowners], all of whom resented the domination of Khurasan by an 'alien' Qaysite-Syrian military elite and its aristocratic Iranian collaborators, and (2) the native Iranian peasantry and mostly assimilated lower class Arabs, who wished to overthrow the landholding aristocracy and who dreamed of an egalitarian society based on a mixture of Islamic and neo-Mazdakite concepts. Through shrewd manipulation of these class antagonisms, the Abbasid propagandists managed to bring about a true mass uprising in Khurasan."[63] These pro-Abbasid groups (Persian and Arab) had developed a common Khorasani cultural identity that transcended their linguistic and ethnic differences, a structural pattern that continues today in northern and western Afghanistan.[64] As their armies moved west, the populations residing in central Iran, Iraq, and Syria certainly viewed them as a single group and one that stayed cohesive as members of the Abbasid Caliphate's new military elite. While many continued to reside in Khorasan, those who moved to the caliphate's new capital of Baghdad and their descendants retained a privileged status as *abna' ahl Khurasan* (sons of Khorasan) and later *abna' al-dawla* (sons of the state).[65]

Events moved quickly after Abu Muslim captured Marv and central Iran fell to the Khorasani troops in March 749. In September they captured Kufa in Iraq and soon named Abdallah Abul-'Abbas al-Saffah as caliph (r. 750–754). Up until this point the top Abbasid leaders had been bystanders in the revolution that bore their name and did not participate directly until joining the final campaigns in Syria, where Abu Muslim defeated the Umayyad caliph Marwan II at the Battle of Zab River in 750. Marwan was killed after he fled to Egypt, and the entire extended Umayyad family was later murdered, with only one survivor escaping to Spain, where a rump Umayyad Caliphate preserved itself until 1031. Thus, in only three years Abu Muslim had moved from being the leader of a small rebel group on the frontier to become the master of an empire whose last Umayyad ruler he had deposed and whose first Abbasid successor he had chosen. He retained the intense loyalty of his Khorasani troops and was the absolute ruler of Khorasan. A later Abbasid caliph, al-Ma'mun (r. 813–833), is reported to have said, "The greatest princes of the earth were three in number: I mean Alexander, Ardashir [founder of the Sasanian Empire], and Abu Muslim."[66] There was some irony here because the second Abbasid caliph and brother to the first, Abu Ja'far 'Abdallah al-Mansur (r. 754–775), was so fearful of Abu Muslim's power and prestige that he murdered him during a visit to the caliphal court in 755. In the aftermath al-Mansur succeeded in buying the political support of Abu Muslim's aggrieved Khorasani army commanders, whose future cooperation was secured by lavish subsidies to them and their heirs. Those of Abu Muslim's followers and their descendants who had been social and religious revolutionaries could not be so easily appeased. Over the coming century they would invoke his name and martyred memory during a series of rebellions that were either explicitly anti-Islamic or based on varieties of heterodox Islam the Abbasids rejected.[67]

G. H. Yusofi summarizes the various debates about what Abu Muslim's plans for the new state might have been since he, like Alexander, died young (thirty-seven) and before he could begin reorganizing the lands he had just conquered:

> Opinions vary on Abū Moslem's ultimate goal in the 'Abbasid revolution. Some claim he wished to establish a national Iranian government and that he fought the Omayyads, under the guise of a religious uprising, to gain control of the caliphate. Others attribute a purely religious motivation devoid of ethnic overtones. One may suggest that he sought simply to destroy the Omayyads and that the social and political aspects of the revolution were stronger than the religious; perhaps he eventually would have moved against the 'Abbasids as well. In any case the revolt marked a revival of Persian culture, which would long dominate the caliphal government; it was also a prelude to the rise of the local dynasties.[68]

What made this a Persian restoration was that its leaders were Iranian and its allies anti-Umayyad Arabs, rather than the reverse. What it did not do was restore a status quo ante in which the Sasanian elite and its cultural values had been dominant. This marked an epochal watershed because every previous Iranian empire from the Achaemenids onward had been under the control of a Zoroastrian Persian aristocratic elite. Although dynasties and empires changed, it was a ruling class and culture that preserved its cohesion and hegemony for 1,200 years. During that time its reign had been interrupted only once, by the Hellenistic Seleucid Empire, which itself was displaced by the Parthians after a century of rule, about the same amount of time that had now elapsed between the Arab conquest of the Sasanian Empire and Abu Muslim's vanquishing the Umayyads. After his victories the Persians were back in power again, but this time with an elite drawn from the ranks of nonaristocratic Iranians who rooted themselves in the Islamic faith rather than Zoroastrianism. It also marked a shift east in the historical locus of Iranian power from cities in Fars and Media (Susa, Ecbatana, Persepolis) to those in Khorasan and Transoxiana (Marv, Herat, Balkh, Bukhara). While the old Achaemenid/Sasanian cultural legacy would later be preserved in Ferdowsi's great Persian-language poetic epic, *The Shahnama*, that late tenth-century work would be read as a glorious account of a vanished world. Had Abu Muslim lived, perhaps he would have made himself (or an heir) the empire's secular ruler and relegated the Abbasid caliphs to a religious status similar to that of the Catholic popes in Rome. Be that as it may, the Iranians initially proved content to let the Arab Abbasid caliphs head the state while they wielded power within it as the viziers and bureaucrats who controlled its administration. This would prove to be a highly adaptable strategy and template for dealing with a later series of nomadic conquerors invading from the northeast that began with the arrival of the Seljuk Turks in the early eleventh century. For the next five hundred years all the region's empires would be founded by dynasties of Turko-Mongolian origin—every one of which would recruit literate Persian-speaking officials to administer their governments and collect their taxes.[69]

The Abbasid Caliphate met all the criteria for an endogenous empire outlined in chapter 1. Perhaps because of the now-stronger role of Iranians, it began employing more administrative institutions used by previous Persian empires. The Abbasids enlarged the historic intelligence-cum-postal system (*barid*) that had been allowed to decline under the Umayyads. Pioneered by the Achaemenids, it was a living legacy of the Sasanians that its caliphal heirs were well aware of and was institutionalized as a separate department under Caliph al-Mutawakkil (r. 847–861) that would be maintained by a series of successor states.[70] The Abbasids also provided the infrastructure for overland trade such as caravansaries and warehouses as well as ports that serviced maritime shipping and expanded Muslim influence throughout the Indian Ocean littoral. Taking a greater role in financing trade and working with merchants, it could perhaps be considered the region's first mercantile-focused empire that exploited its strategic position as the center point linking both the overland and sea routes from the west to China, India, and Southeast Asia.[71] Another of its later innovations was the creation of mamluk armies, "slaves on horseback," which then became a distinguishing feature of later states in the Islamic world. The Abbasid caliphs had begun raising them in the mid-ninth century to counterbalance the Khorasanis and other powerful groups within the empire's elite that were contesting its authority. Recruited from captured or purchased non-Muslim men who came from outside the caliphate, they were converted to Islam but kept their original names and their foreign social identities. Trained to fight as elite units, they had no relatives or home provinces to divide their loyalty but soon evolved into centers of political power in their own right.[72] Like Rome's Praetorian Guard, they could not become caliphs themselves but could determine who did. They famously established their own sultanates as the Abbasid empire unraveled, most successfully in Egypt, where they ruled independently from 1250 to 1517, and as clients of the Ottoman Empire until Napoleon ousted them in 1798.

Of all the transformations that led to the Abbasid Caliphate's becoming an endogenous empire, none was more significant than its elaboration of centralized institutions of governance that were separate and distinct from its rulers. Following a model already well developed by the Sasanians, the Abbasid government was organized around the office of a powerful vizier who supervised a large staff of officials. This centralized body working in Arabic became very efficient at setting empire-wide policies and raising revenue. The most famous of its viziers were drawn from three generations of the Iranian Barmakid family, who wielded unpreceded power during the late eighth century. They came originally from Khorasan, where their ancestors had administered the largest Buddhist shrine in Balkh. The family moved to Syria after the Arab conquest of Balkh, where Barmak, a physician, served the Umayyad caliph Hishem (r. 724–743). Barmak converted to Islam and his son Khalid (705–782) was one of the Abbasid missionaries who helped organize their insurgency against the Umayyads in northern Iran. He went on to become a senior adviser to the first two Abbasid caliphs (al-Saffah and al-Mansur), and under Caliph al-Mahdi (r. 775–785) he held a number of important governorships. Khalid's son Yahya continued his father's work as an official as well as a tutor to the future caliph Harun al-Rashid (r. 786–809), whom he helped to come to power. Al-Rashid made Yahya his vizier and his sons, Fazl and Ja'far, were appointed governors of the east and west, respectively. The family famously supported scholarship and financed the translation of many books from Sanskrit as well as other languages into Arabic, but on a more practical side they reorganized the revenue system so that more money came to the center at the expense of the provinces. In 796, Ja'far was appointed commander of the caliphal bodyguard, manager of the postal (intelligence) service, and supervisor of the mints. For reasons that are still debated, the family experienced a spectacular fall when al-Rashid removed Ja'far from office in 802 and executed him a year later after arresting the other Barmakids and seizing their extensive properties.[73]

As with King Henry VIII's lord chancellor Thomas Cromwell, who wielded similar executive power in sixteenth-century England, the Barmakids may have committed the cardinal sin for a minister in an autocratic regime: appearing more indispensable than his sovereign. State officials who built and administered powerful bureaucratic institutions in any empire were always vulnerable both to the pique of their sovereigns who resented their necessity and to attacks by rivals at court who despised their success. Yet getting rid of such figures invariably came at a high cost. The troubles at the end of al-Rashid's reign and the civil war among his sons for the throne that followed might have been avoided or been less destructive had the Barmakids still been there to maintain good order. In the absence of a strong bureaucratic center, the Turkic mamluk troops would fill the vacuum. In 861 they murdered Caliph al-Mutawakkil and opened a decade of civil unrest that saw five successive caliphs reign for brief periods before the turmoil ended in 870.[74] Better it would seem for an empire to have a set of overpowerful viziers than overpowerful mamluks.

The Abbasid Caliphate is perhaps the finest example of an exogenous empire transforming itself into an endogenous one and, in the process, opening the door to innovations in statecraft, culture, and military organization absent during the initial exogenous period of Umayyad rule. It played to the classic strength of a successful endogenous empire: to manage diversity for the benefit of itself and a broad range of people it governed. Islam now spread throughout the coastal Indian Ocean world, where no Arab army had ever gone but where Muslim merchants, mercenaries, and missionaries did. The distant Bulghar Turks along the Middle Volga River converted to Islam, and Caliph Harun al-Rashid sent Charlemagne an elephant as a diplomatic gift. Little wonder, then, that the first half century of the Abbasid Caliphate was later hailed as Islam's Golden Age. The collection of tales in *A Thousand and One Nights* (*Alfu Laylatin wa-Laylah*) captured the era's mixture of Persian and Arab culture that still has an impact on contemporary culture, albeit with a stronger orientalist bent than it deserves.[75] As in all empires, these benefits were not distributed equally, and slaves reclaiming salty mudflats in Mesopotamia to feed Baghdad can be forgiven for not appreciating that they were basking in the light of a Muslim zenith.[76] This caveat noted, the Abbasid Caliphate was internationally respected as a center of high culture from western Europe to China, and Baghdad was one of the world's largest cities. As the dynasty declined after the death of al-Rashid in 809, the Abbasids found it difficult to maintain their initial highly centralized system of governance and fell into deploying a king-of-kings model in which the outer provinces became autonomous. For example, the Iranian Tahirid dynasty established in 821 ruled Khorasan independently until 873, and its members continued to serve as the governors of Bagdad until 891.[77] In the centuries that followed, a string of independent Iranian (Buyid, Samanid) and Turkic (Ghaznavid, Seljuk, Khwarazmian) empires would emerge but continue to pay homage to the Abbasid caliphs in Baghdad. The non-Muslim Mongols did not share their reverence for the caliphate. After Khubilai Khan's brother Hülegü captured Baghdad in 1258, he executed the thirty-seventh and last of the Abbasid caliphs to end a dynasty that had survived for 579 years.[78]

CHAPTER FIVE

Shadows of the Past

Remembrance of things past is not necessarily the remembrance of things as they were.

—MARCEL PROUST, *IN SEARCH OF LOST TIME*

Empires of Nostalgia

Of all the shadow empires, those based on nostalgia were the most shadowy. Rulers of polities whose imperial authority might otherwise appear threadbare sought to associate themselves with extinct empires imbued with the aura of a former golden age now lost. Based on an invented remembrance of a vanished imperial polity, empires of nostalgia displayed the outward trappings of an endogenous empire without their substance. In particular, they lacked primate urban centers and standing armies. Their existence instead depended on a willing suspension of disbelief by their rulers and elite subordinate subjects who both saw advantages in reviving a fiction of empire that served their mutual interests. It was an empire wished into existence as an idealized political structure whose unique asset was a soft-power authority that could be wielded by whomever became its ruler. They were as rare as vanquisher empires but stood at the opposite end of a power spectrum.

Long-lived endogenous empires left lasting marks on the regions they ruled. In the immediate aftermath of an endogenous empire's demise in Egypt or North China, foreign vulture empires created ad hoc systems of governance by employing survivors of the fallen empire's administration to organize smaller successor states on their behalf. Here nostalgia for the old empire presented an ongoing danger to the rulers of a vulture empire because they were not part of it—indeed their coming to power was viewed by their conquered subjects as symptomatic of a world turned upside down. While vulture empires could offer welcome stability and safety in periods of anarchy, that rationale eroded as conditions improved. The more its foreign frontier rulers adopted the lifestyle and culture of the elites they lived among, the harder it was for them to justify their exclusive domination of state institutions. Nativist political movements therefore presented themselves as the rightful expellers of foreign vulture dynasties that had usurped power in a time of weakness, a rationale that proved particularly potent in China during the rise of the powerful Sui/Tang, Song, and Ming dynasties. A similar pattern of nativist restoration developed in the Iranian world in response to Alexander's vanquisher empire that ultimately led to the expulsion of the Hellenistic Seleucids by the Parthians and later replacement of the Arab-dominated Umayyad Caliphate by the Iranian-backed Abbasid Caliphate. History appeared to be on the side of those seeking imperial restoration in ancient Egypt, China, and Iran, where endogenous empires regularly reemerged and displaced declining exogenous shadow empires. While exploiting nostalgia for empires past proved useful for revanchists seeking to restore endogenous empires in these parts of the world, it was always a stepping stone and never an end state.

Empires of nostalgia therefore emerged only in areas where an endogenous empire could not be restored but where desire to see one return was shared by a large enough number of people to inspire a hope that it would. The authority of rising new rulers and their states was easier to legitimize if they could link themselves to an admired (if long-gone) empire, particularly when its founders replaced dynasties or polities with better pedigrees than their own. However, because empires of nostalgia drew their power from the realm of cultural memory, they did not travel well. The West's past and present infatuation with the Roman Empire has never resonated in China, nor has the epic rise and fall of Chinese dynasties stirred emotions of any kind in the West. Yet such remembrances of empires past could be tenacious within their own cultural spheres. Indeed, it appeared the only way to kill the nostalgia for one was to inculcate a new cultural order. While the memory of Rome remained strong in Europe, it was lost in former Roman North Africa after the Islamic conquest when that region became part of the Arab world. From that point on, the people there focused their nostalgia on the restoration of a universal Islamic caliphate and the cultural memory of their long history as part of the Roman Empire vanished, never to return. But in contemporary Iran, not even its Islamic government has been able to suppress the popular fascination with pre-Islamic Persia and its empires as a source of nostalgic national pride that has greater cultural resonance than the glorification of the caliphate.

A key question that therefore needs to be asked when examining the emergence of an empire of nostalgia is, nostalgia for what? A surprising aspect of the Carolingian Empire (800–888) and its successor, the Holy Roman Empire (962–1806), that I will examine later is that a nostalgia for a Roman imperial past did not emerge in Italy or other parts of the western Mediterranean but instead arose among the Germanic rulers of its successor states who proclaimed themselves its heirs. It was their ancestors, after all, who dismembered the Western Roman Empire during the sixth century and during the first century had prevented Roman expansion into the lands that would become the core territories of these new shadow empires. It would seem that, to reverse William Shakespeare's line about Caesar's death, the good that empires do lives after them; the evil is oft interred with their bones.[1] Part of the explanation is that medieval European elites in the old Roman West were not nostalgic for lost Roman rulers but for their rich and well-ordered empire. Unlike the later Rus' and Russian rulers to the east who attempted to graft a spurious Roman ancestry into their royal genealogies, these Germanic rulers did not seek links with actual Roman emperors but with their empire and then only after Christianity became its state religion. With the cooperation of the Catholic Church, the legitimacy of the Carolingian Empire's rulers would be sanctified by God. Their conquests would simultaneously expand Catholic Christianity north and east into the lands of the Germanic and Slavic pagans and protect western Europe's southern flanks from advancing Muslim forces. By embracing such an imperial project, the new empire's rulers could justify their bloody conquests and suppression of rebellions as more than grubby power plays or opportunities to pillage. Given that the creation of this comparatively short-lived Carolingian Empire is still hailed as a watershed achievement by contemporary Europeans, its founders obviously tapped into a rich vein of cultural memory that is still being mined profitably today.

The Carolingian Empire

BARBARIAN INVASIONS AND THE COLLAPSE OF THE WESTERN ROMAN EMPIRE

The western part of the old Roman Empire was the only part of Eurasia where no successor endogenous empire ever emerged to replace it.[2] This should not be surprising. Uniting the entire Mediterranean Basin was no easy feat even for the immensely powerful Romans and would never be achieved again. Moreover, the Roman Empire's expansion north into the non-Mediterranean European forest zone was never completed. Limiting itself to lines established on the Rhine and Danube Rivers, Rome faced a large reservoir of tribally organized people living beyond its control who potentially threatened the frontier but not the empire as a whole until the fifth century. Unlike China's northern frontier, where peer polity shadow empires like those of the Xiongnu or Turks arose in tandem with the Han and Tang dynasties, Rome never confronted a peer shadow empire that challenged its hegemony. There was, however, a distinction between the political organization of the Germanic tribes on the Rhine frontier that never formed even a nascent state and those on the Danube frontier that did.

Almost a century after Roman emperor Augustus had left them to their own devices, Tacitus described the Germans on the Rhine frontier at the end of the first century A.D. as divided into more than two dozen distinct groups living in widely scattered communities with no towns. As with ibn Khaldun's desert Bedouin, their leaders were selected by their own people and needed to achieve a consensus before taking any action: "Kings they choose for their birth, generals for their valour. But the kings do not have unlimited power without restriction, while the generals lead more by example than command. . . . The leading men take counsel over minor issues, the major ones involve them all; yet even those decisions that lie with the commons are considered in advance by the elite."[3] Rome found the peoples on the Danube frontier better organized. Dacia (today's Romania) was already a well-established mountainous kingdom in 82 B.C. that (unlike Germania) was endowed with mineral resources such as iron for weapons and large deposits of gold and silver. Those resources eventually attracted Rome's attention, and Trajan's conquest of Dacia in 106 yielded the empire 165,000 kg of gold and twice the amount of silver.[4] But the move into Dacia also gave the Romans a frontier with aggressive Sarmatian peoples based in the Carpathian Basin (today's Hungary) who proved more formidable than their Germanic enemies on the Rhine.

The Sarmatians were steppe nomads who had displaced the Scythians on the Pontic steppe in the third and second centuries B.C. and expanded into the grasslands of the Carpathian Basin in the mid-first century A.D., a move that put them directly on Rome's Danube frontier. The Sarmatians were famous for their scaled armor (cataphract) cavalry that used lances instead of bows. They were more centrally organized than the fractious German tribes to the west with whom they established alliances, but the Sarmatians eventually struck an accommodation with Rome as frontier clients.[5] Although China and Iran experienced constant raids and invasions by similar steppe nomads, the Sarmatians (like their Scythian predecessors) never attempted to raid deeply into Roman territory. This relatively stable relationship between Rome and its nomadic neighbors on the Danube frontier and the Pontic steppe to the east was upended by the arrival of the Huns in 370. The Huns had earlier driven the Goths and other defeated peoples westward toward Rome's frontier, where they displaced existing tribes like the Sarmatians and then sought to cross into Roman territory to protect themselves from further attacks. This began a series of migrations that had two long-lasting consequences. The first was a wave of invasions across the whole of Rome's northern frontier that lasted for the next 150 years and led to the resettlement of many Germanic tribes within the empire's western provinces, where they eventually established independent kingdoms.[6] Rome itself was sacked on a number of occasions, although this did not bring the empire down since its capital had been moved to well-fortified Constantinople in 330 just before this period of disruption began. The second major consequence was the replacement of the Iranian steppe nomads who had dominated the Pontic steppe for 1,500 years by Ural-Altaic-speaking nomads (Turkic and Hungarian) whose original homes were far to the east. For the steppe nomads involved, this may have been more of a change in language and identification than way of life, since recent DNA studies have shown that Ural-Altaic-speaking nomads mixed with those already there rather than eliminating them.[7] But if the newcomers' economies and cultures were similar to those of the nomads they settled among, their relationship with neighboring sedentary states was not. The Huns and their Turko-Mongolian successors were practitioners of the violent outer frontier strategy they had first honed in wars with China and now applied to the Iranian and Roman world. That, much more than new languages or alterations in physical appearance that contemporary observers made much of, changed the power dynamics along the steppe frontier and transformed the region's politics and styles of warfare.

While the Huns' pastoral mode of life was the same as the Scythians' and Sarmatians', their interactions with neighboring sedentary societies were more violent. Although there is considerable debate about whether the Huns were the descendants of the northern Xiongnu, there is no doubt they brought a Xiongnu strategy of war, raiding, and extortion to the Roman frontier, uncomfortably close to its eastern capital of Constantinople. The Huns implemented a classic outer frontier strategy that involved fear-inducing raids for loot followed by offers of peace in exchange for large payments in gold and rights to trade. At the height of their power under Attila (r. 434–453), the Huns mounted an ambitious campaign deep into Gaul, where they looted many cities before being defeated at the Battle of Chalons in 451 by a Roman army composed primarily of Germanic tribal axillaries. Since Atilla was intent on raiding rather than conquering, this defeat merely hastened his departure from a province now greatly weakened by the destruction he had wrought. But as with Han China's interactions with the Xiongnu, such damaging raids (particularly earlier ones in the Balkans) were also designed to pressure the Roman government into paying the Huns to stop them, which it did. Over the course of the 440s the Romans paid 900,000 solidi (4,050 kg in gold) for peace agreements that were often broken. Although an impressive sum, it was still a relative bargain for an empire with annual revenues ten times that amount (42,750 kg in gold) that spent 40 percent of it on the military.[8] Unlike the Xiongnu, however, the Huns proved better at war making than state building and their shadow empire dissolved in 469 after Attila's successors (he died suddenly in 453) proved unable to maintain it. A century later, the Avars (567–822) would prove far more capable of transitioning from raiding to diplomatic extortion. They negotiated a long-running series of subsidy treaties with the Byzantines for ever-larger payments: 80,000 solidi annually from 574 to 584, 100,000 solidi from 585 to 597, 120,000 solidi from 598 to 603, 180,000 solidi from 604 to 618, and 200,000 solidi from 623 to 626.[9]

If the Avars proved more politically sophisticated than the Huns, it was likely because they had previously been khagans of the Rouran steppe empire in Mongolia. Established in 402, the Rouran imperial confederacy was defeated by the Kök Türks in 552 during a war in which almost all the members of its ruling clan were killed. However, one surviving royal group, the Avars, escaped and fled west across the Pontic steppe until they eventually reached the Carpathian Basin in 563. Here they settled and established their own long-lived mirror shadow empire at the farthest western end of the Eurasian steppe zone adjacent to Rome's Danube River frontier. Nomadic communities locating themselves in the Carpathian Basin were at one remove from the larger number of pastoral groups remaining on the Pontic steppe and gave primacy to their relationships with neighboring sedentary states and not their nomadic rivals to the east. Like similar imperial confederacies in Mongolia dealing with China, the Avar state financed itself by raiding and extracting subsidy payments from the Byzantine Empire in gold and other luxury goods. But unlike imperial confederacies in Mongolia, those in the Carpathian Basin occupied a region where agriculture was the main economic activity and taxes on its resident nonnomadic population were a significant resource. Unlike seemingly similar vulture empires discussed in the last chapter that expanded out of frontier regions into a neighboring empire's core territories, the steppe nomads who founded states in the Carpathian Basin never abandoned policics that favored raiding and extortion over conquest. As Walter Pohl observes, "The Huns, Avars, and Hungarians in Europe . . . never sought to conquer the heartlands of the empires that they raided but remained in a peripheral area, the Carpathian Basin. This is very much unlike Goths, Vandals, or Franks who occupied core provinces of the Roman Empire in the fifth and sixth centuries, or later Arabs and Berbers in the seventh and eighth, Normans in the tenth and eleventh, and Islamic Turks from the twelfth century onward. Whatever the reason, this difference points to a first-rate structural feature of the polities in question."[10] That reason, I would contend, was the implementation of a strategy long employed by steppe nomads in Mongolia. Kul Tegin, a founding khagan of the Second Kök Türk Empire, left an inscription in the 730s that laid out this strategy explicitly. Warning his people not to get too close to China, where they could be killed in large numbers, he instructed them to extort the Tang Chinese government at a distance from their Orkhon Valley home in central Mongolia: "A land better than the Otukan mountains does not exist at all! The place from which the tribes can be (best) controlled is the Otukan mountains. Having stayed in this place, I came to an amicable agreement with the Chinese people. They (i.e., the Chinese people) give (us) gold, silver, and silk in abundance. . . . If you stay at the Otukan mountains, you will live forever dominating the tribes! If you stay in the land of Otukan, and send caravans from there, you will have no trouble."[11] For the Huns, Avars, and Hungarians, the Carpathian Basin was their Otukan and the Byzantines their Tang China.

THE MEROVINGIANS

The Western Roman Empire dissolved in 476, although some regional Roman cities and provinces maintained its institutions for much longer. These islands of Roman authority did not prevent most of the empire's west from falling under the control of various frontier invaders (Ostrogoths, Visigoths, Vandals, Franks, Angles, and Saxons), many of whom had originally been invited into the empire to protect it from more distant enemies. They formed their own regional states, but most (with the exception of the Franks) were unable to maintain much of the old Roman system of governance. Moreover, despite their success in conquering new places, they had no imperial aspirations of their own. Their leaders instead aspired to become kings (*rex*) of small and then larger regional states. This was a step up from being a simple tribal chieftain or warlord commander, to be sure, but the horizons of these rulers rarely extended beyond the borders of the neighboring kingdoms they fought wars with. What remained of the Roman Empire in the Balkans, Anatolia, Syria, and Egypt was run from Constantinople under Byzantine rule. Though much weaker than the Roman Empire at its height in the second century, the Byzantines considered themselves a continuation of an existing Roman Empire and not a successor to it. Under Emperor Justinian in the mid-sixth century, they recovered many parts of Spain, Italy, and North Africa. Most of this was lost to the Umayyad Caliphate, which had conquered the former Roman provinces of Syria, Egypt, North Africa, and Spain by the mid-eighth century. Moving north from Spain, the Muslims encountered the Franks, who were ruling the old province of Gaul and had created the largest regional state in post-Roman Europe. During the early ninth century this Kingdom of Francia would, with the support of the Catholic Church in Rome, declare Charles the Great (Charlemagne) an emperor, albeit of an empire of nostalgia that did not survive beyond its third generation of rulers.

The Carolingian Empire had its roots in the Kingdom of Francia and the Merovingian dynasty (481–751) that established it. The Franks had long served the Romans as auxiliaries and helped them defeat the Huns just before the western empire formally dissolved. In the period of instability that followed, the Merovingian dynasty's young founder, Clovis, became leader of the Salian Franks (r. 481–511), who ousted the last Roman governor of Gaul in 486. For the next three decades Clovis expanded his kingdom to include the culturally Roman territories in the south and frontier areas occupied by various German tribes in the north. More of a state builder than a tribal leader, he ruthlessly eliminated all rivals who stood in his way, including his own relatives. An ever-larger number of small Germanic tribes and warbands living in Gaul or annexed to it began to identify themselves as Franks to become members of the new state's elite. Like the Manchus on China's frontier I examined earlier, the Franks were a composite ethnic group created by the state they served. By contrast, the neighboring Ostrogoths in Italy, the Visigoths in Spain, the Vandals in North Africa, and the Saxons in England were all well-established ethnic groups before they founded their own kingdoms.

As Heinrich Fichtenau has observed, the Franks as a people and the people they ruled were more diverse than in those other Germanic kingdoms:

> The kingdom of the Franks was founded long before there was such a thing as a Frankish nation. The process of fusion and unification was speeded up by the great opportunities that lay ahead of the nobility of this new monarchy. It was also made easier by the fact that large parts of the Roman administrative system continued to exist. Very little that was really new was created. All that happened was that the masters of the local population of Gaul had changed. These masters did not cold-shoulder the "Romans," as their opposite numbers in other Germanic kingdoms had done, and mixed marriages gave them the necessary influx of strength which had been lacking in the other kingdoms.[12]

One initial barrier to be overcome was the pagan-Christian divide, which Clovis resolved by converting to Christianity near the end of his life. Unlike most of the neighboring Germanic groups (and many members of his own family), who had adopted a simpler but heretical nontrinitarian version of Christianity known as Arianism, Clovis became a Catholic. Theologically this meant he endorsed its orthodox trinitarian Christianity that was also shared by the Byzantines in Constantinople. Whether motivated by theology or politics, the choice proved an astute move that brought Clovis the support of the Catholic bishops in Gaul and made the Franks defenders of their brand of Christian orthodoxy. It gave the new Merovingian dynasty a dual religious and political legitimacy endorsed by the Catholic Church that neighboring Germanic kingdoms lacked. It also provided a way for the Franks to identify themselves with the Church's universalism and hierarchical institutional structure, which had also characterized the empire's government before it collapsed. Indeed Conor O'Brien asserts that "early medieval Christians saw themselves as living in the era founded in the Acts of the Apostles: the passing of the Roman Empire was irrelevant in the face of the essential continuity of the multi-ethnic, universal church that had emerged under it."[13] If empires (even ones relying on nostalgia) specialized in organizing diversity to create multiethnic and multinational states, this was a vital tool in a western European world that was fragmenting into ever-smaller pieces with more parochial identities. Such an expansive vision provided Clovis and his successors with an ideological template that facilitated the incorporation of people different from themselves into their polity. In so doing, the Merovingians became important international political players as well. The Byzantines, who still held the Roman imperial mantle, supported Clovis's construction of a unified Frankish kingdom in Gaul because they had abandoned any thought of recovering northern Europe but still wished to see stability there. When the Byzantines under Emperor Justinian (r. 527–565) later recovered large parts of Italy, Spain, and North Africa, the Merovingian alliance prevented their enemies from regrouping on their territory.

Clovis's conquests created a large new kingdom, but it was one he treated as a common family property. All four of his sons became co-kings with their own courts upon his death, and each inherited a similarly valued set of tax-paying districts. Initially, Clovis's eldest and adult son, Theuderic (r. 511–533), ruled from Rheims, and his three minor half brothers ruled respectively from Orléans (Chlodomer, r. 511–524), Paris (Childebert, r. 511–558), and Soissons (Chlothar, r. 511–561). These original kingdoms were allocated additional territory over the next fifty years after the conquest of Burgundy and the imposition of stronger Frankish control in the south.[14] Their royal centers (Rheims, Paris, Orléans, and Soissons) were remarkably close to one another, and while their proximity may have reduced the possibility of regional division, it elevated the likelihood of conflict among members of its competing royal lines, who were frequently at war with one another.

As the number of potential Merovingian rulers grew over the next century, conflicts among them became a regular part of political life except during the few times there was a single king. Ian Wood argues that Francia's division into these subkingdoms (*Teilungen*) was offset by the Frankish elite's ownership of widely distributed landed estates and other resources that crossed their boundaries. He cites a will drafted in 616 by Bishop Bertram of Le Mans, who was a minor player on both the winning and losing sides in a variety of dynastic contests during his lifetime: "Bertram disposed of lands as far apart as the Seine valley, Lorraine, Burgundy, Provence, the Pyrenees and Bordeaux. It has been estimated that 135 units of land are mentioned in the will, including 62 villae, 13 groups of villae, and other smaller properties, perhaps amounting to some 300,000 hectares. In addition, the bishop had treasure to bequeath, despite the ravages of the civil wars . . . [and] the king gave Bertram a number of estates, including land described as coming from the royal fisc."[15] Given Francia's lack of political centralization and the need for rival royal lines to recruit followers, it is not surprising that such elite helpers might eventually see themselves as replacements for the Merovingians. The main obstacle in their path was the Merovingian dynasty's status as the exclusive source of Frankish kings. As in the ruling golden clans we saw on the steppe, only its members could be promoted to the rank of king, even when their subordinates wielded enough power to replace them. Some lower-ranking rivals attempted to assert a Merovingian lineage that (because past plural marriages and more casual relationships had produced many royal bastard sons) may or may not have been fictitious. A more successful strategy was to rule as a "mayor of the palace" through a figurehead Merovingian king. This position of *major domus* was originally that of a vice-king who could govern in the absence of the monarch and was in charge of the kingdom's administration. During times when the king was a boy, the mayors of the palace ran the kingdom on his behalf. By the mid-seventh century they were the most powerful men in the kingdom, and they often appointed the monarchs they served and chose their own successors. It was from this position that the Carolingians rose to power before they finally made themselves kings.[16]

Members of the Merovingian dynasty had ruled Francia for more than two hundred years as the eighth century began, despite the persistence of perennial low-level civil wars. This was because factions within the kingdom fought for dominance or autonomy rather than independence even though they were organized on a regional basis. Neustria, with its center in Paris, was the most politically powerful and culturally dominant of these regions. Its main rival was Rhineland-based Austrasia, which also controlled the northeastern frontier German duchies of Thuringia, Bavaria, and Alemannia. The kingdom of Burgundy that bordered both Neustria and Austrasia ruled over most of the Rhone River watershed and played a balancing role. The autonomous regions of Aquitaine and Provence farther south swore fealty to Merovingian kings, but neither Austrasia nor Neustria had hegemony there. After a series of back-and-forth struggles, the Austrasian mayor of the palace, Pippin of Herstal, defeated the Neustrians in 687 and occupied Paris to become the *major domus* of all Francia. Pippin held power over the unhappy Neustrians until he died in 714, when a succession struggle within his family allowed them to turn the tables and invade Austrasia. During that turmoil Charles Martel, Pippin's oldest son by a less prestigious wife, escaped his stepmother's imprisonment, raised his own army, and declared himself mayor of Austrasia. After an initial setback, Charles ambushed the Neustrians in April 716 as they were returning home from Cologne with a large treasure extorted from his stepmother. This gave him both the money and momentum to go on the offensive, and he chased his enemies to the outskirts of Paris in March 717 before returning to Cologne to oust his stepmother and declare a new figurehead Merovingian king of Austrasia. The next year Charles beat back a coalition of his enemies fighting in the name of the Neustrian king Chilperic II (r. 715–721), who fled south. Charles then cut a deal with the Duke Odo of Aquitaine (r. ~700–735) to get his hands on Chilperic. Since his own Merovingian king had just died, Charles offered the defeated Chilperic the throne in exchange for recognizing him as mayor of all Francia in 718, the position his father had held when he died.

It was Charles Martel who laid the groundwork for the Carolingian Empire that would be formally declared by his grandson Charlemagne. He did this by first creating a more cohesive Frankish elite united by force, faith, wealth, law, and custom so loyal to him and his heirs that future civil wars (and there would be many) remained family affairs. As significantly, he extended direct Frankish control into frontier regions that had previously been only loosely connected to Francia. In the south this meant expanding into Gallo-Roman Aquitaine and Provence, where Charles repulsed the last Muslim advance north from Spain by defeating the Umayyad amir of Cordova, Abdur Rahman, at Tours in 731. But of greater long-term significance was his incorporation of the German lands that bordered his home region of Austrasia so that, as Paul Fouracre observes, "this period can be said to see the erasure of the Rhine as one of the major cultural boundaries in Europe, that is, as the dividing line between areas more or less influenced by the religion, social structure and bureaucratic traditions of the later Roman Empire." Fouracre continues, "Charles Martel's victories had the effect of exporting this core culture to the lands beyond the Rhine. Two generations later, Charlemagne's ability to address with one voice the common concerns of an elite which was spread throughout most of Western Europe was both a consequence of his grandfather's victories and a mark of how warmly the conquered had embraced Frankish culture. For, as we have just seen, it was a culture which tended to reinforce the power of the elite. It was, in other words, a dual process of conquest and acculturation which made the Frankish empire."[17] There were a number of other steps the Carolingians needed to take before that would happen. While Charles Martel was strong enough to rule without a Merovingian king after Theuderic IV (r. 721–737) died, he did not attempt to become a king himself or name a son as king. Instead he now dated his charters "in the year X after the death of King Theuderic," as if the ghost of a king could serve just as well as a living one. Naming a son king to establish a new dynasty might have been worth the disruption it would entail, but which one? He had two adult sons by his deceased first wife, Rotrude (Carolman and Pippin the Short), and one minor son (Grifo) by his current Bavarian wife, Swanahild, who was now a powerful force at court. Choosing any one of them as king before his own death would have alienated the others at a time when he wanted to keep the family united. But making them all kings would likely have doomed the dynasty to extinction before it could take root. For as Fouracre observes, while there was a long tradition of naming three separate mayors for Austrasia, Burgundy, and Neustria, "dividing the kingship into three sub-kingdoms so soon after taking the throne would have been far more hazardous."[18] Instead, a year before he died, Charles appointed his sons as mayors rather than kings. Carolman would serve as mayor of the palace for Austrasia, Alemannia, and Thuringia while Pippin would serve in the same role for Burgundy, Neustria, and Provence. If Grifo was allotted something, he lost it immediately upon his father's death in 741 when his half brothers imprisoned him and exiled his mother, Swanahild, to a nunnery.

Carolman and Pippin then spent the next five years campaigning together to restore their control over Francia's outlying territories, whose leaders revolted immediately upon the death of Charles Martel. To improve their political legitimacy during this struggle, Carolman appointed a new placeholding Merovingian king, Childeric III, to the throne in 743. From a realpolitik viewpoint, such a move cost the brothers little and wrong-footed their rebel opponents who had long accepted the suzerainty of the Merovingian kings that Carolman and Pippin could now claim to represent. That year the brothers campaigned successfully against the pagan Saxons in the north and the rebellious Aquitanians in the south and forced the Bavarian Duke Odilo (who was married to their sister) to accept them as his overlords. In 746 Carolman executed thousands of Alemanni leaders for treason and redistributed their lands to his own followers. The next year, in a surprise move, Carolman chose to abandon secular life and travel to Rome to become a monk. It was an apparently voluntary decision by a devout man who had close relations with Anglo-Saxon monks like St. Boniface (675–754) whose missions among the pagan German tribes and reform of the Francian church had relied on the patronage of Charles Martel and his sons. It was also a politically opportune time to become a renunciant because all those opposed to the Carolingians had now been defeated and Carolman's seventeen-year-old son Drogo was available to replace him as mayor of the palace in Austrasia. Since Pippin had no children at that time (he married late for a man of his status), Carolman could assume that Drogo's position was secure because he was the only dynastic heir to the brothers' kingdom. That situation shifted dramatically after Pippin's son Charles (Charlemagne) was born in 748. Pippin soon moved to oust his nephew Drogo and released Swanahild's son, his half brother Grifo, to cause problems in Austrasia. All this was in preparation for Pippin's declaring himself king in 751 and ending the 274-year-old Merovingian dynasty, one of the longest lasting in European history.[19]

Replacing a dynasty of such longevity and high status was a usurpation that would require more than the simple assent of a cowed assembly of Franks to be successful. Pippin therefore entered into an alliance that the popes in Rome had long sought with Francia in return for their support. This included an opinion from Pope Zacharias (r. 741–752) that Pippin's proposed transfer of power from the Merovingians would be justifiable and legitimate. The pope also helpfully confined his brother Carolman to his monastery when it appeared he would return to Francia and aid his son Drogo as Pippin consolidated his grip on power there. The Church provided more overt help after Pippin made himself king. In 753 the new pope, Stephen III (r. 752–757), commanded the Franks to recognize Pippin as their king or suffer perdition. It was a threat that carried great weight because, as Marc Bloch observes, "the fear of hell was one of the great social forces of the age."[20] Most impressively, in 754 Pope Stephen traveled to Paris personally in the company of Carolman, where he anointed Pippin, his wife Bertrada, and their two sons Charlemagne and Carolman and "solemnly declared that in future only the descendants of Pippin should be the kings of the Franks."[21] To tie up loose ends, Pippin then dispatched Drogo to a monastery, killed Grifo as he attempted to ally with the Lombards in Italy, and imprisoned his brother Carolman, who died a year later. Pippin kept his end of the bargain with the popes by mounting a war against the Lombards although that was unpopular with the Frankish elite. After two successful invasions of northern Italy in 754 and 756, Pippin arranged for the transfer of the formerly Byzantine Exarchate of Ravenna and some other territories in central Italy to the Vatican, laying the groundwork for what would become the Papal States that would last (with a couple of disruptions) until 1929. But Pippin did not seek to displace the Lombard rulers of northern Italy and instead turned his attention to Aquitaine, where he engaged in bitter wars with its recalcitrant duke during the mid-760s that finally brought it and neighboring Basque Gascony under Francia's control in 768, the last year of his reign.

Pippin the Short left a stable Francia to his two sons, Charlemagne and Carolman, who each inherited different parts of the kingdom and its client territories to administer as joint rulers. This division of the kingdom among a new set of heirs upon the death of the king was the continuation of a Merovingian Frankish tradition that had long been a source of political instability, and Pippin's failure to modify this system of inheritance left his new Carolingian dynasty just as vulnerable to the same problems. Like a fatal recessive gene that lay dormant in one generation only to debilitate another later, preserving a unitary kingdom and then empire from the consequences of dividing its territory anew in each generation among a set of rivalrous co-kings proved more a matter of luck than planning. Pippin the Short only got to rule a unified kingdom because his more powerful older brother Carolman became a monk; Charlemagne only avoided a brewing civil war with his younger brother Carolman because he died of natural causes in 771; and Charlemagne's son Louis the Pious would become the sole ruler of his father's empire in 814 only because all his brothers predeceased him. That luck ran out even before Louis's death in 840 when his surviving sons began fighting one another in a civil war that ended only when they agreed to divide the empire into three sovereign kingdoms in 843 so that each could be an independent ruler.

CHARLEMAGNE AND LOUIS THE PIOUS

As soon as Charlemagne became sole ruler of Francia, he began a series of military campaigns that would double the size of his kingdom over the next twenty-five years to create what became the Carolingian Empire (map 5.1). He took Lombardy first (773–774), followed by campaigns in 778 that created a marchland south of the Pyrenees in northern Spain and retook control of a breakaway Bavaria in the east. However, Charlemagne's most long-lasting wars would be with the pagan Saxons in the north, who had the strongest military of any of his opponents. They vehemently resisted their incorporation into his empire and Charlemagne's policies of forcible conversion to Christianity. Charlemagne mounted almost annual campaigns against the Saxons from 777 to 797, most intensively in the mid-780s, that were conducted with great violence, including large-scale massacres and deportations of civilians that in turn laid the groundwork for fresh revolts when Charlemagne was busy fighting elsewhere. To the east Charlemagne found himself on the edge of a forested vacuum zone running from the Baltic to the Balkans inhabited by German-speaking tribes in the north and Slavic-speaking ones in the south along a line west of the Oder and Danube Rivers. Here there were no real states or even strong tribal confederations like the Saxons, so the Carolingians pursued a policy not unlike that of the contemporaneous Khazar Khaganate in its forest zone by creating client rulers who were then expected to deliver regular tribute collected from their own people. (Over time these client rulers would develop their own independent states much as the Kievan Rus' did.)

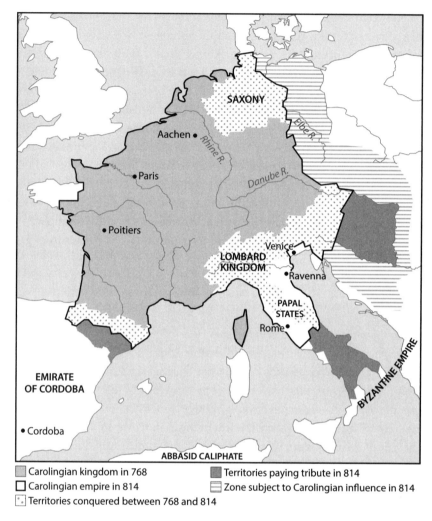

MAP 5.1. The Carolingian Empire. From Burbank and Cooper, 2010.

Employing a policy unlike the one of forcible conversion to Christianity that was applied to the Saxons, Charlemagne looked to achieve the same end in the east voluntarily by supporting the work of Catholic missionaries there and by offering greater benefits to those of his client rulers who became Christian. One practical reason for not seeking a total conversion to Christianity was that captured pagans could be sold as slaves but Christians (at least Catholic Christians) could not, and the slave trade of people from the forest zone to the Muslim world was as profitable here as it was for the steppe nomads farther to the east.[22] Those two worlds briefly intersected when the Carolingians invaded a crumbling Avar Khaganate in 796 and captured its vast royal treasury accumulated over two centuries, the value of which astounded the Franks.

Charlemagne was crowned emperor by the pope in 800, but his government still relied on the inherited institutions of governance it had developed as a much smaller and less diverse kingdom. As Rosamond McKitterick describes it,

> The central administration of the Carolingian monarchy was extremely rudimentary. To the king was attached his household, many members of which had duties and responsibilities that extended beyond the palace. The household was not just a court, but an organ of administration. Except for the last few years of Charlemagne's reign, the king and his household were itinerant; they travelled from palace to villa to monastery to civitas. There was no one place where the king could be expected to be at any one time, albeit a number of royal residences, Ingelheim, Herstal, Attigny, and after 796 Aachen, were more often favoured with the king's presence than others.[23]

Charlemagne successfully ruled his immense holdings without a developed administrative infrastructure because he did not govern it directly but instead delegated that authority to local powerholders, approximately six hundred secular counts and an equal number of Catholic bishops and monastic abbots. Both counts and clerics were appointed by Charlemagne, and he could remove them at will but rarely did so because that would have required a level of micromanagement beyond the capacity of his court. He divided the core of the empire into inspection circuits (*missatica*) to which teams of two *missi* (one lay, one cleric) were dispatched on a regular basis to evaluate local governance and deliver imperial edicts. They had the independent power to investigate injustice or malfeasance and hold their own court sessions to rectify it, or they could request guidance directly from Charlemagne. In newly conquered areas like Lombardy and Saxony, Charlemagne replaced the local elite with Franks whose loyalty he could better rely on. In older but historically fractious Frankish territories like Bavaria and Aquitaine, he appointed his relatives as subkings to watch over the restive nobles who continued to administer their own hereditary territories. In this way Charlemagne made himself master of a network of counts and clerics through which his policies were implemented. If we assume that their likely number was under 1,500 people, it would be a small enough network for Charlemagne to have known most of its important members personally and easily obtain needed information about the rest from members of his court or his *missi*.[24] Subordinates were expected to pay regular visits to his court (sometimes annually) and participate in military campaigns where he could observe them. And unlike capital-bound emperors elsewhere in the world who knew the details of their realms only secondhand, Charlemagne had personally visited virtually every corner of his empire on multiple occasions.

As Jennifer Davis explains,

> The empire was centralized from the start by the extent to which the political networks fostered by the Carolingians coalesced around the person of the king. The eventual use of Aachen as a real capital during the second half of the reign only heightened these processes of central-ization. When we look at the empire from a top-down perspective, from the vantage point of the royal court, what the king and his men were attempting was to focus and center all political life on themselves. This did not mean destroying pre-existing networks; it simply meant rerout-ing them centripetally around Charlemagne and eventually his capital. Charlemagne's vision of centralization thus did not require, nor in fact encourage, uniformity.[25]

Davis continues, "What held this unwieldy empire together was a careful balancing of unity and diversity. The king and his men tried to centralize, but rarely to standardize. They built on the regional diversity they could not have eliminated. They insisted on an ultimate overarching political culture centered on the court, but then nuanced their efforts to rule to local circumstance, and often first attempted their most innovative techniques of rule in the conquered regions."[26] With an empire eventually encom-passing an area of 1.2 million km^2 with a population of between ten mil-lion and twenty million people, Charlemagne used the last two decades of his forty-six-year reign attempting to transform it into a minimally func-tioning imperial polity. During this period the number of decrees focusing on the reorganization of the legal system, instructions for counts to follow, and demands for oaths of loyalty increased markedly. Charlemagne also reformed the Church's administration of its extensive landholdings and ordered the convening of synods to create more uniformity in religious practices as well. Although he had been crowned emperor in 800, Char-lemagne rarely used the title afterward except in his international rela-tions. While he saw the value of adopting administrative techniques that empires had long used to organize the diversity of the people they ruled, Charlemagne remained at heart a king who viewed his vast conquests as a personal patrimony. Rather than creating a singular imperial admin-istration, he would appoint his sons as subkings of different parts of the empire with the expectation that they would then rule it together upon his death. While this might superficially appear to be a Persianate king-of-kings model, it was not. Subordinate kings in that system were outsiders with strong local roots and never members of the ruling dynasty. Since there could be only one ruling sovereign at the top, fights among royal contenders over who would succeed a dead emperor had only two possible outcomes: the emergence of a single winner who then ruled an indivisible state or the dissolution of that state.

Yet perhaps Charlemagne's view of his polity as a collection of kingdoms (the title he most often employed in state documents was "King of the Franks and Lombards") was a realistic one. Three centuries after the fall of the Western Roman Empire and despite a growing population and a reviving economy, medieval Francia was still a place where tracts of forests were more extensive than tilled land, towns were few, and roads were bad or nonexistent. There were no great urban centers anywhere comparable to Muslim Spain's Cordova, which boasted a population of 160,000, or Byzantine Constantinople with 250,000 inhabitants, or Abbasid Baghdad or China's Tang dynasty Chang'an with a million-plus residents each. The Carolingian capital of Aachen was more of an overgrown palace complex with impressive public architecture than city, a "place of power" whose small population (probably less than 20,000) did not reflect its political importance.[27] This made Aachen functionally more similar to Mongol Karakorum (with a population of only 10,000) than to Constantinople or Baghdad. Both were shadow empire capitals that owed their importance to being the residence of an imperial elite that commanded others to do business with them there. Beyond Aachen, the empire's civilian imperial footprint was light, consisting of scattered palace complexes that only came to life when they housed Carolingian royalty or their agents. (North of the Alps, Charlemagne had 25 major and 125 minor palaces sustained by seven hundred different royal estates in German areas located along the region's lakes and rivers.) Alongside these and elsewhere in the empire were a rapidly growing number of landowning monasteries, bishoprics based in towns, and ducal estates. The often-itinerant Carolingian court would park itself in one of these if a purpose-built palace was not available, a move that would inevitably drain the surplus of any monastery or ducal estate blessed with such a royal visit.[28]

Although the Carolingian Empire lacked many of the structural characteristics common to endogenous empires, it did meet both the population and territorial size thresholds (table 5.1). This has prompted historians to treat it as a poorly organized endogenous empire when it

Table 5.1. Endogenous empire organizational components in Charlemagne's
Carolingian Empire

Present	Partial	Absent
Size: 1.2 million km²	Monopoly of force within their territories, and military force projected outward (Carolingians had no standing army or centralized military command structure)	Centralized institutions of governance that were separate and distinct from the rulers
Population: 10–20 million	Systems of communication that allowed administration of all subject areas from the center directly (Carolingian decrees were often more hortatory than imperative)	A primate imperial center with transportation systems designed to serve it militarily and economically
Organized to administer and exploit diversity		
Imperial project that imposed some type of unity throughout the system (Catholic Christianity)		

is better seen as an exogenous empire that, like other shadow empires, functioned despite the absence of many standard components that endogenous empires possessed.

Throughout this book I have argued that exogenous empires were not defective endogenous empires but instead employed alternative structures to create imperial peer polities with their own distinct characteristics. Empires of nostalgia were distinct in their emphasis on soft power, creating a polity in which its elite (at least) saw itself as engaged in a common enterprise. For the Carolingians this was the restoration of a Christian Roman Empire, a project that ennobled its leaders and convinced its subjects that they were doing God's work. Like all empires, the Carolingian Empire was created and maintained by military force, but it is striking how few domestic rebellions Charlemagne faced (three in forty years and none that threatened his grip on power). Davis has argued that this was because he sought political centralization without standardization, allowing him to accept a considerable amount of diversity at the local level. But perhaps more importantly, she contends that he was guided by a set of soft-power ideas that included Christian salvation and creating a common community at the elite level in what I have defined as an appeal to nostalgia.[29]

Charlemagne's alliance with the Catholic Church and its declaration that he was "a new Constantine" would prove a propaganda bonanza in this regard since the Catholic Church was the link to that past. During what is sometimes described as the first Carolingian renaissance during his reign, the model being revived was of a fourth-century Christian Rome by which an ethnic Frankish elite was broadened and transformed into a universal Christian one that transcended regional and linguistic differences.[30] However, Charlemagne never saw himself as anything other than a mighty king whose accomplishments had led the pope to reward him with an emperor's crown. He was now the third and most successful in a line of remarkable Carolingian warrior rulers that began with Charles Martel and whose political authority rested on their personal power, not titles or institutions. Although perhaps devaluing his status as emperor a little more than Charlemagne himself might have, McKitterick accurately notes that "the title was of little practical importance":

> It is difficult indeed to see the imperial title as anything more than a bold attempt by the Papacy to describe the achievements and stature of Charlemagne, cock a snook at Byzantium, and define the peculiar relationship that had evolved between the Papacy and the Frankish rulers over the preceding century. A strong argument in favour of this view is the *Divisio regni* of 806, which is devoid of any idea of Empire, let alone of unity, and cheerfully splits Charlemagne's vast realm into kingdoms for each of his three sons. No reference is made to the imperial title. The acquisition of the imperial title in 800 simply added a name rich in tradition to a well-developed theory of Christian kingship, of which the duties of protection of Rome and the Pope were a part, and which was itself largely the outcome of the actual practice of the early Carolingian kings. Only under Louis the Pious was a theory of Empire and imperial office elaborated.[31]

Because all his full brothers had predeceased him, Louis the Pious became the Carolingian Empire's sole ruler upon Charlemagne's death in 814, and he was immediately faced with the daunting task of keeping it united. As F. L. Ganshof describes it, the empire he inherited was ridden with problems: "During the last years of Charlemagne's reign, the results of bad administrative organization were everywhere evident: inefficient functioning of the public services; corruption; individual and collective violence; insecurity of life and property, both for individuals and corporate bodies; a general tendency to disregard the law and more particularly to avoid military service; frequent disorders and irregularities in the Church.

Altogether, the Empire was internally in a very unsatisfactory state, to say nothing of the external anxieties caused by the Bretons, Saracens, Slavs and Danes along the borders or the coasts."[32] Many of these problems stemmed from Charlemagne's failure to grasp the structural differences between a large kingdom and an empire. As Ganshof compared the two men's approaches to governance, he concluded that Charlemagne believed royal kingly power was the only type that had any reality and that "this power over people and land was traditionally held to be part of the patrimony of the king and of his dynasty, rather than the prerogative of some theoretical being which was permanent and independent of the actual person of the monarch. The abstract notion of the state, of the *respublica*, seems to have been as foreign to Charlemagne as to his predecessors." By contrast, he argues, Louis the Pious "had the intellectual capacity for grasping an abstraction and his frequent intercourse with learned clerics must have familiarized him with the 'non-historic' notion of the Empire which had developed in Church circles since the time of Gregory the Great [r. 590–604]," concluding that it is only in his reign that a Carolingian emperor attempted to act like one: "According to this notion the emperor—and this meant, of course, the Roman Emperor—was endowed with a universal authority destined to protect the universal Church against the dangers which might threaten her, to spread the Christian faith, and to preserve its purity. Such an abstract conception of imperial authority was of course incompatible with the traditional, almost patrimonial idea of royal power. The result was that all mention of this royal power disappeared, as early as 814, from the title of Louis the Pious: *Hludowicus* [Louis] *divina odinante providential imperator augustus*."[33] While few people may have taken notice of a title change that dropped any mention of Francia and Lombardy, which Charlemagne had insisted on including, they could not help but notice the changes to the law of succession in Louis's *Ordinatio Imperii* of 817. Promulgated soon after Louis luckily survived an Aachen building collapse, it declared an end to the partition of the empire's territories among the sons of the ruler at his death and created a system of unitary government headed by a singularly powerful emperor. After seeking God's guidance through prayer, Louis crowned his eldest son, Lothar, coemperor and sole heir. Lothar's younger brothers Pippin and Louis (the German) could only inherit the throne if Lothar died without heirs of his own. Pippin was made king of Aquitaine and Louis king of Bavaria, consolation prizes that would be forfeited to Lothar if they failed to produce legitimate sons. Emphasizing their inferiority to Lothar was his right to punish his brothers if they abused their power, as well as requirements that they seek Lothar's permission to marry and that they present him with gifts during annual visits to his court. Louis the Pious justified these breaks with previous Frankish tradition as an implementation of God's divine will that could not be abrogated by man.[34]

In the original Christianized Roman Empire of Constantine and his successors, the emperors protected the Church but were not bound by its religious norms when wielding secular power. On occasion Christian Roman emperors accepted criticism and even chastisement from clerics who deemed their actions sinful or violations of religious norms, but the obligations of statecraft required the regular employment of un-Christian violence and cruelty. As Machiavelli observed, a ruler was safer being feared than loved, and the Church had long depended on such hard men to preserve the political order in which it preached the milder Christian virtues of mercy, forgiveness, and redemption.[35] And despite the Catholic Church's praise of the many Christian Roman emperors who helped preserve the faith, none was ever made a saint. When Louis succeeded Charlemagne on the throne, he envisioned himself ruling a true Christian Roman Empire in which the emperor too would govern using Christian values. His model of leadership was that of a Benedictine abbot overseeing a monastery who followed the same rules as did his brother monks. This was a sharp departure from the Frankish warrior-king model in which killing in battle and crushing foes took precedence. They might declare themselves defenders of Christian values, but they would not willingly allow themselves to be judged by them in the political realm. Louis was because it allowed him to meld the state with the clerical establishment to give the empire a stronger institutional base that had been missing under Charlemagne. He was also a deeply religious man with a puritanical streak keen to see Christian norms imposed and observed more widely. Upon becoming emperor, he immediately ended the lively party scene in Aachen that had flourished under his father, banning German drinking songs, expelling prostitutes from the city, and dispatching his fun-loving unmarried sisters to nunneries.

For previous Carolingian rulers, politically motivated killings, massacres, and the forceful relocation of relatives to monasteries were the ordinary tools of statecraft that brought the empire into being. If this troubled their souls, they could, like Pippin the Short's elder brother Carolman, renounce secular life and become monks. Louis the Pious, by contrast, suffered deep pangs of guilt for taking actions his predecessors would not have lost much sleep over. The one that seemed to most trouble him was his culpability in the 818 death of his nephew Bernard. Then the king of

Italy, Bernard was found guilty of planning a revolt against Louis and sentenced to death. In an act of clemency, Louis commuted the sentence to blinding, but the procedure was botched and his nephew died in agony as a result. Louis felt such remorse for this, as well as for relegating his illegitimate half brothers to various monasteries, that he invited the pope and a council of clergy to join with a delegation of nobles to attend a ceremony at his palace of Attigny where he did public penance for his sins in 822. Louis then reconciled with his half brothers by making them bishops and freed a number of former enemies in an exuberance of forgiveness. Performing this unprecedented ritual of penance brought immediate praise from the clerical establishment, a godly act by a godly ruler. By contrast, the secular elite viewed the whole performance with some wariness and as evidence of Louis's increasing domination by churchmen and an implicit rejection of their own martial code of conduct.[36] Louis was now moving to a model of rulership borrowed from the Church in which he would be a shepherd to his flock, protecting it from predators, leading it to new pastures, and recovering any strayed sheep. Should this appear to be unrealistically naïve, we should not overlook a more coldblooded aspect of shepherding: the shepherd spares no effort tending to his flock because each sheep is eventually butchered for his benefit.

Louis maintained the stability of the empire against outside attacks and avoided internal rebellions throughout the 820s. It appeared that he might succeed well enough to create a stable endogenous empire in which Christian unity would transcend existing sets of ethnic and regional identity in a manner similar to how the Roman Empire employed citizenship to unify its diverse population. His eldest son and coemperor, Lothar, was poised to inherit an intact empire and would likely have put more distance between himself and the clerical establishment, which would have appeased critics of his father who complained Louis was *too* pious. As king of Italy, Lothar had already gotten one pope to reinforce his imperial rights by crowning him emperor in 823 and the next year forced a successor to accept the *Constitutio Romana*, which reaffirmed the supremacy of the empire over the papacy. But Louis would bring about the collapse of his own imperial project by undermining its unitary political structure in the wake of the birth of a new royal heir, Charles (the Bald), to his young and strong-willed second wife, Judith, in 823. She was determined to see her son receive a kingdom on par with those of his much older half brothers. Such a grant would not have necessarily threatened Lothar's status as coemperor and sole heir as outlined in the *Ordinatio Imperii* of 817, but Lothar suspected that Judith was laying the groundwork for a greater power grab. Thus, when Louis announced in August 829 that the seven-year-old Charles would receive land in Alemannia, where his mother's family lived, Louis's other sons (Pippin of Aquitaine, Louis the German, and Lothar) all united to oppose him. In April 830 they intervened to separate their father from Judith (whose reputation they then thoroughly blackened), and Lothar began ruling the empire in Louis's name. Lothar quickly discovered that his brothers' motives were different from his own when they restored Louis to the throne after he promised to bequeath them independent kingdoms. In February 831 Louis announced that upon his death the empire would be split into four equal kingdoms.[37]

What had been a family inheritance dispute was now a constitutional crisis that pitted those who saw the division of the empire among its royal heirs as a welcome return to a centuries-old Frankish legal tradition against those who wished to preserve a united empire. Lothar led the imperial camp and raised a powerful coalition that included his full brothers (who now believed Judith was out to take their kingdoms), the pope, and a coterie of bishops that Lothar planned to use to undermine his father's clerical support. Louis raised his own army and the two forces met in June 833 in Alsace, where Louis's supporters infamously deserted him despite their oaths of loyalty. Lothar then used Louis's own precedent-breaking 822 atonement ritual against his father by staging a show trial in October during which bishops loyal to him forced Louis to confess to a litany of sins that, they declared, exposed him as an unfit ruler. He was sentenced to perpetual penance and imprisoned in the monastic complex of Saint-Denis outside Paris. Lothar declared himself sole emperor but underestimated the opposition that move would provoke. As the contemporary historian Nithard recounted,

> Pepin and Louis saw that Lothair intended to seize the whole empire and make them his inferiors, and they resented his schemes. . . . They began to quarrel, and, since each of them looked out for his own, they entirely neglected the government. When the people saw that, they were distressed. Shame and regret filled the sons for having twice deprived their father of his dignity, and the people for having twice deserted the emperor. Therefore, they all now in 834 agreed on his restoration and headed for St.-Denis, where Lothair was then holding his father and Charles [the Bald].[38]

Lothar decamped to his kingdom in Italy, where he stayed thereafter. Louis recrowned himself emperor at Metz in 835 and continued to rule unopposed until he died in 840. While he soon reconciled with Lothar, who was once again recognized as coemperor, the imperial structure was broken. When Pippin died in 838, Louis ignored his heirs and gave Aquitaine to Judith's son Charles the Bald. Charles the German's unsuccessful attempts to reduce the size of his half brother Charles the Bald's allocation of lands in Germany left him confined to Bavaria. Lothar stayed out of these fights because he expected to become sole emperor after his father's death but found his way blocked by both Charles the German and Charles the Bald. After a period of civil war among them, the empire was divided into three independent kingdoms by the Treaty of Verdun in 843. It gave Charles the Bald West Francia, Charles the German East Francia, and Lothar Middle Francia along with the title of emperor and control of the imperial cities of Aachen and Rome. Since Lothar had no power over his brothers, that title was symbolic, though it would be fought over for the next thirty years. The kingdoms then drifted apart from one another culturally, linguistically, and politically, with the western parts eventually becoming France and the eastern parts Germany.

Nostalgia 2.0: The Holy Roman Empire

The Carolingian Empire dissolved, but the belief that there should be a transnational Roman Catholic Christian empire whose singular emperor ranked above kings, protected the Church, and preserved political order did not die with it. It was reestablished in northern Italy and Germany by the Ottonians (919–1024), who gave it new life in what became known as the Holy Roman Empire (see map 5.2). Founded by Duke Henry the Fowler, the Ottonian dynasty was Saxon in origin and replaced the last Frankish rulers of East Francia. Henry's son, Otto the Great (912–973), became the king of East Francia (Germany) in 936 and was crowned emperor by the pope in Rome in 962. And if nostalgia had proved an inadequate foundation for a successful endogenous empire for the Carolingians, the persisting ideal of a Christian Roman Empire proved spectacularly successful as an organizing principle for a successor exogenous empire in the fragmented German lands. From the Ottonians down to its last Austrian Habsburg ruler in 1806, the Holy Roman Empire would endure for almost nine centuries through seven dynastic changes, even when its emperor-kings were never formally crowned as such by the pope (table 5.2).

The structure of the Holy Roman Empire had its origins in the empire of nostalgia pioneered by the Carolingians but took that model in the opposite direction, except for its development of a real bureaucracy that maintained itself no matter who became emperor. Charlemagne had

MAP 5.2. The Holy Roman Empire

Table 5.2. Imperial reigns and German kings

Time frame	Dynastic era	Number of kings	Total years	Years with an emperor
800–918	Carolingians	8	119	52
919–1024	Ottonians	5	105	50
1024–1125	Salians	4	101	58
1125–1137	Lothar III	1	12	4.5
1138–1254	Staufers	7	116	80
1254–1347	"Little Kings"	8	93	20
1347–1437	Luxembourgs	4	90	27
1438–1806	Habsburgs	18	368	365

Source: Wilson, *Heart of Europe,* 37.

conquered a vast contiguous territory with a population of over ten million people that put it on the cusp of becoming an endogenous empire. Had his heirs been able to maintain it as a unified polity, they might have succeeded in transforming it into one. Instead dissolution of the united Carolingian Empire left Europe divided into a large number of kingdoms that were themselves subdivided into smaller units ruled by autonomous dukes, counts, barons, marquises, and other holders of aristocratic titles. Ambitious kings in France, England, and Spain therefore focused their attention on building unified nation-states by subduing their own nobles, conquering neighboring frontier lands, and keeping rival kings at bay. While they employed the tools of empire pioneered by the Carolingians to create these more powerful states, none displayed Europe-wide imperial ambitions. The political situation in Germany and northern Italy provided fewer opportunities for the emergence of unified regional states. Germany was still more a cultural and geographical concept than a political one, consisting as it did of a patchwork of autonomous duchies. Italy was even more decentralized because it had devolved into rivalrous city-states, none of which had the capacity to permanently dominate the others or resist periodic invasions by stronger outside powers. (Neither Germany nor Italy would be united into nation-states similar to those in France, the Netherlands, Britain, or Spain until the late nineteenth century.) Instead, beginning with the Ottonians, ambitious kings here focused on reviving a Christian Roman Empire in which local autonomy was maintained within what resembled a much weaker version of a Xiongnu imperial confederacy. Rulers of its component parts recognized the authority of a singular elected emperor who left them otherwise independent. They only need agree that one of their number should be raised to the rank of emperor and contenders for that role were not limited to a single descent group as had been the practice among the Carolingians.

If the organizational components found within the Carolingian Empire (see table 5.1) appear to show an exogenous empire in the process of becoming endogenous, those of the Holy Roman Empire (table 5.3) display an evolution into a more purely exogenous one. The latter now attempted to organize its diverse people and places almost entirely through soft-power levers by stressing its sacred transnational mission to protect a universal Catholic Christian church even when its leaders were at odds with the popes in Rome. Unlike polities in western parts of Europe where monarchical power became associated with ruling a distinct people and territory, the Empire (as it was most commonly called) lacked a contiguous territory, singular national group, or imperial capital

Table 5.3. Endogenous empire organizational components in the Holy Roman Empire

Present	Partial	Absent
Organized to administer and exploit diversity		A primate imperial center with transportation systems designed to serve it militarily and economically
Imperial project that imposed some type of unity throughout the system		Monopoly of force within their territories, and military force projected outward
Centralized institutions of governance that were separate and distinct from the rulers		Systems of communication that allowed administration of all subject areas from the center directly

city. The one thing it did accomplish that the Carolingians did not was to create centralized institutions of governance separate and distinct from that of the ruler. The position of emperor was now permanent and independent of the actual person of the monarch, and the empire itself was indivisible. It could shift from one dynastic line to another with no loss of legitimacy, permitting rising new elites to replace declining older ones without a dissolution of the polity. That flexibility was reinforced by a system of electors who were empowered to choose a new emperor, the number of which was eventually limited to seven by the Golden Bull of 1356. While the electors normally just confirmed the existing emperor's heir, they did have the power to recognize a new line of rulers if the political conditions changed.

Kings already had an existing power base before they made a bid for the imperial title. As Peter Wilson explains, "Otto and his successors never regarded the Empire as a German nation state. In their eyes, what made them worthy to be emperor was that they already ruled such extensive lands. By the early eleventh century it had become accepted that whoever was German king was also king of Italy and Burgundy, even without separate coronations. The title King of the Romans (*Romanorum rex*) was added from 1110 in a bid to assert authority over Rome and reinforce claims that only the German king could be emperor."[39] By the late fifteenth century, the emperor's rule was confined largely to the German lands and their margins. That was eventually reflected in its 1512 name change to the Holy Roman Empire of the German Nation (Sacrum Romanum

Imperium Nationis Germanicae), although that designation slighted its Slavic subjects in central Europe. What made this system work was the willingness of the aristocracy to support the Empire in return for a say in its governance. This included participation in the policy-making Imperial Diet (Dieta Imperii, Reichstag), which originally met only periodically but had become institutionalized by the sixteenth century. If kings in France or England were centralizing power at the expense of their feudal nobility, the Empire granted its aristocracy defined liberties that helped preserve their privileged political status for centuries longer than in the west. As Wilson observes,

> The most important liberty was the right of lords to participate in the greater affairs of the Empire by having a voice in forming the political consensus. Rather than a constant battle between centralism and princely independence, the Empire's political history is better understood as a long process of delineating these rights and fixing them with greater precision. . . . The Empire's hierarchy was not a chain of command, but a multilayered structure allowing individuals and groups to disobey one authority whilst still professing loyalty to another. Imperial rule was not hegemonic, despite periodic moves towards a more command-style monarchy, notably under the Salians, but was characterized more by brokerage and negotiation. It worked because the main participants usually had more to gain from preserving the imperial order than by overturning or fragmenting it.[40]

The legal system employed by the Empire reflected this multilayered tapestry of intertwined threads.[41] Here counts and dukes judged disputes in their own sovereign territories while the Empire's courts focused on cases between such units or their rulers, dealt with complaints that involved conflicts over rights or status, and could examine charges against rulers accused of abusing their power. The Empire's legal system differed from those developing in neighboring nation-states that focused on implementing a fixed set of laws designed to be applied universally. The Empire's system focused instead on delivering equity: Would the decision rendered be deemed fair by the community given the context of the dispute and the motives of those involved? Given the inability of the Empire's courts to enforce their decisions if opposed, reflecting such community norms was important. Courts commonly accepted the validity of local customary practices unless they were deemed "bad." In many cases courts avoided the necessity of making definitive judgments by pressuring disputants to agree to mediation or arbitration. The time consumed and expense involved in keeping legal proceedings alive provided a strong incentive to settle disputes outside the court system. Appeals were common (there were two equal and parallel supreme courts), and in extreme situations cases lingered for generations, although they could be handled speedily when necessary. But by providing independent legal forums where different classes of people and individuals could publicly air their grievances, the Empire was better able to deal with social and political problems before they provoked violence. As Andreas Osiander observes, "One of the most interesting aspects of the legal order of the empire is that anyone within it could take their ruler to court (only the emperor himself was immune)."[42] Emphasis on seeking equity and consensus, plus having multiple paths for dispute resolution, helped the Empire preserve order within its vast territories with a minimal degree of intervention.[43]

If anything should have killed this long-lived polity, it was the violent divisions spawned by the Protestant Reformation in Germany during the sixteenth century. For a Christian empire that justified its existence as the defender of a universal church, the expanding schism between a rising number of Protestant sects and the Roman Catholic Church in Rome put its foundational rationale in doubt. Moreover, because the Empire relied on consensus-brokered political deals to govern, it was ill-equipped to cope with an ideological struggle where clerics on both sides urged their followers to brook no compromise. Yet the Empire did survive, first by accepting at face value both sides' affirmations that there was only "one, holy, catholic and apostolic Church," as proclaimed in the Christian Nicene Creed of 325. The Empire could reasonably maintain it was still defending that single universal church, particularly against the expanding Muslim Ottoman Empire, whose Sultan Suleiman the Magnificent (r. 1520–1566) had unsuccessfully laid siege to Vienna in 1529. Second, its Catholic emperor Ferdinand I (r. 1556–1564) took the view that his job was to maintain peace and order within the Empire, not resolve religious doctrinal disputes or ecclesiastical governance issues. Abandoning the hardline policies of his abdicating brother and king of Spain, Charles V, Ferdinand had earlier gone to the Imperial Diet in 1555 and hammered out the Peace of Augsburg. It recognized both Lutheranism and Catholicism as legitimate religious choices but put off reconciling them to some future date. A ruler was free to impose his own religion on his subjects, and those not agreeing could leave without penalty. Free imperial cities without such rulers could remain mixed.[44] This was a compromise that kept the peace among the Empire's component states for the next half century but had defects that eventually led to its breakdown. The most significant was its unwillingness to recognize the legitimacy of Calvinist sects whose rapid expansion was displacing Lutherans as the dominant Protestant group in many regions. The second was that assigning a ruler the power to impose his own religion on his subjects created perverse incentives. If Protestant rulers ousted Catholic ones (or vice versa), they could add new territories to those of their own faith. Third, because of unclarity about the dates to be applied or an inability to enforce the rules, the status of many expropriated Catholic Church properties remained subject to litigation and was still a topic of acrimonious debate at the Imperial Diet of 1608 a half century later.

None of these issues alone was enough to destabilize the Empire, but they did create fault lines that emerged with particular force during periods of political uncertainty. Both Protestants and Catholics had established their own military leagues and foreign alliances that could be mobilized against one another in a crisis. One of these would spark the Thirty Years' War (1618–1648) and devastate Germany as marauding armies, plagues, and famines killed off half the population in many places. It began with the death of a childless Emperor Matthias (r. 1612–1619) and a dispute over who should succeed him. A Protestant coup in Bohemia had just ousted his likeliest successor, the Catholic Hapsburg Archduke of Austria Ferdinand II, from his kingship there in 1618. The Bohemians then attempted to elect a Protestant, the Palatine elector Frederick V, as Holy Roman Emperor, but the other German Protestant electors refused to back him even though they constituted a majority. Indeed, as an elector, Frederik found himself forced to join their unanimous elevation of Ferdinand to the emperorship (r. 1619–1637), which put aside religious differences in favor of continuing the tradition of Hapsburg dynastic rule that was now in its 180th year. They only turned against Ferdinand when he tried to strip Frederick and other Protestant nobles who had opposed him of their lands and titles. Aided by the Spanish, the Catholic League and an imperial mercenary army recruited by Albrecht von Wallenstein (a wealthy Bohemian Catholic convert who proved himself a remarkably talented general) soon took control of major Protestant territories in central and northern Germany. Wallenstein was rewarded with land in the Protestant territories he conquered, a grant that alienated the aristocracy regardless of religion because it threatened the status of their own inherited estates. In 1629 Ferdinand issued the Edict of Restitution requiring the return of seized Church property, which his commanders on the ground were not keen to enforce because of the trouble it would cause. While the defeated Protestants were now too weak to defend themselves, they did have support from surrounding states that were not part of the Empire—France, the Netherlands, England, Denmark, and Sweden. They all shared a common hostility to the Habsburg kings of Spain and Austria and wished to see their gains rolled back. France's Cardinal Richelieu (staunchly anti-Protestant at home) financed an invasion of Germany by Protestant Sweden's King Gustavus Adolphus, whose advances deep into the south beginning in 1630 only ended when he was killed on the battlefield in 1632. (Whether he might have established a new Swedish empire in Germany had he lived is still debated.) After these setbacks to the Catholic cause and facing mounting financial problems, Ferdinand reconciled with his old enemies by agreeing to the Peace of Prague in 1635, which withdrew his Edict of Restitution, disbanded both Catholic and Protestant military leagues, and gave amnesty to those who had fought against the Empire. The agreement failed to end the war entirely because the French and Swedes fought on seeking territorial concessions from the Empire, a goal they achieved in the 1648 Peace of Westphalia, which ceded Metz and Alsace to France and parts of the southern Baltic coast to the Swedes.[45]

Although the Peace of Westphalia is commonly viewed as establishing the modern system of sovereign and equal territorial states, Osiander has demonstrated that it is better seen as the last of the great compromises that had long kept the Empire stable, noting that "compared to the religious-political deadlock that had paralyzed the empire during the decade or two preceding the war, it emerged from the peace congress unchanged in its conception, but in a better working condition."[46] The Peace of Westphalia fixed the defects of the Peace of Augsburg by depriving rulers of their power to determine the religious affiliations of their estates: the official religion of each was now frozen in place based on its status (Catholic, Protestant, or mixed) as of January 1, 1624. It also guaranteed the private exercise of religion for Catholics, Lutherans, and Calvinists alike and mandated some protection for members of minority faiths. As the laws were promulgated by the whole Empire, individual rulers and free cities could not abrogate them. As before, the estates within the Empire remained responsible for governing their own territories and could make alliances with outside powers as long as they were not detrimental to the Empire and did not pose a danger to public peace. The Empire's courts continued to hear cases that, even in the absence of a centralized government, provided protection of the Empire's smaller estates (more than three hundred) against more powerful ones and let the weak confront the strong on a relatively equal basis. Osiander observes,

> Stephan Putter, an eighteenth-century authority on German constitutional law, wrote in 1777 that "the constitution of the German empire indeed shows itself in favourable light, since every estate of the empire is free to do good in his lands, but can be prevented from doing evil by a higher power." August Ludwig von Schlozer, a professorial colleague of Pitter at Gottingen and a prominent enlightenment figure, in 1793 spoke of "happy Germany, the only country where, without prejudice to their dignity, one can prevail against one's rulers through legal action before an external tribunal, rather than before their own one."[47]

This positive assessment was not shared by the Empire's many critics who viewed its patchwork sovereignty and lack of centralization as out of sync with the times. France, Britain, Sweden, Denmark, and the Netherlands were all building centralized national governments with powerful militaries, primate cities, and clear lines of internal political authority. Nor was the structure of the Empire at all similar to that of the still-growing autocratic empires to its east, where Europeans deemed the authority of an Ottoman sultan and Russian tsar the acme of despotism. Unable to fit the Holy Roman Empire into any of their usual categories, post-Westphalian political philosophers made it a target of attack. In his excoriating 1667 book, *De statu imperii Germanici*, which saw more than one hundred thousand copies printed, Samuel Pufendorf declared that "*Germany* is an Irregular Body, and like some mis-shapen Monster, if it be measured by the common Rules of Politicks and Civil Prudence."[48] By "Irregular Body" he meant that its sovereignty was mixed, and for him that constituted a fundamental weakness. But it was Voltaire's 1756 evisceration that is best remembered: "This agglomeration that was called and which still calls itself the Holy Roman Empire is neither Holy, nor Roman, nor an Empire," a snarky putdown that is now better remembered than the Empire itself.[49] The first part of Voltaire's attack was misdirected, however, because "Holy Roman" did not designate two categories but one: the fourth-century Christian Roman Empire. Unlike the later caliphate, whose ruler was both head of state and head of the religion, the Christian Roman model envisioned secular rulers governing the state separate from an autonomous clerical establishment that maintained its own hierarchical leadership. Though this template was ancient and largely forgotten, its basic structure was still evident its two top positions, emperor and pope. Voltaire's assertion that it was not an empire was on stronger ground, but only because he assumed that "real empires" were those I have categorized as endogenous. The Holy Roman Empire was not that, but it was a successful exogenous shadow empire that functioned as an imperial polity for close to a millennium. Like other exogenous empires, it was organized along a different set of principles from endogenous ones—here based on a nostalgia for having an empire that people wished to maintain rather than break up. Despite its critics, the Empire remained fully functional for another 150 years after the Peace of Westphalia.

What finally killed the Holy Roman Empire was the emergence of a new ideology that replaced one set of universal ideals with an entirely different set inspired by the French Revolution. The Holy Roman Empire had used the universality of the Christian Church as its rationale to unite a large part of Europe otherwise fractured by language, nationality, and geography that survived even the Protestant-Catholic schism. But when the idea of building an equalitarian polity without a religious base seized the popular imagination, nostalgia for a lost past where Christianity reigned supreme and an aristocratic class ran the state could not compete with it. As Alexis de Tocqueville noted, it was an ideology whose scope and attraction closely resembled those of a religious movement, but one whose universal secular dogma concerned itself with the here and now and not some afterlife to come:

> The French Revolution proceeded with respect to this world in precisely the same way that religious revolutions proceeded with respect to the other. It took an abstract view of the citizen, outside any particular society, just as religions treated man in general, independent of country and time. It did not seek to determine the particular rights of the French citizen but rather the general rights and duties of man in the political realm.
>
> The French Revolution always sought out what was least particular and, so to speak, most *natural* in regard to social state and government. That is why it was able to make itself comprehensible to all, and why it could be imitated in a hundred places at once.
>
> Since it appeared to aim at the regeneration of the human race even more than at the reform of France, it kindled a passion that not even the most violent political revolutions had ever aroused before. It inspired proselytism and propaganda and therefore came to resemble a religious revolution, which was what contemporaries found so frightening about it. Or, rather, it itself became a new kind of religion—an imperfect religion, to be sure, without God, cult, or afterlife—yet a religion that, like Islam, inundated the earth with its soldiers, apostles, and martyrs.[50]

The greatest challenge this revolutionary ideology presented to the Empire was less its rejection of Christianity as a unifying principle than its rejection of feudal hierarchy and the organization of society into distinct corporate groups, each with unequal rights and privileges. This was reflected in the Empire's political structure, where electors, ecclesiastical estate holders, nobles, and free cities might make policy in Reichstag but the vast majority of its people remained simple subjects with no right to rule themselves. The French Revolution had in 1789 abolished the old estate organization that recognized the nobility and clergy (about 2 percent of the population) as separate and superior classes, replacing them with a single body of politically equal citizens. The structure it destroyed was the very heart of the Empire's organization and its primary rationale for existing. Even if the new French Empire under Napoleon (who had himself declared emperor in 1804) did not immediately seek to impose this level of citizen equality on the territories it overran, the French did force the Empire to restructure itself at the expense of its small estates, ecclesiastical duchies, and free cities. The most powerful German states within the Empire, such as Prussia, Bavaria, and Saxony, gained from this policy and either allied themselves with Napoleon or were forced to sign treaties that put them under the control of the French Empire. After losing a series of battles and seeing Vienna occupied in 1805, Emperor Francis II released all his subjects from any obligation to the Empire (effectively abolishing it) on August 6, 1806, and retitled himself emperor of Austria. While the French Empire would itself collapse in the wake of Napoleon's disastrous invasion of Russia in 1812, the 1815 Congress of Vienna that redrew the boundaries of Europe to again make the world safe for monarchies did not attempt to restore the Holy Roman Empire.

Tocqueville argues, however, that the Empire may have reached its sell-by date well before the French army arrived at the gates of Vienna because it could exist only as long as its subjects accepted their subordinate status within it as natural. The French revolutionary insistence that the Empire's hierarchy was neither natural nor sustainable was a spark that found ready fuel in German lands:

> In order for arguments of this type to provoke revolutions, the minds of men must be prepared to accept them by certain prior changes in social conditions, customs, and mores. There are times when men are so different from one another that the idea of a single law applicable to all is almost incomprehensible. There are other times when it is enough to show them the vague and distant image of such a law for them to

recognize it instantly and hasten after it. The most extraordinary thing was not that the French Revolution employed the methods or conceived the ideas that it did. The great novelty was that so many nations had reached the point where such methods could be used effectively and such maxims could be readily accepted.[51]

As utopian dreams for the future gained ground over veneration for tradition, the empires restored by the Congress of Vienna in Europe—and elsewhere in the world—would find themselves fighting a rearguard battle over the next century to preserve themselves before being swept way in the aftermath of the First World War.

CHAPTER SIX

Shadows in the Forest

I have no way to defend my borders but to extend them.

—CATHERINE THE GREAT, EMPRESS OF RUSSIA (1762–1796)

Vacuum Empires

Vacuum empires arose in the sparsely settled forest and forest steppe zones of northeastern Europe that were previously without even nascent state-level political structures. They were vacuums not because no people lived there but because they sucked in would-be empire builders who realized the potential of unifying such a vast region (over 2 million km²) once it had achieved a sufficient level of economic development, a task its indigenous population either had no interest in undertaking or lacked the capacity to accomplish. For many millennia these forest areas were inhabited only by dispersed communities engaged in subsistence farming, foraging, hunting, and animal husbandry with little urbanization or political centralization. They interacted only with other communities like themselves or with foreign traders transiting between the Baltic and the Black Seas. Nor was the northern forest zone initially a very attractive target for invaders because of its low population density, the absence of towns to occupy, and the lack of precious metals to plunder—not to mention bitterly cold winters and swarms of blood-sucking summer insects. Divided by many rivers and dotted with extensive marshlands and bogs, its dense forests presented serious obstacles to any potential attackers because the local inhabitants could use their knowledge of a seemingly trackless wilderness to hide from invaders or ambush them. Moreover, with the exception of parts in western Europe, the Eurasian forest zone lay far from any powerful agrarian states and had only steppe nomadic polities on its southern frontiers.

The forest areas located from watersheds of the Dniester River in the west to the Volga River in the east saw the first development of state-level organizations in the middle of the ninth century. At that time and afterward, a series of successive exogenous empires arose as a product of interaction with nomadic empires on their southern steppe borders during the medieval period. These included the Kievan Rus' (862–1242), the Grand Duchy of Lithuania and Polish-Lithuanian Commonwealth (1251–1795), and the Grand Duchy (later Tsardom) of Moscow (1283–1721). The last transformed itself into the endogenous Russian Empire under Peter the Great (r. 1682–1725), which eventually came to rule over almost 23 million km^2 until its dissolution in 1917. All these exogenous empires were characterized by their expansion into territorial vacuums in which they became the dominant power in the absence of other rivals where the local populations lacked the ability to resist them. Until the late eighteenth century none proved able to incorporate the many powerful steppe nomadic tribes on their southern and eastern frontiers. Nor did they achieve parity with the Byzantine (and later Ottoman) Empire to their south or displace the more established European states to their west, a deficiency they would compensate for with treaties and marriage alliances. Only during the reign of Catherine the Great (1762–1796) would the Russian Empire break out of its northern forest confines to incorporate both the steppe tribal confederations and the Polish Lithuanian Commonwealth to give it frontiers with the Ottoman Empire and Iran in the south and Prussia and the Hapsburgs in the west.

The Kievan Rus' Empire

THE KHAZARS AND OPENING OF THE FOREST ZONE

It was the Khazar Khaganate (650–969) that would initially have the greatest impact on the lives of the forest peoples to the north, particularly the communities closest to the steppe. It facilitated the expansion of trade networks that transformed what had been an economic backwater into a commercial hub for the exportation of furs and slaves in exchange for silver dirhams minted by the Muslim Caliphate and its successor states.[1] As Eric Wolf has shown, long-distance trade in furs or slaves could have a transforming impact on the organization of the societies that provided them, even when they lay beyond the control of the states generating that demand.[2] By focusing on fur production, forest communities that had formerly been exclusively subsistence oriented entered a cash economy and participated in a trading system that lasted many centuries.[3] The slave trade had a similar if more pernicious impact, and it too would continue for many centuries. Although the population densities in these regions were relatively low, communities lacking enough political organization to protect themselves (or living in polities too weak to provide it) were easy targets. Steppe nomads in particular had the capacity to mount raids on farming villages to obtain captives who were then sent south for sale. They also targeted each other to meet the Islamic world's demand for mamluks, since pagan Turkic peoples were believed to be the best source of these slave soldiers.[4] So large was this trade that the word for *slave* in English and other European languages was derived from "Slav," the name of the predominant inhabitants of the southern steppe-forest zone, who were its main victims.[5] Indigenous populations had a strong incentive to develop stronger political and military institutions in response to such violent acts either to defend their communities or to become slave raiders themselves. It was this economic and political transformation that laid the foundation for vacuum empires that would make the forest zone itself the center of their new states. Its indigenous peoples were not empire builders themselves but adapted themselves to working with people who were.

The Khazar Khaganate (map 6.1) established itself as an imperial confederacy on the North Caucasian steppe when it ousted the Onoghur-Bulghars in 670. Khazar khagans were members of the nonnative royal Ashina lineage that had earlier led the western part of the Kök Türk Empire. At its height in the mid-ninth century the Khazar Khaganate ruled over at least two dozen subject peoples across a territory of 3 million km² between the Black and Caspian Seas that included other steppe nomads such as the Pechenegs, Magyars, Bulgars, Sabirs, and Oghuz, who had no imperial ambitions of their own.[6] It also ruled over a variety of sedentary peoples that included the Alans and other indigenous groups living in the Caucasus as well the Don Alans and numerous Finnic communities in the Volga-Don interfluve: Mordva, Cheremis, and Burtas (who were mainly hunters).

The Khazar Khaganate began as a classic mirror shadow empire that responded to both the threats and opportunities of being the steppe neighbor to two powerful endogenous empires. As Peter Golden notes, this had both military and economic consequences: "Lying on the borders of Byzantium and Sâsânid Iran, and more importantly the latter's dynamic successor, the Arabian Caliphate, Khazaria was in close contact with the

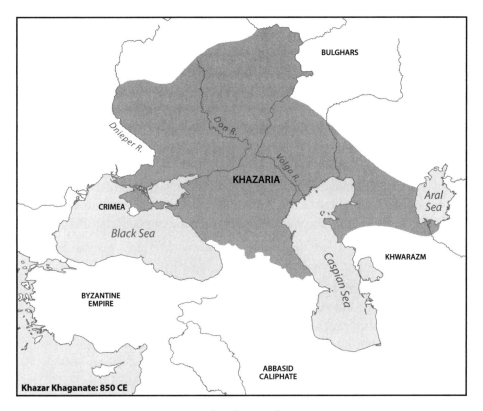

MAP 6.1. The Khazar Khaganate.

two greatest sedentary powers of the Mediterranean world. The Khazars also sat astride the most important East-West trade routes. This pattern of intimate political and economic interaction with the sedentary world was the driving force behind the efflorescence of Khazar statehood."[7] The Khazars were indeed ideally located to extract revenue from the international trade that passed through their territories. Their political center of Itil somewhere north of the Volga River delta (its location has never been precisely determined) lay at the juncture of the north–south riverine trade network and the east–west overland caravan routes from central Asia. With the emergence of the Abbasid Caliphate in 750, the volume of trade flowing through Khazaria grew exponentially. The khaganate's most significant source of revenue was a 10 percent customs duty imposed on the transit trade that the mid-tenth-century Arab geographer Istakhri described as "dues and tithes on merchandise, according to certain usages of theirs, from every land route and sea and river," of which the maritime customs fees were the most important for the "wellbeing and wealth of the king of the Khazars," according to the slightly later Persian *Hudud al-'Alam (Boundaries of the World)*.[8] Of the goods traded, the most lucrative were slaves and furs that came from the forest zones in the north, Istakhri explaining that "the beaver-skins which are taken to all parts of the world are found only in those rivers in the territory of Bulghar and the [Rus'] and Kiev, and not anywhere else so far as I know."[9] He went on to add that the Khazar country itself "produces nothing which can be exported to other lands except isinglass. As to the slaves, honey, wax, beaver—and other skins, they are imported to Khazaria."[10]

Thomas Noonan argues that it was the value of these furs and slaves that made the previously ignored forest regions targets of intense exploitation and produced the revenue needed to support a powerful state like that run by the Khazars:

> The economy of the khaganate experienced a long period of growth precisely because Khazaria dominated the Islamic trade with the north and derived great revenues from it. The wealth coming from this commerce allowed the khaganate to hire large numbers of Islamic mercenaries from Khwārizm (the al-Lārisiya). With this additional force, the Khazars were able to impose their control over many neighboring peoples and force them to pay tribute as well as furnish troops. The revenues coming from the Islamic trade with northern Europe thus formed the foundation for the expansion of Khazar power into such areas as the middle Volga, the Oka basin, and the middle Dnepr. The reports, discussed above, of the numerous dependent peoples in the khaganate reflect this period of growing political power based on the revenues from the Islamic trade.[11]

Little attention has been paid to just how unique this strategy of northern expansion was. Steppe empires historically displayed far less interest in the forest peoples to their north than in the agrarian empires to their south. Their populations were dispersed and the value of what could be taken from them meager in comparison to rich and densely populated agricultural states. It was also more work. Dealing with the agrarian empires was a wholesale one-stop-shopping experience: their centralized governments were responsible for collecting the demanded goods or precious metals and delivering them to steppe leaders for redistribution or reexport. Extracting resources from the forest zone was a retail business that required obtaining the desired goods from the local population, a task that was often left to the Khazar vassals (such as the upstream Volga Bulgars) who bordered them. And what they could provide might not justify the effort involved in extracting it—just how many furs or slaves were really required to meet the domestic needs of their steppe overlords? This calculus changed significantly when the demand for northern products was not local but international and when the price paid by the ultimate consumers was far higher than the costs of acquisition and transport. This favorable exchange ratio (and weight-to-value ratio) had long existed for silk from China or spices from Southeast Asia. It was now driving the expansion of the trade in furs and slaves out of the Eurasian forest zone as they too began to generate similarly supercharged profits. The demand came largely from the Muslim world and secondarily from the Byzantine Empire, not the poorer post-Roman western European states, which had few export items to sell, or Tang China, where furs were associated with uncouth barbarians.

The scale of this increased trade was as breathtaking as its impact on local economies. Noonan has estimated that the "trade of northern Europe with the Islamic world resulted in the export of some 100,000,000 to 200,000,000 whole dirhams into European Russia and the Baltic."[12] So when Islamic trade routes shifted north toward the lands of the Bulgars on the middle Volga in the tenth century with the rise of the Samanid Empire in Transoxiana and Khorasan, whose coinage became the dominant currency of the trade, the Khazar Khaganate saw its share of that trade decline substantially. And because the Khazar Khaganate remained dependent on tapping foreign trade for its survival, this declining revenue seriously undermined its stability. Khazar tributaries began looking for other alternatives, and one was provided by the arrival of Scandinavian merchant warriors from the Baltic Sea region. In search of business opportunities, they were also quick to realize that there were political gains to be had as they expanded south into the frontier territories formerly ruled by the Khazars. It would be the Rus' from today's Sweden who would within a few generations unite the entire forest zone and rule it until the arrival of the Mongols in the thirteenth century (map 6.2).

THE RISE OF THE RUS' AND THEIR VACUUM EMPIRE

Vacuum empires emerged in peripheral areas that lacked indigenous polities capable of expanding their rule beyond a single region and the people who lived within it. What made them possible in the northern forest zone beginning in the ninth and tenth centuries was the transformation of the regional economy from one based on low-value foraging and subsistence agriculture into one that exported high-value furs and

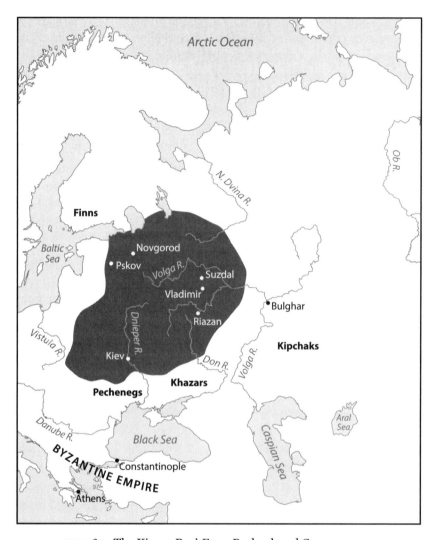

MAP 6.2: The Kievan Rus'. From Burbank and Cooper, 2010.

slaves in exchange for silver. This attracted in-migrating Viking maritime merchant-warrior groups known as the Varangians from the Baltic Sea who had previously focused their attention to the west and south. Here they encountered two types of societies. The first were scattered Finno-Ugric foraging communities that were active participants in their frontier fur trade because they had access to the best pelts but were too far north to fall under the control of any steppe polities. The second were a variety of settled agricultural peoples with towns whose indigenous political leaders were bound in some way to the Khazar Khaganate as tributaries. It would be these groups that combined with the Scandinavians to create a shadow empire using a Khazar tributary and trade template, but one that centered itself within the forest zone. The Varangians, also known as the Rus', would take the lead militarily and politically, but the region's indigenous elite would prove itself capable of ensuring that the resultant exogenous empire served its own interests as well.

The Scandinavians first arrived in the far north during the middle of the eighth century when they established the trading settlement of Lagoda, located at the southern end of Europe's largest lake near today's Russian-Finnish border. Their initial plan may have been simply to barter manufactured items (iron knife blades, kettles, needles, beads, etc.) to the region's dispersed foraging communities, where these goods were in high demand. But Lagoda took on a larger, starring role when silver dirhams first began appearing in large numbers, produced by the expanding fur and slave trade with the Islamic world. For the Vikings, Noonan explains, that turned what had been an insect-infested backwater into a rich target of opportunity:

> The lack of indigenous sources of silver in both medieval Russia and Scandinavia gave these dirhams a special value. An examination of the earliest dirham hoards from Russia and the Baltic shows that dirhams initially reached Russia in the late eighth century and soon after a growing number of dirhams regularly found their way into both Russia and the Baltic. Most of the dirhams to reach Russia seem to have been kept there for a variety of purposes. Many of these dirhams came to the Dnepr and Volga basins as payment to the local peoples for their furs. But, a significant number of dirhams, perhaps as high as 36% on average, were re-exported from Russia to the Baltic. . . . But, while many peoples of the Baltic may have been attracted to Ladoga, the available evidence suggests very strongly that only the Vikings ventured into the interior of Russia to seek out the source of silver coins. By 839, these Viking adventurers had become so familiar with the interior of Russia that they had reached Constantinople. Their appearance here indicates that it took the Vikings about one generation, ca. 800–ca. 840, to discover how to travel south across Russia using the great water routes of eastern Europe.[13]

The Vikings were maritime traders and warriors whose lightweight boats could be portaged from one river drainage system to another or around impassible cataracts. This gave them access to most of the communities in the region as well as external connections to the Baltic Sea in the north and the Black and Caspian Seas in the south. There was plenty of good wood to build more boats when they were needed, and additional settlers or warriors could join them from Scandinavia on short notice. Because rivers were natural travel routes for the boat-going Vikings, they could more easily exploit the forest zone and its inhabitants than could the steppe nomadic Khazars, for whom rivers were barriers to movement except when they froze over in the winter. In this regard, the Vikings were fortunate in their timing because they expanded at the beginning of the Medieval Warm Period (800–1200), when there was less ice and higher water levels than previously, facilitating their movement through the forest zone and reducing that of steppe nomadic rivals.[14] The Vikings' ax- and sword-wielding infantry was also better adapted to fighting in heavily wooded areas and marshlands than the steppe nomads, whose preferred battlegrounds were treeless open plains where their mobility was unrestricted and targets for their arrows easily spotted.

The Khazars projected their power into the forest zone by employing frontier tributaries, although there is no historical documentation about how they organized and managed this system. Nevertheless, its consequences were profound because the relationship created a new class of indigenous political leaders who acted as intermediaries between their communities and the outside world. Their first task was to organize their own people into tax-paying units and collect the required tribute payments in furs from them, a task that increased their own power too. The process created a more complex surplus-producing economy that attracted Volga Bulghar middleman merchants (among others) to the forest zone. They were willing to pay in silver to acquire additional furs and other goods (lumber, honey, beeswax, and slaves) that could be fed into the international trade system.[15] As silver coins entered these local economies at an ever-accelerating rate, many tributary communities switched to paying their taxes in cash. In regions where farming was the economic mainstay, that cash rate was set at one silver dinar per plow in lieu of a fur pelt.[16] As the entire regional economy grew, towns like Novgorod and Kiev emerged as political and trading centers in their own right. Nor did paying tribute come without substantial benefits, the most important of which was a broad Pax Khazarica that ensured that travel and trade across the khaganate's steppelands and river systems were safe and secure. Being tributaries had another important benefit for the settled farming communities as well: preventing neighboring steppe nomads who were under Khazar control from raiding their villages and markets. That alone would have been worth the price of admission in a world where the danger of such raiding had previously precluded the development of otherwise good agricultural land. Indeed, a number of farming groups expanded eastward into areas under Khazar protection in what is now central Russia, where they were free of such danger. On a more prosaic level, the Khazars ensured day-to-day peace by reducing conflict between their subject peoples and providing them with a formal system of justice to resolve disputes.[17]

By the early ninth century the Vikings had established enough of an autonomous presence in the north to begin portraying themselves as a peer polity with the Khazars when they sent a diplomatic mission to Byzantium in 838 that identified their ruler as a khagan, and there are also a number of Arab accounts that described a "Rus' khagan." Just who these Rus' khagans were (they are never named) remains uncertain, but the ministers at the court of Louis the Pious who received the homeward-bound embassy opined that they were a variety of Swedes.[18] The title of khagan was an imperial one among Turko-Mongolian peoples, and whether the Vikings simply appropriated it to stake a claim of independence from the Khazars or had it granted to them by the Khazars is subject to debate. Later Rus' rulers used the local title of *kniaz*, a nonexclusive rank that is usually (and unhelpfully) translated as "prince." Their top leadership position was the grand kniaz, which was somewhat equivalent to a *rex* (king) in medieval western European states or *archon* (governor) for the Byzantines.[19] As we will see, part of the problem interpreting the meaning of such titles in regard to the Rus' was that the grand kniaz and the shadow empire he ruled was organized quite differently from other imperial polities, including the steppe empires that it appeared to most closely resemble. The relationship between the center and its component parts, between its Viking ruling elite and its Slavic and Finno-Ugric subjects, and the autonomy of its towns and cities from its rulers gave it an unusually decentralized political dynamic even for a shadow empire.

According to the *Russian Primary Chronicle*, the earliest written history of the Rus', their polity began with an invitation to rule after a successful revolt in 860 against a previous set of Viking rulers (the aforementioned khagans?):

> The tributaries of the Varangians drove them back beyond the sea and, refusing them further tribute, set out to govern themselves. There was no law among them, but tribe rose against tribe. Discord thus ensued among them, and they began to war one against another. They said to themselves, "Let us seek a prince who may rule over us and judge us according to the Law." They accordingly went overseas to the Varangian Russes. . . . The Chuds, the Slavs, the Krivichians, and the Ves' then said

to the people of Rus', "Our land is great and rich, but there is no order in it. Come to rule and reign over us." They thus selected three brothers, with their kinsfolk, who took with them all the Russes and migrated. The oldest, Rurik, located himself in Novgorod [on Lake Ilmen]; the second, Sineus, at Beloozero [on Lake Beloye]; and the third, Truvor, in Izborsk [on Lake Peipus]. On account of these Varangians, the district of Novgorod became known as the land of Rus'. The present inhabitants of Novgorod are descended from the Varangian race, but aforetime they were Slavs. After two years, Sineus and his brother Truvor died, and Rurik assumed the sole authority. He assigned cities to his followers, Polotsk to one, Rostov to another, and to another Beloozero. In these cities there are thus Varangian colonists, but the first settlers were, in Novgorod, Slavs; in Polotsk, Krivichians; at Beloozero, Ves', in Rostov, Merians and in Murom, Muromians. Rurik had dominion over all these districts.[20]

The claim that these diverse ethnic groups invited the Rus' to rule them is often dismissed as improbable, but the reasons for doing so were sound given the structure of the societies making the offer. In his seventeenth-century treatise on the perils of political anarchy, Thomas Hobbes famously concluded that people without a common ruler to protect life and property are doomed to "continual fear, and danger of violent death; and the life of man, solitary, poor, nasty, brutish, and short."[21] In reality, governance without institutionalized leadership was workable but often proved inadequate as groups grew more diverse or were attacked by outsiders, conditions that emerged as the region's trading economy expanded and private stores of wealth attracted raiders. Yet here no one group was powerful enough to create a larger indigenous regional state by conquering the others, and none was willing to submit voluntarily to the authority of a neighboring people no stronger than themselves. This dilemma made the choice of an outsider—a stranger king—to rule over them all equally an attractive option, particularly when they were proven warriors who could defend their territories more effectively than the locals. Recruiting a stranger king was a widespread political phenomenon cross-culturally. Marshall Sahlins has argued that it produced polities in which the immigrants held the political offices but could not alienate the long-standing rights of the indigenous people who had invited them to assume power:

> Summarising and at some risk generalising, in these stranger-kingships, two forms of authority and legitimacy coexist in a state of mutual dependence and reciprocal incorporation. The native people

and the foreign rulers claim precedence on different bases. For the underlying people it is the founder-principle: the right of first occupancy—in the maximal case, the claim of autochthony. Earth-people by nature, often characterised as "the owners," their inherent relation to the land gives them unique access to the divine and ancestral sources of its productivity—hence their indispensable "religious" authority and ritual functions. But the stranger-kings trump these claims of priority in aggressive and transgressive demonstrations of superior might, and thus take over the sovereignty. Typically, then, there is some enduring tension between the foreign-derived royals and the native people. Invidious disagreements about legitimacy and superiority may surface in their partisan renderings of the founding narratives, each claiming a certain superiority over the other.[22]

One consequence of Rurik being recruited as a Rus' stranger king was that only his descendants were deemed eligible to become rulers after he died. This laid the foundation for a seven-hundred-year line of Rurikid rulers whose authority was based less on the details of their specific genealogical lineages than on their accepted membership in a royal "golden clan" that held the exclusive right to compete for the office of grand kniaz and were deemed legitimate when they succeeded.[23] Nonmembers could and often did wield de facto power, but it needed to be cloaked in some relationship to a figurehead ruler who did hold the correct status. This type of political exclusivity was well rooted in the political cultures of the Khazars and other hierarchically organized Turko-Mongolian peoples but was absent among the Vikings. But even if other Scandinavians refused to believe that Rurikids were their superiors, it proved impossible to replace them once the dynasty took root because no one would recognize a ruler who did not have this descent. A Rus' grand kniaz never feared replacement by non-royal outsiders but instead looked to foil plots hatched by his own patrilineal relatives (particularly paternal uncles, brothers, half brothers, and nephews), who needed only to kill him to become a legitimate replacement. With morbid regularity, this led either to the deaths of such potential rivals or to the assassination of the ruler himself.[24]

In spite of this Rurikid exclusivity as titular rulers, during its first century of its existence the Kievan Rus' polity owed its survival to the efforts of three generations of powerbrokers who acted on their behalf: Oleg, the foster father of Rurik's young son Igor; Olga, widow of Igor and long-reigning regent for her son Sviatoslav; and Dobrynia, Saint Vladimir the Great's maternal uncle, guardian, and military governor (*voevoda*) of

Novgorod, who engineered his seizure of the throne. Indeed, it might be said that the greatest danger to the stability of the Rus' polity before the reign of Vladimir (980–1015) came from its own unrestrained Rurikid rulers, whose rash actions precipitated their untimely deaths. Vladimir's grandfather Igor would be murdered by Slavic tributaries after exceeding the customary bounds of extortion; his father, Sviatoslav, would lose his head to Pecheneg nomads after a failed military campaign on the Byzantine frontier; and his half brother Yaropolk would be betrayed by his own allies once they came to believe it was in their interests to do so.

Oleg became the de facto ruler of the nascent Rus' state in 879 when, "on his deathbed, Rurik bequeathed his realm to Oleg, who belonged to his kin, and entrusted to Oleg's hands his son Igor, for he was very young."[25] (To be kin enough to rule the state on Igor's behalf but not royal enough to rule it himself may have meant that he was Rurik's brother-in-law.) Rurik had been content with his territories in the north, and he encouraged other Viking groups to seek their fortunes farther south along the Dnieper River trade route, which led to the Black Sea and the imperial realms of the Khazar Turks and the Byzantine Greeks. The most important of these were Askold and Dir, "two men who did not belong to his [Rurik's] kin, but were boyars [aristocrats]."

> They obtained permission to go to Tsar'grad [Constantinople] with their families. They thus sailed down the Dnieper, and in the course of their journey they saw a small city on a hill [Kiev]. Upon their inquiry as to whose town it was, they were informed that three brothers . . . had once built the city, but that since their deaths, their descendants were living there as tributaries of the Khazars. Askold and Dir remained in the city, and after gathering together many Varangians, they established their dominion over the country of the Polyanians at the same time that Rurik was ruling at Novgorod.[26]

In Kiev they built a powerful city-state, organizing a two-hundred-ship raid on Constantinople in 860 in which they pillaged the area around it before returning home.[27] They also likely traded with Khazars via the Don River trade route, where a portage led to the lower Volga River delta, although whether they were ever Khazar tributaries is unclear. After Rurik died, Oleg was keen to expand into this wealthier and more densely populated part of the middle and lower Dnieper. With an army composed of Varangians and local tributaries, Oleg struck south and seized Smolensk before taking Kiev by treachery in 882. Presenting himself as a traveling stranger and an official envoy on his way to Constantinople, he invited

Askold and Dir to meet him outside the city where his boats were moored. They agreed to come and pay their respects, unaware that Oleg had prepared an ambush. "Then all the soldiery jumped out of the boats, and Oleg said to Askold and Dir, 'You are not princes nor even of princely stock, but I am of princely birth.' Igor' was then brought forward, and Oleg announced that he was the son of Rurik. They killed Askold and Dir, and . . . Oleg set himself up as prince in Kiev, and declared that it should be the mother of Russian cities."[28] Rus' was now an exogenous empire ruled from its southern capital of Kiev (hence Kievan Rus') and Novgorod declined to secondary status. More aggressive than Askold and Dir, within a few years Oleg forced the Polyanians, the Drevlians, the Severians, and the Radimichians (all nearby Slavic groups) to cut their ties to the Khazars and pay that tribute to the Rus'. By the 890s he had taken control of the areas bordering the Danube delta as well. The Khazars were in no position to prevent this because invading Pecheneg nomads had forced their clients in the region, the Magyars, to decamp for Hungary. Oleg followed up on this consolidation of Rus's control over the whole forest region between the Baltic and the Black Sea by mounting an attack on Constantinople in 907, reportedly ten times the size of the 860 raid. In addition to the loot they picked up pillaging, the Rus' received a large cash payment to go home plus a trade agreement that was ratified in 911. It allowed Rus' merchants to trade freely with the Byzantines and paid for their stays in Constantinople when they traveled there.[29] Oleg could take credit for having created an empire from the base bequeathed to him by Rurik that his ward Igor finally got to rule when he died in 913.

For Igor such wars proved less successful than those of Oleg. The Rus' organized raids on the eastern Caspian seacoast with the cooperation of the Khazar khagan in 913–914, but the project ended in failure when, upon their return to the Volga delta, many were killed in a battle with the Muslim Khazar royal guard, who were outraged by their khagan's unseemly deal.[30] In 941 Igor attacked Constantinople only to meet with failure when his ships were destroyed by the Byzantines' famed Greek fire. What loot the Rus' and their allies obtained pillaging the city's outskirts was also lost when the Byzantine fleet intercepted their remaining ships on the way home, and in 944 the trade treaty Igor ratified with the Byzantines was less favorable than the one negotiated by Oleg.[31] That winter Igor collected a large tribute payment from the forest-dwelling Derevlians northwest of Kiev. Seemingly in need of more funds to reward his own warrior entourage (*druzhina*), who had been complaining about his stinginess, Igor impulsively returned to the Derevlian capital of Iskorosten to collect an additional round of payments accompanied by only a small number of men. There the angry Derevlians, fearing that there would be no end to his exactions, killed him and his men and buried them outside the town.[32]

The murder of a grand kniaz by his Slavic tributaries was an act of rebellion that exposed the weakness of Rus' governance, whose traditional mode of tax collection (*poliudie*) required that the ruler and his men come each winter to extract the payments personally. Far from fearing retribution, "the Derevlians then said, 'See, we have killed the Prince of Rus'. Let us take his wife Olga for our Prince Mal, and then we shall obtain possession of [Igor's son] Svyatoslav, and work our will upon him." Upon arriving before Olga in Kiev, their envoys announced the killing of Igor and demanded she marry their ruler. Rather than rejecting these demands outright and threatening retaliation, Olga appeared to believe herself in such a weak position that she feigned agreement, saying, 'Your proposal is pleasing to me; indeed, my husband cannot rise again from the dead. But I desire to honor you tomorrow in the presence of my people. Return now to your boat, and remain there with an aspect of arrogance. I shall send for you on the morrow, and you shall say, "We will not ride on horses nor go on foot; carry us in our boat." And you shall be carried in your boat.' Thus she dismissed them to their vessel."[33] The site of the planned meeting was a stone reception hall outside the city near the river that was part of a tomb and temple complex where Olga had ordered a large trench be dug overnight. In the morning a group of Kievans bewailing their fate arrived to carry the twenty Derevlians in their boat to the place where Olga now awaited them. "The latter sat on the cross-benches in great robes, puffed up with pride. They thus were borne into the court before Olga, and when the men had brought the Derevlians in, they dropped them into the trench along with the boat. Olga bent over and inquired whether they found the honor to their taste. They answered that it was worse than the death of Igor'. She then commanded that they should be buried alive, and they were thus buried."[34] That these gruesome theatrics followed the template of an iconic Viking ship burial and took place in an elite tomb complex was a bit of irony undoubtedly lost on their Derevlian victims but not on their Rus' organizers. Before news of the massacre could reach the Derevlians, Olga sent a messenger demanding they send her a delegation composed of their most distinguished men because otherwise her people would not consent to her leaving Kiev. Upon the delegation's arrival, Olga suggested they use her sauna and clean themselves. Once they entered the steam bath, she ordered the doors barred and the building set ablaze, incinerating the second Derevlian delegation.

She was not yet finished.

Olga then sent to the Derevlians the following message, "I am now coming to you, so prepare great quantities of mead in the city where you
killed my husband, that I may weep over his grave and hold a funeral
feast for him." When they heard these words, they gathered great quantities of honey and brewed mead. Taking a small escort, Olga made the
journey [of 150 km] with ease, and upon her arrival at Igor's tomb, she
wept for her husband. She bade her followers pile up a great mound
and when they had piled it up, she also gave command that a funeral
feast should be held. Thereupon the Derevlians sat down to drink, and
Olga bade her followers wait upon them.
    The Derevlians inquired of Olga where the retinue was which they
had sent to meet her. She replied that they were following with her
husband's bodyguard. When the Derevlians were drunk, she bade her
followers fall upon them, and went about herself egging on her retinue
to the massacre of the Derevlians. So they cut down five thousand of
them; but Olga returned to Kiev and prepared an army to attack the
survivors.[35]

After losing an initial battle, the Derevlians retreated behind the wooden
walls of their towns since the Rus' lacked the skills and equipment needed
to take them by direct assault. Olga chose to focus her attention on Iskorosten and settled in for a siege. It was still ongoing a year later, at which
point she employed a trick to set the town ablaze and then "took the city
and burned it, and captured the elders of the city. Some of the other captives she killed, while she gave others as slaves to her followers. The remnant she left to pay tribute. She imposed upon them a heavy tribute."[36]
    While Olga's revenge restored Rus' hegemony over its restive tribu-
taries, her major contribution was reforming the polity's institutions of
governance as regent for her young son Svyatoslav from 945 through the
early 960s. She was aided in this task by the powerful Varangian warlord
Sveinald, who commanded the army for the entire time she was regent
and went on to serve Svyatoslav when he began ruling in his own right. In
the year following her victory over the Derevlians, Olga reorganized their
territories and put them under the direct control of Kiev with a new capital at Vruchiy. She replaced the customary piratical mode of tribute collection here and elsewhere with a more law-based institutional process in
which appointed officials set up shop in local strongholds (pogosts) to collect taxes at fixed rates, administer the law, and provide secure places for
merchants to trade. Although the Rus' polity had its origins in Novgorod

and the north, the south had overshadowed it after Oleg transferred its capital to Kiev six decades earlier. As a northerner from Pskov herself, Olga appeared keen to better integrate the two regions. Beginning in 947 she reorganized Novgorod's administrative structure by setting up pogosts, fixing territorial boundaries, setting tax rates, and encouraging more trade. According to Greek records, Svyatoslav was sent to Novgorod as well. Despite this, the areas beyond the surrounding Kievan plains (Polyania) and forests (Derevlia) were only loosely governed by the Rus' until much later, even when they paid tribute. Olga then turned her attention to foreign affairs, making a state visit in 957 to Constantinople, where her conversion to Christianity made her a welcome guest who was personally hosted by the Byzantine imperial family. (The Orthodox Church would declare her a saint in 1547.) Thus, after a beginning bathed in blood, Olga's policies produced two decades of peace and prosperity and she remained in Kiev running its domestic affairs until her death in 969 while her son engaged in a series of far-flung wars.[37]

Svyatoslav was keen to prove himself a successful warrior after Olga relinquished her regency, spending the entire decade of his rule on the move with his druzhina companions-in-arms. He was a staunch pagan, rejecting his mother's Christianity as unbefitting a warrior like himself. "When Prince Svyatoslav had grown up and matured, he began to collect a numerous and valiant army. Stepping light as a leopard, he undertook many campaigns. Upon his expeditions he carried with him neither wagons nor kettles, and boiled no meat, but cut off small strips of horseflesh, game, or beef, and ate it after roasting it on the coals. Nor did he have a tent, but he spread out a horse-blanket under him, and set his saddle under his head; and all his retinue did likewise."[38] Unlike his father, Igor, Svyatoslav had a natural talent for war and won victories over two great (if declining) powers: the steppe Khazar Khaganate in the east and the Balkan Bulgarian Empire in the southwest. He advanced against the Khazars from the north along the middle Volga River in 964 rather than from the west along the Don River, which was the more usual Rus' invasion and trade route. This required subduing the Slavic Vyatichi living around today's Moscow before attacking and defeating the Volga Bulghars. The Rus' then headed south and took control of the Khazar fortress at Sarkel, which guarded the portage between the Don and lower Volga Rivers, before battling the Khazar khagan near his capital of Itil, which the Rus' destroyed. Svyatoslav then took his troops south, sacking Khazar towns and cities along the Caspian Sea. As a steppe nomadic polity, the Khazar Khaganate could lose such battles and still survive, but it could not restore its previous hegemony over the entire Pontic steppe and was eventually displaced by the Oghuz (the Torki of Russian chronicles and Ghuz of Islamic sources) and some Pechenegs who took control of the Pontic steppe. Svyatoslav returned to Kiev with his loot in 967, but he lacked the capacity to expand into the neighboring steppelands, which remained under the control of hostile Pecheneg nomads. Impressed by his victories over the Khazar Khaganate, the Byzantines sent an embassy to Kiev promising Svyatoslav a payment of 680 kg in gold if he would attack the Bulgarian Empire on its Balkan frontier. The Greeks only wished to weaken the Bulgars (and divert Rus' attention from themselves), but Svyatoslav proved overly successful. Soon after he arrived on the Danube frontier in 968, the Bulgar ruler died unexpectedly and his army defected to the Rus'. Svyatoslav then declared the Balkans part of his realm and suggested the Byzantines withdraw from their European provinces if they could not defend them.[39]

Returning briefly to Kiev in 969 to deal with Pecheneg nomad attacks on the city that had erupted during his absence, Svyatoslav appeared before his dying mother, Olga, to explain that the lands of the Rus' were too poor for a man of his ambitions. "Svyatoslav announced to his mother and his boyars, 'I do not care to remain in Kiev, but should prefer to live in Pereyaslavets on the Danube, since that is the centre of my realm, where all riches are concentrated; gold, silks, wine, and various fruits from Greece, silver and horses from Hungary and Bohemia, and from Rus' furs, wax, honey, and slaves.'"[40] Svyatoslav was quite right about this; the Avars had built their own wealthy exogenous empire here, but in the long run it would have meant abandoning the Rus' forest zone territories that had never been governed from a state based in the Balkans. As with Alexander the Great's leaving Macedonia behind, it was a move that explicitly redefined Svyatoslav's Rus' homeland as the future backwater of a more powerful state and perhaps one that could be abandoned to its own devices. Unlike Alexander, however, Svyatoslav faced a Byzantine Empire that would successfully thwart his ambitions. Taking advantage of lax defenses, the Byzantines retook the old Bulgarian capital in 971 and installed a puppet ruler. The two sides then engaged in a series of hard-fought battles that ended with a peace agreement that allowed the Rus' to withdraw with their booty. The Byzantines informed the Pechenegs that Svyatoslav was returning to Kiev with a vast treasure, so they blocked the Dnieper River portage to prevent his passage. In the spring of 972 Svyatoslav attempted to fight his way through and was killed. The Pechenegs made his skull into a gold-lined drinking cup, a steppe honor given to great enemies going back to Scythian times.[41]

After Svyatoslav's unexpected death, it was non-Rurikid power brokers who ensured the peaceful transfer of power to his son Yaropolk. The most significant of these was the old Varangian warlord Sveinald, who had led Olga's campaign against the Derevlians in 945 and was still serving as Svyatoslav's chief commander in Bulgaria a quarter century later. His position was so prominent that the official Byzantine treaty ending that war began by stating it was "concluded by Svyatoslav, Prince of Rus' and by Sveinald."[42] Before leaving for Bulgaria, Svyatoslav had appointed his elder son Yaropolk to command Kiev, given his younger son Oleg Derevlia to rule, and dispatched a third son, Vladimir (born to a maidservant of his mother, Olga), to Novgorod. As Yaropolk's military commander and chief adviser, Sveinald ensured that the young man sat securely on his new throne and should have provided advice that would have kept him there unchallenged. But things began to unravel when Sveinald's son Lyut was murdered by Oleg while hunting in Derevlia in 974. Not surprisingly, "there sprung up a feud between Yaropolk and Oleg, and Sveinald was continually egging Yaropolk on to attack his brother and seize his property, because he wished to avenge his son." In 976 Yaropolk did go to war and was victorious in their first encounter. Unfortunately for Oleg, the panicked mass of troops fleeing the battlefield for the safety of Derevlia's walled capital of Vruchiy crowded the narrow bridge across the city's moat and he and many others fell to their deaths in the melee. While Yaropolk expressed remorse at Oleg's death, he also seized his property. When Vladimir got word of this, he fled to Scandinavia and Yaropolk dispatched his own officials to Novgorod, making him sole ruler of Rus'.[43]

Vladimir had been sent to Novgorod in 969 when he was only about eleven years old because the people there insisted that they too were entitled to a Rurikid ruler of equal status to the ones being appointed in the south as Svyatoslav was departing for Bulgaria:

At this time came the people of Novgorod asking for themselves a prince. "If you will not come to us," said they, "then we will choose a prince of our own." Svyatoslav replied that they had need of a prince, but Yaropolk and Oleg both refused, so that Dobrynya suggested that the post should be offered to Vladimir. For Vladimir was son of Malusha, stewardess of Olga and sister of Dobrynya. Their father was Malk of Lyubech, and Dobrynya was thus Vladimir's uncle. The citizens of Novgorod thus requested Svyatoslav to designate Vladimir to be their prince, and he went forth to Novgorod with Dobrynya, his uncle.[44]

Svyatoslav appointed Dobrynya the military governor (*voevoda*) of Novgorod and Vladimir's tutor. Dobrynya was a trusted member of Svyatoslav's druzhina and likely either a Derevlian or Severian who saw an opportunity to further his own career by suggesting a good use for his sister's boy, whose status, though a Rurikid through his father, Svyatoslav, fell well below that of his two half brothers. Because Svyatoslav was in the prime of his life, he was not devolving power to his sons, who were being left behind largely as symbols of Rurikid authority in his absence.

Mothers' brothers and affines (relatives through marriage) could play prominent political roles in patrilineal societies because while they were ineligible to hold political positions inherited from father to son or elder brother to younger brother, they were directly tied to those who could. Winning political competitions involving half brothers, all of whom of course had the same father and so competed for the support of the same patrilineal kin, often hinged on the aid supplied by maternal and affinal relatives, who naturally favored the sons and husbands of their own sisters or daughters. In societies practicing varieties of tanistry where the path to power was littered with the corpses of patrilineal rivals, maternal relatives not only made the best allies in succession battles but were the safest choices as regents or guardians when the heir was too young to wield power in his own right. Vladimir's non-Rurikid maternal uncle Dobrynya had every incentive to keep him alive and build a coalition to support him because he could never sit on the throne himself. (Oleg had the same incentive to keep Igor alive as he ruled in his name for three decades.) The opposite was true for paternal uncles, who might legitimately inherit the throne if their nephews disappeared, as the audience of William Shakespeare's play *Richard III* quickly learns. In Kievan Rus' there was additional advantage. In mixed marriages (or less formal relationships) in which the mother was a native and the father Scandinavian, the maternal relatives had better success in mobilizing support from their larger ethnic groups (Krivichians, Polyanians, Derevlians, Severians, Radimichians, etc.) than the Scandinavians, who could only fall back on networks of scattered kin who were both fewer in number and minorities in the lands they ruled.[45]

Fearing he might be next after receiving word of his half brother Oleg's death, Vladimir abandoned Novgorod and fled to Scandinavia in 977. In the ensuing two years he managed to recruit an army of Varangian mercenaries for an invasion of Rus' with a promise of payment upon victory. Although Yaropolk's agents had taken control of Novgorod when he left, Vladimir had no trouble evicting them and raising more troops there, undoubtedly facilitated by his uncle Dobrynya's many connections as its former governor. Because the relationship between Novgorod and Kiev had long been brittle, there would have been few in the north sympathetic to Yaropolk's cause. As his forces moved south, Vladimir sought to arrange a marriage alliance with Rogvolod, the Scandinavian ruler of Polotsk, a strategic fortified town in the lands inhabited by the Slavic Krivichians. However, Rogvolod had already accepted a competing offer of marriage from Yaropolk and was not inclined to change his mind, in part because his daughter Rogneda objected to Vladimir's low social status, saying that she did not intend to "draw off the boots of a slave's son."[46] The "slave" in question was Dobrynya's sister, an insult to him and his nephew he chose not to ignore. As commander of Vladimir's army, Dobrynya took his revenge in 980 by capturing Polotsk, where Vladimir raped Rogneda and killed her whole family before marrying her. Turning south, his army reached the neighborhood of Kiev but stayed at some distance from it, unsure who its residents would support.

Vladimir's unhindered advance on Kiev, but without enough confidence to take the city, gives some idea of just how weak the power bases of both Yaropolk and Vladimir really were. Neither side commanded enough resources to win a civil war. In similar situations in the past, Rus' contenders for power had found that employing guile and treachery was more effective than fighting, and so it proved here. Old Sveinald had apparently died earlier, because Yaropolk's main adviser was now a man named Blud whose background the *Primary Chronicle* never bothers to describe. Vladimir made him an offer: "Be my friend; if I kill my brother, I will regard you as my father, and you shall have much honor from me."[47] Why Blud was open to betraying Yaropolk is unclear, but he immediately began doing so very effectively by convincing him that the people of Kiev were in communication with Vladimir to hand him over. In truth, Blud believed he could not kill Yaropolk inside Kiev because of the support he had in the city, a reason that Vladimir also hesitated to attack. But Yaropolk swallowed the lie and fled Kiev for the small town of Rodnya on the Pecheneg frontier, where he withstood a siege that resulted in the starvation of the people there. Here Blud again worked to undermine Yaropolk's confidence by telling him he could not possibly win this war with Vladimir. "Do you see what a large force your brother has? We cannot overcome them. Make peace with your brother."[48] Another of his advisers, Varayazhko, warned Yaropolk that such a surrender would only result in his murder and argued that a better course would be to seek sanctuary on the steppe among the Pechenegs, from where he could raise a new army. Instead

Yaropolk agreed to return to Kiev with Blud and meet with Vladimir to hear what terms his half brother might offer. Once he entered the stone hall meeting place, the door was barred to keep Yaropolk's bodyguards out and two Varangians stabbed him to death. Vladimir was now the sole ruler of Rus' less than two years after returning from exile in Scandinavia. His coup marked the third time a Rus' ruler had used treachery to deal with stronger rivals: Oleg's ambush and murder of Askold and Dir in 882, Olga's slaughter of the Derevlians in 945–946, and now Vladimir's killing of Yaropolk in 980—all cases in which the victims had been lured to their deaths by the promise of peaceful meetings. And Blud? There is no further mention of him.

Although the Rus' Empire had existed for a century when Vladimir became grand kniaz, he is traditionally seen as the ruler who made it a stable Great Power. It was a remarkable accomplishment for a man whose regime was so weak when he took power, but he possessed what Turkic steppe nomads called *qut*, a heaven-granted good fortune that they believed was a necessary quality in an imperial leader. While Vladimir made many of his most significant decisions for ad hoc and tactical reasons, they had positive strategic consequences that left the Rus' polity much stronger than he found it and were maintained by his dynastic descendants. These included adopting Eastern Orthodox Christianity as a state religion; using military force internally while relying on diplomacy and trade externally; vastly increasing the size of the Rurikid royal descent group, which allowed the Rus' government thereafter to be a family-run enterprise; and developing Kiev into a proper capital city with new architecture, cultural institutions, and a denser population surrounding it.

Vladimir was the first Rus' ruler to use religion to buttress his authority, beginning with the construction of pagan temple complexes in both Kiev and Novgorod, the latter overseen by his uncle Dobrynya, who had been sent there as its governor.[49] Previous rulers who were believers in these gods swore oaths by them in treaties with the Byzantines but saw no need to employ religion in politics. Vladimir's sponsorship of these temple complexes, where children chosen by lot were sacrificed and where he made personal ritual offerings after returning from wars, had two objectives. The first was to link himself and his authority to the gods by participation in, or sponsorship of, ritual events that validated his leadership. The second was to impose a state-sponsored cult on the diverse pagan communities to demonstrate his power. Such communities may well have recognized these gods, but they ordinarily preferred to sacrifice to local deities rather than to more distant ones worshiped by many people. Distant and universal deities were the selling points of the proselyting monotheistic religions being adopted by an ever-growing number of neighboring peoples. This made Vladimir and the Rus' targets for conversion by the Jews, Muslims, Latin Catholic Christians, and Greek Orthodox Christians, who all sent envoys expounding on the merits of their own faiths and the faults of the others. Vladimir sent his own envoys to their lands to observe their religious practices, but when he queried his boyars in 987 as to whether they were willing to convert to any of these religions, they politely suggested that any such decision rested with him. That would occur in 988, not, it appears, because Vladimir doubted his pagan beliefs but because an opportunity arose to marry a Byzantine princess. He had just taken the Byzantine city of Kherson in the Crimea and was demanding a marriage to the Emperor Basil II's sister Anna to make peace. Because Basil was engaged in a civil war that threatened his throne, he needed allies and was open to this proposition. The sticking point was a Byzantine refusal to marry a princess to a pagan, but that obstacle was overcome when Vladimir agreed to convert to Eastern Orthodox Christianity. After his marriage, he destroyed the pagan idols and converted the people of Rus' to that religion en masse.[50] It was a good trade. A universal religion proved much better suited to the needs of a state builder like Vladimir than paganism. With its literate clergy, churches, and monasteries, the Orthodox Church became a powerful state-supporting institution and, in turn, the state became the protector of the Church's religious monopoly and an enforcer of its beliefs against dissidents. The adoption of Eastern Orthodox Christianity laid the foundation for the development of a common religious culture that would eventually be shared by diverse groups of people previously divided by ethnicity and distance. It would survive the political structure that generated its growth and forge a cultural identity so intertwined with the Orthodox religion that not even the concerted seventy-year efforts of the atheist USSR in the twentieth century could uproot it.

Perhaps the biggest shift in Rus' policy under Vladimir was his focus on consolidating power within Rus' rather than seeking to conquer new lands. His father, Svyatoslav, had done the opposite, leaving the lands of Rus' to their own devices while he attacked the Khazar Khaganate and attempted to create a new state in Bulgaria. Unlike his father, Vladimir did not attempt to expand Rus' much beyond the forest and forest steppe zones except for some strategic trade depots in Crimea. Instead Vladimir harked back to his grandmother Olga's policies and imposed direct rule over previously autonomous tributaries, eventually distributing their governance among his many sons. After an attempt to conquer the rich Volga Bulghar steppe nomads in 985 fell short of its goal despite capturing a lot of people, his uncle Dobrynya remarked to Vladimir, "I have seen the prisoners, who all wear boots. They will not pay us tribute. Let us rather look for foes with bast [bark fiber] shoes."[51] It was advice Vladimir took to heart: Rus' would conquer more bast-shoe-wearing people in the forest zone, but its wars with the steppe nomads were henceforth exclusively defensive. Similarly, taking a lesson from his father's failure in Bulgaria, where he had too few troops dislodge the Byzantines, Vladimir turned to diplomacy and alliance making, the first fruit of which was his marriage to the Byzantine princess Anna. He then rid himself of the Scandinavian mercenaries who had helped him come to power by dispatching six thousand of them to aid his new brother-in-law Basil in Constantinople. They stayed on in that wealthy city to become the famous Varangian Guard, an institution that protected succeeding Byzantine emperors for the next three centuries. Vladimir thus avoided wars in the Balkans and did not attempt to expand westward against Poland, Hungary, or Germany, instead making marriage alliances with their rulers. One explanation for this change, and why the policy was maintained by his successors, was that Vladimir understood that the revenue derived from trade did not require the conquest of other lands, merely the ability to control the networks that linked them. Rus' now held a unique position to do this as an exogenous empire that linked both east–west and north–south trade routes.[52] This adjustment also reflected the declining flow of silver dirhams from the Muslim world, which made a shift to stronger trade ties with the Byzantines and Europeans opportune. And unlike the warring kingdoms in western Europe or the Byzantine Empire, Rus' had no external enemies other than disunited steppe nomads who were dangerous but lacked the ability to conquer the forest zone.

Under Vladimir's rule, Rus' became a family enterprise, and in succeeding generations Vladimir's descendants had such large families that the number of people who could claim royal Rurikid descent became so large that not even their murderous succession struggles did more than lop off a few branches. While not usually seen as an innovation, Vladimir's prodigious production of children resulted in a quantum shift in the dynasty's demographic profile when compared with its previous century of rule, during which Rurikid heirs were so few in number that it is surprising the dynasty survived. Igor was the sole Rurikid in his generation, as was his surviving son Svyatoslav. At Svyatoslav's death there were only three Rurikid heirs, two of whom were murdered during the fratricidal struggle in which Vladimir emerged the victor—and so he was again the sole surviving Rurikid of his generation. Vladimir resolved this problem by having as many children as possible both inside and outside his many marriages. The Orthodox Church may have declared him a saint, but this did not stop the monks who later wrote the *Primary Chronicle* from complaining that "Vladimir was overcome by lust for women. . . . He was insatiable in vice. He even seduced married women and violated young girls, for he was a libertine like Solomon."[53] It is unlikely that Vladimir would have rationalized his compulsion to bed as many women as possible by claiming it was a strategy to remedy his dynasty's demographic deficit, but it did. By the end of his reign, every important region was ruled by one of his twelve sons, who served as transferable representatives of his government in Kiev, a form of administration that his successors would continue. Vladimir also made good political use of his daughters by marrying two of them to the rulers of Hungary and Poland, respectively. This began a series of marriage alliances that would grow ever wider under his successors, with Rus' princesses in the next generation marrying kings in Norway, Denmark, Hungary, and France. While Rus' is commonly seen as more closely attached to the Byzantine world than to western Europe, marriage alliances with so many powerful courts from there show a more balanced policy. Of the fifty-two known dynastic marriages the Rus' made between the late ninth and mid-twelfth centuries, Christian Raffensperger found that forty of them were with European kingdoms.[54]

After Vladimir consolidated Rus' control over rebellious or previously unincorporated territories, he decided that the region around Kiev itself needed a stronger agricultural base to support the city's growing size. Previously raids by the Pecheneg nomads had made this land too dangerous for farmers to settle safely. And because the Pechenegs lacked any centralized leadership, it was not possible to secure an enforceable peace agreement with them because at least one subgroup would always see an advantage in breaking it. Vladimir therefore organized the construction of large defensive earthworks and a series of forts designed to create a zone of security into which farming communities could expand. To this end he "gathered together the best men of the Slavs, and Krivichians, the Chuds, and the Vyatichians, and peopled these forts with them," an example of population transfers not previously used by the Rus'.[55] Such a defensive policy required almost constant wars with the Pecheneg steppe nomads to keep them from encroaching on these newly settled lands, but it proved to be a price worth paying because it facilitated Kiev's growth as a major urban center. In the early eleventh century Kiev grew to between 300 and

320 hectares in size with a population of between thirty-six thousand and forty thousand people.[56] It was adorned with new churches in the Byzantine style, built to make it a place minimally acceptable as the residence of a Byzantine princess used to finer things, but the city also had many workshops and markets as well as monasteries that served as centers of high culture. While Kiev may not have approached the size of medieval mega-cities like Constantinople (two hundred thousand people) or Baghdad (over a million), it was on par with the largest cities in Christian western Europe in the year 1000.

Under Vladimir and his successor Yaroslav the Wise (r. 1016–1054), Kievan Rus' reached the zenith of its power and, despite a long series of tanistry-driven wars of succession, remained a united empire for another century before it devolved into a looser federation of autonomous polities. Their Rurikid kniazes determined who among them would hold the position of grand kniaz in Kiev based on a complex calculus of descent and principles of lateral succession, all of which could be trumped by the use of force. During this period the northeastern region of Suzdalia (which would later become the Grand Duchy of Muscovy) grew to rival Kiev and Novgorod in importance. As with other shadow empires, the Rus' vacuum empire lacked many of the most important institutions that characterized endogenous empires but created a model well adapted to governing a large territory with a low population density that was adopted by successor polities in the northern forest zone (table 6.1).

JELLYFISH STATES: ON THE POLITICAL ORGANIZATION OF VACUUM EMPIRES

Of all the shadow empires we have reviewed to this point, vacuum empires displayed the least well-developed political structures despite encompassing large territories. Although the Rus' focus on trade and their strategic use of boats in some ways resembled the strategies of a maritime empire, they never developed a home mega-center like Athens, Carthage, Venice, London, or Amsterdam from which they projected power outward. They instead abandoned their Scandinavian homeland and distributed themselves widely throughout the forest zone as a dominant class of colonial settlers who (unlike other imperial maritime elites) merged with the local people by adopting their language and culture in a process similar to that of the Mughal conquerors of Bengal in India. Nor did the Rus' polity follow a steppe imperial confederacy model where nomad autocrats devolved power to subordinate local rulers but monopolized foreign relations and sat at the

Table 6.1. Endogenous empire components in the Rus' vacuum empire

Present	Partial	Absent
Size: 2.1 million km²		Centralized institutions of governance that were separate and distinct from the rulers
Population: 5.5 million		A primate imperial center with transportation systems designed to serve it militarily and economically
Organized to administer and exploit diversity		Systems of communication that allowed administration of all subject areas from the center directly
Imperial project that imposed some type of unity throughout the system (Eastern Orthodox Christianity)		
Monopoly of force within their territories, and military force projected outward		

apex of a system that redistributed prized goods and trading opportunities to the leaders of its component parts. Rus' subordinates expected to have their own direct links with the outside world that required no mediation. In trade treaties with the Byzantines, they signed on as equal participants together with the Rus' ruler. Unlike vulture or vanquisher empires, the Rus' moved into regions that had no existing state structures and so built their own by combining elements drawn from a variety of cultures—Turkic, Byzantine, Slavic, and Scandinavian—that scholars have often sought to disentangle rather than seeing how they were woven together. From the Turkic Khazars we see the Rus' adoption of a khagan supreme leader position filled by a member of an exclusive Rurikid royal descent group in which brothers often took precedence over sons. From the Byzantines we see the Rus' adoption of Eastern Orthodox Christianity, which brought with it a hierarchical clerical establishment and a tradition of governance where state authority was based on laws and institutions. The Rus' incorporated from the Slavs existing political institutions that included decision-making councils in towns and regions (*veche*), indigenous local rulers (kniaz), and a class of aristocratic military commanders (*voevoda*). The Rus' readily intermarried with the indigenous elite and eventually adopted their Slavonic language. From the Scandinavians they retained an almost unique capacity to shift from being warriors and raiders to peaceful long-distance traders as conditions warranted and did so with breathtaking speed, a trait they shared with many other seafaring peoples. Land-based warrior and aristo-cratic classes, by contrast, disdained personal engagement in commerce as beneath their dignity, and land-based merchants had no military capacity, instead purchasing protection or seeking out patrons who could provide it. The Scandinavians also displayed a willingness (rivaled only by that of the steppe nomads) to relocate themselves and forget about where they had come from. They constantly tested themselves against new foes in the belief that they could become the rulers of any place their boats landed—a hubris well adapted to people creating an empire where none had existed before. It gave them a cosmopolitan view of the world missing in more homebound groups.

What they created was a jellyfish-like state that was able to absorb enough resources to sustain itself without requiring either a strong impe-rial center or autocratic leadership and where no single part was critical to the survival of the whole. Lacking a brain, jellyfish depend on a distrib-uted neural network composed of integrated nodes that together create a highly responsive nervous system. As a result, jellyfish can survive the loss of parts of their bodies and regenerate them quickly. Because this regeneration is designed to restore damaged symmetry rather than simply replace the lost parts, a jellyfish cut in half becomes two new jellyfish as each half regenerates what is missing. Without carrying the comparison too far, vacuum empires displayed a similar capacity to maintain them-selves after losing almost any of their parts, along with a similar ability to reconstitute themselves after such losses although their boundaries might shift in the process. The Rus' leadership structure also resembled a dis-tributed neural network in which Kiev and its grand kniaz was only the biggest node in a system of nodes rather than an exclusive one. Each city had its own veche that could oust a Rurikid kniaz if aggrieved.[57] Its non-Rurikid voevoda also wielded considerable power, and Nora Chadwick goes so far as to argue that this created a type of partnership between the Rus' and the peoples they ruled: "The evidence would seem to suggest that the voevodas with their Slavonic names and titles, their hereditary rights and high, even princely rank, their paramount prestige and heroic ide-als, were, in fact, the native Russian hereditary aristocracy. The evidence suggests further that this native Russian aristocracy was not abolished or even displaced by the coming of the Norse rulers. On the contrary, the Norse rulers were largely dependent on them, not only for their position, but also for their maintenance and organisation."[58] While such a generalization likely underestimates the independent power the Rurikids actually wielded in the Rus' polity, it is compatible with a political system in which local nodes of production and political authority were overlain by an imperial structure and not destroyed by it. This was in sharp contrast to other types of empires, even ones that devolved power using a king-of-kings template. As ibn Khaldun had observed of Sasanian Iran, such empires collapsed when they lost their centers because the "center is like the heart from which the (vital) spirit spreads."[59] Vacuum empires had no such irreplaceable vital centers.

Muscovy to Russia: Transformation from Exogenous to Endogenous Empire

RUSSIAN TRIBUTARIES UNDER MONGOL RULE

After the Mongols completed their conquest of North China in 1234, their Great Khan Ögedei convened a *qurultai*, a meeting if the empire's elite members, that approved plans to expand westward with an invasion of Europe. This expedition mustered 140,000 troops and included a skilled technical corps equipped with siege engines. The Mongols arrived on the Volga Bulghar frontier in early 1236 and set about subjugating all the steppe nomads in the region. After securing their rear and adding locally recruited troops to their ranks, the Mongols commenced their invasion. The Rus' campaign was well planned and carried out in two phases over the course of three years. It began with the swift conquest of the middle Volga in the winter of 1237–1238 and concluded with a second campaign against the south and southwest that ended with the capture of Kiev in late 1240.[60] The Mongols then proceeded to invade central Europe on multiple fronts. One army upended a coalition of Poles, Czechs, and Teutonic Knights at the Battle of Liegnitz on April 9, 1241, and three days later a second army routed the Hungarians and their allies at the Battle of Mohi. The Mongol invasion ended abruptly, however, when its commanders received word that the Great Khan Ögedei had died unexpectedly, and decided that determining who would inherit the empire's throne was more important than continuing the war in Europe. They withdrew their troops east to the Pontic steppe in mid-1242. While the Mongols threatened to come back, the empire's later rulers instead deployed imperial troops against South China and the Near East.[61] As a result, Batu (the leader of the Jochid lineage descended from Chinggis Khan's eldest son) established his own autonomous khanate on the lower Volga. The Golden Horde (1242–1501), as it was better known in the West, was infinitely more powerful than the Khazar Khaganate that preceded it, making use of a wide-ranging set of common administrative structures, tax systems, and data-collection policies that were implemented throughout the Mongol Empire by government bureaucrats. Although elsewhere the Mongols raised revenue and troops from subject populations directly, in the forest zone they employed local intermediaries to deliver these and govern their people as Mongol clients. The intermediaries they chose for the job in Russia were the very Rurikids they had just annihilated as independent rulers a few years previously.

The Mongols, whom the Russians insisted on calling Tatars, initially interfered very little with the governing of their Russian holdings. Members of the Rurikid elite who had survived the initial massacres of their relatives got their ruling positions back upon receiving a Mongol letter of appointment (*yarliq*). While the Mongol Empire eliminated ruling dynastic elites in territories under its direct control (the Jurchen Jin and Song dynasties in China, the caliphate in Iraq, and the Khwarazm Shahs in central Asia), it preferred to retain established rulers with local legitimacy as clients in areas it chose to rule more indirectly, such as Russia, Caucasian Georgia, or Iranian Khorasan. The Mongols relied on them to manage the local population, and they relied on the Mongols to maintain themselves in power. However fraught and unequal the relationship, it produced a durable governmental structure.

Leaders seeking Mongol appointments had to travel to the ruler's court in Sarai on the lower Volga steppe to acknowledge Mongol sovereignty in person and leave close relatives behind as hostages to ensure their good behavior. Their people were required to submit to a census, and both they and the client leaders were supervised by a Mongol-appointed resident (*darughachi*). They were responsible for maintaining local postal relay stations (*jam*) that were established throughout the entire empire to facilitate communication and trade. Mongol taxes were high and included not only regular tribute payments but also levies on commerce and agriculture. Rigorous Mongol censuses assessed how much a district was required to pay in taxes, how many troops it was required to supply, and what corvée labor duties could be assigned to it. The existence of an exact written record of a region's assets made it difficult for people to avoid Mongol exactions and ensured that client rulers could not easily divert this revenue for their own use.[62]

Rurikid kniazes were often forced to choose between defending the autonomy of the local population or implementing harsh Mongol policies. The winners chose the Mongols, who backed their clients with force and preserved the authority of a preinvasion class of Rurikid rulers whose interests soon became firmly aligned with those of the Golden Horde. God too was on the Mongol side. Clerics of all religions in the Mongol Empire and their institutional property were free of tax liability, and the Russian Orthodox Church avidly sought written exemptions for its holdings from the pagan (and later Muslim) rulers of the Horde.[63] This proved to be the beginning of a very long-lasting relationship because, as John Fennell explains, "from Saray, for the next 138 years, the khans of the Golden Horde, as [Batu's] empire came to be known as, were to exercise political control over all the Russian principalities, and, for a further 100 years, from 1380 to 1480, were to continue to demand, though not always to get, tribute from their Russian 'vassals.'"[64]

The division of Russia into weak principalities and the never-ending succession disputes among their Rurikid rulers served Mongol interests well. The Mongols did not have to worry about the emergence of new power centers or rebel leaders, allowing the Horde to administer a vast territory in Russia without the need for Mongol military garrisons. The Horde soon felt secure enough to replace resident Mongol political agents (*basqaq, darughachi*) with envoys (*posol*) who traveled out to deal with problems only when needed, much like the Athenian Empire's overseers (*episkopos*). In Fennell's opinion, this resulted "in the growing enthrallment of Suzdalia by the Tatars": "There was no longer any question of resistance to Tatar domination. Instead, the Russians were beginning to look to the Horde for military aid in their own internal squabbles, and the Tatars were beginning to show an increasing interest in Russian affairs and to realize that the wealth of the Russian land was there to be ravished. The last quarter of the thirteenth century was to witness a series of particularly ruinous Tatar interventions, raids and invasions."[65] The Golden Horde retained a strong grip on its Russian principalities until the mid-fifteenth century, invading them when necessary but mostly shifting its patronage among the competing sets of Rurikid kniazes who looked to the Horde as the final arbiter in succession disputes. Victory in conflicts between rival Russian principalities was largely determined by which could bring the Horde's power to its side. The situation changed only when the Horde itself was torn apart by internal disputes that reached a peak after Tamerlane's destruction of its capital of Sarai in 1395.

But the relationship benefited the long-ruling Rurikids too, since they could not be driven from power as long as the Mongols protected them. There were other advantages, though not ones anticipated by either side. First, working for the Mongols gave the Rurikids new tools of governance that included an efficient and thoroughgoing system of taxation and conscription that could be used to build their own polities. Second, the Russians learned Mongol war tactics while serving as auxiliaries, eventually gaining military parity with them. Both advantages would be used by Muscovy first to build a new shadow empire in the fifteenth and sixteenth centuries under Tsars Ivan III (the Great) and Ivan IV (the Terrible) that then grew into the world largest endogenous empire in the eighteenth century under Emperors Peter and Catherine (both the Great) once the power of the steppe nomads declined and then collapsed across all of Eurasia during the early modern period.

TSARIST RUSSIA

As Mongol power slowly waned, two new vacuum empires emerged and divided the forest zone between them for many centuries: the Grand Duchy of Lithuania (1236–1795) in the west and the Grand Duchy of Muscovy (1283–1478) in the east.

With their capital in Vilnius, the Lithuanians had avoided the Mongol onslaught and began expanding into the Dnieper River watershed in the early fourteenth century at a time when the Horde was content to let them do so (map 6.3). The largest empire in Europe at the time, the Grand Duchy of Lithuania (GDL) was founded by pagans whose rulers later became Catholic Christians, although the GDL's population remained religiously diverse.[66] What was so striking about the emergence of the GDL and the territories it occupied was how closely the Lithuanians followed the pattern of the Rus' as foreigners moving into a power vacuum produced by the decline of a steppe nomadic power and how they superimposed themselves on an existing political system too fractured to unite from within. Like the Rus', they created a jellyfish polity with many integrated nodes of production and authority without a true metropole, any one of which could be lost without necessarily bringing about the collapse of the polity. It was the region's dominant power for a short period after Tamerlane destroyed the Golden Horde's capital of Sarai in 1395.

The other emerging power in the forest zone was the Grand Duchy of Muscovy, which became the center of a vacuum empire in the east when the Horde's power fractured. In 1476 Ivan the Great rejected a tribute demand

MAP 6.3. The Grand Duchy of Lithuania, thirteenth to fifteenth century.

by the Great Horde, which had succeeded the Golden Horde as ruler of
the lower Volga steppe, and beat back a retaliatory invasion in 1480. This
occurred about halfway through his reign (1462–1505, the longest of any
Russian ruler), during which he built an autocratic state by annexing as
many neighboring Russian principalities as he could. It was a policy that
laid the foundation for an exogenous empire that would be proclaimed by
his grandson Ivan IV (the Terrible) when he made himself the first tsar of all
Russia in 1547. Although Ivan IV's father and grandfather had occasionally

referred to themselves as tsars, the Russians previously applied that title only to Byzantine emperors (basileus) and Chinggisid Great Khans. The capture of Constantinople (Tsargrad) by the Muslim Ottomans in 1453, which resulted in the death of the last Byzantine emperor, led some, particularly in the Orthodox Church, to assert that Moscow was now a "Third Rome" and that its ruler had an obligation to assume that imperial title, particularly since Ivan IV's grandmother was the niece of that last Byzantine emperor. But as Michael Cherniavsky argues, the stronger imperial influence on Ivan was the model of tsar as khan:

> If the image of the basileus stood for the orthodox and pious ruler, leading his Christian people toward salvation, then the image of the khan, perhaps, was preserved in the idea of the Russian ruler as the conqueror of Russia and of its people, responsible to no one. If the basileus signified the holy tsar . . . then the khan, perhaps, stood for the absolutist secularized state, arbitrary through its separation from the subjects. The two images were not really synthesized; both existed separately, if in a state of tension which the first Russian Tsar, Ivan IV, exemplified so tragically: killing by day and praying by night.[67]

The establishment of Russia as a tsardom was designed in part to facilitate the conquest of the Chinggisid-ruled Kazan and Astrakhan Khanates, which was achieved in 1552 and 1556. Ivan needed to present himself as a peer sovereign of the Chinggisid khans he was eliminating by promoting himself from grand kniaz to tsar. Usurping their khan titles for himself was not an option because he was not a Chinggisid, a barrier that had caused even the great Tamerlane to choose the title of amir and caused the Ottomans to call themselves sultans because neither were of Chinggisid descent. The title of tsar filled the bill for Ivan because it was an imperial rank of Roman origin and not derived from either a Turko-Mongolian or Islamic lexicon. Cherniavsky points out that even after their incorporation into the Muscovite state, the "titulature of the Russian tsar confirmed the special role of the Tatar successor states: 'Great Sovereign, Tsar and Grand Prince of all Russia, of Vladimir, of Moscow, of Novgorod, Tsar of Kazan, Tsar of Astrakhan, Sovereign of Pskov, Grand Prince of Smolensk, Tver.'"[68]

Ivan IV's declaring himself a tsar also marked Russia's formal assertion of imperial status on the world stage and began its first attempt to become an endogenous empire. Despite Ivan's powerful impact, however, that effort would fail: at the end of his reign, Russia would be an enormously larger vacuum empire, but one that remained largely confined to the forest

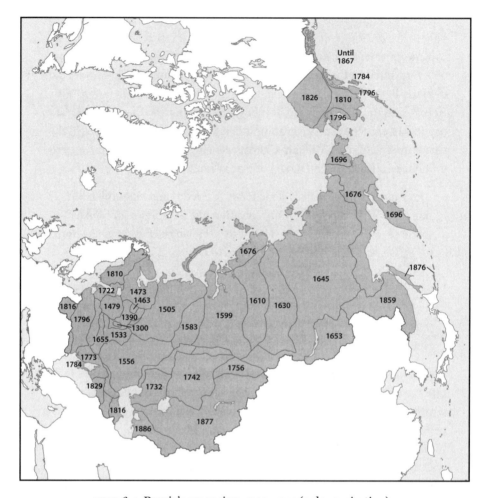

MAP 6.4. Russia's expansion, 1300–1914 (polar projection).

zone, unable to displace either the GDL and Sweden in the west or the Crimean Khanate and stateless Nogay steppe nomads in the south (map 6.4). But if Ivan ruled a vacuum empire, it was as a self-identified autocrat who believed his God-given right to command his subjects granted him even more authority than that commonly attributed to Ottoman sultans, Chinese emperors, or Mongol khans. While the reforms he implemented during the early part of his reign were not unlike those of his grandfather Ivan III, in the 1560s he instigated a decade-long reign of terror and radical political reorganization known as the *oprichnina* that for a modern observer recalls that of the Soviet Union's Joseph Stalin in the 1930s or China's Mao Zedong in the 1960s. Not surprisingly, well-informed historians split on whether Ivan's actions and policies should be regarded as the calculated acts of a harsh but realpolitik monarch consolidating power who let nothing and no one stand in his way or as the warped products of a paranoid and sadistic psychopath whose delusions drove his decision making.[69] By the time Ivan ended his *oprichnina*, Novgorod lay in ruins and Russia was defending itself against invasions rather than mounting them against others. Moscow was burned to the ground by the Crimean Tatars in 1571, and between 1577 and 1583 Ivan lost the Baltic territories that he had captured years earlier to Poland's elected king Batory, who was originally from Hungary.

Ivan's death in 1584 opened a period of unrest in Russia from which it barely survived. His son Feodor inherited the throne but died childless in 1598, ending the line of Rurikid grand kniazes and tsars that had continuously filled these positions for seven centuries. His death marked not just the extinction of a dynasty but the beginning of Russia's infamous Time of Troubles, a two-decade period of economic, political, and demographic disruptions so severe it would have collapsed any normal state. Tsar Feodor's capable brother-in-law, Boris Godunov, had been Russia's de facto ruler for his entire reign and made himself tsar when Feodor died. Boris had the misfortune to be governing when a transitory oscillation in weather patterns (1601–1603) generated intense cold that resulted in the worst crop failures in Russian history. The ensuing famines generated economic chaos and reduced Russia's population by a third. Yet despite famine, population decline, rising banditry, and demands for more tax revenue, Tsar Boris remained firmly in charge of Russia as the worst conditions finally began easing. He crushed boyar plots, maintained order in Moscow under famine conditions, kept the military financed with new taxes, and limited peasant population movements with policies that would lay the groundwork for serfdom.[70]

Boris died of a stroke in April 1605. Many ordinary Russians who already believed the bad weather and famines were signs of God's displeasure saw Boris's unexpected death as proof that his occupation of the throne was illegitimate. A mob in Moscow looted his palace and his family was murdered. In the countryside rebels flocked to support a pretender claiming to be Dmitry, a son of Ivan IV who had died under mysterious circumstances in 1591. Boris had come close to eliminating this populist revolt but his death gave it new life. The so-called False Dmitry entered Moscow at the head of his army in June and was crowned tsar in July. A clique of boyars murdered Dmitry in May 1606 but were unable to quell the ensuing anarchy. Swedish and Polish troops invaded Russia in support of different factional leaders and another replacement Dmitry. Only in 1612 was there enough cohesion to expel the Poles from Moscow and convene a Zemsky Sobor (Assembly of the Land) the next year to elect a sixteen-year-old Michael Romanov (r. 1613–1645) as tsar and end the civil war. In doing so they were replicating a pattern begun 750 years earlier with the foundation of the Rurikid dynasty they were now replacing, and for the same reasons.[71] As the authors of the *Russian Primary Chronicle* wrote of those times, "Discord thus ensued among them, and they began to war one against another. They said to themselves, 'Let us seek a prince who may rule over us and judge us according to the Law.'"[72] The new Romanov dynasty took on that role, establishing itself as a new golden clan that would rule Russia until 1917.

That Russia survived the Time of Troubles as an intact empire with only a marginal loss of territory and a tsar still ruling from Moscow bordered on the amazing. A more likely outcome would have been its destruction and dismemberment by the Polish-Lithuanian Commonwealth and Sweden or its devolution back into the rival petty states that existed before Ivan III and his successors unified them into one exogenous empire. The explanation for its avoiding the first fate may lie in the peculiarity of Tsarist Russia (and Kievan Rus' before it) as a jellyfish state whose vast and sparsely populated territory was seemingly impervious to wholesale occupation by invaders (as Napoleon would later discover). Neither winning battles nor capturing important places proved a successful formula for conquering Russia when its defenders simply reconstituted themselves in ever more distant territories. While early modern European powers had the military strength to defeat Russia on the battlefield, they lacked the manpower to occupy and administer its vast territory directly and were too parochial to do so indirectly with proxies as did the Golden Horde. Even after occupying Moscow for two years (1610–1612) and putting their prince on the throne, the Poles discovered this did not give them control of Russia and they eventually went home. Normally, having an enemy occupy the capital of an empire led to that empire's demise, but Russia's distributed political networks continued to function even without its biggest node. To be effective a new imperial power would have to occupy these other nodes as well, something the Mongols and the GDL had proved capable of doing centuries earlier but not the more western-oriented Swedes or Polish-Lithuanian Commonwealth. For the Commonwealth's Catholic kings in Warsaw, already involved in sectarian wars with rising Protestant powers in central, northern, and western Europe, the price of winning in Russia and annexing its hostile Orthodox population proved higher than they were willing to pay, a calculus that might have been different if the Commonwealth had been run from Lithuanian Vilnius. Sweden too saw little in Russia worth owning outside the coastal Baltic zone that it already occupied, although it was now well positioned to set itself up as the potential ruler of the northern forest zone and would make a bid to do so a century later.

Internally, despite the persistence of strong regional identities, no part of Tsarist Russia attempted to become independent during the Time of Troubles, nor did any city attempt to replace Moscow as Russia's center (albeit a Russia that did not yet include the Baltic territories in the north or the Kievan Ukrainian lands in the southwest). This was in sharp contrast to the failing caliphate and the later Mongol Empire, where a host of regional centers broke away and established new states and new dynasties. Novgorod, long at odds with Moscow but ruined by Ivan IV's devastation of its economy during the *oprichnina*, was in no condition to strike out on its own. The old Volga khanates of Kazan and Astrakhan, in spite of their distance from Moscow, Tatar populations on the surrounding steppe, and a previous history of statehood, did not throw the Russians out either. And the immense swath of Russian territory in Siberia appeared unaffected by whoever ruled Moscow. When regional populations were involved in rebellions, it was in support of, or opposition to, larger political movements that were "all-Russia" oriented, such as that led by False Dmitry. Such revolts split existing elites and military forces rather than pitting one corporate or regional group against another. Again, this was a pattern that dated back to Rus' times when regions and their local elites first became parts of larger political systems run by stranger kings and accepted their superimposed order because it freed them from endemic wars with neighboring polities. Michael Romanov was accepted as tsar of all Russia not because he imposed his authority on it but because recognizing him ended the Time of Troubles anarchy. This should not be attributed to some innate culture of political passivity, however. Many of these same people had joined Dmitry's fight to become tsar even when the threat of retribution and death was high and continued that fight for a decade. What it did demonstrate was a cultural predisposition for people in Russia to see themselves in a reciprocal relationship with a sacral ruler so that their rebellions were directed at the person holding the position, a false tsar, rather than the institution itself. For the next 150 years the most significant regional rebellions in Russia would follow the model pioneered by Dmitry. A pretender claiming to have escaped death at the hands of a supposedly false tsar would declare himself the rightful tsar and lead his forces against the false tsar (or tsarina), asserting that he was not disrupting Russia's God-given political order but restoring it.

IMPERIAL RUSSIA

Under the first Romanov tsars, Russia not only recovered from its civil war but expanded rapidly until by the late seventeenth century it had reached the limits of its capacity as a vacuum empire. In the northwest it risked being replaced by a newly aggressive Sweden as the ruler of the forest zone, and its attempts to expand southward into the steppe were stymied by the Crimean Khanate and the Ottoman Empire. These foreign threats emerged as the Romanov court in Moscow was losing cohesion after the death of Tsar Alexis in 1676 when a series of three youthful tsars were put on the throne. In a situation that would have been familiar to Ivan IV more than a century earlier, rival boyar advisers, regents, in-laws, mothers, sisters, and maternal relatives all formed factions whose power rested on their ability to wield power in the name of a tsar who could not wield it himself. This period ended when Peter the Great (r. 1682–1725) took power in his own right in 1689 and began a series of foreign wars and internal reforms that transformed Russia. In 1713 he moved the capital to his new city of St. Petersburg and proclaimed Russia an empire in 1721 after winning the Great Northern War with Sweden (1700–1721), which had established Russia as a Baltic power.[73] This marked the last major shift in forest zone political capitals from Rus' Kiev to GDL Vilnius to Tsarist Moscow and now imperial St. Petersburg. With denser farming populations expanding into the south and Russia's imperial court in the Baltic north, Moscow's status receded from center of everything to just one of Russia's many regional centers. Such a relocation was only possible in a networked nodal system in which capitals like Kiev or Moscow were political centers only as long as governing regimes continued to make them so. By contrast, no English king could rule from anywhere other than London any more than a French king could move farther from Paris than Versailles.

Although battles with the Ottoman Empire and Sweden take pride of place in most historical accounts of Russia's eighteenth-century growth, its more piecemeal expansion south into the steppe zone and replacement of the pastoral nomadic population there with settled farmers were more significant. For the previous thousand years the steppe nomadic powers had dominated the peoples who lived in the northern forest zone. While the Rus', the GDL, and Muscovy all eventually broke free of steppe nomads' control and became autonomous, they were unable to occupy the steppe zone (Dikoe Pole, the Wild Field) even after the Khazar Empire and the Golden Horde had collapsed. This only began to change after Ivan IV conquered Kazan and Astrakhan, but those campaigns relied on Russia's

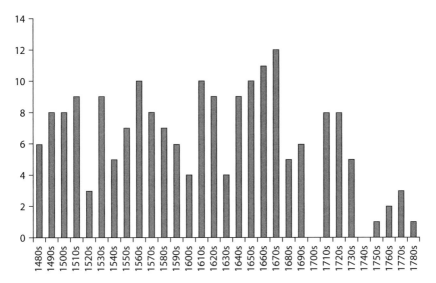

FIGURE 6.1. Frequency of nomad raids on Russia by decade, 1480–1780s.
Source: Matranga and Natkhov, "All Along the Watchtower," 36.

ability to move troops along the Volga River by boat, not march across the steppe. Outside that narrow riverine corridor, stateless nomads like the Nogay Tatars and the later in-migrating Mongol Kalmyks from western Mongolia roamed freely across the adjacent ungoverned grasslands. Moreover, as long as the Crimean Khanate remained independent and hostile, it could employ a devastating outer frontier strategy of raiding and extortion that put the Russian state itself in danger (figure 6.1).

Ivan IV, responding to what he saw as an existential threat after the Crimean khan Devlet Giray burned Moscow to the ground and returned home with an immense number of captives in 1571, ordered the construction of a series of wooden linear barriers designed to keep the nomads out (map 6.5). These were originally built along the Oka River to protect Moscow itself and then expanded southward with the construction of the Tula Line about 180 km south of Moscow in the late sixteenth century. By the 1630s these integrated defense lines spanned 500 km and included more than forty forts, barriers of cut timber along the edge of the forest zone, and numerous watchtowers. Finding the needed thirty-five thousand troops and supporting them in place presented a problem for a vacuum empire like Muscovy, as Andrea Matranga and Timur Natkhov have outlined:

> The need for protection required large military forces that should permanently reside on the defense line and patrol the "wild fields." Given the primitive state of the economy, and the taxation technologies

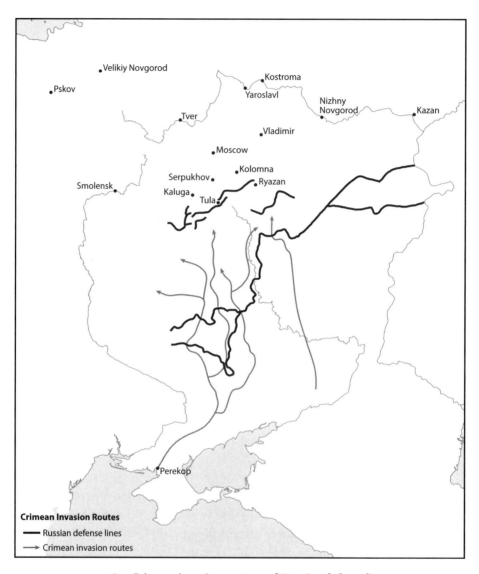

MAP 6.5. Crimean invasion routes and Russian defense lines.
From Matranga and Natkhov, "All Along the Watchtower," p. 47.

available at the time, the state found it impossible to support the military from tax revenues alone. Hence, the government began to assign lands on the southern frontier to the high ranked solders, in exchange for military service. They were expected to support themselves by the means of peasant labor on their lands. This device, later called the *pomest'e* system, permitted the creation of an army of a nearly maximum size given the low fiscal capacity of the state. . . . Hence, the enserfment of Russian peasantry was in large part a consequence of the external military threat faced by the Muscovy state, which required the maintenance of [a] large feudal army on the permanent basis in a particular geographic location.[74]

Unlike China, where the location of the Great Wall was static because the steppes north of it were deemed useless for farming, the Dikoe Pole was potentially highly productive agricultural land. Russia therefore had every incentive to expand its defensive lines ever farther south and transferred troops there to extend the length of the east–west fortification lines. By the late seventeenth century these southern defense lines lay 700 km south of the original barriers first erected by Ivan IV. The territories on either side of these lines were converted to farmland and the old forts eventually became regional urban centers. What began as a military response to fend off nomad attacks evolved into a colonial economic development program designed to replace the nomads and their pastoral economy with immigrant farmers whose grain surpluses could feed Russia's growing population.[75] As figure 6.2 illustrates, the percentage of Russia's population living in the forest zone declined significantly, and by the mid-nineteenth century the population inhabiting the former frontier steppelands exceeded it.

At any given time, this static defense and settlement policy could be criticized for failing to end the nomad raids that continued to capture people for ransom or sale as slaves well into the last half of the eighteenth century. But just as in the United States, where the horse-riding Comanches and Sioux could still terrify frontier settler communities even as their territories were being reduced by American military expansion after the Civil War, nomadic societies that dominated the Pontic and Caspian steppes a century earlier now found themselves on the losing end of an occupation policy that ultimately brought them under Russian control.[76] Nomadic groups like the Mongolian Kalmyks signed treaties with the Russians in 1655 in return for handsome gift payments and were autonomous steppe allies against the Crimean Khanate in the early eighteenth century. Fifty years later under the rule of Catherine the Great, they found their lands increasingly occupied by colonial farmers protected by Russian soldiers and found themselves the targets of exploitation so severe that they decided to return to Manchu-ruled Zungharia in 1771. Only one-third of the 150,000 people who left Russia made it to the Chinese frontier.[77]

Light field cannons in particular wreaked havoc on nomad horse cavalries, putting an end to a military superiority that had made them masters of the steppe for more than two millennia. The nomads found themselves

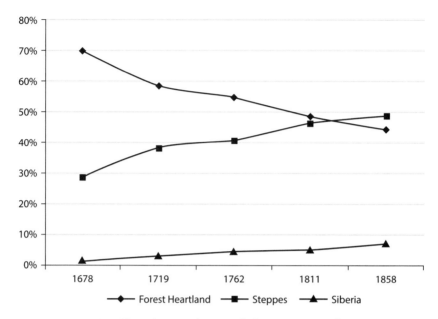

FIGURE 6.2. Changing Russian population percentages by region.
Source: Matranga and Natkhov, "All Along the Watchtower," 35.

increasingly unable to raid for goods and slaves, the source of external
revenue that had supported them for centuries, making them dependent on Russian markets to meet their needs. More significantly, the
Russian government began extending its control over the nomads' traditional pasturelands so that they now needed the goodwill of the Russian authorities to conduct their annual migrations. As the nineteenth
century opened, the steppe nomads found themselves trapped within a
colonial system that stripped them of the right to rule themselves and
took control of the lands that had previously been theirs alone. But
imposing Russian colonial authority on the steppe (unlike in Siberia) was
long in coming and the nomads there did not go down without a fight. The
Crimean Khanate, the last of the nomad successor states to the Golden
Horde, remained a potent threat until the end of the eighteenth century.
By Michael Khodarkovsky's calculations, the cost that Russia paid in blood
and treasure was staggering:

> In the first half of the seventeenth century alone, the Crimeans received
> from Moscow 1 million rubles in various forms of tribute and taxes.
> During the same time, they captured as many as 150,000 to 200,000
> Russians. A conservative estimate of 100,000 people redeemed at an
> average price of 50 rubles per person would require a sum of 5 million

rubles. Thus, over a period of fifty years, Moscow poured into the Crimea alone 6 million rubles. By comparison, 1 million rubles spent between 1600 and 1650 could have provided for the construction of four small towns annually. In other words, in the first half of the seventeenth century, Russia was short 1,200 small towns. That Russia was under urbanized in comparison to its Western European neighbors is an undisputed fact, but that this shortage of urban centers may, in no small degree, be related to the nature of Russia's southern frontier is poorly understood.[78]

Like other former shadow empires that became fully endogenous, Russia retained a number of its earlier exogenous characteristics. It continued to display a preference for expansion into adjacent vacuum areas that lacked states capable of resisting during its nineteenth-century annexation of territories in the Caucasus, the vast Kazakh steppe, and the central Asian khanates. It stopped when it confronted other peer polities: the Ottoman Empire, Safavid Iran, Qing China, and British India. Later Russian attempts to expand farther south into a weakening Iran and Ottoman Empire were stymied by rival European powers that protected them, such as when France and Britain allied with the Turks in the Crimean War (1853–1856), which ended in Russia's defeat. As part of its later alliance with France and Britain against Germany in the First World War, Russia was promised Constantinople and control of northern Iran, a postwar colonial division of the spoils, but the endogenous empire established by Peter the Great was dissolved by revolution in 1917 before that could happen.[79]

CHAPTER SEVEN

Shadows' End

For each age is a dream that is dying,
Or one that is coming to birth

—ARTHUR O'SHAUGHNESSY, *ODE*, 1873

THIS BOOK HAS OUTLINED the many varieties of shadow exogenous empires that emerged in response to the expansion of endogenous empires in Eurasia beginning in ancient times. While not every endogenous empire found itself interacting directly with an exogenous shadow empire, no exogenous shadow empire existed without a relationship to one or more other empires. It was like fleas on a dog: while you might find a dog without fleas, you would never find fleas without a dog. Yet having successfully coevolved with endogenous empires over the course of two and half millennia, and still playing a prominent historical role at the beginning of the eighteenth century, all varieties of shadow empires were extinct by the beginning of the nineteenth century. How did this happen? The answer is somewhat surprising. Over the course of a little more than a century, three different types of shadow empires concurrently evolved into endogenous empires of immense size. The Manchu Qing dynasty, the only vulture empire to succeed in conquering all of China and its entire Inner Asian frontier, created an empire almost three times the size of the Tang dynasty. The vacuum empire of Tsarist Russia, previously restricted to the forest zone by a southern belt of powerful steppe nomadic polities, slowly displaced these nomads and tripled its already large size, repopulating their lands with farmers. The maritime British Empire in India, which began in the eighteenth century as a merchant company serving the Mughal dynasty from three small ports, by the mid-nineteenth century had become the master of the entire subcontinent, an area that encompassed more than 4 million km². Perhaps this dynamism should have been anticipated. The only two previous examples of shadow empires becoming endogenous empires had emerged just as rapidly with the rise of the Abbasid Caliphate in the mid-eighth century and the Mongol Empire in the mid-thirteenth, both of which were of unprecedented size and power during their heydays. The parallel transformation of three former exogenous empires, two land based and one sea based, profoundly reordered Eurasian geopolitics and would eventually pit them against one another during the nineteenth century. Only the singular Holy Roman Empire, a shadow empire of nostalgia, failed to even attempt such a transformation and was dissolved by its own emperor in 1806.

Death or Apotheosis: Two Paths to Extinction for Shadow Empires

The emergence and continued existence of shadow empires depended on a delicate set of relationships without which they could not survive. If the rest of the world vanished overnight, an endogenous empire could continue functioning. The vast bulk of its revenue was internally generated, and the loss of international trade would be offset by the elimination of costly frontier defenses. A shadow empire would not be so fortunate. It depended on the exploitation of external resources to finance itself, and their disappearance would spell its doom. Moreover, because a shadow empire's internal cohesion was also based on the protection it provided against external aggression, that glue would be gone too. Thus, shadow empires can never be analyzed in isolation but must instead be placed within a context that defines the particular niches they occupied and what sustained them. A new shadow empire of the same type could arise to replace one that was destroyed as long as its niche continued to exist, but not if that niche were destroyed. Instead, if another shadow empire emerged at all, it would be of a different type better adapted to the changed conditions.

This is perhaps easiest to grasp by way of examples. In an ancient Mediterranean world that consisted largely of city-states, the Athenians created a maritime empire in 478 B.C. that was dissolved after it lost the Peloponnesian War in 404 B.C. In the aftermath, no other city-state in the eastern Mediterranean ever replaced Athens as a hegemonic maritime power, but one in the western Mediterranean did: Carthage. Like the Athenians, the Carthaginians were a naval power that sought economic advantage rather than territorial conquest. Located in today's Tunisia, Carthage lay beyond the reach of the Alexandrian successor states that dominated the eastern Mediterranean in the third century B.C. It was a peer polity with the rising endogenous Roman Empire, with which it fought two wars (264–241, 218–201 B.C.), the second of which destroyed its empire but left the city and its economy intact. Not content with this victory, the Romans mounted a third war (149–146 B.C.) that completely destroyed Carthage and accelerated the process of turning the Mediterranean into what the Romans then called Mare Nostrum (Our Sea). Only after the Roman Empire collapsed in the west and its eastern Byzantine successor lost direct control over northern Italy was it possible for the Venetians to establish a new Mediterranean maritime empire in A.D. 697 as they exerted their hegemony over the Adriatic Sea and traded even more widely. Like the Athenians and Carthaginians, the Venetians built a strong navy to project power and improve their economic position without seeking much territorial expansion. Not endangered by neighbors strong enough to destroy it until the late eighteenth century, Venice sustained this maritime empire for 1,100 years.

China's northern frontier provides many examples of one shadow empire being succeeded by another over the course of 2,000 years, but it also displayed an alternating pattern in which different types of shadow empires replaced each other in turn (see table 3.3). Large mirror steppe empires emerged and prospered when China was unified under long-ruling native dynasties that established linear bipolar frontiers with Mongolia where nomadic imperial confederacies had established their own peer polities. The unity of these steppe empires was coterminous with the Chinese dynasties that funded them. When economic and political crises brought about the collapse of major dynasties in China, their steppe counterparts (now without a source of outside revenue) also collapsed. Shadow vulture empires emerged in these periods of anarchy and economic breakdown following the demise of the Han dynasty in the third century and the Tang dynasty in the tenth. Founded by frontier leaders who had previously been under the tight control of either China or a steppe empire, their polities lacked both the administrative sophistication of the Chinese dynasties and the raw military power of steppe empires they replaced. During periods of disunion in China and on the steppe, however, their second-best talents sufficed to bring political order and economic renewal to the parts of North China they controlled while keeping the steppe tribes divided. One-eyed kings in a land of the blind, they had difficulties retaining power after their rebellious Chinese subjects regained their sight and the steppe nomads started to reorganize themselves. At these times, their second-best talents proved inadequate to meet new challenges. The unification of China under the Sui and Tang dynasties at the end of the sixth century and the rise of the Mongol Empire in the thirteenth ushered these vulture shadow empires off the world stage. Conditions for their reemergence would not occur again until the seventeenth century when the collapse of China's Ming dynasty opened a period of anarchy that enabled the rise of the Manchus.

One way for exogenous shadow empires to break free of their dependency on external relationships was to transform themselves into endogenous empires through large-scale territorial expansion. This required them to take on the responsibility of ruling very large populations whose economies and cultures were very different from their own. Although these expansions were often serendipitous rather than carefully planned, they produced empires of unprecedented size: the mid-eighth-century Abbasid Caliphate was 11.1 million km², the mid-thirteenth-century Mongol Empire was 24 million km², the mid-eighteenth-century Qing dynasty in China was 14.7 million km², and late eighteenth-century Russia was 15.5 million km². While these land-based empires occupied contiguous territories, the maritime British Empire acquired a string of worldwide colonies that encompassed 33 million km² by 1920, of which the most heavily populated was its Indian raj acquired from the Mughals beginning in the late eighteenth century. These empires adapted their own styles of governance to the new places they now ruled, creating hybrids that contained elements drawn from their own exogenous shadow empire traditions and the preexisting imperial structures of the lands they conquered.

The extent of these empires, the largest in world history, raises the question of why those of shadow origin were so much larger than historic endogenous empires. While the latter averaged between 4 million and 6 million km² in size, the former were two or three times larger. My suggestion would be that endogenous empires deliberately restricted their growth based on what they deemed worth conquering. Areas with low population densities and no concentrated resources would not repay the cost of administration, particularly if the peoples there were prone to revolt to preserve their independence. Even more attractive places might be written off in response to military disasters such as Persia's failed second invasion of Greece, Rome's loss of three legions in Germania, or the Xiongnu nomads' humiliation of the founder of the Han dynasty in China. Cultural factors were also at work. Rulers of endogenous empires firmly believed that there were some lands and peoples that they could not successfully integrate, permanent outsiders not deserving the opportunity of membership. Once having decided which territories or peoples should not be incorporated into the empire, or did not justify the cost of doing so, endogenous empires then drew lines that they would defend but not expand beyond. Thus, the Romans put the limits of their northern frontier at the Rhine and Danube Rivers rather than attempting to incorporate the people inhabiting the forest zones beyond them. Similarly, while they fought with the Parthians and Sasanians over borderlands in the upper Euphrates in the east, the Romans never sought to conquer Persia itself as Alexander had done. At the other end of Eurasia, China famously built the Great Wall that marked the line between what it deemed the southern civilized lands worth governing and the northern "ungovernable" barbarian lands inhabited by steppe nomads in Mongolia and forest tribes in Manchuria. By contrast, the Mongol Yuan and the Manchu Qing dynasties saw both as eminently governable and, labeled barbarians themselves by the Chinese, viewed both sides of the frontier as indivisible parts of a single culturally pluralistic empire. Having themselves originated in places with much lower population densities, they possessed the tools to govern similar places as their strength grew and added ever-larger numbers of them to their expanding empires, in some cases by treating them as allies rather than subjects.

The lands that lay beyond the frontiers of endogenous empires were the natural breeding grounds of shadow empires. While they may have envied the wealth of endogenous empires, their success in remaining shadow empires required keeping a distance from them. However, on the rare occasions when they became endogenous empires themselves, their governments combined centers and peripheries together by using different modes of administration for each. This meant that not only was the territory they ruled immensely large but the people within it were remarkably diverse. The caliphate combined regions as distant as Spain and central Asia that had never been part of the same cultural and political world previously. The Mongol Empire was even more diverse, with central Asian Muslim officials collecting taxes in China and Chinese siege specialists fighting in the lands of the former caliphate and Russia. The Manchu, Russian, and British empires similarly combined the most amazing range of peoples together in a single polity. In this respect endogenous empires of shadow origin demonstrated a far greater capacity for growth than more parochial endogenous empires. This was key to their success and long duration. As described in detail in the individual case studies, their transformation into endogenous empires required radical changes to their administrative structures that often saw the relocation of their centers of power. Because the members of the ruling elites who implemented these changes were keen to stress the continuity of tradition rather than their break from it, it is easy to overlook how disjunctive the changes were.

Rulers of these new endogenous empires retained a keen appreciation of how shadow empires came into being and did their best to preempt the formation of rival new ones. The exogenous Muslim Umayyad Caliphate mobilized the Arab tribes in Arabia to create an empire and rewarded them with new lands and high political positions. It resisted attempts by non-Arabs to become Muslims and discriminated against those who did. Its endogenous Abbasid successor reversed this policy by encouraging non-Arabs to become Muslims, making Islam a world religion. In their brand-new capital of Baghdad, the Abbasids also adopted former Sasanian bureaucratic institutions that relegated the descendants of the empire's Arab founders to the margins. Arabia always retained its primacy as a center of religious pilgrimage but lost its political significance. No new shadow empire came out of Arabia thereafter.

The Mongols created a steppe shadow empire under Chinggis Khan and his son Ögedei that relied on extracting external revenue. Tribute and loot from across its vast conquests were sent to the Mongol capital of Karakorum, where all significant political decisions were made. Chinggis's grandson Khubilai shifted the base of Mongolian power to North China and created an endogenous empire by establishing the Yuan dynasty, which came to rule all of China and Mongolia from his capital there. Khubilai did this by winning a civil war in which he cut off the supplies sent from China to his traditionalist nomad opponents who had sought to maintain Mongolia as the empire's center. He reduced the steppes of Mongolia to provincial status within his endogenous redesign of the universal Mongol Empire. The steppe tribes there would not become autonomous again until after the Ming dynasty ousted the Mongols from China in 1368 and restored the classic bipolar frontier with the steppe.

Both the Manchus and Russians prevented the rise of new steppe shadow empires by occupying their lands. The Manchus used eastern Mongol client princes to campaign against the independent Zunghar nomads in western Mongolia who were attempting to create such a new steppe shadow empire. Over the course of one hundred years, the Qing dynasty conducted a series of wars that led to the utter destruction of the Zunghars in 1757 and to the incorporation of Tibet, Xinjiang, and western Mongolia into the Qing empire. More or less concurrently, the Russians began expanding south into the Pontic and Caspian steppes, the former home of the Golden Horde, and brought the steppe tribes living there into their empire. In the nineteenth century the Russians expanded east to conquer the Kazakh steppe and did not stop until they reached the borders of the Qing empire in Mongolia and Xinjiang. With the entire Eurasian steppe now divided between China and Russia, there was no place for any new steppe shadow polity to develop, and none did—ending a steppe shadow empire tradition that had endured for two thousand years.

Empires' Last Stands

As the nineteenth century progressed, the world of empires was an "endogenous only" club whose members still ruled the majority of Eurasia's people and territory. In so doing they were the keystone species within the larger political ecosystems that developed around them. While critics of empires might prefer to see them as apex predator polities atop an economic and military food chain with no natural enemies other than similar empires or wannabe empires, even they viewed the existence of empires as normative, not exceptional. Yet by the end of the twentieth century's First World War, every empire in Eurasia had collapsed with no prospect of returning. The European colonial empires that avoided collapse at that time dissolved in the decades after the Second World War. What happened to end the long age of these political dinosaurs, and what filled the niche they formerly occupied? A detailed answer to that question would require a monograph as substantial as this one, so here I will only suggest some of the main forces at play that led to their extinction and then examine how the structural elements of empires past—particularly shadow empires—remain surprisingly relevant for understanding Great Powers in the twenty-first century.

Endogenous empires were classically centralized tribute- and tax-extracting machines that put a high premium on preserving internal political order and social stability. They were willing to sacrifice innovations in technology or trade that might increase economic growth if these threatened that stability. Large-scale private ownership of land, goods, or money could only exist within the limits they set, curbing the emergence of an autonomous economic elite. Endogenous empires regularly confiscated private wealth when they needed to raise revenue or feared that its holders were growing too powerful. Among ancient empires, China was the most suspicious of those who made profits through trade and Rome the least, but all relied primarily on taxing people and agricultural production. Increasing the size of the farming population rather than expanding the commercial sector was their preferred path for economic growth. This was in sharp contrast to shadow steppe and maritime empires that saw trade as a vital resource to be protected and encouraged, as well as an activity in which the state itself might profitably participate.[1]

The rapid technological changes initiated by the Industrial Revolution in the late eighteenth century undermined the steady state economic equilibria that agrarian endogenous empires sought to preserve. It is not that empires were unaware of the positive role they could play in economic development. Early endogenous empires had taken the lead in transforming regional production systems with mega-projects that included road, canal, and port building; mining complexes and metal production; irrigation; and land reclamation. Indeed, for most of history only endogenous empires had the necessary capital, technical expertise, and mass forced labor needed to undertake such projects. One could therefore have imagined a similar possibility for state-centered industrial development, but the dynamism required to make that happen was entirely absent in the Ottoman, Austrian, Spanish, Russian, Mughal, and Qing empires in the early nineteenth century. The dynasties that ruled these empires were by the mid-nineteenth century well past their prime even by agrarian empire standards. They were no longer making large-scale infrastructure investments and were laggards in appreciating the potential of factory-based production of goods and steam power. These innovations were being pioneered in northwestern Europe, where Walter Scheidel argues that the failure of an empire to reemerge in the West after the fall of the Roman Empire created the preconditions for the Industrial Revolution and capitalism.[2] Only here was there a private sector with individuals who possessed enough capital and expertise to finance transformative industrial development, and only here were there states that either were too weak to prevent them or saw advantages in outsourcing economic development to them.

Still, existing endogenous empires might have remained economically competitive if it had been just a question of adopting a new set of technologies one time. What endogenous empires proved unable to manage were serial technological changes that disrupted the world economy and its power balances not once a century but once every few decades. These were accompanied by regular cycles of economic booms and busts that were politically disruptive even for states that attempted to insulate themselves from them. This capitalist assault on the existing world order was led by a new and growing bourgeois class. They were not members of the old political elite anywhere and had no loyalty to it. Privileging the acquisition of profit over inherited social status or holding government positions, the bourgeoisie presented a challenge that conservative empires were ill-prepared to meet. Karl Marx and Friedrich Engels condemned capitalism in their *Communist Manifesto* but stood in awe of its wrecking-ball dynamism that was constantly reinventing itself so that "all fixed, fast-frozen relations, with their train of ancient and venerable prejudices and opinions, are swept away, all new-formed ones become antiquated before they can ossify."[3]

Eurasian land empires were initially able to ward off such challenges to a degree not possible in fragmented Europe. Their nascent bourgeois classes were easier to control since they still existed within patrimonial economic systems. Access to markets and permission to develop new industries were gifts of the state that could be awarded to individuals or classes of people in return for political subservience and withdrawn just as easily. This proved progressively more difficult to maintain after European imperialists began making colonies of weak polities in Asia and Africa and forced existing empires to grant them economic concessions that opened their markets to wider competition. Fearful that they could not survive without upgrading their own infrastructures, existing empires gave priority to military improvements and state-strengthening technologies like railways and telegraphs but with some misgivings about the consequences.[4] While empires continued to exist within their historical borders, they found themselves becoming secondary players within a capitalist economic world system.

The exception to this general rule were maritime empires that were at home in such an environment and could even be said to have pioneered it. As we saw in chapter 2, the more conservative Greek city-states accused the ancient Athenians of being "born into the world to take no rest themselves and to give none to others" as they built an empire based on economic hegemony rather than territorial conquest.[5] But while the Athenians could revolutionize a regional commercial economy, they remained dependent on existing sources of energy (human, animal, wind, and water), methods of craft production, metallurgy, and transport. None of these would undergo radical transformation until the late eighteenth and nineteenth centuries when ever-newer sources of energy (steam, electricity, internal combustion) and increasingly sophisticated machines produced goods on an unprecedentedly large scale.[6] These commodities were sold to a world market connected by fast-moving steamships and railways that could carry bulk cargoes of goods that were often cheaper or better quality than those produced locally. Trains and ships also transported raw materials extracted from one side of the world to be processed in another, changing the dynamics of international trade. Information too began to flow at the unprecedented speed of light with the introduction of the electric telegraph, and keeping track of time to the exact hour and minute became normal. The disruptive technologies of the nineteenth century would themselves be disrupted and displaced by innovations in the twentieth century instead of plateauing in some end state. Perhaps unsurprisingly, it was the British maritime empire that became the leading power of the nineteenth-century Industrial Age, and the world set its clocks to Greenwich Mean Time.

Despite experiencing severe challenges throughout the nineteenth century, the empires of Austro-Hungary, Russia, the Ottomans, and Qing China still ruled over the majority of Eurasia's territory as the twentieth century dawned. By 1920 they were all gone. The Manchu Qing dynasty, established in 1644, was overthrown by Chinese nationalists in 1911. Having barely survived one revolution in 1905, Tsarist Russia succumbed to a second in 1917 in the midst of the First World War only four years after the Romanov dynasty had celebrated its tricentennial. The Austro-Hungarian Empire, whose Habsburg rulers boasted a lineage dating back to the thirteenth century, dissolved in 1918 after it ended up on the losing side of the First World War. The Ottoman Empire too was on the losing side of that war and stripped of almost all its territory in 1920 by the victorious Allies. It was formally abolished in 1922 by a new nationalist Turkish state that wrested back most of the empire's lost territory in Anatolia and ended the reign of the 880-year-old Osmanli dynasty. The entire Eurasian temperate zone was now divided among independent nation-states of various sizes, some old and some new. The overseas colonial empires of Britain and France survived intact, although the immense cost of the war and the exhaustion of their peoples left both in a weakened state. While the British and French colonial empires reached their greatest extent during the interwar years, they and the smaller Dutch, Belgian, and Portuguese colonial empires all dissolved in the decades following the end of the Second World War. The United States and the Soviet Union, which emerged from that war as the two dominant powers, were both hostile to colonialism and, for very different reasons, keen to see the rise of new nation-states that could become members of their competing blocs.

Endogenous empires thrived as masters of agrarian economies with technological and transportation infrastructures that changed in only minor ways after they first emerged in the mid-first millennium B.C. They extracted the bulk of their revenue from an illiterate farming population rather than from trade or manufacturing and had low rates of urbanization despite sometimes impressively large capital cities. Under these conditions they were indeed wonders of their age, unmatched by any other type of polity except for shadow empires that emulated them in some way. But the technological and economic innovations wrought by the Industrial Revolution that Britain embraced destabilized them during the nineteenth century. Agrarian-based empires struggled to maintain their hegemony in a rearguard action that pitted their seemingly immovable inertia against an equally irresistible tide of change. That they ultimately succumbed was no surprise, but their ability to remain intact and functional until the second decade of the twentieth century was quite amazing. I say amazing since these empires lacked the needed tools to run economies where industry and trade superseded agriculture in importance, where their societies were increasingly urban and literate, and where the global population was rising exponentially.

The Legacy of Empires in the Twenty-First Century

The age of the imperial dinosaurs ended not because empires did something wrong but because they could not adapt themselves to a new world that was quite unlike the one that produced them. Whether any large states in the post–Second World War era could be called empires has remained a topic of much debate, and employing the terminology of empire to describe the enormously large but quite different political entities that resembled them in the twenty-first century is both anachronistic and structurally inadequate. (Perhaps by the twenty-second century a clearer social science framework will have emerged that does them justice.) Nevertheless, contemporary Great Powers have borrowed many of the tools developed by now-extinct empires, to a surprising extent, particularly shadow ones. Indeed, it could be said that a good knowledge of past shadow empires is a necessary foundation for understanding international relations in the first quarter of the twenty-first century.

Because the empire label is a pejorative one in the twenty-first century, no polity today calls itself an empire as many proudly did earlier. For this reason, categorizing large polities like the United States or the People's Republic of China as empires has proved more provocative than enlightening. (During the Cold War both the United States and the Soviet Union took to calling each other empires while indignantly rejecting the term's application to themselves.) The debate assumes a binary answer—they are or they aren't—and forecloses the opportunity of investigating what different types of past imperial models they may have adopted for projecting power on the world stage today. Like Charles Maier, I too am agnostic on the question of whether any contemporary states deserve to be called empires, but it is clear to me that the many different strategies empires developed in the past are on full display in world politics today and are worth examining in that light.[7] This is an exercise more likely to appeal to international relations specialists than historians since those of us who have lived most of our lives in the twentieth century find it hard to think of the twenty-first as anything other than current events.

As the twenty-first century opened, there were 191 sovereign member states in the United Nations. International law no longer recognized military conquest of territory as legitimate, and fear of nuclear weapons limited armed conflicts to marginal places where they were unlikely to be employed in response. The pressure to create new smaller states by dividing older ones remained far greater than the desire to merge into larger ones (German reunification in 1990 being the exception). But the legacy of empire was not fully extinguished because major world powers like the United States, the European Union, China, and Russia continued to rely on structures and strategies derived from them. Each drew on different models with unique sets of strengths and weaknesses that were part of their own historical DNA but quite distinct from each other. Three employed shadow empire templates (the United States, the European Union, and Russia), and one was rooted in the endogenous empire tradition (China). These templates set the parameters for how each governed domestically and how each organized its foreign relations. And because they were grounded in different sets of largely unarticulated economic and cultural principles, the potential for misinterpreting each other's motives and ambitions was considerable.

THE UNITED STATES: SUSTAINING AMERICA'S *ARCHE*

The United States of America in 2020 governed a territory of 10 million km^2 with a population of 331 million and was the world's largest economy. It was the first nation designed around principles of governance rather than inherited institutions, but in its foreign policy it drew on a maritime empire template that it had acquired as a colony of Great Britain but implemented more along the lines of imperial Athens to create its own *arche* in the post–Second World War era.

Although by 1853 the United States possessed all the enormous territories between its Atlantic and Pacific Coasts, it never thought of itself as a land power. (Even in the twenty-first century its demographic and economic centers of gravity remain on the East and West Coasts, not its much vaster inland regions.) Instead, outside North America, it drew on a maritime empire template for its international relations that gave sea power priority over land power, viewed economic hegemony as more desirable than territorial hegemony, and deemed indirect political domination more sustainable than direct political domination. This first displayed itself in the 1823 Monroe Doctrine, which declared the Americas to be the exclusive sphere of influence of the United States—a policy that could only be implemented by a maritime power. However, this maritime empire template would not display itself fully until after the Second World War when the United States faced off against the land-based Soviet Union as one of the world's two superpowers. Using an indirect maritime strategy that would have been familiar to the Athenians, the Americans sought economic rather than territorial hegemony through an alliance system that protected its member states from possible Soviet aggression and allowed their economies to grow rapidly. Unlike the maritime Athenian Empire, however, the United States possessed a large and self-sustaining domestic economy in continental North America that could bankroll its high defense spending without extorting payments from allies. Nor was it interested in re-creating a closed trading system with subject colonies like that of the now-dissolved maritime British Empire that required considerable military force to maintain. Instead the United States constructed a postwar international system from which it benefited militarily and economically but that also benefited its allies enough to make it self-sustaining. Less elegantly, the United States was happy to manage an Adam Smith free market casino where all had a fair chance to win but where the odds favored the house and all bets were in its dollar-denominated chips that replaced gold and the British pound as the world's reserve currency.

The American *arche* consisted of overlapping networks of military and economic alliances that spanned the globe. The military alliances were designed to provide protection against the Soviet bloc through mutual defense treaties, including the 1949 North Atlantic Treaty Organization (NATO) in Western Europe, and bilateral agreements with Japan (1951, 1960) and Korea (1953) in Northeast Asia. These were the linchpins of a system that allowed the stationing of its troops within these sovereign allied nations, which also fell under the protection of an American nuclear umbrella. It was part of a much vaster system of secondary alliances that even a quarter century after the collapse of the Soviet Union included eight hundred military bases of various types in seventy countries. Connected by sea and air routes, this network allowed the United

States to project its power worldwide without maintaining an excessively large number of troops abroad. Its success in the aftermath of the Second World War was based on turning former enemies, Germany and Japan, into close allies and major economic powers after installing democratically run governments and financing their reconstruction. It did the same for the rest of Western Europe as well, laying the groundwork for the Common Market and the future European Union. The economic side soon eclipsed the military side in importance, buttressed by new multilateral institutions such as the World Bank (1944), the International Monetary Fund (1945), and the General Agreement on Tariffs and Trade (1947). This was less a matter of altruism than the employment of a maritime empire strategy that sought to minimize control of territory by tying states into an economic system from which it benefited. In an improvement on ancient Athens's approach, the United States relied as much on the self-interest of its members to keep the system functioning as it did on its own power. This dual military-economic network would see off the Soviet Union and maintain itself afterward. Its success as a strategy was best appreciated by contrasting it with failed American policies that veered from the maritime empire template and drew the United States into counterproductive land wars in Vietnam, Iraq, and Afghanistan, costly misadventures that weakened it domestically and internationally. When Donald Trump began braying about an American First policy in 2016 and questioning the need for alliances like NATO or keeping U.S. troops in Korea, it was members of the alliance who were most appalled that he would not see its value. The Russian invasion of Ukraine in 2022 revived both the alliance's rationale and America's central role as its leader.

In one important area the United States broke with the maritime template that had created cosmopolitan economies with insular ruling elites in Athens, Venice, Holland, and Britain. In the United States universal birthright citizenship, immigration, and capitalist economic disruption combined to produce a more open political system in which the elites who set American policy eventually reflected the diversity of the population, albeit with a considerable lag time. That diversity was also reflected in America's soft-power influence similar to that of Athens in the ancient Greek world because, beginning in the mid-twentieth century, the United States became the place to be for those producing culture. Part of the attraction was its rich economy and freedom of expression, but it benefited just as much from the arrival of artists, scholars, scientists, and entrepreneurs who left their own homelands and eventually became American citizens themselves. This put the United States at the forefront of many fields that it would have been unlikely to develop (or develop as quickly) without them. Whether in Hollywood, New York, or Silicon Valley, the ability to attract talented people who became American citizens by choice was an opportunity missing in even the most economically cosmopolitan maritime empires of the past. It was certainly the first to make culture itself a profitable export.

THE EUROPEAN UNION: A NOT-SO-HOLY ROMAN EMPIRE

In 2020 the European Union had a population of around 450 million people divided among twenty-seven sovereign nations encompassing 4.2 million km² that together constituted the world's third-largest economy after the United States and China. It emerged as a post–Second World War aspirational project designed to avoid the conflicts that had devastated the continent for centuries, first by integrating Western Europe into a single market and then by creating a common political structure to administer it without eliminating the nationally sovereign governments of its member states. (Member states continued to maintain their own armies, foreign policies, and parliaments and could choose to withdraw from the EU.) It expanded into central and eastern Europe after the dissolution of the Soviet Union in 1991. Intellectually the EU rooted itself in the idea that there was a common European culture that transcended the continent's many different languages, national divisions, and religions. It would be a union with a formidable regulatory bureaucracy and court system, but one without a military or single capital. Imaginary European-style buildings and bridges illustrated its euro banknotes to avoid having to choose among real ones. If the main advantage of empires over other polities was their ability to organize diversity, then the EU would obtain the same result without also creating a unitary state in the process—a caffeine-free espresso, if you will. It did so by employing a striking number of shadow elements found in the Holy Roman Empire, particularly its high tolerance for subsidiary sovereignty among its member states. It is not that the founders of the EU took the Holy Roman Empire as a model, but rather that complexities the EU faced were so similar that they developed in parallel ways.

Because a problem solved is a problem soon forgotten, it is barely remembered that the initial rationale for the nascent union was to end a Franco-German hostility that had led to three consecutive conflicts in seventy years: the Franco-Prussian War (1870–1871), the First World War (1914–1918), and the Second World War (1939–1945). This began with the integration of their coal and steel industries in 1951 and took political shape in 1957 when the Treaty of Rome created the European Common Market, which was more formally merged in 1965. Its six founding members (Belgium, France, Luxembourg, Italy, the Netherlands, and West Germany) occupied the same territories as Charlemagne's Carolingian Empire had during the ninth century, the only previous time that the German and French worlds shared a single governing institution with common cultural aspirations. The new entity had no single capital but instead split its institutions among the cities of Brussels, Strasbourg, and Luxembourg. They were all nondescript places located in borderlands that the French and Germans had long fought over and that lacked any taint of the invidious past glory that characterized Paris, Rome, or a then-divided Berlin. By the 1970s both Germany and France had so thoroughly embraced the integration of the community's economies that any notion that it was designed to reduce hostility between them was relegated to a historical footnote. Their common vision now was to expand into other parts of Europe and create an entity that could compete more equally with the United States and the Soviet Union, something no European state could hope to achieve alone.

Enlargement began with the addition of Great Britain, Ireland, and Denmark (1973); Greece (1981); and then Spain and Portugal (1986). In 1993 it was reorganized into the European Union before adding Sweden, Finland, and Austria in 1995. The withdrawal of Soviet troops from central Europe allowed Germany to reunite in 1990, and the collapse of the Soviet Union itself led to a further wave of new members in 2004: Estonia, Latvia, Lithuania, Poland, the Czech Republic, Slovakia, Hungary, and Slovenia. These were followed by Romania and Bulgaria in 2007 and Croatia in 2013. (Great Britain, after an unexpected negative referendum vote in 2016, left the EU in 2020.) But the successful establishment of the EU also depended on a fortuitous alignment in world politics. The United States, following its maritime empire alliance template, was supportive of European unity and the creation of a large new economic bloc. It not only did not hinder its emergence, but through NATO the United States provided the EU with the security framework that left it free to focus entirely on economic affairs. The Soviet Union, by contrast, had ensured that not even a modicum of economic or political autonomy would emerge in the areas it occupied after the Second World War—the default position historically when large land-based states were in a position to dominate smaller ones.

It may be remembered that in 1667 Samuel Pufendorf declared the Holy Roman Empire a "misshaped monster" because it lacked sovereignty over its component states.[8] It also lacked a capital city and an army that emerging national states (and all other types of empires) deemed foundational. It turns out that this structure, so ill-adapted to a world of emerging nation-states that drove it to extinction, was perfectly designed for a union of sovereign states that governed as a supranational polity largely through administrative regulation and a rules-enforcing judicial system. It had its own revenue sources that included customs receipts, required member contributions, and a percentage of nationally assessed value-added taxes. Typical of modern states but not empires, most of the EU's income was redistributed through subsidies and capital investments tilted toward its poorer members. The EU parliament resembled the Diets of the Holy Roman Empire in their multiple meeting places and the disconnection between that body and a weak executive. While the Holy Roman Emperor was faulted for his inability to command the obedience of member states, the EU refused even to create a single chief executive officer. Instead it had three separate presidencies whose priority depended on the issues involved: a rotating council of ministers' presidency filled by a different member country every six months, a president of the European Commission, and a president of the EU parliament. A similarly decentralized Holy Roman Empire lasted nine hundred years in the German world and northern Italy but stood in sharp contrast to the centralized systems of government that developed in countries such as France or Britain where the state's chief executive was the most important player. One reason for the lack of focus on an executive office in the EU was that it had no military forces to command. Defense responsibilities rested with national states themselves and with NATO on a Europe-wide basis. While the EU's major players were members of the NATO alliance during the Cold War, smaller states with nonaligned policies were not. And while NATO had its large headquarters in Brussels and defending Europe was its core mission, it was distinct from the EU because it had many non-EU partners, including the United States (its dominant member), Canada, Iceland, Norway, and Turkey. When the EU expanded eastward in 1994, all its new member states sought to join the NATO alliance to protect themselves from future Russian aggression. They were joined by Finland and Sweden in 2022 when that threat became more real with Russia's invasion of Ukraine.

There were of course significant differences between the EU and its shadow empire predecessor, the most distinctive of which was that the EU was resolutely secular. Its concept of European unity was cultural and economic rather than religious, but resistance to accepting Muslim

Turkey as European enough to join demonstrated the persisting legacy of Europe's long Christian history. Nor was the EU rooted in a nostalgia for the past that had most recently produced violent nationalisms that left millions of people dead in the Second World War. Seeking to end such violence demanded new ways of thinking and a future orientation. Appeals to nostalgia were left to anti-EU nationalist parties fighting a rearguard battle to dissolve it in order to make their own countries great again. It was an ambition that became ever more difficult to achieve as the majority of Europe's population could no longer imagine a world in which it did not exist. The turmoil that Britain endured to leave the EU looked less likely to restore its former glory than to lead to its own dissolution. Scotland, where 62 percent of the people had voted to remain, renewed its push for independence to rejoin, and the once-unthinkable prospect that the people of Northern Ireland might choose to reunify with EU member Ireland rather than stick with Britain became a distinct possibility after 56 percent of its people voted to remain. But perhaps the greatest difference of all was that the EU was a product of voluntary alliance and treaty making, unlike empires that were created in wars of conquest. Empires may have improved the lives of those who lived in them as they evolved, but these benefits were appreciated only by the descendants of those who survived their violent formation.

CHINA: TANG OR SONG?

The People's Republic of China (PRC) was established in 1949 after the Communists defeated the ruling nationalist Kuomintang in a civil war. During the twenty-first century it became a world power that governed a territory of 9.3 million km^2 with a population of 1.4 billion people. In 2020 it had the world's second-largest economy after the United States, although its per capita income was far lower ($11,000 versus $63,000).[9] The PRC was the only one of the imperial afterlife examples that based itself on models drawn from an endogenous empire template despite Mao Zedong's goal of wiping out that past through the radical reorganization of China's society and economy. The first few decades of PRC rule proved so ruthless and disruptive that they can only be compared to the similarly turbulent period following the Qin unification of China in 220 B.C. As in 206 B.C. when the Han dynasty abandoned the most destructive Qin policies to create a more stable state, Mao's vision of a China in constant revolution was reversed after Deng Xiaoping (1904–1997) took power in 1978. PRC policies shifted to building China economically and improving its standard of living without any accompanying political liberalization. A challenge to development by diktat arose in 1989 when mass demonstrations in Beijing's Tiananmen Square, the symbolic heart of state power, demanded political reforms similar to those then occurring in the Soviet bloc. The Chinese Communist Party called in the People's Liberation Army to crush the demonstrations—which it did with great violence—and began a policy of political suppression that included wiping this event from the country's historical memory with severe censorship. In the years that followed, the Communist Party would also begin glorifying China's imperial past, which Mao had condemned, because it wished to restore China to the dominant role it had previously occupied in those eras.

China had many past imperial templates to draw inspiration from. The most universal but least acceptable were those created by the frontier minority rulers of China, which included the Mongol Yuan and Manchu Qing dynasties, because Han Chinese nationalists viewed them as aliens. Instead the PRC looked to emulate the longest-lived empires run by native Chinese dynasties, the Han and Tang, both of which were hegemonic East Asian powers for many centuries. As we saw in chapter 1, their organization lay at the extreme end of the centralization and state control axis when compared with other contemporary endogenous empires. It was a model that privileged centralized rule and institutions run by the state, attributes that the PRC wished to maintain in its own government. Even after China ended collectivized agriculture in the 1980s, it was the state rather than the farmers that retained legal title to the land. And although by 2020 there were four hundred billionaires in China, their private property rights were not secure and depended on the sufferance of the state—a situation that was the norm in China for most of its history. These empires had also produced well-functioning state bureaucracies that could serve as a model for any successor state even if the criteria of recruitment changed from knowledge of the Confucian classics to those of Mao Zedong or Xi Jinping thought.

Another feature of endogenous empires the PRC retained was the assumption that its people were subjects to be ruled and not participants in government. This was a universal characteristic of endogenous empires but not of the polities that had replaced them in the twentieth century. It made the PRC a political outlier in a twenty-first-century global system where its main rivals had some kind of popular domestic electoral system that either chose its leaders, as in the United States and EU, or at least validated authoritarian ones, as in Russia. Even theocratic Iran had an elected parliament and president, although its ruling clerics vetted who could run. China left the choice of its leaders to the two hundred members of the Communist Party's Central Committee, who elected a two-dozen-member Politburo that actually wielded power and selected a president who set policy. Such a system of governance was normative for agrarian empires where peasants provided the bulk of the state's revenue and expected to receive only security from violence and economic stability in return. Peasant rebellions in China occurred when the state failed to maintain one or both of these conditions. But while China's economy still had a much higher percentage of farmers than its peers, by 2020 its urban population constituted a majority of 60 percent, up from a base of less than 20 percent when China began its economic reforms in the 1980s. In other parts of the world, such rapid population shifts from rural to urban areas and the rise of a literate wage-earning class led to the demise of agrarian empires. China's Communist Party calculated that it could avoid such a fate by undertaking policies that raised hundreds of millions of poor rural peasants out of poverty, that progressively improved the standard of living of urban dwellers, and that rewarded entrepreneurs with prospects of extreme wealth. In return the Communist Party expected to be accepted as a political golden clan where competition for state power would remain restricted to its own members. Whether a system originally designed to rule over a vast number of rural peasants could be retrofitted to govern a far more sophisticated urban population in an industrial economy without giving them the right of political participation will certainly test the limits of that template in the future.

China had two possible endogenous empire models to emulate for dealing with the outside world. The first was characteristic of dynasties located in North China's Yellow River watershed such as the Han (206 B.C.–A.D. 220) and Tang (618–907) that asserted their "emperor of all under heaven" could have no equal. China could therefore have only tributaries that acknowledged its supremacy or enemies that did not. It recognized no peer polities—a position that caused the Han dynasty to engage in decades of costly warfare with the Xiongnu nomads that began in 134 B.C. to reverse the agreement its founder, Han Gaozu, made that had recognized them as an equal state in 198 B.C. It was a policy that produced strong armies and sought the conquest of neighboring agrarian territories that would then be integrated into the empire. Annexed lands were peopled with colonial settlers administered by centrally appointed officials who were also expected to assimilate the local population by transforming them into Han Chinese culturally. Although generally successful in extending Chinese power, the policy had its limitations. Repeated attempts to assimilate Vietnam and

Korea failed even though their elites adopted many aspects of Chinese culture. The steppe nomads north of the Great Wall never adopted anything culturally Chinese other than its luxury goods, and the peoples in today's Xinjiang and Tibet proved too distant and culturally different to make them easy candidates for assimilation.

A second endogenous model developed in southern China's Yangtze and Pearl River watersheds where the Song dynasty (960–1279) had reconciled itself to living in a political world of equals after North China fell under the rule of foreign dynasties.[10] It flourished during a period when the center of China's population and wealth had shifted south, leaving the now-poorer north far less significant. The Song dynasty gave precedence to economic development and deployed its relatively weak military forces defensively—a decision made easier because it lay far from the traditional steppe nomad conflict zone along the Great Wall. The Song encouraged international trade and its ports in the Pearl River delta connected China to the Indian Ocean economic sphere. The Song period was renowned for its economic and technological innovations, including the introduction of gunpowder weapons and paper money, which Philip Curtin praises in lavish terms: "Between the foundation of the Song dynasty in 960 and the conquest of northern China by the Jurchen nomads in 1127, China passed through a phase of economic growth that was unprecedented in earlier Chinese history, perhaps in world history up to this time. It depended on a combination of commercialization, urbanization, and industrialization that has led some authorities to compare this period in Chinese history with the development of early modern Europe six centuries later."[11] Deng Xiaoping's strategy for building China's power implicitly relied on the Song southern model that avoided alienating other world powers who might slow China's rise if they deemed it a possible military danger. South China became the crucible in which the PRC's new relationship to the global economy was forged, and that region remains China's most dynamic.

This strategy changed after Xi Jinping assumed the presidency in 2013 with the goal of restoring China's previous hegemony by seeking to position itself as a successor Great Power to the United States on the world stage. Under Xi's rule the PRC became more nationalistic and aggressive in its foreign relations, following a Tang template in which China would again have tributaries and enemies but no peers. (Indeed, it is hard to think of any country today that China views as a true friend or vice versa.) This included building up China's military forces and making extravagant and legally dubious claims over disputed neighboring territories and sea lanes. This shift had domestic repercussions as well. At its founding the

PRC recognized its vast but sparsely populated non–Han Chinese territories in Inner Mongolia, Xinjiang, and Tibet as semiautonomous regions in a country where more than 90 percent of the population was Han Chinese. The government also granted China's fifty-odd minority peoples (*minzu*) special status to ensure their distinctiveness was respected.[12] Under Xi attitudes toward such minority groups shifted dramatically from one where their languages and cultures received special protections to one in which they were expected to assimilate into the dominant Han culture. These policies were especially severe in Xinjiang and Tibet. In addition to settling millions of Han people in Xinjiang to make the native Uighurs minorities in their own lands (already the case in Manchuria and Inner Mongolia), local officials implemented coercive policies designed to increase the use of the Chinese language in all aspects of public life and eradicate indigenous religious beliefs. Islamic communities were a particular target of attack. Many mosques and shrines were damaged or destroyed and the use of Arabic script and language was discouraged.[13] The roots of this policy were to be found not in China's socialist ideology but in the legacy of the earlier dynasties that had dealt with minority populations in similar ways.

Xi's policies have given rise to speculation about a potential Great Power conflict that would pit the American maritime empire template against China's endogenous empire template.[14] But the Tang template may be as obsolete as the empire that produced it. It allowed China to become hegemonic in an agrarian East Asia that was a closed system in which it faced no significant rivals other than shadow nomadic empires that were happy to make symbolic tributary visits as long as they profited from them. It was never designed to function in an open system that included peer polities that did not share its cultural values and whose economies and armed forces matched or exceeded China's own. While pursuing a militaristic Tang model might restore China's status as the hegemonic power in East Asia, it would ultimately fail if China's ambitions were global rather than regional. Its most likely outcome would be the emergence of a more fragmented economic world that would slow China's economic growth rate at a time when its per capita income was still between 30 and 40 percent lower than that in the United States, the EU, or Japan.

By contrast, the more cosmopolitan and economically oriented Song southern China model was well designed to accommodate China's emergence as a major player on the world stage. The Song had always supported links between China's economy and the non-Chinese world that went in both directions: China's large overseas population today (an estimated forty million in Southeast Asia alone) had its origins in migrations from the country's southern provinces that began during the Song dynasty itself. These communities lived as minorities in other societies but retained their own cultural identity. Their networks of merchants linked back to China when it was open to trade but could remain viable within their own prosperous regional economic spheres when it was not. And unlike communities back home, they were free to act without the heavy hand of the Chinese state restricting their actions. Deng Xiaoping's reforms put the south in a dominant economic position domestically as the twenty-first century progressed, but China's political center of power remained in Beijing, its quintessentially northern capital since the time of the Mongols. Over the course of eight hundred years, the Yuan, Ming, and Qing dynasties all financed their imperial ambitions and subsidized the poorer north by exploiting southern resources that included the construction of major infrastructure projects like the Grand Canal that supplied Beijing (literally "northern capital"). Xi's ambitious policies designed to make China great again appeared to follow that old northern pattern and threatened to disrupt what had been the south's remarkably successful integration into the world economy at ever-higher levels of sophisticated production. If disruptions in international economic relationships were the price of an aggressive foreign policy, these would hit the south harder than the north, where China's aging heavy-industry rust belt remained dependent on loss-making state-owned enterprises. Those with a long historical memory might remember the Ming dynasty had closed all its southern ports to trade and ordered China's navy destroyed in the fifteenth century so that it could focus on its Great Wall wars with the Mongols, whose attacks threatened Beijing.

While which long-term path China will take is uncertain, it is worth noting that unlike the Communist Party–led Soviet Union, whose ruling elite lacked significant private assets and whose children did not succeed them in top posts, the families of the PRC's Communist Party rulers have both amassed great private wealth and established multigenerational political dynasties. They would be personally harmed by economic disruptions, and the emergence of international hostility toward China would put their extensive foreign investments and ability to travel in jeopardy. For these people a softer Song power model that permits China to prosper and play a larger cooperative role in world affairs has significant attractions over a harder Tang power model. Within China the Song model is the one with dynamism: since the 1960s when the north and south contributed about equally to China's economy, the regions have diverged sharply, with the south now contributing 65 percent of China's GDP and just two of its southern provinces (Guangdong and Jiangsu) having accounted for more than 20 percent of China's total GDP in 2020.[15] Moreover, the south remains the center of the innovative technological economy that China sees as its future. In a world where economic power has become more significant than military power in determining a country's relative influence, it may be only a matter of time before proponents of a southern template that prioritizes economic growth and global outreach seek to replace Xi's northern template, which is bad for business and alienates the rest of the world. Germany and Japan both grew wealthier and more influential after getting out of the dominate-your-neighbor business. In addition, Great Power political games pay far fewer dividends today than they once did, so the dynamics that drove them may no longer be applicable to a world where transnational private corporations with assets of a trillion dollars have more clout than most nation-states.

RUSSIA: RETURN TO THE SHADOWS

Russia emerged as the Soviet Union's primary successor state after it collapsed in 1991. Although shorn of about 5.5 million km^2 of former Soviet territory, Russia remained the world's largest country, with 17.1 million km^2. Its status as a peer power with the United States, the European Union, and China rested on its possession of the Soviet Union's nuclear arsenal and robust spending on military forces that amounted to around 3 or 4 percent of its GDP from 2010 to 2020, but in other respects Russia was not in their league. As the third decade of the twenty-first century opened, the Russian economy formed only 1.79 percent of the world's total GDP, more than an order of magnitude smaller than that of the United States (24.8 percent), China (18.2 percent), or the EU (17 percent).[16] Its GDP was smaller than South Korea's, a country less than 100,000 km^2 in size whose top exports were advanced electronics, machinery, and motor vehicles. Russia's main exports, by contrast, were oil, natural gas, coal, grain, timber, minerals, and metals (iron, steel, and aluminum). While the Soviet Union's population when it dissolved was larger than that of the United States, Russia's population of 146 million in 2020 was less than half that of the United States and declining.

Of the imperial afterlife examples presented here, Russia most closely resembled an exogenous shadow empire that depended on external resources to maintain its power. Abandoning the Soviet Union's closed economy that sought self-sufficiency, Russia returned to a Muscovite (and even Rus') pattern of exporting its natural resources to sustain itself. These exports financed the military spending that maintained Russia's parity with other world powers and the welfare services that were now expected by its citizens. Its mere survival in the decade after the Soviet Union collapsed was an impressive feat. Russia could have experienced a cascade of further breakups as occurred in the former Yugoslavia but did not because the regions with the strongest desire to be independent became so when the Soviet Union dissolved (Chechnya being the major exception). In the aftermath Russia appears to have retained its resilient jellyfish structure that could reconstitute itself from whatever damaged parts survived, albeit on a smaller scale. Despite having been part of a centralized Soviet command economy for seventy years, Russia remained a network of economic and political nodes where no single part was critical to the survival of the whole.

Both the Tsarist Russian Empire and its Soviet Union successor employed political structures designed to govern the diverse range of peoples they ruled over and celebrated that diversity as evidence of their greatness. Post-Soviet Russia was a far less cosmopolitan polity and apparently happy to be so. Under Vladimir Putin's leadership after 2000, Russia increasingly defined itself in nationalist cultural terms that linked an imagined premodern past to a unique contemporary transnational Russkiy Mir (Russian World). Seeking to unite Russian language speakers and championing conservative Christian values, proponents of a Russkiy Mir rejected both the Soviet Union's atheism and its universalist socialist ideology as well as the liberal values of Western democratic societies. This was exemplified by Putin's growing engagement with the Russian Orthodox Church, to which he presented himself as the defender of traditional values—a tsar equivalent protecting Holy Mother Russia from the evils of the outside world. More pragmatically, Putin made the continued possession of great wealth dependent on personal loyalty to him—creating a patrimonial political system that better resembled that of the tsars and their boyars than a modern capitalist economy. As a consequence, many talented Russians chose to make their mark abroad by emigrating. Putin's Russia thereby forfeited the opportunity to remain on the technological cutting edge that China, the United States, and the European Union all saw as the economic battleground of the future. But one virtue of adopting a shadow empire template was that Russia need not compete in these areas to remain relevant. Russia only needed to maintain its military strength, and its standing as the world's second-largest nuclear power with the fourth-largest defense budget and fifth-biggest army achieved that goal.

As the twenty-first century opened, Russia was a nuclear-armed Muscovy with frontiers that would have been familiar to Ivan the Terrible. Refusing to accept that any part of the Russkiy Mir had a right to maintain its independence, Putin adopted two templates used by shadow empires to assert Russia's dominance. Drawing on an idealized vision of bygone eras characteristic of empires of nostalgia, he asserted that Russia's future greatness lay in reclaiming its past glory—that of the tsars and not the Soviet Union. Such an appeal attracted people who shared his cultural Russkiy Mir vision of the world but had nothing to offer those who did not, one of the severe limitations of all empires of nostalgia. Putin also adopted the vacuum empire template of piecemeal expansion (characteristic of the Rus', the Grand Duchy of Lithuania, and Muscovy) in which stronger polities first dominated and then annexed weaker polities on their frontiers, stopping only when they encountered polities capable of resisting them or that had allies capable of doing so. The dissolution of the maximalist Soviet Union created a large number of such states on Russia's new borders and Putin wanted them back. Sensitive to this danger, the ex-Soviet Baltic states of Estonia, Latvia, and Lithuania, along with the former Warsaw Pact member countries of Poland, the Czech Republic, Hungary, Romania, Bulgaria, and Slovakia, joined both the NATO defense alliance and the European Union between 1999 and 2007. Putin was unable to prevent this stampede to join the West, but he did assist local secessionist groups in establishing client enclaves elsewhere with the help of Russian troops in Moldova (2004) and Georgia (2008) after their governments indicated they too wished to be part of the EU and NATO.

The 2004 Orange Revolution in Kiev risked putting Ukraine in that category, but the installation of pro-Moscow oligarchs as presidents kept that country in the Russian sphere until the 2013–2014 Maidan Revolution ousted them and enshrined the goal of EU and NATO membership in the Ukrainian constitution. Putin then used his Russkiy Mir ideology as a rationale for the dismemberment of neighboring post-Soviet states he viewed as part of it. He illegally annexed Crimea to Russia in 2014 and aided separatists occupying land in Ukraine's eastern Donbas region by claiming he was only protecting Russian speakers there. These actions provoked only a survivable series of sanctions from the West, and Putin spent the next eight years upgrading Russia's military capacity to make it capable of seizing all of Ukraine in a blitzkrieg war. The plan assumed that Ukraine was a vacuum zone Russia could easily fill because its people would not resist and the West would not respond in any ways that might stop him. This proved a monumental miscalculation on both counts after Russia attacked Ukraine in 2022.

Putin justified his invasion of Ukraine as an act of domestic house cleaning that the world had no business objecting to by defining the Ukrainians as a variety of wayward Russians—sheep who had strayed now being brought back into the fold. (He made it illegal for Russians to call it a war.) But it also replicated Tsarist Russia's vacuum empire history of expanding into frontier territories held by states that other world powers considered marginal to their own interests. Much to Putin's and the world's surprise, the Ukrainians repulsed the Russian attack on Kiev and inflicted heavy casualties that forced a Russian retreat with the aid of antitank and anti-aircraft weapons provided by NATO countries. More significantly from a strategic perspective, the invasion reinvigorated a NATO alliance that had been questioning its own relevance. Sweden and Finland—Baltic states with long histories of neutrality—agreed to join the alliance as full members, and NATO deployed a much larger number of troops into eastern Europe to bolster defenses there. A broad coalition of Western states provided billions of dollars' worth of advanced weapons and financial support to Ukraine. The EU and United States also imposed severe sanctions on Russian assets abroad and reduced its ability to export oil and gas. Putin then shifted to a more limited strategy of annexing smaller border territories and proclaiming them parts of the Russian Federation, only to be driven out of them by Ukrainian counterattacks.

A lesson drawn from the history of vacuum empires is that Russia has never been the inevitable victor in such wars of expansion. There were a series of shadow empires that held these lands before Russia became an endogenous empire in the eighteenth century, after which they were largely forgotten except by the people who lived there. The collapse of the Soviet Union allowed for their reemergence. Ukraine's aligning with the West has re-created the old Polish-Lithuanian Commonwealth frontiers that had halted Russian expansion for centuries. While Putin saw himself as a new Peter the Great, he was risking Ivan the Terrible's fate of losing the gains he had earlier achieved when he overreached in the sixteenth century—a failure that preceded Russia's debilitating Time of Troubles a generation later. However, what could undermine Russia more is not winning or losing a war, even badly, but being on the wrong side of the transition to carbon-free wind, geothermal, and solar energy technologies that might leave its oil and gas resources stranded without buyers, a process accelerated by Europe's eliminating Russian gas and oil imports on which it was previously dependent. Shadow empires losing their accustomed flow of outside revenues, however differently they obtained them, rarely survived their disappearance.

A Few Afterwords

I began this book by asserting that empires were organized to administer and exploit diversity, whether economic, political, religious, or ethnic. In comparison to smaller parochial polities that organized themselves on the basis of sameness, they were cosmopolitan and saw that as a strength and not a weakness. In the nineteenth century that cosmopolitanism was deemed a fatal flaw as ethno-nationalist movements seeking independence provoked empires to lash out violently against them, bringing unrest to lands they had previously ruled for centuries without difficulty. Midsize nation-states like Britain, France, Germany, and Japan appeared to be their natural successors—large enough in area and population to support a strong industrial base and military but homogeneous enough to create a common national identity. But what became clear after the world's old empires collapsed at the end of the First World War was that such midsize national states had no way to maintain a global political and economic order. Their emphasis on the uniqueness of sovereign nation-states provided little basis for cooperation and encouraged rivalries inflamed by the rise of ultranationalist regimes that ended in the conflagration of the Second World War. The post-1945 world attempted to avoid this problem in two ways. One was idealistically through the establishment of global institutions such as the United Nations and similar international bodies. But as these lacked the power to enforce their rulings and had no independent sources of revenue to finance themselves, they did not constitute a world government. The other was in the hard-power politics of a bipolar world divided between the USSR and United States as rival nuclear-armed superpowers. They filled the roles of world-organizing superstates, maintaining a dangerous type of mutually assured destruction stability. But the USSR and United States were not rivals of the same type but rather proponents of two very different and opposed models of economic organization, socialist versus capitalist, that divided the globe into two blocs. Interaction between them was minimal because they created such separate worlds politically and economically. Conflicts were largely via proxy wars in distant lands and less violent competitions to recruit Third World client states to their own side.

The collapse of the Soviet Union in 1991 ended that bipolar world order and replaced its socialist command economies with capitalist ones worldwide. These became more economically integrated in the succeeding decades, but while medium-sized national states could thrive economically, they could not remake the rules in this new system without first achieving closer parity with the United States, the surviving superpower. In the twenty-first century the EU and China entered that competitive arena using the tools of empires to make themselves more politically and economically equal to the United States. This required the return of a cosmopolitan ethos that characterized past empires but not nation-states, something the EU and China achieved using very different models. This in turn created new niches for the equivalent of shadow empires like Russia that could remain peer powers by having one or two strengths but not the complete set that the United States, the EU, and China possessed. At the same time there was an opposing anticosmopolitan devolutionary trend away from diversity in which larger national states split into smaller ones based on internal ethnic, religious, and regional divisions. Minnows greatly exceeded whales in the world political ecosystem as the number of UN member states rose to 193 in 2020, but large polities still stood at its center as empires had previously done, perhaps to be joined by India or some rising new power from Africa or South America. Insight into how these mega-polities develop and the political templates they adopt to organize themselves and compete with others can best be gained by appreciating the legacy of the empires they replaced. As I hope this book has demonstrated, this is a legacy far richer in variety than is normally acknowledged. Empires may be gone, but it would be foolish to forget a history of 2,500 years from which there is still much to learn.

Eurasian and North African Mega-empires in the Historical Record by Region

Date (peak)	Empire name	Type	World region	Area (million km²)
−1300	Egypt (New Kingdom)	Endogenous	Africa	1.00
350	Axum	Exogenous Maritime	Africa	1.25
969	Fatimid	Endogenous	Africa	4.10
1120	Almoravid	Exogenous Periphery-Vulture	Africa	1.00
1200	Almohad	Exogenous Periphery-Vulture	Africa	2.00
1380	Mali	Endogenous	Africa	1.10
1400	Mameluk	Endogenous	Africa	2.10
−176	Xiongnu	Exogenous Steppe	Central Asia	9.00
405	Rouran	Exogenous Steppe	Central Asia	2.80
557	Turks (Göktürk)	Exogenous Steppe	Central Asia	6.00
800	Uighur	Exogenous Steppe	Central Asia	3.10
800	Tufan (Tibet)	Endogenous	Central Asia	4.60
850	Khazar	Exogenous Steppe	Central Asia	3.00
1100	Xi Xia	Exogenous Periphery-Vulture	Central Asia	1.00
1210	Khwarazm	Endogenous	Central Asia	2.30
1210	Kara-Khitai	Endogenous	Central Asia	1.50

(Continued on next page)

Date (peak)	Empire name	Type	World region	Area (million km²)
1270	Mongol	Exogenous Steppe becomes Endogenous during Eurasian conquests- with 3 imperial successor states**	Central Asia	24.00
1310	Golden Horde**	Endogenous Mongol successor state	Central Asia	6.00
1350	Chagatai**	Endogenous Mongol successor state	Central Asia	3.50
1405	Timurid	Endogenous	Central Asia	4.40
−50	China-Early Han	Endogenous	East Asia	6.00
579	Liang	Endogenous	East Asia	1.30
715	China-Tang	Endogenous	East Asia	5.40
947	Khitan Liao	Exogenous Periphery-Vulture	East Asia	2.60
980	China-Song	Endogenous	East Asia	3.10
1126	Jurchen Jin	Exogenous Periphery-Vulture	East Asia	2.30
1280	Yuan**	Endogenous Mongol successor state	East Asia	11
1450	China-Ming	Endogenous	East Asia	6.50
1790	Qing-Manchu	Exogenous Periphery-Vulture that becomes endogenous	East Asia	14.70
117	Rome	Endogenous	Europe	5.00
441	Huns (Atilla's)	Exogenous Steppe	Europe	4.00
555	East Roman	Endogenous	Europe	2.70
814	Carolingian	Exogenous Nostalgia	Europe	1.20
1000	Kievan Rus'	Exogenous -Vacuum	Europe	2.10
1025	Byzantine	Endogenous	Europe	1.35
1480	Lithuania-Poland	Exogenous Vacuum	Europe	1.10
1683	Ottoman	Endogenous	Europe	5.20
1800	Russia	Endogenous from earlier exogenous vacuum Tsardom	Europe	15.50
1290	Khmer	Endogenous	Southeast Asia	1.00
−250	Mauryan	Endogenous	South Asia	5.00
200	Kushan	Endogenous	South Asia	2.00
400	Gupta	Endogenous	South Asia	3.50

Date (peak)	Empire name	Type	World region	Area (million km^2)
648	Harsha (Kanyakubia)	Endogenous	South Asia	1.00
1312	Delhi	Endogenous	South Asia	3.20
1690	Mughal	Endogenous	South Asia	4.00
1760	Maratha	Endogenous	South Asia	2.50
−670	Assyria	Endogenous	Southwest Asia	1.40
−585	Media	Endogenous	Southwest Asia	2.80
−500	Achaemenid Persia	Endogenous	Southwest Asia	5.50
−323	Hellenistic (Alexander)	Exogenous Periphery Vanquisher	Southwest Asia	5.20
−301	Seleucid	Exogenous Periphery Vanquisher	Southwest Asia	3.90
0	Parthian	Endogenous	Southwest Asia	2.80
550	Sasanian Persia	Endogenous	Southwest Asia	3.50
750	Caliphate	Exogenous Periphery Vanquisher becomes Endogenous with Abbasids	Southwest Asia	11.10
928	Samanid	Endogenous	Southwest Asia	2.85
980	Buyid	Endogenous	Southwest Asia	1.60
1029	Ghaznavid	Endogenous	Southwest Asia	3.40
1080	Seljuk	Endogenous	Southwest Asia	3.90
1190	Ayyubids	Endogenous	Southwest Asia	2.00
1310	Il-Khanate**	Endogenous Mongol successor state	Southwest Asia	3.75

Source: Adapted from Turchin, "Theory for Formation," 202–3.

** Indicates endogenous successors to the Mongol Empire.

NOTES

Introduction

1. "Cent disques, cent films."

2. Barfield, "Shadow Empires."

3. Turchin, "Theory for Formation."

4. Weber, *Economy and Society*; Kalberg, *Max Weber's*, 288.

5. The former: Doyle, *Empires*; Burbank and Cooper, *Empires in World History*. The latter: Darwin, *After Tamerlane*.

6. Steinmetz, "Return to Empire," 342, 344.

7. Doyle, *Empires*, 93–98.

8. Scheidel, *Escape from Rome*.

9. To look ahead: the Abbasid Caliphate experienced this transition when it replaced the Umayyad Caliphate in 750; the Mongol Empire accomplished it under Khubilai Khan in 1263 when he moved the empire's center to northern China; the Qing dynasty's Emperor Kangxi did so when he used Chinese troops to put down a rebellion that the Manchu ruling elite had failed to suppress in 1683; Peter the Great promoted Russia from tsardom to empire in 1721 after a series of draconian reforms; and the British in India transitioned themselves from clients to masters of the Mughal Empire after defeating its emperor in 1765. Of these, only the Abbasid Caliphate crossed any type of Caracallan threshold when it made Islam a universal religion and not an exclusively Arab one; the rest always maintained a sharp distinction between themselves and the people they ruled.

10. Thucydides, *History*, 1.22.

11. Wolf, *Europe and the People*; Sahlins, *Islands of History*.

12. Ibn Khaldūn, *Muqaddimah*.

13. Barfield, "Turk, Persian and Arab"; Barfield, "Tribe and State Relations."

14. Braudel, *Mediterranean*.

Chapter One

1. Population figures cited are drawn from McEvedy and Jones, *Atlas of World Population History*. All such figures need to be seen as estimates that are more accurate in their trend lines than as hard facts.

2. Territory size estimates here and below are from Taagepera, "Size and Duration of Empires"; and Turchin, "Theory for Formation." See also "Global History Databank," Seshat, accessed November 4, 2022, http://seshatdatabank.info/data/index.html.

3. Barfield, "Shadow Empires," 29–33.

4. Aristotle, *On the Cosmos*, 398a; Xenophon, *Cyropaedia*, 2.8.10–12.

5. As lasting remains, road systems have generated many studies. For those examples mentioned here, see Needham, *Shorter Science*, 1–25; Briant, "From the Indus"; Hitchner, "Roads, Integration, Connectivity"; Julien, "Chinchaysuyu Road."

6. Erdkamp, *Grain Market*, 143–257.

7. Needham, *Shorter Science*, 172–254.

8. Mundy, *Death of Aztec Tenochtitlan*, 25–31.

9. Smailes, *Geography of Towns*, 9–23.

10. Herodotus, *Histories*, 8.98.

11. Needham, *Shorter Science*, 25. When I first observed a ruined line of beacon towers running across some desert wastelands in Xinjiang in the far west of China, I must admit that my first thought was not of their ingenuity but rather that the small crews manning each of them must have had the most boring and career-ending military assignments imaginable.

12. Aristotle, *On the Cosmos*, 298b.

13. For an excellent compilation of original source material, see Kuhrt, *Persian Empire*.

14. Herodotus, *Histories*, 1.136.

15. Herodotus, 1.125.

16. Barth, *Nomads of South Persia*; Beck, *Qashqa'i of Iran*; Digard, *Techniques*.

17. Ibn Khaldūn, *Muqaddimah*. The Arab Abbasid Caliphate adopted a Persian ruling structure to create a long-lived dynasty that did rule an immensely large empire (see chapter 4).

18. Scott, *Against the Grain*.

19. Xenophon, *Cyropaedia*, 2.8.14.

20. Xenophon, 2.8.19.

21. Xenophon, 2.8.7.

22. Mauss, *Gift*, 83.

23. Briant, *From Cyrus to Alexander*, 129–30.

24. Herodotus, *Histories*, 1.134.

25. Briant, *From Cyrus to Alexander*, 179–83.

26. Briant, 77.

27. Briant, 79.

28. Briant, 50–61, 65.

29. Xenophon, *Cyropaedia*, 2.8.22.

30. Briant, *From Cyrus to Alexander*, 731.

31. Ibn Khaldūn, *Muqaddimah*, 122.

32. Thucydides, *History*, 5.84–116.

33. Bosworth, *Conquest and Empire*, 178–79.

34. Barfield, "Turk, Persian and Arab."

35. Ahmed, *Pukhtun Economy and Society*.

36. Moorey, *Cemeteries*, 128.

37. Caroe, *Pathans*, 23.

38. Pines, *Envisioning Eternal Empire*.

39. Sima, *Records of the Grand Historian: Qin Dynasty*, chap. 68; Mark Edward Lewis, *Early Chinese Empires*.

40. Pines, "Legalism in Chinese Philosophy."

41. Shang, *Book of Lord Shang*, 243.

42. Han, *Han Fei Tzu*; Bodde, *China's First Unifier*; Mark Edward Lewis, *Early Chinese Empires*, 32–34.

43. Sima, *Records of the Grand Historian: Qin Dynasty*, chaps. 5, 6.

44. Sima, 43–45.

45. Mark Edward Lewis, *Early Chinese Empires*, 47–54; Hulsewé, *Remnants of Ch'in Law*.

46. Elvin, *Retreat of the Elephants*.

47. Waldron, *Great Wall of China*; Barfield, *Perilous Frontier*.

48. Sima, *Records of the Grand Historian of China: Han Dynasty*, vol. 2, chaps. 46, 51, 52; Mark Edward Lewis, *Early Chinese Empires*, 15–17.

49. Yates, "State Control of Bureaucrats"; Bielenstein, *Bureaucracy of Han Times*; Mark Edward Lewis, *Writing and Authority*.

50. Michael W. Doyle's justly praised work on comparative empires, for example, draws on Western examples exclusively and uses Roman history as his basic template for the structure of empires in general. Doyle, *Empires*, 93–98.

51. Finley, *History of Sicily*.

52. Goldsworthy, *Fall of Carthage*; Harris, *War and Imperialism*, 50–53

53. Taagepera, "Size and Duration of Empires," 125–26.

54. Gabba, "Rome and Italy."

55. Adrian Sherwin-White, *Roman Citizenship*; Wiseman, *New Men*.

56. Oliver, "Ruling Power," 901–2.

57. Scheidel, "Quantifying the Sources"; Scheidel, "Human Mobility in Roman Italy," 79; Bradley, *Slaves and Masters*.

58. Ando, *Imperial Ideology*; Goody, "Adoption in Cross-Cultural Perspective," 59–61.

59. Sands, *Client Princes*; Cheesman, *Auxilia*; Adrian Sherwin-White, *Roman Citizenship*, 247–50; Luttwak, *Grand Strategy of the Roman Empire*, 25–44.

60. Suetonius, *Lives of the Caesars*, 1.3.26.

61. Wells, *Barbarians Speak*.

62. Luttwak, *Grand Strategy of the Roman Empire*, 51–126.

63. Goffart, *Barbarians and Romans*; Yu, *Trade and Expansion*.

64. Ibn Khaldūn, *Muqaddimah* (unabridged), 2.242.

Chapter Two

1. Bigourdan, "Neolithic"; Caspers, "Harappan Trade."

2. Mark, "Ship- and Boatbuilding."

3. Wachsmann, *Seagoing Ships*.

4. Starr, "Myth."

5. Mark, *Homeric Seafaring*.

6. Oren, *Sea Peoples*.

7. Homer, *Iliad*, 2.484–785; Crossett, "Art of Homer's Catalogue."

8. Casson, *Ships and Seamanship*, 49.

9. Wallinga, "Trireme and History"; Wallinga, *Ships and Sea-Power*.

10. Herodotus, *Histories*, 7.114; Thucydides, *History*, 2.13.

11. Thucydides, *History*, 3.17, 1.117.

12. Morris, "Greater Athenian State," 119.

13. Herodotus, *Histories*, 1.143.

14. Herodotus, 3.34.

15. Briant, *From Cyrus to Alexander*, 77, 405.

16. Herodotus, *Histories*, 7.22. Even if the figure is exaggerated—many believe the actual number of Persian ships was closer to six hundred—Persian fleets appear always to have been about twice the size of any enemy.

17. Shahbazi, "Darius I the Great."

18. Briant, *From Cyrus to Alexander*, 151.

19. Herodotus, *Histories*, bks. 6, 8–16.

20. Briant, *From Cyrus to Alexander*, 496–98.

21. Herodotus, *Histories*, bks. 5, 42.

22. Holladay, "Medism in Athens"; Graf, "Medism."

23. Herodotus, *Histories*, 7.1.

24. Herodotus, bks. 7–9.

25. Kagan, *New History*, 41; Meritt, Wade-Gery, and McGregor, *Athenian Tribute Lists*, 3:223–24.

26. Aristotle, *Athenian Constitution*, chaps. 23–24.

27. Thucydides, *History*, 1.141–43, 19.

28. Thucydides, 1.98; italics added.

29. Hansen, *Athenian Democracy*, 91–93; Moreno, *Feeding the Democracy*, 30–31. Athens's disproportionately large and diverse population was typical of primate cities in later maritime empires as well.

30. Thucydides, *History*, 1.98; Kallet, "Origins."

31. Meiggs, "Crisis of Athenian Imperialism."

32. Cawkwell, "Foundation"; Cawkwell, "Notes on the Failure"; Cawkwell, "Athenian Naval Power."

33. Thucydides, *History*, 1.76.

34. Smith, *Inquiry into the Nature*, chap. 7, pt. 3.

35. The Portuguese Empire appears to have been the only exception, being ruled by monarchs from its establishment in 1415, albeit ones with strong commercial interests. Aristotle praised Carthage's republic (480–146 B.C.), in which its leaders proposed actions but "the people have the sovereign decision and anybody who wishes may speak against the proposals." Aristotle, *Politics*, 2.8. Venice (810–1797) and Holland (1588–1795) were both famously republics, and Britain's maritime empire (1601–1997) was overseen by a parliament that wielded executive power after the English Civil War.

36. Thucydides, *History*, 1.23.

37. Marx and Engels, *Communist Manifesto*, 82.

38. Thucydides, *History*, 1.70.

39. Thucydides, 2.41.

40. Thucydides, 5.89.

41. Kallet, "Origins," 55–56.

42. Thucydides, *History*, 2.38.2.

43. Morris, "Greater Athenian State," 144–54; Kallet, "Origins."

44. Herodotus, *Histories*, 5.23.

45. Herodotus, 6.46–47.

46. Kallet, "Origins," 49n.44.

47. Thucydides, *History*, 1.100.2.

48. Kallet, "Origins," 50.

49. Moreno, "'Attic Neighbour.'"

50. Morris, "Greater Athenian State," 148.

51. Zelnick-Abramovitz, "Settlers and Dispossessed."

52. Moreno, *Feeding the Democracy*, 316–17.

53. Moreno, "'Attic Neighbour,'" 214.

54. Aristophanes, *Wasps*, lines 700–715. A *choenix* was a dry measure of 1.1 liters that constituted a daily ration of grain for one person.

55. Moreno, "'Attic Neighbour,'" 216.

56. Balcer, "Imperial Magistrates"; Balcer, "Athenian Episkopos."

57. Wallbank, "Proxeny and Proxenos"; Mack, *Proxeny and Polis*.

58. Meiggs, "Crisis of Athenian Imperialism," 19.

59. "Decree Enforcing Use of Athenian Coins, Weights and Measures," ca. 414 B.C. [?], Attic Inscriptions Online, https://www.atticinscriptions.com/inscription/OR/155.

60. David Lewis, "Athenian Coinage Decree"; Samons, *Empire of the Owl*, 331–32.

61. Morris, "Greater Athenian State," 147.

62. Morris, 147.

63. Pseudo-Xenophon, *Constitution of Athens*, 2.3.

64. Pseudo-Xenophon, 2.11–13.

65. Pseudo-Xenophon, 1.10–11.

66. Ste Croix, "Notes on Jurisdiction" (pt. 1); Ste Croix, "Notes on Jurisdiction" (pt. 2).

67. Pseudo-Xenophon, *Constitution of Athens*, 1.16–18. Six thousand Athenian citizens were chosen annually for paid service in the law courts, where their members constituted both jury and judge.

68. Kallet, *Money*, 160–64, 201–4. In later eras sea raiders who operated with state sponsorship were deemed pirates by their victims but legitimate privateers by those who licensed them, a source of continual conflict between England's Elizabeth I and the Spanish in the late sixteenth century.

69. Harlan, *Central Asia*, 127.

70. Thucydides, *History*, 7.28.

71. Moreno, *Feeding the Democracy*, 144–205.

72. Thucydides, *History*, 2.65.12.

73. Cook, *Born to Die*.

74. Cañeque, *King's Living Image*.

75. Flynn and Giráldez, "Cycles of Silver."

76. Goodman, *Spanish Naval Power*; Storrs, *Resilience*, chap. 2.

77. Newitt, *History*.

78. Subrahmanyam and Parker, "Arms and the Asian."

79. Subrahmanyam, "Written on Water."

80. Burnet, *East Indies*.

81. Irwin, "Mercantilism."

82. Vieira, "Mare Liberum."

83. Israel, *Dutch Primacy*, 71.

84. Masselman, "Dutch Colonial Policy."

85. Vink, "'World's Oldest Trade.'"

86. Annual sales in Amsterdam during the 1620s amounted to 225,000–250,000 kg of cloves, 200,000 kg of nutmeg, and 40,000 kg of mace. Glamann, *Dutch-Asiatic Trade*, 91–94.

87. Parthesius, *Dutch Ships*; Blussé, "No Boats to China"; Glamann, *Dutch-Asiatic Trade*.

88. Bond, *Speeches of the Managers*, 15.

89. Richards, *Mughal Empire*; Dyson, *Population History of India*, 61–62.

90. Brown and Rowse, *Itinerant Ambassador*, 96–98.

91. Hunter, *History of British India*, 57–58.

92. Hunter, 242. Ramsay, *English Overseas Trade*, 92, explains that "dead payes" referred to the common practice of company commanders pocketing the wages of dead soldiers whose names remained on the active payroll.

93. Richards, *Mughal Empire*, 212–24.

94. Vaughn, "John Company Armed."

95. Wink, *Land and Sovereignty*, 155–56.

96. Tabatabai, *Translation*, 2:384.

97. Dalrymple, *Anarchy*, 208. Rs 2.6 million, or £325,000, in 1773 was equivalent in purchasing power to about £49 million in 2019 (US$63 million); the tax revenue of Bengal's twenty million people generated between £2 million and £3 million a year in the 1770s.

98. Damodaran, "Famine in Bengal."

99. Dalrymple, *Anarchy*, xxxvi. In 1773 £1 million was equivalent in purchasing power to £151 million in 2019 (US$194 million).

100. Travers, "British Empire by Treaty," 135–36.

101. Duffy, "World-Wide War," 196–202.

102. Doran, "Spartan Oliganthropia."

103. Aristotle, *Politics*, 26.4. Years later Pericles himself would fall afoul of his own law and have to seek an exception to get citizenship for the children he had by his consort, Aspasia of Miletus.

104. Rhodes, *Athenian Democracy*, 18–24, 225–36.

105. Except perhaps for its monarchs: after the Stuarts (themselves originally Scottish) were deposed in 1689, British monarchs were recruited thereafter from Holland and then Germany, a far more diverse group in origin than its aristocracy or members of the British Parliament.

106. Athens, at more than 300,000 people, was an order of magnitude larger than the next-biggest Greek city-states and had a resident alien population of 40,000. London's population grew from approximately 740,000 in 1760 to 1.1 million in 1801. By 1815, when it had its first census, it was world's largest city, with 1.4 million people, and grew to 3.1 million in 1860 and to over 7 million by the 1910s. In the mid-nineteenth century 38 percent of Londoners were born somewhere else and the city had immigrant communities from all corners of the world. "London and Its Hinterlands," Proceedings of the Old Bailey, March 2018, https://www.oldbaileyonline.org/static/London-life.jsp.

107. Boswell, *Life of Samuel Johnson*, 131.

108. Wickwire and Wickwire, *Cornwallis*, 89–90.

Chapter Three

1. Barfield, *Nomadic Alternative*, chap. 5.

2. Damgaard et al., "137 Ancient Human Genomes."

3. McEwen, Miller, and Bergman, "Early Bow Design."

4. Anthony and Brown, "Secondary Products Revolution," 156. Note that we saw a similar transition in maritime societies from undecked boats owned and sailed by heroes to state-owned multidecked galleys manned by anonymous rowers.

5. Scott, *Against the Grain*, 244.

6. Khazanov, *Nomads*.

7. Irons, "Political Stratification," 362.

8. Barfield, "Hsiung-nu Imperial Confederacy."

9. Sima, *Records of the Grand Historian: Han Dynasty*, 2:144–45.

10. Yu, *Trade and Expansion*, 41–42.

11. Some of the defeated Yuezhi tribes that fled west in a series of stages to escape the Xiongnu would eventually resettle in today's Uzbekistan and Afghanistan, where their descendants founded the Kushan Empire in the first century B.C.

12. Sima, *Records of the Grand Historian: Han Dynasty*, 2:140–41.

13. Sima, 140–41.

14. Sima, 140–41.

15. Yu, *Trade and Expansion*, 92–105. In some respects, the Xiongnu demands and use of violence were similar to those later employed by Western maritime empires dealing with China in the nineteenth century, which also went to war for trading rights rather than territory.

16. Sima, *Records of the Grand Historian: Han Dynasty*, 2:148.

17. Yu, *Trade and Expansion*, 11.

18. Sima, *Records of the Grand Historian: Qin Dynasty*.

19. Loewe, "Campaigns of Han Wu-ti"; Barfield, "Steppe Empires."

20. Sima, *Records of the Grand Historian: Han Dynasty*, 2:157.

21. Wylie, "History of the Heung-Noo," 43.

22. Wylie, 44.

23. Yu, *Trade and Expansion*, 45–46.

24. Wylie, "History of the Heung-Noo," 47–48.

25. Wylie, 62–63.

26. Barfield, *Perilous Frontier*, 70–80; Yu, *Trade and Expansion*, 60–64.

27. Barfield, *Perilous Frontier*, 85–130, 164–86.

28. Togan, *Flexibility and Limitation*.

29. Barfield, *Perilous Frontier*, 189–97.

30. H. Desmond Martin, *Rise of Chingis Khan*.

31. Rachewiltz, *Secret History*, sec. 248, p. 167.

32. Rachewiltz, sec. 251, p. 168.

33. Juzjani, *Tabakat-i-Nasiri*, 2:965.

34. H. Desmond Martin, *Rise of Chingis Khan*.

35. Ho, *Estimate of the Total*; Bielenstein, "Chinese Historical Demography," 85–88.

36. Bartol'd, *Turkestan*, p. 469.

37. Rachewiltz, "Yeh-lu Ch'u-ts'ai."

38. Allsen, "Guard and Government"; Allsen, *Mongol Imperialism*; Morgan, *Mongols*.

39. Mote, *Imperial China*, 448–64.

40. Halperin, *Russia*.

41. Rossabi, *Khubilai Khan*, 76–152.

Chapter Four

1. Gibbon, *History of the Decline*; Yang, "Toward a Study"; Usher, "Dynastic Cycle."

2. Barfield, *Perilous Frontier*, chaps. 3, 5, 7.

3. Wittfogel and Feng, *History of Chinese Society*, 398–400.

4. Wittfogel and Feng, 142.

5. Wittfogel and Feng, 576.

6. Wittfogel and Feng, 473.

7. Tao, "Barbarians or Northerners."

8. Wittfogel and Feng, *History of Chinese Society*, 286, 377, 406.

9. Mote, *Imperial China*, 222–49.

10. Chan, *Legitimation in Imperial China*, 57–83; Mote, *Imperial China*, 222–49.

11. Crossley, *Translucent Mirror*, 157–65; Rawski, *Last Emperors*, 99–101.

12. Wakeman, *Great Enterprise*, 53–55.

13. Wakeman, 65–74; Roth, "Manchu-Chinese Relationship," 1–21.

14. Li, "Rise," 85.

15. Li, 171–72.

16. Li, 120.

17. Roth, "Manchu-Chinese Relationship," 21–33.

18. Di Cosmo, "From Alliance to Tutelage."

19. Wakeman, "Shun Interregnum of 1644."

20. Crossley, *Translucent Mirror*, 30.

21. Oxnam, *Ruling from Horseback*.

22. Kessler, "Chinese Scholars," 180.

23. Kessler, *K'ang-Hsi*, 74–136; Di Cosmo, *Diary of a Manchu Soldier*, 7–31.

24. Rawski, "Presidential Address"; Barfield, *Perilous Frontier*, chap. 7.

25. Black swan events are those lying outside the realm of regular expectations (i.e., nothing in the past suggested they were possible) and that have an extreme impact when they occur. Explanations for them concocted after the fact, however, invariably assert they were explainable and predictable. Taleb, *Black Swan*, xxii.

26. Bloody tanistry is a succession system that presumes "the most talented male member of the royal dynasty should inherit the throne, commonly by murder and war. . . . Among the Turks and the Mongols tanistry worked so well that no regular, ascriptive, and automatic succession principle, such as primo-geniture or levirate (in the wider sense of the term), ever replaced it on anything more than a temporary basis." Although seemingly disruptive, it produced strong and long-lived dynasties, such as the Ottomans (more than eight hundred years), where one brother would kill all the others to take the throne, both proving his superiority and preempting the emergence of collateral royal lines that might cause trouble for his own future heirs. Fletcher, "Turco-Mongolian Monarchic Tradition," 239.

27. Briant, *From Cyrus to Alexander*, chap. 15; Bosworth, *Conquest and Empire*.

28. Briant, *Alexander the Great*, 43.

29. Herodotus, *Histories*, 7.1.

30. Bosworth, *Conquest and Empire*, 35–104.

31. Curtius Rufus, *History of Alexander*, 7.9.22.

32. Bosworth, *Conquest and Empire*, 107–19; Holt, *Alexander the Great*. It has not been lost on recent commentators that British, Soviet, and American armies found themselves in similar situations in this region during the nineteenth, twentieth, and twenty-first centuries. See Holt, *Into the Land of Bones*.

33. Collins, "Royal Costume."

34. Briant, *Alexander the Great*, 125. In the nineteenth century a similar issue arose between Great Britain and China over whether its envoys would be required to kowtow before the emperor, and the loanword retains its very negative connotation in English.

35. Briant, 151–55.

36. Briant, 156.

37. Briant, 157.

38. Sherwin-White and Kuhrt, *From Samarkhand to Sardis*.

39. Ibn Khaldūn, *Muqaddimah*, 120–21; Barfield, "Tribe and State Relations"; Lindholm, "Kinship Structure."

40. See Josephus, *Jewish War*; and Crone, *Iranian Reception of Islam*, 1–49.

41. Shia Islam did later create a hierarchical clerical establishment similar to that of the Catholic and Orthodox Christian churches when the Safavid dynasty came to power in Iran in 1500. Within Christianity, Protestant Christians moved in the opposite direction by rejecting the institutionalized hierarchy of the Catholic Church and its popes beginning in 1517 to create a decentralized and egalitarian system similar to that found in Sunni Islam. Interestingly, these moves to reverse the existing patterns of religious organization occurred contemporaneously.

42. Lindholm, *Islamic Middle East*.

43. Nöldeke, *History of the Qur'an*, 135–88, quote on 17.

44. Ibn Khaldūn, *Muqaddimah*, 120–21. The steppe nomadic tribes with hierarchical tribal systems had no need of a religion to unite them, and groups like the Turks and Mongols adopted new religions only after they established their empires.

45. Sahlins, "Segmentary Lineage."

46. Crone, *Meccan Trade*, 242, 247.

47. Shalem, "Fall of Al-Madāʾin."

48. Specifically, Abu Bakr was the father of Aisha, the prophet's favorite wife, and Umar was the father of Hafsa, another of the prophet's wives. Uthman married two of Muhammad's daughters, Ruqayya and later Umm Kulthum, and Ali married Fatima, who was also a patrilineal cousin since his father was Muhammad's uncle.

49. Donner, *Early Islamic Conquests*, 82–91.

50. Greatrex and Lieu, *Roman Eastern Frontier*, 167–228.

51. Sharon, "Decisive Battles"; Fisher and Wood, "Writing the History."

52. Kaegi, *Byzantium*, 87.

53. Morony, "'ARAB ii."

54. Ibn Khaldūn, *Muqaddimah*, 128–29. An exception should be noted, however, in cases where one endogenous empire captured the capital of a rival and then

withdrew after extracting a favorable political deal. The Romans took Ctesiphon from the Parthians three times (116, 165, and 198), but unlike Alexander or the Arabs, their goal was to exert dominance over a rival, not replace it. Similarly, Heraclius stopped short of taking the city in 628 after the Sasanians agreed to his political demands.

55. For those intrigued by this analogy of a seemingly culturally specific business successfully going transnational, see Watson, *Golden Arches East*.

56. Kennedy, *Prophet*, 83.

57. Kennedy, 87–88; Luttwak, *Grand Strategy of the Byzantine Empire*, 201–5.

58. Luttwak, *Grand Strategy of the Byzantine Empire*, 206.

59. Gibbon, *History of the Decline*, 1.2.1.

60. Kennedy, *Prophet*, 94–100.

61. Duri, "Notes on Taxation."

62. Most Shi'ites believed that a legitimate caliph must be a direct descendant of Ali through his marriage to the prophet's daughter Fatima, although some expanded that to include the descendants of Ali's children by other wives. The Abbasids argued that all the members of the prophet's broader Hashemite clan were eligible to serve as caliph, a much larger group that included themselves as descendants of one of the prophet's younger uncles, al-Abbas (d. 653). Both factions agreed that the Umayyad caliphs were illegitimate because they were not descendants of the prophet's family, however narrowly or broadly that was defined.

63. Daniel, *Political and Social History*, 26.

64. There are still tribally organized self-identified Arab pastoralists here who claim descent from the Arab tribes of this period who have long been native Persian speakers, often bilingual in Uzbeki, with no knowledge of Arabic. Persian is also widely spoken by the region's large number of Turkic speakers, and intermarriage is common. Barfield, *Central Asian Arabs*.

65. Turner, "Abna' al-Dawla."

66. Daniel, *Political and Social History*, 106.

67. Crone, *Nativist Prophets*.

68. Yūsofī, "Abu Moslem Korasani."

69. See Barfield, "Turk, Persian and Arab."

70. Silverstein, *Postal Systems*, chaps. 2, 3.

71. Bennison, *Great Caliphs*, chap. 3.

72. Crone, *Slaves on Horses*, 74–81.

73. El-Hibri, *Reinterpreting Islamic Historiography*, 31–53; Abbas, "Barmakids"; Van Bladel, "Bactrian Background."

74. Gordon, *Breaking*.

75. Mahdi, *Thousand and One Nights*.

76. As James Scott has subversively argued, such people may have often found themselves better off during periods of state collapse when they could escape the burdens of forced labor and high taxes on their grain harvests. Scott, *Against the Grain*.

77. Kennedy, "Decline and Fall."

78. Gilli-Elewy, "Al-Ḥawādit al-Ǧāmiʿa." The caliph was rolled up in a carpet and trampled to death, a style of execution favored by the Mongols as a mark of respect for high-ranking people because no blood was spilled. It was a courtesy unlikely to have been appreciated by its victim.

Chapter Five

1. Cf. Shakespeare, *Julius Caesar*, act 3, scene 2.

2. Scheidel makes a powerful case that the emergence of a polycentric European political order after the collapse of the Roman Empire in the west was almost inevitable given its geography and interaction with other parts of Eurasia and North Africa rather than a historical accident. Scheidel, *Escape from Rome*.

3. Tacitus, *Germania*, 80–81.

4. Oltean, *Dacia*, 38–39.

5. Istvánovits and Kulcsár, *Sarmatians*; Bârcă, "Nomads of the Steppes."

6. Halsall, *Barbarian Migrations*.

7. Damgaard et al., "137 Ancient Human Genomes."

8. Maenchen-Helfen, *World of the Huns*, 180–89.

9. Pohl, *Avars*, 403.

10. Pohl, 201–2.

11. Levi, *Islamic Central Asia*, 52.

12. Fichtenau, *Carolingian Empire*, 2.

13. O'Brien, "Chosen Peoples," 1008.

14. Wood, *Merovingian Kingdoms*, 55–70.

15. Wood, 208–9.

16. Hen, "Merovingian Polity," 226–28.

17. Fouracre, *Age of Charles Martel*, 178–79.

18. Fouracre, 166.

19. Fouracre, 167–74.

20. Bloch, *Feudal Society*, 94.

21. Fouracre, *Age of Charles Martel*, 172.

22. McCormick, "New Light."

23. McKitterick, *Frankish Kingdoms*, 78.

24. For an academic reader, this would be comparable to the number of administrators and department chairs in a large research university, whose tenured faculty bear a close resemblance to their medieval forbears in the difficulty of dislodging them and their resistance to following policy diktats from above.

25. Davis, *Charlemagne's Practice of Empire*, 335.

26. Davis, 432.

27. Nelson, "Aachen." Nelson and other scholars of the Carolingian Empire universally avoid estimating the number of people permanently living there, so the guess is mine based on its documented city plan and comparisons to places like Paris at the time.

28. Wilson, *Heart of Europe*, 331–34.

29. Davis, *Charlemagne's Practice of Empire*, 128–64, 397–403.

30. Ullmann, *Carolingian Renaissance*.

31. McKitterick, *Frankish Kingdoms*, 72.

32. Ganshof, "Louis the Pious Reconsidered," 173.

33. Ganshof, 174.

34. Ganshof, "Some Observations."

35. Machiavelli, *Prince*, chap. 17: "Therefore a prince, so long as he keeps his subjects united and loyal, ought not to mind the reproach of cruelty; because with a few

examples he will be more merciful than those who, through too much mercy, allow disorders to arise, from which follow murders or robberies; for these are wont to injure the whole people, whilst those executions which originate with a prince offend the individual only."

36. Jong, "Power and Humility."

37. For a concise summary of factions and actions, see Riché, *Carolingians*, 148–58.

38. Nithard, *Carolingian Chronicles*, 134.

39. Wilson, *Heart of Europe*, 37.

40. Wilson, 44.

41. Wilson, chap. 12.

42. Osiander, "Sovereignty, International Relations," 274.

43. For how such a similar system works under far more challenging conditions, see Barfield, "Culture and Custom."

44. Soen, "Treaty of Augsburg."

45. Osiander, "Sovereignty, International Relations," 253–60.

46. Osiander, 272.

47. Osiander, 276–77.

48. Pufendorf, *Present State of Germany*, 279.

49. Voltaire, *Essai sur les moeurs*, 3:338–39.

50. Tocqueville, *Ancien Régime*, 20; italics in the original.

51. Tocqueville, 20.

Chapter Six

1. Noonan, "Why Dirhams."

2. Wolf, *Europe and the People*, chaps. 6, 7.

3. Janet Martin, *Treasure of the Land*.

4. Seeley, "Russia and the Slave Trade." No similar slave trade emerged in Mongolia because China's high population required no augmentation. Steppe nomads there might capture people for domestic service, but there was no export market.

5. Kłosowska, "Etymology of Slave."

6. Golden, "Stateless Nomads." Steppe empires in this region were invariably established and ruled by the dynastic heirs of the Turkic and Mongol empires that first emerged on China's steppe frontier.

7. Golden, *Introduction to the History*, 238.

8. Dunlop, *History*, 93; Minorsky, *Hudud Al-Alam*, 168.

9. Dunlop, *History*, 93.

10. Dunlop, 96. Isinglass is a substance obtained from the dried swim bladders of fish used to make glue, brew beer, make confections, and preserve eggs.

11. Noonan, "Some Observations," 239.

12. Noonan, 236–37. A dirham's value in Islamic law was set at 2.275 grams of silver.

13. Noonan, "Why the Vikings," 346–47.

14. Lamb, "Early Medieval Warm Epoch"; Helama, "Viking Age."

15. Curta, "Steppe Empires?," 148.

16. Noonan, "Why the Vikings," 342.

17. Noonan, "Khazar Qaghanate," 90–91.

18. Golden, "Question of the Rus Qaganate"; Halperin, "'Now You See Them.'"

19. Raffensperger, *Kingdom of Rus'*. The specific title of grand kniaz appears to have developed only later and was projected backward by Rus' chroniclers, but paramount leaders clearly existed in those times and so we use it here.

20. Nestor, *Russian Primary Chronicle*, 59–60.

21. Hobbes, *Leviathan*, 1.13.9.

22. Sahlins, "Stranger-King," 183–84.

23. One might compare this to Muslim sayyids who, in theory, can all trace their descent directly back to the prophet but owe the recognition of that status to the fact that their fathers and grandfathers held it, not because they are personally able to trace the specific links. Inheriting such a status is like receiving a baton in a relay race where a runner is disqualified only if the baton is dropped or deemed to have been passed on improperly.

24. Feldbrugge, *History of Russian Law*, chap. 13.

25. Nestor, *Russian Primary Chronicle*, 60.

26. Nestor, 60.

27. Vasiliev, *Russian Attack*.

28. Nestor, *Russian Primary Chronicle*, 61.

29. Vasiliev, "Second Russian Attack."

30. Minorsky, *History of Sharvān*, chap. 8, annex 3. Some scholars have argued that it was Oleg who led this attack and was killed during it. See Larsson, "Contacts between Scandinavia."

31. Kaiser, "Kievan Rus-Byzantium."

32. Zuckerman has argued that Igor's reign is misdated in the *Russian Primary Chronicle* and that he only ruled from 941 to 945, the time of these failed military campaigns, explaining the absence of detailed activities for the first thirty years of his supposed reign. If correct, that would make the argument here stronger since his desire to make a personal reputation and his untimely end would be concentrated into this short time period. Just who would have been ruling in his name before that (or if a generation has been skipped) is unclear. Zuckerman, "On the Date."

33. Nestor, *Russian Primary Chronicle*, 79.

34. Nestor, 79.

35. Nestor, 80.

36. Nestor, 80–81.

37. Nestor, 80–87; Constantine, *De Administrando Imperio*, chap. 9.

38. Nestor, *Russian Primary Chronicle*, 84.

39. Basilevsky, *Early Ukraine*, 99–102.

40. Nestor, *Russian Primary Chronicle*, 86.

41. Basilevsky, *Early Ukraine*, 102–8.

42. Nestor, *Russian Primary Chronicle*, 89.

43. Nestor, 90–91.

44. Nestor, 87.

45. See Raffensperger, "Shared (Hi)stories."

46. Nestor, *Russian Primary Chronicle*, 91.

47. Nestor, 92.

48. Nestor, 92.

49. Zaroff, "Organized Pagan Cult."

50. Nestor, *Russian Primary Chronicle*, 110–19.

51. Nestor, 96.

52. Raffensperger, *Reimagining Europe*, chap. 4.

53. Nestor, *Russian Primary Chronicle*, 94.

54. Raffensperger, *Reimagining Europe*, 91.

55. Nestor, *Russian Primary Chronicle*, 119.

56. Mezentsev, "Territorial and Demographic Development," 160.

57. Hanak, *Nature*, chap. 5.

58. Chadwick, *Beginnings of Russian History*, 117.

59. Ibn Khaldūn, *Muqaddimah*, 128–29.

60. Fennell, *Crisis of Medieval Russia*, 75–76.

61. Jackson, *Mongols and the West*, chap. 3; Voegelin, "Mongol Orders."

62. Allsen, "Mongol Census Taking," 50.

63. Halperin, *Russia*, 21–43.

64. Fennell, *Crisis of Medieval Russia*, 84.

65. Fennell, 141.

66. Rowell, *Lithuania Ascending*, 82–117; Norkus, *Unproclaimed Empire*; Norkus, "Grand Duchy of Lithuania." Lithuanian rulers used the title of grand duke or king in dealing with European powers and grand kniaz with Russians, reflecting their place between two worlds.

67. Cherniavsky, "Khan or Basileus," 476.

68. Cherniavsky, 474.

69. For Ivan as a realpolitik monarch, see Perrie and Pavlov, *Ivan the Terrible*. For Ivan as a psychopath, see De Madariaga, *Ivan the Terrible*. A more balanced picture that focuses on his period of terror can be found in Halperin, *Ivan the Terrible*.

70. Dunning, *Russia's First Civil War*, 60–71.

71. Dunning, 404–60.

72. Nestor, *Russian Primary Chronicle*, 59.

73. Rogers and Wilson, "Great Northern War."

74. Matranga and Natkhov, "All Along the Watchtower," 8–9. Also see Hellie, *Enserfment and Military Change*.

75. Sunderland, *Taming the Wild Field*.

76. See Hämäläinen, *Comanche Empire*; and Hämäläinen, *Lakota America*.

77. Khodarkovsky, *Russia's Steppe Frontier*, 135–47.

78. Khodarkovsky, 223–24.

79. For a detailed overview, see Rieber, *Struggle*.

Chapter Seven

1. Barfield, "Steppe Empires." Also see the section in chapter 2 titled "The Logic of Maritime Empires."

2. Scheidel, *Escape from Rome*.

3. Marx and Engels, *Communist Manifesto*.

4. For examples of railroads, see Demirci and Coşar, "Modernisation through Railways"; Huenemann, *Dragon and the Iron Horse*; and Schmid and Huang, "State Adoption."

5. Thucydides, *History*, 1.70.

6. Landes, *Unbound Prometheus*.

7. Maier, *Among Empires*.

8. Pufendorf, *Present State of Germany*, 279.

9. "Projected GDP Ranking," Statistics Times, October 26, 2021, http:// statisticstimes.com/economy/projected-world-gdp-ranking.php.

10. Rossabi, *China among Equals*.

11. Curtin, *Cross-Cultural Trade*, 109.

12. Ge, *What Is China?*

13. Zhao and Leibold, "Ethnic Governance"; Klimeš, "Advancing 'Ethnic Unity.'"

14. There are dozens of good books on this topic, but see Allison, *Destined for War*.

15. "China's Regional Gap Is Worsening," *Economist*, January 23, 2021, https:// www.economist.com/finance-and-economics/2021/01/23/chinas-regional-gap-is -worsening.

16. "Projected GDP Ranking."

Abbas, Ihsan. "Barmakids." *Encyclopaedia Iranica* 3, no. 8 (1988): 806–9.

Ahmed, Akbar S. *Pukhtun Economy and Society: Traditional Structure and Economic Development in a Tribal Society*. London: Routledge, 1980.

Allison, Graham. *Destined for War: Can America and China Escape Thucydides's Trap?* Boston: Houghton Mifflin Harcourt, 2017.

Allsen, Thomas T. "Guard and Government in the Reign of the Grand Qan Möngke, 1251–59." *Harvard Journal of Asiatic Studies* 46, no. 2 (1986): 495–521.

———. "Mongol Census Taking in Rus', 1245–1275." *Harvard Ukrainian Studies* 5, no. 1 (1981): 32–53.

———. *Mongol Imperialism: The Policies of the Great Qan Möngke in China, Russia, and the Islamic Lands, 1251–1259*. Berkeley: University of California Press, 1987.

Ando, Clifford. *Imperial Ideology and Provincial Loyalty in the Roman Empire*. Berkeley: University of California Press, 2000.

Anthony, David W., and Dorcas R. Brown. "The Secondary Products Revolution, Horse-Riding, and Mounted Warfare." *Journal of World Prehistory* 24, no. 2 (July 21, 2011): 131–60.

Aristophanes. *Wasps*. Translated by Eugene O'Neill. New York: Random House, 1938.

Aristotle. *On the Cosmos*. Translated by Edward Forster and D. J. Furley. Cambridge, MA: Harvard University Press, 1955.

———. *Politics*. Cambridge, MA: Harvard University Press, 1932.

Balcer, Jack Martin. "The Athenian Episkopos and the Achaemenid 'King's Eye.'" *American Journal of Philology* 98, no. 3 (1977): 252–63.

———. "Imperial Magistrates in the Athenian Empire." *Historia: Zeitschrift für alte Geschichte* 25, no. 3 (1976): 257–87.

Bârcă, Vitali. "Nomads of the Steppes on the Danube Frontier of the Roman Empire in the 1st Century CE: Historical Sketch and Chronological Remarks." *Dacia*, n.s., 57 (2013): 99–125.

Barfield, Thomas. *The Central Asian Arabs of Afghanistan: Pastoral Nomadism in Transition*. Austin: University of Texas Press, 1981.

———. "Culture and Custom in Nation-Building: Law in Afghanistan." *Maine Law Review* 60, no. 2 (2008): 347–73.

———. "The Hsiung-nu Imperial Confederacy: Organization and Foreign Policy." *Journal of Asian Studies* 41 (1981): 45–61.

———. *The Nomadic Alternative*. Upper Saddle River, NJ: Prentice Hall, 1993.

———. *The Perilous Frontier: Nomadic Empires and China*. Cambridge, MA: Blackwell, 1989.

———. "The Shadow Empires: Imperial State Formation along the Chinese-Nomad Frontier." In *Empires*, edited by Susan E. Alcock, Terence N. D'Altroy, Kathleen D. Morrison, and Carla M. Sinopoli, 11–41. Cambridge: Cambridge University Press, 2001.

———. "Steppe Empires, China and the Silk Route: Nomads as a Force in International Trade and Politics." In *Nomads in the Sedentary World*, edited by Anatoly M. Khazanov and André Wink, 234–49. London: Curzon, 2001.

———. "Tribe and State Relations: The Inner Asian Perspective." In *Tribes and State Formation in the Middle East*, edited by Philip Khoury and Joseph Kostiner, 153–85. Berkeley: University of California Press, 1991.

———. "Turk, Persian and Arab: Changing Relationships between Tribes and State in Iran and along Its Frontiers." In *Iran and the Surrounding World: Interactions in Culture and Cultural Politics*, edited by Nikki Keddie, 61–88. Seattle: University of Washington Press, 2002.

Barth, Fredrik. *Nomads of South Persia: The Basseri Tribe of the Khamseh Confederacy.* Boston: Little, Brown, 1961.

Bartol'd, V. V. *Turkestan Down to the Mongol Invasion.* 3rd ed. London: Luzac, 1968.

Basilevsky, Alexander. *Early Ukraine: A Military and Social History to the Mid-19th Century.* Jefferson, NC: McFarland, 2016.

Beck, Lois. *The Qashqa'i of Iran.* New Haven, CT: Yale University Press, 1986.

Bennison, Amira K. *The Great Caliphs the Golden Age of the 'Abbasid Empire.* New Haven, CT: Yale University Press, 2009.

Bielenstein, Hans. *The Bureaucracy of Han Times.* Cambridge: Cambridge University Press, 1980.

———. "Chinese Historical Demography AD 2–1982." *Museum of Far Eastern Antiquities Bulletin*, no. 59 (1987): 1–288.

Bigourdan, Nicolas. "Neolithic and Early Bronze Age Reed Boats and Watercraft from Mesopotamia and the Persian Gulf: An Overview." *Journal of the Australasian Institute for Maritime Archaeology* 33 (2009): 63–71.

Bloch, Marc. *Feudal Society.* Translated by L. A. Manyon. New York: Routledge, 2014.

Blussé, Leonard. "No Boats to China: The Dutch East India Company and the Changing Pattern of the China Sea Trade, 1635–1690." *Modern Asian Studies* 30, no. 1 (1996): 51–76.

Bodde, Derk. *China's First Unifier: A Study of the Ch'in Dynasty as Seen in the Life of Li Ssŭ (280?–208 B.C.).* Leiden: Brill, 1938.

Bond, E. A., ed. *Speeches of the Managers and Counsel in the Trial of Warren Hastings.* Vol. 1. London: Longwood, 1859.

Boswell, James. *The Life of Samuel Johnson.* London: J. M. Dent, 1914.

Bosworth, Albert B. *Conquest and Empire: The Reign of Alexander the Great.* Cambridge: Cambridge University Press, 1993.

Bradley, Keith R. *Slaves and Masters in the Roman Empire: A Study in Social Control.* Brussels: Latomus, 1984.

Braudel, Fernand. *The Mediterranean and the Mediterranean World in the Age of Philip II.* New York: Harper and Row, 1972.

Briant, Pierre. *Alexander the Great and His Empire: A Short Introduction.* Princeton, NJ: Princeton University Press, 2010.

———. *From Cyrus to Alexander: A History of the Persian Empire.* Winona Lake, IN: Eisenbrauns, 2002.

———. "From the Indus to the Mediterranean: The Administrative Organization and Logistics of the Great Roads of the Achaemenid Empire." In *Highways, Byways, and Road Systems in the Pre-modern World*, edited by Susan E. Alcock, John P. Bodel, and Richard J. A. Talbert, 185–201. Malden, MA: Wiley-Blackwell, 2012.

Brown, Michael J., and A. L. Rowse. *Itinerant Ambassador: The Life of Sir Thomas Roe*. Lexington: University Press of Kentucky, 2014.

Burbank, Jane, and Frederick Cooper. *Empires in World History: Power and the Politics of Difference*. Princeton, NJ: Princeton University Press, 2010.

Burnet, Ian. *East Indies: The 200 Year Struggle between the Portuguese Crown, the Dutch East India Company and the English East India Company for Supremacy in the Eastern Seas*. Dural, New South Wales: Rosenberg, 2013.

Cañeque, Alejandro. *The King's Living Image: The Culture and Politics of Viceregal Power in Colonial Mexico*. New York: Routledge, 2004.

Caroe, Olaf. *The Pathans, 550 B.C.–A.D. 1957*. New York: St. Martin's, 1959.

Caspers, Elisabeth C. L. During. "Harappan Trade in the Arabian Gulf in the Third Millennium B.C." *Proceedings of the Seminar for Arabian Studies* 3 (1973): 3–20.

Casson, Lionel. *Ships and Seamanship in the Ancient World*. Princeton, NJ: Princeton University Press, 1971.

Cawkwell, George. "Athenian Naval Power in the Fourth Century." *Classical Quarterly* 34, no. 2 (1984): 334–45.

———. "The Foundation of the Second Athenian Confederacy." *Classical Quarterly* 23, no. 1 (1973): 47–60.

———. "Notes on the Failure of the Second Athenian Confederacy." *Journal of Hellenic Studies* 101 (1981): 40–55.

"Cent disques, cent films et cent livres pour un siècle." *Le Monde*, no. 17019 (October 15, 1999): 32–33.

Chadwick, Nora K. *The Beginnings of Russian History: An Enquiry into Sources*. New York: AMS, 1977.

Chan, Hok-lam. *Legitimation in Imperial China: Discussions under the Jurchen-Chin Dynasty (1115–1234)*. Seattle: University of Washington Press, 1984.

Cheesman, George. *The Auxilia of the Roman Imperial Army*. Hildesheim, Germany: G. Olms, 1971.

Cherniavsky, Michael. "Khan or Basileus: An Aspect of Russian Mediaeval Political Theory." *Journal of the History of Ideas* 20, no. 4 (1959): 459–76.

Collins, Andrew W. "The Royal Costume and Insignia of Alexander the Great." *American Journal of Philology* 133, no. 3 (2012): 371–402.

Constantine. *De Administrando Imperio*. Greek text edited by Gyula Moravcsik. English translation by R.J.H. Jenkins. Washington, DC: Dumbarton Oaks Center for Byzantine Studies, 1967.

Cook, Noble David. *Born to Die: Disease and New World Conquest, 1492–1650*. Vol. 1. Cambridge: Cambridge University Press, 1998.

Crone, Patricia. *The Iranian Reception of Islam*. Leiden: Brill, 2016.

———. *Meccan Trade and the Rise of Islam*. Princeton, NJ: Princeton University Press, 1987.

———. *The Nativist Prophets of Early Islamic Iran: Rural Revolt and Local Zoroastrianism*. New York: Cambridge University Press, 2012.

———. *Slaves on Horses: The Evolution of the Islamic Polity*. Cambridge: Cambridge University Press, 2003.

Crossett, John. "The Art of Homer's Catalogue of Ships." *Classical Journal* 64, no. 6 (1969): 241–45.

Crossley, Pamela Kyle. *A Translucent Mirror: History and Identity in Qing Imperial Ideology*. Berkeley: University of California Press, 2002.

Curta, Florin. "Steppe Empires? The Khazars and the Volga Bulgars." In *Eastern Europe in the Middle Ages (500–1300)*, 128–51. Leiden: Brill, 2019.

Curtin, Philip D. *Cross-Cultural Trade in World History*. Cambridge: Cambridge University Press, 1984.

Curtius Rufus, Quintus. *History of Alexander*. Translated by John Carew Rolfe. Cambridge, MA: Harvard University Press, 1946.

Dalrymple, William. *The Anarchy: The Relentless Rise of the East India Company*. London: Bloomsbury, 2019.

Damgaard, Peter de Barros, Nina Marchi, Simon Rasmussen, Michaël Peyrot, Gabriel Renaud, Thorfinn Korneliussen, J. Víctor Moreno-Mayar, et al. "137 Ancient Human Genomes from across the Eurasian Steppes." *Nature* 557, no. 7705 (2018): 369–74.

Damodaran, Vinita. "Famine in Bengal: A Comparison of the 1770 Famine in Bengal and the 1897 Famine in Chotanagpur." *Medieval History Journal* 10, no. 1–2 (2006): 143–81.

Daniel, Elton L. *The Political and Social History of Khurasan under Abbasid Rule, 747–820*. Minneapolis: Bibliotheca Islamica, 1979.

Darwin, John. *After Tamerlane: The Global History of Empire since 1405*. New York: Bloomsbury, 2008.

Davis, Jennifer R. *Charlemagne's Practice of Empire*. Cambridge: Cambridge University Press, 2015.

De Madariaga, Isabel. *Ivan the Terrible*. New Haven, CT: Yale University Press, 2005.

Demirci, Sevtap, and Nevin Coşar. "Modernisation through Railways: Economic and Social Change in the Ottoman Empire in the Nineteenth Century." *Journal of Balkan and Near Eastern Studies* 23, no. 5 (2021): 684–94.

Di Cosmo, Nicola. *The Diary of a Manchu Soldier in Seventeenth-Century China: "My Service in the Army," by Dzengseo*. London: Routledge, 2007.

———. "From Alliance to Tutelage: A Historical Analysis of Manchu-Mongol Relations before the Qing Conquest." *Frontiers of History in China* 7, no. 2 (2012): 175–97.

Digard, Jean Pierre. *Techniques des nomades baxtyâri d'Iran*. Cambridge: Cambridge University Press, 1981.

Donner, Fred McGraw. *The Early Islamic Conquests*. Princeton, NJ: Princeton University Press, 1981.

Doran, Timothy. "Spartan Oliganthropia." *Brill Research Perspectives in Ancient History* 1, no. 2 (2018): 1–106.

Doyle, Michael W. *Empires*. Ithaca, NY: Cornell University Press, 1986.

Duffy, Michael. "World-Wide War and British Expansion, 1793–1815." In *The Oxford History of the British Empire*, vol. 2, *The Eighteenth Century*, edited by P. J. Marshall, 185–206. Oxford: Oxford University Press, 1998.

Dunlop, Douglas Morton. *The History of the Jewish Khazars*. Princeton, NJ: Princeton University Press, 1954.

Dunning, Chester S. L. *Russia's First Civil War: The Time of Troubles and the Founding of the Romanov Dynasty*. University Park: Pennsylvania State University Press, 2010.

Duri, 'Abdal 'Aziz. "Notes on Taxation in Early Islam." *Journal of the Economic and Social History of the Orient* 17 (1974): 136–44.

Dyson, Tim. *A Population History of India: From the First Modern People to the Present Day*. Oxford: Oxford University Press, 2018.

El-Hibri, Tayeb. *Reinterpreting Islamic Historiography: Hārūn al-Rashīd and the Narrative of the 'Abbāsid Caliphate*. Cambridge: Cambridge University Press, 1999.

Elvin, Mark. *The Retreat of the Elephants: An Environmental History of China*. New Haven, CT: Yale University Press, 2004.

Erdkamp, Paul. *The Grain Market in the Roman Empire: A Social, Political and Economic Study*. Cambridge: Cambridge University Press, 2005.

Feldbrugge, F.J.M. (Ferdinand Joseph Maria). *A History of Russian Law: From Ancient Times to the Council Code (Ulozhenie) of Tsar Aleksei Mikhailovich of 1649*. Leiden: Brill, 2017.

Fennell, John. *The Crisis of Medieval Russia, 1200–1304*. London: Longman, 1983.

Fichtenau, Heinrich. *The Carolingian Empire*. Vol. 1. Toronto: University of Toronto Press, 1978.

Finley, M. I. *A History of Sicily: Ancient Sicily to the Arab Conquest*. New York: Viking, 1968.

Fisher, Greg, and Philip Wood. "Writing the History of the 'Persian Arabs': The Pre-Islamic Perspective on the 'Naṣrids' of al-Ḥīrah." *Iranian Studies* 49, no. 2 (2016): 247–90.

Fletcher, Joseph. "Turco-Mongolian Monarchic Tradition in the Ottoman Empire." *Harvard Ukrainian Studies* 3/4 (1979): 236–51.

Flynn, Dennis, and Arturo Giráldez. "Cycles of Silver: Global Economic Unity through the Mid-Eighteenth Century." *Journal of World History* 13, no. 2 (2002): 391–428.

Fouracre, Paul. *The Age of Charles Martel*. London: Routledge, 2016.

Gabba, Emilio. "Rome and Italy: The Social War." *Cambridge Ancient History* 9 (1994): 104–28.

Ganshof, François-Louis. "Louis the Pious Reconsidered." *History* 42, no. 146 (1957): 171–80.

———. "Some Observations on the Ordinatio Imperii of 817." In *The Carolingians and the Frankish Monarchy: Studies in Carolingian History*, 273–88. Ithaca, NY: Cornell University Press, 1971.

Ge, Zhaoguang. *What Is China? Territory, Ethnicity, Culture, and History*. Cambridge, MA: Harvard University Press, 2018.

Gibbon, Edward. *The History of the Decline and Fall of the Roman Empire*. London: F. Westly and A. H. Davis, 1835.

Gilli-Elewy, Hend. "Al-Ḥawādiṯ al-Ǧāmi'a: A Contemporary Account of the Mongol Conquest of Baghdad, 656/1258." *Arabica* 58, no. 5 (2011): 353–71.

Glamann, Kristof. *Dutch-Asiatic Trade, 1620–1740*. 2nd ed. The Hague: Nijhoff, 1981.

Goffart, Walter A. *Barbarians and Romans, AD 418–584: The Techniques of Accommodation*. Princeton, NJ: Princeton University Press, 1980.

Golden, Peter B. *An Introduction to the History of the Turkic Peoples: Ethnogenesis and State-Formation in Medieval and Early Modern Eurasia and the Middle East*. Wiesbaden, Germany: Otto Harrassowitz, 1992.

———. "The Question of the Rus Qaganate." *Archivum Eurasiae Medii Aevi* 2 (1982): 77–97.

——. "The Stateless Nomads of Central Eurasia." In *Empires and Exchanges in Eurasian Late Antiquity: Rome, China, Iran, and the Steppe, ca. 250–750*, edited by Nicola Di Cosmo and Michael Maas, 317–32. Cambridge: Cambridge University Press, 2018.

Goldsworthy, Adrian Keith. *The Fall of Carthage: The Punic Wars 245–146 B.C.* London: Cassell, 2003.

Goodman, David. *Spanish Naval Power, 1589–1665: Reconstruction and Defeat*. Cambridge: Cambridge University Press, 2003.

Goody, Jack. "Adoption in Cross-Cultural Perspective." *Comparative Studies in Society and History* 11, no. 1 (1969): 55–78.

Gordon, Matthew S. *The Breaking of a Thousand Swords: A History of the Turkish Military of Samarra (AH 200–275/815–889 CE)*. Albany: State University of New York Press, 2001.

Graf, David F. "Medism: The Origin and Significance of the Term." *Journal of Hellenic Studies* 104 (1984): 15–30.

Greatrex, Geoffrey, and Samuel N. C. Lieu. *The Roman Eastern Frontier and the Persian Wars, AD 363–630*. London: Routledge, 2005.

Halperin, Charles J. *Ivan the Terrible: Free to Reward and Free to Punish*. Pittsburg: University of Pittsburgh Press, 2019.

——. "'Now You See Them, Now You Don't': A Note on the First Appearance of the Rhos (Rus') in Byzantium." *Canadian-American Slavic Studies* 7, no. 4 (1973): 494–97.

——. *Russia and the Golden Horde: The Mongol Impact on Medieval Russian History*. Bloomington: Indiana University Press, 1987.

Halsall, Guy. *Barbarian Migrations and the Roman West, 376–568*. Cambridge: Cambridge University Press, 2007.

Hämäläinen, Pekka. *The Comanche Empire*. New Haven, CT: Yale University Press, 2008.

——. *Lakota America: A New History of Indigenous Power*. New Haven, CT: Yale University Press, 2019.

Han Fei. *Han Fei Tzu: Basic Writings*. Translated by Burton Watson. UNESCO Collection of Representative Works, Chinese Series. New York: Columbia University Press, 1997.

Hanak, Walter K. *The Nature and the Image of Princely Power in Kievan Rus', 980–1054: A Study of Sources*. Leiden: Brill, 2013.

Hansen, Mogens Herman. *The Athenian Democracy in the Age of Demosthenes: Structure, Principles, and Ideology*. Norman: University of Oklahoma Press, 1999.

Harlan, Josiah. *Central Asia: Personal Narrative of General Josiah Harlan, 1823–1841*, edited by Frank E. Ross. London: Luzac, 1939.

Harris, William V. *War and Imperialism in Republican Rome, 327–70 BC*. Oxford: Oxford University Press, 1985.

Helama, Samuli. "The Viking Age as a Period of Contrasting Climatic Trends." In *Fibula, Fabula, Fact: The Viking Age in Finland*, edited by Joonas Ahola, Frog, and Clive Tolley, 117–30. Helsinki: Finnish Literature Society, 2014.

Hellie, Richard. *Enserfment and Military Change in Muscovy*. Chicago: University of Chicago Press, 1971.

Hen, Yitzhak. "The Merovingian Polity." In *The Oxford Handbook of the Merovingian World*, edited by Bonnie Effros and Isabel Moreira, 217–37. Oxford: Oxford University Press, 2020.

Herodotus. *The Histories*. Translated by A. D. Godley. Cambridge, MA: Harvard University Press, 1921.

Hitchner, R. Bruce. "Roads, Integration, Connectivity, and Economic Performance in the Roman Empire." In *Highways, Byways, and Road Systems in the Pre-modern World*, edited by Susan E. Alcock, John P. Bodel, and Richard J. A. Talbert, 222–34. Malden, MA: Wiley-Blackwell, 2012.

Ho, Ping-ti. *An Estimate of the Total Population of Sung-Chin China*. Chicago: University of Chicago Press, 1967.

Hobbes, Thomas. *Leviathan: 1651*. South Bend, IN: Infomotions, 2001.

Holladay, James. "Medism in Athens 508–480 B.C." *Greece and Rome* 25, no. 2 (1978): 174–91.

Holt, Frank Lee. *Alexander the Great and Bactria: The Formation of a Greek Frontier in Central Asia*. Leiden: Brill, 1988.

———. *Into the Land of Bones: Alexander the Great in Afghanistan*. Berkeley: University of California Press, 2012.

Homer. *The Iliad*. Translated by A. T. Murray and William F. Wyatt, revised by William F. Wyatt. Cambridge, MA: Harvard University Press, 1924.

Huenemann, Ralph William. *The Dragon and the Iron Horse: The Economics of Railroads in China, 1876–1937*. Cambridge, MA: Council on East Asian Studies, Harvard University, 1984.

Hulsewé, A.F.P. *Remnants of Ch'in Law*. Sinica Leidensia, vol. 17. Leiden: Brill, 1985.

Hunter, William Wilson. *A History of British India: To the Union of the Old and New Companies under the Earl of Godolphin's Award [1708]*. Vol. 2. London: Longmans, Green, 1900.

ibn Khaldūn. *The Muqaddimah: An Introduction to History* (unabridged). 3 vols. Translated by Franz Rosenthal. London: Routledge & K. Paul, 1958.

———. *The Muqaddimah: An Introduction to History*. Edited by N. J. Dawood. Translated by Franz Rosenthal. Abridged ed. Princeton, NJ: Princeton University Press, 1969.

Irons, William. "Political Stratification among Pastoral Nomads." In *Pastoral Production and Society*, 361–74. Cambridge: Cambridge University Press, 1979.

Irwin, Douglas A. "Mercantilism as Strategic Trade Policy: The Anglo-Dutch Rivalry for the East India Trade." *Journal of Political Economy* 99, no. 6 (1991): 1296–314.

Israel, Jonathan I. *Dutch Primacy in World Trade, 1585–1740*. Oxford: Oxford University Press, 1990.

Istvánovits, E., and V. Kulcsár. *Sarmatians: History and Archaeology of a Forgotten People*. Mainz: Römisch-Germanisches Zentralmuseum, 2017.

Jackson, Peter. *The Mongols and the West, 1221–1410*. London: Routledge, 2018.

Jong, Mayke de. "Power and Humility in Carolingian Society: The Public Penance of Louis the Pious." *Early Medieval Europe* 1, no. 1 (1992): 29–52.

Josephus, Flavius. *The Jewish War*. Cambridge, MA: Harvard University Press, 1927.

Julien, Catherine. "The Chinchaysuyu Road and the Definition of an Inca Imperial Landscape." In *Highways, Byways, and Road Systems in the Pre-modern World*, edited by Susan E. Alcock, John P. Bodel, and Richard J. A. Talbert, 148–67. Malden, MA: Wiley-Blackwell, 2012.

Juzjani, Minhaj Sinaj. *Tabakat-i-Nasiri (A General History of the Muhammadan Dynasties of Asia)*. 2 vols. Translated by H. G. Raverty. New Delhi: Oriental Books Reprint, 1970.

Kaegi, Walter Emil. *Byzantium and the Early Islamic Conquests*. Cambridge: Cambridge University Press, 1992.

Kagan, Donald. *New History of the Peloponnesian War*. Ithaca, NY: Cornell University Press, 2012.

Kaiser, Daniel H. "Kievan Rus-Byzantium: Treaties of 907, 911, 944 and 971." *Jus Gentium: Journal of International Legal History* 1 (2016): 627–38.

Kalberg, Stephen. *Max Weber's Comparative-Historical Sociology Today: Major Themes, Mode of Causal Analysis, and Applications*. Burlington, VT: Ashgate, 2012.

Kallet, Lisa. *Money, Expense, and Naval Power in Thucydides' History 1–5.24*. Berkeley: University of California Press, 1993.

———. "The Origins of the Athenian 'Arche.'" *Journal of Hellenic Studies* 133 (2013): 43–60.

Kennedy, Hugh. "The Decline and Fall of the First Muslim Empire." *Der Islam* 81, no. 1 (2004): 3–30.

———. *The Prophet and the Age of the Caliphates: The Islamic Near East from the Sixth to the Eleventh Century*. 2nd ed. London: Routledge, 2015.

Kessler, Lawrence D. "Chinese Scholars and the Early Manchu State." *Harvard Journal of Asiatic Studies* 31 (1971): 179–200.

———. *K'ang-Hsi and the Consolidation of Ch'ing Rule: 1661–1684*. Chicago: University of Chicago Press, 1976.

Khazanov, Anatoly M. *Nomads and the Outside World*. 2nd ed. Madison: University of Wisconsin Press, 1994.

Khodarkovsky, Michael. *Russia's Steppe Frontier: The Making of a Colonial Empire, 1500–1800*. Bloomington: Indiana University Press, 2002.

Klimeš, Ondřej. "Advancing 'Ethnic Unity' and 'De-extremization': Ideational Governance in Xinjiang under 'New Circumstances' (2012–2017)." *Journal of Chinese Political Science* 23, no. 3 (2018): 413–36.

Kłosowska, Anna. "The Etymology of Slave." In *Disturbing Times: Medieval Pasts, Reimagined Futures*, edited by Catherine Karkov, Vincent W. J. van Gerven Oei, and Anna Kłosowska, 151–214. Goleta, CA: Punctum Books, 2020.

Kuhrt, Amelie. *Persian Empire: A Corpus of Sources from the Achaemenid Period*. New York: Routledge, 2007.

Lamb, H. H. "The Early Medieval Warm Epoch and Its Sequel." *Palaeogeography, Palaeoclimatology, Palaeoecology*, no. 1 (1965): 13–37.

Landes, David S. *The Unbound Prometheus: Technological Change and Industrial Development in Western Europe from 1750 to the Present*. Cambridge: Cambridge University Press, 1969.

Larsson, Gunilla. "Contacts between Scandinavia and the Caucasus in Viking Age." In *Between East and West: Early Contacts between Scandinavia and Caucasus*, edited by Gunilla Larsson, 41–61. Uppsala: Uppsala Universitet, 2013.

Levi, Scott C. *Islamic Central Asia: An Anthology of Historical Sources*. Bloomington: Indiana University Press, 2009.

Lewis, David. "The Athenian Coinage Decree." In *The Athenian Empire*, edited by Polly Low, 118–41. Edinburgh: Edinburgh University Press, 2008.

Lewis, Mark Edward. *The Early Chinese Empires: Qin and Han*. Cambridge, MA: Harvard University Press, 2007.

———. *Writing and Authority in Early China*. Albany: State University of New York Press, 1999.

Li, Gertraude Roth. "The Rise of the Early Manchu State: A Portrait Drawn from Manchu Sources to 1636." PhD diss., Harvard University, 1975.

Lindholm, Charles. *The Islamic Middle East: Tradition and Change*. Rev. ed. Malden, MA: Blackwell, 2002.

———. "Kinship Structure and Political Authority: The Middle East and Central Asia." *Comparative Studies in Society and History* 20 (1986): 334–55.

Loewe, Michael. "The Campaigns of Han Wu-Ti." In *Chinese Ways in Warfare*, edited by Frank Kierman and John King Fairbank, 67–122. Cambridge, MA: Harvard University Press, 1974.

Luttwak, Edward. *The Grand Strategy of the Byzantine Empire*. Cambridge, MA: Harvard University Press, 2009.

———. *The Grand Strategy of the Roman Empire: From the First Century CE to the Third*. Rev. ed. Baltimore: Johns Hopkins University Press, 2016.

Machiavelli, Niccolò. *The Prince*. Translated by W. K. Marriott. Minneapolis: First Avenue Editions, 2015.

Mack, William Joseph Behm Garner. *Proxeny and Polis: Institutional Networks in the Ancient Greek World*. Oxford: Oxford University Press, 2015.

Maenchen-Helfen, Otto. *The World of the Huns: Studies in Their History and Culture*. Berkeley: University of California Press, 1973.

Mahdi, Muhsin S. *The Thousand and One Nights*. Leiden: Brill, 1995.

Maier, Charles S. *Among Empires: American Ascendancy and Its Predecessors*. Cambridge, MA: Harvard University Press, 2006.

Mark, Samuel. *Homeric Seafaring*. College Station: Texas A&M University Press, 2005.

———. "Ship- and Boatbuilding in Ancient Egypt." In *Encyclopaedia of the History of Science, Technology, and Medicine in Non-Western Cultures*, 2nd ed., edited by Helaine Selin, 2:3967–80. Berlin: Springer, 2008.

Martin, H. Desmond. *The Rise of Chingis Khan and His Conquest of North China*. Baltimore: Johns Hopkins University Press, 1950.

Martin, Janet. *Treasure of the Land of Darkness: The Fur Trade and Its Significance for Medieval Russia*. Cambridge: Cambridge University Press, 2004.

Marx, Karl, and Friedrich Engels. *The Communist Manifesto*. 1848. Translated by Samuel Moore. London: Penguin, 1967.

Masselman, George. "Dutch Colonial Policy in the Seventeenth Century." *Journal of Economic History* 21, no. 4 (1961): 455–68.

Matranga, Andrea, and Timur Natkhov. "All Along the Watchtower: Defense Lines and the Origins of Russian Serfdom." Unpublished manuscript, 2019. https://www.econ.ucdavis.edu/events/papers/copy2_of_1029Matranga.pdf.

Mauss, Marcel. *The Gift: The Form and Reason for Exchange in Archaic Societies*. New York: W. W. Norton, 2000.

McCormick, Michael. "New Light on the 'Dark Ages': How the Slave Trade Fuelled the Carolingian Economy." *Past and Present*, no. 177 (2002): 17–54.

McEvedy, Colin, and Richard Jones. *Atlas of World Population History*. Harmondsworth, UK: Penguin Books, 1978.

McEwen, Edward, Robert L. Miller, and Christopher A. Bergman. "Early Bow Design and Construction." *Scientific American* 264, no. 6 (1991): 76–83.

McKitterick, Rosamond. *The Frankish Kingdoms under the Carolingians, 751–987*. London: Routledge, 2018.

Meiggs, Russell. "The Crisis of Athenian Imperialism." *Harvard Studies in Classical Philology* 67 (1963): 1–36.

Meritt, Benjamin Dean, H. T. Wade-Gery, and Malcolm Francis McGregor. *The Athenian Tribute Lists*. Cambridge, MA: Harvard University Press, 1939.

Mezentsev, Volodymyr I. "The Territorial and Demographic Development of Medieval Kiev and Other Major Cities of Rus': A Comparative Analysis Based on Recent Archaeological Research." *Russian Review* 48, no. 2 (1989): 145–70.

Minorsky, V. V. *Hudud Al-Alam: The Regions of the World—A Persian Geography, 372 A.H.–982 A.D.* London: E.J.W. Gibb Memorial Trust, 2015.

Minorsky, Vladimir. *A History of Sharvān and Darband in the 10th–11th Centuries*. Cambridge, UK: Heffer, 1958.

Moorey, Peter. *Cemeteries of the First Millennium B.C. at Deve Hüyük*. Oxford: B.A.R., 1980.

Moreno, Alfonso. "'The Attic Neighbour': The Cleruchy in the Athenian Empire." In *Interpreting the Athenian Empire*, edited by John Ma, Nikolaos Papazarkadas, and Robert Parker, 211–21. London: Duckworth, 2009.

———. *Feeding the Democracy: The Athenian Grain Supply in the Fifth and Fourth Centuries BC*. Oxford: Oxford University Press, 2007.

Morgan, David. *The Mongols*. Oxford: Blackwell, 1991.

Morony, M. "ARAB ii. Arab Conquest of Iran." In *Encyclopaedia Iranica*, vol. 2, fasc. 2, pp. 203–10. London: Encyclopaedia Iranica Foundation, 1987.

Morris, Ian. "The Greater Athenian State." In *The Dynamics of Ancient Empires: State Power from Assyria to Byzantium*, edited by Ian Morris and Walter Scheidel, 99–177. Oxford: Oxford University Press, 2009.

Mote, Frederick W. *Imperial China, 900–1800*. Cambridge, MA: Harvard University Press, 1999.

Mundy, Barbara E. *The Death of Aztec Tenochtitlan, the Life of Mexico City*. Austin: University of Texas Press, 2015.

Needham, Joseph. *The Shorter Science and Civilisation in China: An Abridgement of Joseph Needham's Original Text*. Vol. 5. Cambridge: Cambridge University Press, 1978.

Nelson, Janet L. "Aachen as a Place of Power." In *Topographies of Power in the Early Middle Ages*, edited by Mayke de Jong and Frans Theuws, 217–37. Leiden: Brill, 2001.

Nestor. *The Russian Primary Chronicle: Laurentian Text*. Translated by Samuel Hazzard Cross and Olgerd P. Sherbowitz-Wetzor. Cambridge, MA: Mediaeval Academy of America, 1953.

Newitt, Malyn. *A History of Portuguese Overseas Expansion, 1400–1668*. London: Routledge, 2004.

Nithard. *Carolingian Chronicles: Royal Frankish Annals and Nithard's Histories*. Translated by Bernhard W. Scholz and Barbara Rogers. Ann Arbor: University of Michigan Press, 1970.

Nöldeke, Theodor. *The History of the Qur'an*. Edited and translated by Wolfgang Behn. Leiden: Brill, 2013.

Noonan, Thomas S. "The Khazar Qaghanate and Its Impact on the Early Rus' State: The Translatio Imperii from Itil to Kiev." In *Nomads in the Sedentary World*, edited by Anatoly M. Khazanov and André Wink, 76–102. London: Curzon, 2001.

———. "Some Observations on the Economy of the Khazar Khaganate." In *The World of the Khazars*, edited by Peter B. Golden, Haggai Ben-Shammai, and András Róna-Tas, 207–44. Leiden: Brill, 2007.

———. "Why Dirhams First Reached Russia: The Role of Arab-Khazar Relations in the Development of the Earliest Islamic Trade with Eastern Europe." *Archivum Eurasiae Medii Aevi* 4 (1984): 151–282.

———. "Why the Vikings First Came to Russia." *Jahrbücher für Geschichte Osteuropas* 34, no. 3 (1986): 321–48.

Norkus, Zenonas. "The Grand Duchy of Lithuania in the Retrospective of Comparative Historical Sociology of Empires." *World Political Science* 3, no. 4 (2007). https://doi.org/10.2202/1935-6226.1031.

———. *An Unproclaimed Empire: The Grand Duchy of Lithuania: From the Viewpoint of Comparative Historical Sociology of Empires*. London: Routledge, 2017.

O'Brien, Conor. "Chosen Peoples and New Israels in the Early Medieval West." *Speculum* 95, no. 4 (2020): 987–1009.

Oliver, James H. "The Ruling Power: A Study of the Roman Empire in the Second Century after Christ through the Roman Oration of Aelius Aristides." *Transactions of the American Philosophical Society* 43, no. 4 (1953): 871–1003.

Oltean, Ioana A. *Dacia: Landscape, Colonization and Romanization*. London: Routledge, 2007.

Oren, Eliezer D. *The Sea Peoples and Their World: A Reassessment*. Philadelphia: University of Pennsylvania Press, 2000.

Osiander, Andreas. "Sovereignty, International Relations, and the Westphalian Myth." *International Organization* 55, no. 2 (2001): 251–87.

Oxnam, Robert B. *Ruling from Horseback: Manchu Politics in the Oboi Regency, 1661–1669*. Chicago: University of Chicago Press, 1975.

Parthesius, Robert. *Dutch Ships in Tropical Waters*. Amsterdam: Amsterdam University Press, 2010.

Perrie, Maureen, and Andrei Pavlov. *Ivan the Terrible*. London: Taylor and Francis, 2003.

Pines, Yuri. *Envisioning Eternal Empire: Chinese Political Thought of the Warring States Era*. Honolulu: University of Hawai'i Press, 2009.

———. "Legalism in Chinese Philosophy." In *The Stanford Encyclopedia of Philosophy*, edited by Edward N. Zalta, Spring 2017 ed. Metaphysics Research Lab, Stanford University. https://plato.stanford.edu/archives/spr2017/entries/chinese-legalism/.

Pohl, Walter. *The Avars*. Ithaca, NY: Cornell University Press, 2018.

Pseudo-Xenophon. *A Loeb Constitution of the Athenians*. London: Heinemann, 1968.

Pufendorf, Samuel. *Present State of Germany*. Translated by Edmund Bohun. London: printed for Richard Chriswell, 1696.

Rachewiltz, Igor de. *The Secret History of the Mongols: A Mongolian Epic Chronicle of the Thirteenth Century*. Leiden: Brill, 2013.

———. "Yeh-lu Ch'u-ts'ai (1189–1243): Buddhist Idealist and Confucian Statesman." In *Confucian Personalities*, edited by A. Wright and Denis Twitchett, 189–216. Stanford, CA: Stanford University Press, 1962.

Raffensperger, Christian. *The Kingdom of Rus'*. Kalamazoo, MI: ARC Humanities, 2017.

———. *Reimagining Europe*. Cambridge, MA: Harvard University Press, 2012.

———. "Shared (Hi)stories: Vladimir of Rus' and Harald Fairhair of Norway." *Russian Review* 68, no. 4 (2009): 569–82.

Ramsay, George D. *English Overseas Trade during the Centuries of Emergence*. London: Macmillan, 1957.

Rawski, Evelyn S. *The Last Emperors: A Social History of Qing Imperial Institutions*. Berkeley: University of California Press, 1998.

———. "Presidential Address: Reenvisioning the Qing: The Significance of the Qing Period in Chinese History." *Journal of Asian Studies* 55, no. 4 (1996): 829–50.

Rhodes, Peter John. *Athenian Democracy*. Oxford: Oxford University Press, 2004.

Richards, John F. *The Mughal Empire*. Cambridge: Cambridge University Press, 1995.

Riché, Pierre. *The Carolingians: A Family Who Forged Europe*. Philadelphia: University of Pennsylvania Press, 1993.

Rieber, Alfred J. *The Struggle for the Eurasian Borderlands*. Cambridge: Cambridge University Press, 2014.

Rogers, Clifford, and Peter H. Wilson. "Great Northern War (1700–1721)." In *Wars That Changed History*, by Spencer C. Tucker, 182–93. Santa Barbara, CA: CLIO-ABC, 2015.

Rossabi, Morris, ed. *China among Equals: The Middle Kingdom and Its Neighbors, 10th–14th Centuries*. Berkeley: University of California Press, 1983.

———. *Khubilai Khan: His Life and Times*. Berkeley: University of California Press, 2009.

Roth, Gertraude. "The Manchu-Chinese Relationship, 1618–1636." In *From Ming to Ch'ing: Conquest, Region, and Continuity in Seventeenth-Century China*, edited by Jonathan D. Spence and John Elliot Wills, 1–38. New Haven, CT: Yale University Press, 1979.

Rowell, S. C. *Lithuania Ascending: A Pagan Empire within East-Central Europe, 1295–1345*. Cambridge: Cambridge University Press, 1994.

Sahlins, Marshall. *Islands of History*. Chicago: University of Chicago Press, 1985.

———. "The Segmentary Lineage: An Organization for Predatory Expansion." *American Anthropologist* 63 (1960): 332–45.

———. "The Stranger-King or, Elementary Forms of the Politics of Life." *Indonesia and the Malay World* 36, no. 105 (2008): 177–99.

Samons, Loren J. *Empire of the Owl: Athenian Imperial Finance*. Stuttgart: Franz Steiner Verlag, 2000.

Sands, Percy. *The Client Princes of the Roman Empire under the Republic*. New York: Arno, 1975.

Scheidel, Walter. *Escape from Rome: The Failure of Empire and the Road to Prosperity*. Princeton, NJ: Princeton University Press, 2019.

———. "Human Mobility in Roman Italy, II: The Slave Population." *Journal of Roman Studies* 95 (2005): 64–79.

———. "Quantifying the Sources of Slaves in the Early Roman Empire." *Journal of Roman Studies* 87 (1997): 156–69.

Schmid, Jon, and Jonathan Huang. "State Adoption of Transformative Technology: Early Railroad Adoption in China and Japan." *International Studies Quarterly* 61, no. 3 (2017): 570–83.

Scott, James C. *Against the Grain*. New Haven, CT: Yale University Press, 2017.

Seeley, Frank Friedeberg. "Russia and the Slave Trade." *Slavonic and East European Review* 23, no. 62 (1945): 126–36.

Shahbazi, A. Shapur. "Darius I the Great." In *Encyclopaedia Iranica*, vol. 7, fasc. 1, pp. 41–50. London: Encyclopaedia Iranica Foundation, 1994.

Shalem, Avinoam. "The Fall of Al-Madā'in: Some Literary References Concerning Sasanian Spoils of War in Mediaeval Islamic Treasuries." *Iran* 32, no. 1 (1994): 77–81.

Shang Yang. *The Book of Lord Shang: Apologetics of State Power in Early China*. Translated by Yuri Pines. New York: Columbia University Press, 2017.

Sharon, Moshe. "The Decisive Battles in the Arab Conquest of Syria." *Studia Orientalia Electronica* 101 (2007): 297–358.

Sherratt, Andrew. "The Secondary Exploitation of Animals in the Old World." In *Economy and Society in Prehistoric Europe*, edited by Andrew Sherratt, 199–208. Princeton, NJ: Princeton University Press, 1997.

Sherwin-White, Adrian. *The Roman Citizenship*. 2nd ed. Oxford: Clarendon, 1973.

Sherwin-White, Susan M., and Amélie Kuhrt. *From Samarkhand to Sardis: A New Approach to the Seleucid Empire*. Vol. 13. Berkeley: University of California Press, 1993.

Silverstein, Adam J. *Postal Systems in the Pre-modern Islamic World*. Cambridge: Cambridge University Press, 2007.

Sima Qian. *Records of the Grand Historian: Han Dynasty*. 2 vols. Rev. ed. Hong Kong: Research Centre for Translation, Chinese University of Hong Kong, 1993.

———. *Records of the Grand Historian: Qin Dynasty*. Rev. ed. Hong Kong: Research Centre for Translation, Chinese University of Hong Kong, 1993.

Smailes, Arthur E. *The Geography of Towns*. 5th rev. ed. London: Hutchinson, 1966.

Smith, Adam. *An Inquiry into the Nature and Causes of the Wealth of Nations*. Dublin: Whitestone, 1776.

Soen, Violet. "The Treaty of Augsburg." In *Encyclopedia of Martin Luther and the Reformation*, edited by Mark A. Lamport, 770–72. Lanham, MD: Rowman and Littlefield, 2017.

Starr, Chester G. "The Myth of the Minoan Thalassocracy." *Historia: Zeitschrift für alte Geschichte* 3, no. 3 (1955): 282–91.

Ste Croix, G.E.M. de. "Notes on Jurisdiction in the Athenian Empire. I." *Classical Quarterly* 11, no. 1 (1961): 94–112.

———. "Notes on Jurisdiction in the Athenian Empire. II." *Classical Quarterly* 11, no. 2 (1961): 268–80.

Steinmetz, George. "Return to Empire: The New U.S. Imperialism in Comparative Historical Perspective." *Sociological Theory* 23, no. 4 (2005): 339–67.

Storrs, Christopher. *The Resilience of the Spanish Monarchy, 1665–1700*. Oxford: Oxford University Press, 2006.

Subrahmanyam, Sanjay. "Written on Water: Designs and Dynamics in the Portuguese Estado Da India." In *Empires: Perspectives from Archaeology and History*, edited by Susan E. Alcock, Terence N. D'Altroy, Kathleen D. Morrison, and Carla M. Sinopoli, 42–69. Cambridge: Cambridge University Press, 2001.

Subrahmanyam, Sanjay, and Geoffrey Parker. "Arms and the Asian: Revisiting European Firearms and Their Place in Early Modern Asia." *Revista de Cultura* 26 (2008): 12–42.

Suetonius. *Lives of the Caesars*. Translated by John Carew Rolfe. Vol. 1. London: W. Heinemann, 1920.

Sunderland, Willard. *Taming the Wild Field: Colonization and Empire on the Russian Steppe*. Ithaca, NY: Cornell University Press, 2016.

Taagepera, Rein. "Size and Duration of Empires: Growth-Decline Curves, 600 B.C. to 600 A.D." *Social Science History* 3, no. 3/4 (1979): 115–38.

Tabatabai, Ghulām Husain Khān. *A Translation of the Sëir Mutaqharin: Or, View of Modern Times, Being an History of India, from the Year 1118 to the Year 1195*. Vol 2. Calcutta: James White, 1790.

Tacitus, Cornelius. *Germania*. Translated by J. B. Rives. Oxford: Clarendon, 1999.

Taleb, Nassim Nicholas. *The Black Swan: The Impact of the Highly Improbable*. 2nd ed. New York: Random House, 2010.

Tao, Jing-shen. "Barbarians or Northerners: Northern Sung Images of the Khitans." In *China among Equals: The Middle Kingdom and Its Neighbors, 10th–14th Centuries*, edited by Morris Rossabi, 63–88. Berkeley: University of California Press, 1983.

Thucydides. *History of the Peloponnesian War*. Translated by Charles Forster Smith. Cambridge, MA: Harvard University Press, 1911.

Tocqueville, Alexis de. *The Ancien Régime and the French Revolution*. Translated by Arthur Goldhammer. New York: Cambridge University Press, 2011.

Togan, Isenbike. *Flexibility and Limitation in Steppe Formations: The Kerait Khanate and Chinggis Khan*. Leiden: Brill, 1998.

Travers, Robert. "A British Empire by Treaty in Eighteenth-Century India." In *Empire by Treaty: Negotiating European Expansion, 1600–1900*, edited by Saliha Belmessous, 132–60. Oxford: Oxford University Press, 2014.

Turchin, Peter. "A Theory for Formation of Large Empires." *Journal of Global History* 4, no. 2 (2009): 191–217.

Turner, J. P. "The Abna' al-Dawla: The Definition and Legitimation of Identity in Response to the Fourth Fitna." *Journal of the American Oriental Society* 124, no. 1 (2004): 1–22.

Ullmann, Walter. *The Carolingian Renaissance and the Idea of Kingship*. London: Routledge, 2010.

Usher, Dan. "The Dynastic Cycle and the Stationary State." *American Economic Review* 79, no. 5 (1989): 1031–44.

Van Bladel, Kevin. "The Bactrian Background of the Barmakids." In *Islam and Tibet—Interactions along the Musk Routes*, edited by Anna Akasoy, Charles Burnett, and Ronit Yoeli-Tlalin, 57–102. London: Routledge, 2016.

Vasiliev, Aleksandr Aleksandrovich. *The Russian Attack on Constantinople in 860.* Cambridge, MA: Mediaeval Academy of America, 1946.

———. "The Second Russian Attack on Constantinople." *Dumbarton Oaks Papers* 6 (1951): 161–225.

Vaughn, James M. "John Company Armed: The English East India Company, the Anglo-Mughal War and Absolutist Imperialism, c. 1675–1690." *Britain and the World* 11, no. 1 (2018): 101–37.

Vieira, Mónica Brito. "Mare Liberum vs. Mare Clausum: Grotius, Freitas, and Selden's Debate on Dominion over the Seas." *Journal of the History of Ideas* 64, no. 3 (2003): 361–77.

Vink, Markus. "'The World's Oldest Trade': Dutch Slavery and Slave Trade in the Indian Ocean in the Seventeenth Century." *Journal of World History* 14, no. 2 (2003): 131–77.

Voegelin, Eric. "The Mongol Orders of Submission to European Powers, 1245–1255." *Byzantion* 15 (1940): 378–413.

Voltaire. *Essai sur les moeurs et l'esprit des nations; et sur les principaux faits de l'histoire, depuis Charlemagne jusqu'à Louis XIII.* Vol. 3. Nouv. éd., conforme à l'éd. de Genève. Neuchatel, 1773.

Wachsmann, Shelley. *Seagoing Ships and Seamanship in the Bronze Age Levant.* College Station: Texas A&M University Press, 2009.

Wakeman, Frederic E. *The Great Enterprise: The Manchu Reconstruction of Imperial Order in Seventeenth-Century China.* Berkeley: University of California Press, 1985.

———. "The Shun Interregnum of 1644." In *From Ming to Ch'ing: Conquest, Region, and Continuity in Seventeenth-Century China,* edited by Jonathan D. Spence and John Elliot Wills, 39–87. New Haven, CT: Yale University Press, 1979.

Waldron, Arthur. *The Great Wall of China: From History to Myth.* Cambridge: Cambridge University Press, 1990.

Wallbank, Michael. "Proxeny and Proxenos in Fifth-Century Athens." In *The Athenian Empire,* edited by Polly Low, 132–39. Edinburgh: Edinburgh University Press, 2008.

Wallinga, Herman T. *Ships and Sea-Power before the Great Persian War: The Ancestry of the Trireme.* Leiden: Brill, 1993.

———. "The Trireme and History." *Mnemosyne* 43, no. 1/2 (1990): 132–49.

Watson, James L. *Golden Arches East: McDonald's in East Asia.* 2nd ed. Stanford, CA: Stanford University Press, 2006.

Weber, Max. *Economy and Society.* Berkeley: University of California Press, 1978.

Wells, Peter S. *The Barbarians Speak: How the Conquered Peoples Shaped Roman Europe.* Princeton, NJ: Princeton University Press, 1999.

Wickwire, Franklin B., and Mary B. Wickwire. *Cornwallis: The Imperial Years.* Chapel Hill: University of North Carolina Press, 2017.

Wilson, Peter H. *Heart of Europe: A History of the Holy Roman Empire.* Cambridge, MA: Harvard University Press, 2016.

Wink, André. *Land and Sovereignty in India: Agrarian Society and Politics under the Eighteenth-Century Maratha Svarājya.* Cambridge: Cambridge University Press, 1986.

Wiseman, T. P. *New Men in the Roman Senate, 139 B.C.–A.D. 14.* London: Oxford University Press, 1971.

Wittfogel, Karl August, and Chia-sheng Feng. *History of Chinese Society: Liao, 907–1125.* New York: American Philosophical Society, 1949.

Wolf, Eric R. *Europe and the People without History.* Berkeley: University of California Press, 1982.

Wood, Ian. *The Merovingian Kingdoms, 450–751.* London: Routledge, 2014.

Wylie, Alexander. "History of the Heung-Noo in Their Relations with China." *Journal of the Anthropological Institute of Great Britain and Ireland* 5 (1876): 41–80.

Xenophon. *Cyropaedia.* Translated by Walter Miller. Vol. 2. Cambridge, MA: Harvard University Press, 1914.

Yang, Lien-sheng. "Toward a Study of Dynastic Configurations in Chinese History." *Harvard Journal of Asiatic Studies* 17, no. 3/4 (1954): 329–45.

Yates, Robin. "State Control of Bureaucrats under the Qin: Techniques and Procedures." *Early China* 20 (1995): 331–65.

Yu, Ying-shih. *Trade and Expansion in Han China.* Berkeley: University of California Press, 1967.

Yūsofī, Ġ. Ḥ. "Abu Moslem Korasani." In *Encyclopædia Iranica*, edited by E. Yarshater, vol. 1, fasc. 4, pp. 341–44. New York: Columbia University, Center for Iranian Studies, 2011. http://www.iranicaonline.org/articles/abu-moslem-abd-al-rahman-b.

Zaroff, Roman. "Organized Pagan Cult in Kievan Rus': The Invention of Foreign Elite or Evolution of Local Tradition?" *Studia Mythologica Slavica* 2 (2015): 47–76.

Zelnick-Abramovitz, Rachel. "Settlers and Dispossessed in the Athenian Empire." *Mnemosyne* 57, no. 3 (2004): 325–45.

Zhao, Taotao, and James Leibold. "Ethnic Governance under Xi Jinping: The Centrality of the United Front Work Department & Its Implications." *Journal of Contemporary China* 29, no. 124 (2020): 487–502.

Zuckerman, Constantin. "On the Date of the Khazars' Conversion to Judaism and the Chronology of the Kings of the Rus Oleg and Igor: A Study of the Anonymous Khazar Letter from the Genizah of Cairo." *Revue des études byzantines* 53, no. 1 (1995): 237–70.

INDEX

Page numbers in *italics* refer to figures and tables.

Athenian Empire (*continued*)
endogenous empire, *68*; governance
of, 89, 92–94, 278, 329n67; legal
system, 96–97; map of, *80*; maritime
empire, 67, 73–74, 99, 294; origin and
expansion of, 84, 88; Peloponnesian
War, 11, 53–54, 82, 84, 87, 100; Persia
and, 82–83, 88–89, 100; revenue of,
97–99; Thrace and, 88–90, 114. *See also*
Greece
Attila (Hun leader), 185, 216
Augustus (Roman emperor), 28, 52, 59–60,
78, 214
Aurangzeb (Mughal emperor), 109
Austro-Hungarian Empire, 6, 301
Axum empire, 3
Aztec and Incan empires, 3, 23, 102

Balcer, Jack Martin, 93
Barmakid, Khalid, 208
Barmakid family, 208–9
Batu (Golden Horde founder), 276–78
Bedouins, 12, 189, 193, 214
Bernard (Louis's nephew), 233–34
black swan events, 173, 332n25
Bloch, Marc, 224
bloody tanistry, 174, 332n26
Braudel, Fernand, 12
Briant, Pierre, 34–36, 74, 176, 180, 182
British East India Company (EIC): depen-
dent state treaties, 113; expansion of,
108–9, 111, 113, 116; failure and bailout,
112; military operations, 330n92;
Mughals and, 106–8, 111, 330n97;
Mughals and Mughal Empire, 67;
private chartered company, 66, 103–4;
Treaty of Allahabad, 111–12
British Empire: citizenship in, 115–17;
elites of, 115; endogenous transformation, 295; governing elite, 115, 328n35,
330n105; India and, 38, 67, 105–6, 109,
113, 115; London in, 115, 330n106;
maritime empire, 14, 66, 100; Mughals
and, 295; North America and, 107, 116;
origin and expansion of, *106*, 238, 292;
South Asia and, 105
Burke, Edmund, 106
Byzantines and Byzantine Empire: Arabian
tribes and, 186, 192–99; Avars and, 216;
Battle of Yarmouk, 185; Constantinople,

191, 194–95, 215, 218–19, 229, 260–61,
264, 281; decline of, 26; endogenous
empire, 52; furs and slave trade, 253;
Islamic Caliphate, 187, 190; Muslims
and, 15; origin and expansion of, 220;
Ottoman Empire and, 63; Papal States,
224; religion and, 273; religion of,
204, 219; Roman Empire and, 218;
Rus' empire and, 265–66, 269–71, 274;
Sasanian Empire and, 39, 184–85;
steppe nomadic empires and, 16;
Varangian Guard, 271; Venetians and,
294; wars of, 191–95

Cambyses II (Persian emperor), 29, 31,
34–35, 74–75
Caroe, Olaf, 40
Carolingian Empire: Aachen, capitol of,
227–29, 335n27; Avars and, 216, 226–27;
Catholic Church and, 213, 218–19, 226,
230–31, 233–34; empire of nostalgia,
4, 229–30; end of, 236; EU territory,
307; exogenous to endogenous empire,
238; expansion of, 225; Germanic
tribes and, 214; governance of, 227–29,
335n24; Huns and, 9, 31, 185, 215–18;
map of, *226*; origin and expansion of,
218, 225; outer frontier strategy, 215;
Sarmatians and, 214–15; Saxons and,
225; succession in, 232–37, 335n35;
Treaty of Verdun, 236; Umayyads
and, 222
Carolman, 222–25, 233
Carthage: Arabs and, 197; governance of,
328n35; maritime empire, 3, 14, 53, 66,
293; naval power, 73, 294–95; Persia
and, 75; Punic Wars, 53–56
Casson, Lionel, 70
Catherine the Great (Russian empress),
249, 279, 289
Cavafy, Constantine P., 152
Chadwick, Nora, 275
Chagatai Khanate, 148
Charlemagne (Holy Roman emperor), 9,
16, 218, 222–33, 236, 307
Charles the Bald (Carolingian emperor),
235–36
Cherniavsky, Michael, 281
Childeric III (Merovingian king), 223
Chilperic II (Neustrian king), 222

INDEX [359]

China: border of, 139, 296; diversity of, 57; dynasties of, *139*; elites of, 40, 46, 50; foreign dynasties and, 140; military of, 139–40, 144; mirror empires and, 294; northeastern frontier dynasties, 155, 157; transportation systems of, 22–23; uniform governance of, 27–28, 51; vulture empires and, 294–95; Warring States period, 19, 40–*41*, 46–47, 49, 201; Yellow Turban Rebellion, 137. *See also* Han dynasty; Jurchen Jin dynasty and people; Khitan Liao dynasty; Manchu Qing dynasty; Ming dynasty; Mongol Yuan Empire; Qin dynasty; Song dynasty; Tang dynasty; Toba Wei dynasty; Xiongnu Empire; Zhou dynasty

China, People's Republic (PRC): empire label, 302; endogenous models of, 311–12; governance of, 310–11; imperial templates of, 310–11; military of, 312–13; minority treatment, 313; non-Chinese world and, 313–14; origin and expansion of, 309; ruling elite, 314–15

Chinggis Khan, 13, 15, 119, 122, 140–42, 145–47, 277, 297

Claudius (Roman emperor), 61

Clive, Robert, 111–13

Clovis (Merovingian founder), 218–20

Communist Manifesto (Marx, Engles), 86, 300

Confucianism, 22, 50–51, 149

Constantine (Roman emperor), 62, 233

Cornwallis, Charles, 116

Croesus (king of Lydia), 32–33

Cromwell, Thomas, 209

Crone, Patricia, 189

Cyrus the Great (Persian emperor), 10, 29, 31–35, 37, 52, 73–74

Dalrymple, William, 112

Daniel, Elton, 205

Darius III (Persian emperor), 52, 175–79, 195

Darius the Great (Persian emperor), 10, 29, 31, 33–34, 74–78, 180

David, Jacques-Louis, 2

Davis, Jennifer, 228, 230

Deng Xiaoping, 309, 312, 314

De statu imperii Germanici (Pufendorf), 244

Digunai (Wanyan Liang), 162–63

Diocletian (Roman emperor), 62

dirhams, 197–98, 249, 253, 255, 271, 336n12

Distribution of the Eagle Standards, The (David), 2

Dmitry (Russian tsar), 283, 285

Dobrynya (Rus' military governor), 266–69, 271

Dorgon (Manchu Qing regent), 167, 169

Doyle, Michael, 10

Drogo, 223–24

Duke Xiao (emperor), 43

Dutch United East India Company (VOC), 103–5, 330n86

Economy and Society (Weber), 7

Egypt: agricultural exports, 23, 32, 99; Athenians and, 83, 99; elites of, 20; endogenous empire of, 20, 211–12; Macedonians and, 178; mamluk subjects of, 208; Medes and, 19; Old Kingdom, 18; Persians and, 29, 34–35, 73–74, 175, 191; Portuguese and, 103; religion of, 199; ships and shipping, 68; wars and rebellions, 72, 74, 77–78, 83, 176

empires, endogenous: agrarian empires of, 301–2; American or Swiss cheese governance model, 26–27, 37–38, 47; centralized governance of, 21–22; citizenship in, 113–14; collapse of, 153, 333n54; communication systems of, 23–24; definition of, 2–3; dissolution of, 298–301; diversity and, 20–21; early history, 18; evolution to, 292; Industrial Revolution and, 299; languages of, 24–25; military monopoly, 25–26; rebels in, 37–38; templates for, 63; transportation systems of, 22–23; uniform governance of, 26–27; uniform projects in, 26; vanquisher empires and, 183–84

empires, exogenous: collapse of, 64; definition of, 2, 4; Empires of nostalgia, 4; endogenous transformation, 295; extortion by, 146; mirror nomadic steppe empires, 4, 292; periphery empires, 4; shadow empires, 3; vacuum empires, 5

empires of nostalgia, 4–5, 15–16, 211–12, 230, 317

Engels, Friedrich, 300

A NOTE ON THE TYPE

———

THIS BOOK has been composed in Miller, a Scotch Roman typeface designed by Matthew Carter and first released by Font Bureau in 1997. It resembles Monticello, the typeface developed for The Papers of Thomas Jefferson in the 1940s by C. H. Griffith and P. J. Conkwright and reinterpreted in digital form by Carter in 2003.

Pleasant Jefferson ("P. J.") Conkwright (1905–1986) was Typographer at Princeton University Press from 1939 to 1970. He was an acclaimed book designer and AIGA Medalist.